CW00766706

The Watermills of Buckinghamshire

The Watermills of Buckinghamshire

A 1930s account by Stanley Freese
with original photographs

Edited by Michael Farley, Edward Legg and James Venn

with a contribution by Martin Watts

Buckinghamshire Papers No. 12

Buckinghamshire Papers No. 12
Buckinghamshire Archaeological Society
c/o County Museum, Church Street
Aylesbury
HP20 2QP

© Buckinghamshire Archaeological Society 2007

ISBN 978-094900324-9

Typeset by Avocet Typeset, Chilton, Buckinghamshire
Printed by Halstan & Co. Ltd., Amersham, Buckinghamshire

Contents

Stanley Freese 1902–1972 by James Venn

Stanley Harman Freese and his twin brother Cyril were born in Kentish Town, London in 1902, where they lived until 1908 when the family moved to The Kraal, South Heath, Great Missenden. Both boys attended Dr Challoner's School, Amersham, on leaving which their father hoped that they would join his business of a manufacturing pharmaceutical chemist. However both boys showed little enthusiasm for this, but soon developed a marked talent for drawing and painting and by the mid 1920s were established as successful commercial artists with a studio in Shaftesbury Avenue, London.

Four or five times a year they set off on extensive cycling tours of East Anglia, the West of England, Wales and Yorkshire, returning home with perhaps twenty or more sketches most of which were done very rapidly with the intention of finishing them at home. Stanley Freese in particular was a prolific recorder of country scenes, filling forty sketch books in the period c 1925–33. His subjects included churches, cottages, village streets, farm buildings, agricultural implements, wind and watermills. Most were impressionistic style sketches taking not more than ten or fifteen minutes to complete, drawn with a fountain pen in books 7" × 5".

In 1933, both brothers acquired cameras, which from then onwards tended to replace their sketching activities. This was an important development for over the next six or seven years they took hundreds of 120 size photographs covering the same subjects as before but now including railways and other forms of transport. As might be expected of artists, their photographs were always carefully composed and pictorially attractive, but what makes their work so interesting is that it gives glimpses of a way of rural life that had endured for generations, but would soon disappear under the pressure of social and economic change in the post 1945 era. This element is particularly noticeable in their pictures of agricultural work, in which, quite remarkably, the horse still remained the main source of power long after the internal combustion engine was in general use in road transport. Together with detailed views of implements and farm buildings there are the workers in their old worn clothes tied at the knees, their heads invariably covered with a cloth cap. Likewise there are the cottages in which they lived, most of them ancient and in varying degrees of neglect all of which illustrates the poverty and hardship common in agricultural communities at that time.

Stanley Freese is probably best known for his book *Windmills and Millwrighting* published by Cambridge University Press in 1957, though his first published work *In search of English Windmills* written jointly with Thurston Hopkins, appeared in 1932. Freese drew the sketches and wrote several chapters, one of which describes some Buckinghamshire windmills. Hopkins was clearly a professional writer and wrote a number of popular books, his topics including London, Cornwall, the moated houses of England, Kipling, and George Borrow. Freese, was to illustrate for Hopkins *The Man who was Sussex* (1933).

Freese himself, had an early venture into print but on a completely different topic. In 1932 Cecil Palmer, who also published Hopkin's works, published for him *The Ten-Year Plan: a Dream of 1940*. This book, a novel, has a hero Martin J. Allen, who is clearly Freese's alter ego. The plot, such as it is, revolves around Allen's attempts to bring to the authorities his master plan for re-locating overcrowded London to one or more new towns based around linear transport structures, in particular railway lines. Trains, buses etc would run at a low level, the remainder of the town being at the surface along the route. There are several illustration drawn by the author. One of Allen (Freese's) visionary illustrations has in the background a 'great wind-driven power station' (reproduced here as Fig 4). In the book, opposition to the vision, and responsibility for the poor state of London, comes from a series of bodies and individuals who are to later figure in one way or another in his mills manuscript. They include 'indifferent and incompetent officials – largely 'German-Americans and Russians of the most unscrupulous type', and one Silas Blobbs, a 'typical county councillor'.

Freese became friends with the Reverend Drury, Rector of Binsted, Sussex, who founded the English Linear Cities Association. Freese was to become Secretary and a letter of his to *The Times* (13th July

1938), titled 'The Linear City' refers to the concept. The Association's blueprint, presaged in the 1932, novel, was for 'an extended industrial city, such as from London to Birmingham or Liverpool, flanked by a series of crescents ….'

Freese became friendly with H.E.S Simmons who at that time was working on a detailed historical survey of Sussex windmills and it seems likely this influenced Stanley Freese to embark on a similar one for Buckinghamshire. This was indeed fortuitous for he began systematic research into both wind and watermill history just in time to record the final generation of Buckinghamshire millers and many other old people whose personal recollections went back as far as the 1850s. Within a decade, this unique and irreplaceable source of information had gone forever, thereby making Stanley Freese's manuscript the only reasonably complete and definitive record now existing of this industry in Buckinghamshire.

The combined wind and watermill manuscript was finished by about August 1939 but it was then impossible to find a publisher for such a lengthy, specialised and detailed project. The war prevented further attempts at publication and likewise ended the Freese's photography and their careers as commercial artists. After a short period working on a smallholding at Cranleigh in Surrey, Stanley joined the staff of the Bucks War Agriculture Committee in Aylesbury. After the Bucks W.A.C. was wound up he worked for a while on rating valuations work with the High Wycombe Valuation Office of the Inland Revenue and from there he moved to the Eastern Electricity Board with whom he worked as a draughtsman at their Pinner office until he retired in 1963.

In 1964 he moved from The Kraal, Great Missenden to Wenhaston in Suffok where once more he became involved in the repair of local windmills. At the same time he resumed work, begun in the 1930s, on a history of Suffolk windmills. This had hardly begun when he died, suddenly and unexpectedly on his 70th birthday, 1st June 1972.

Latterly he was remembered as somewhat eccentric in his habits, but this impression should not detract from his contribution to local history. However, his research is open to criticism for the neglect to quote his sources of information. In common with many other writers of similar background in the 1930s, he failed to appreciate the

FIGURE 1 *Stanley Freese*

importance of stating exact and verifiable references. At that time the academically disciplined, analytical approach to the study of local and industrial history as we know it today had hardly begun, other than in universities. In any case, research into the history of individual mills, especially windmills where there was little documentary evidence, had to rely on oral sources which could never be verified and had to be accepted solely on the basis of probability.

Introduction to Freese's Mills Manuscript

Michael Farley and Edward Legg

In the 1950s Stanley Freese deposited the typescript of a volume entitled 'A Topographical and Historical Account of the Windmills and Watermills of Buckinghamshire' at Buckinghamshire County Museum together with many photographs. The manuscript consists of three parts: Part I Windmills of Buckinghamshire, Part II The Ouse watermills in Buckinghamshire and Part III The Thames watermills in Buckinghamshire. The present publication includes parts II and III of the manuscript with his proposed order of chapters slightly re-arranged. Part I (on windmills) is being revised by one of us (JHV) and it is hoped to publish this at a later date elsewhere.

The manuscript was apparently substantially complete just before the outbreak of the Second World War although a few wartime events are recorded. For example Bury Field at Newport Pagnell is noted as going under the plough, the drowning of Harry Alderman, miller of Whitchurch Mill in a stream apparently is a result of the "blackout", and Upper Glory Mill, Wooburn where photographic paper etc was manufactured 'in considerable secrecy', had 'half a mile of heavy wire and barbed wire fencing …added to the defences' at the 'outbreak of hostilities'. The chimney of Gunpowder/ Eggams Green Mill at Wooburn was also reported to have been camouflaged. Seeing an opportunity for reviving traditional milling in a wartime economy, Freese berates the authorities for not making better use of its potential. He notes, for example, that Westbury had its machinery cleared in September 1939 'just when it could have embarked on a new and more useful sphere of life.' During the 1930s when he was visiting mills, most had already ceased to be used for their original purpose, or if in use were not powered by water. The latest recorded date in the manuscript is a pencilled note to a typist in 1947.

It was the author's intention to publish the whole manuscript as a book illustrated with his photographs, but the war put an end to this aspiration. Subsequently he passed a copy of the typescript to his friend H.E.S. Simmons, who in turn incorporated much of it word for word into his own typescript on watermills, adding some additional historical detail from, for example, Royal Exchange Fire Insurance policies.

Stanley Freese died in 1972. In 1974 Simmon's own papers were passed by his widow to the Library of the Science Museum, London, and catalogued as 'The Simmons collection of records relating to British windmills and watermills'. A copy of the Buckinghamshire section of Simmon's manuscript was later supplied to the Local History Collection of the County Reference Library (subsequently the Centre for Buckinghamshire Studies) where it is bound as three volumes on watermills and one on windmills (ref. 000:84).

Two introductory chapters are missing from the watermills section of the Freese manuscript: 'Some Notes concerning Corn-watermill History' and 'Some Notes concerning Papermill History'. However, the succeeding chapters 'Introduction to Corn Watermill History' (incomplete) and the 'Introduction to Paper and Millboard Mills' are present, and are here included as appendices. Four of Freese's own appendices which dealt with 'The Posse Comitatus', 'The Future of Wind and Watermills', 'Wind and Watermill Fires in Buckinghamshire', and 'Horse mills and Treadmills' survive, but since they largely refer to both wind and watermills have been omitted from the present publication. His proposed preface to the whole volume covering both kinds of mill has, however, been included since it eloquently describes his attitudes to mills and also expresses his gratitude to a number of informants. For convenience his joint bibliography on both wind and watermills is also published here. Unfortunately several diagrams referred to in his text are missing. The whole manuscript is now deposited with the Buckinghamshire Archaeological Society.

The typescript has on it many of his corrections and deletions in ink. An example of a page is given here (Fig.2). This published version has accepted these corrections, as well as his punctuation and capitalisations. A few spelling mistakes of common words have been corrected. Most of his amendments to the manuscript were intended to reduce its length and in a few instances he deleted small amounts of descriptive material of value. For example, he sometimes removed compass points indicating relationships between buildings and fittings. Researchers on specific mills are advised to refer to the original manuscript since deleted material can often be read beneath the scoring out.

The manuscript is of particular importance for Freese's first-hand descriptions of the mechanisms of mills, most of which have long since disappeared. He also spent much time interviewing millers and millwrights for their own accounts of mills and memories of their predecessors. For the early history of mills he relies largely on the *Victoria County History* – particularly for mills no longer extant – but he also uses early printed county maps, manuscript maps then in the archives of the Buckinghamshire Archaeological Society, and early Ordnance Survey editions. These are listed by date at the commencement of each entry. He uses local histories where they were available and adds a number of details from trade directories and sale catalogues, although he does not always source the latter.

His principal interest was in traditional watermills. Where such mills had subsequently acquired supplementary or replacement power-sources such as a 'Cornish engine' or a gas engine he notes the evidence but clearly his heart was with unmodernised mills and he relished their often idyllic situations, writing sadly of those neglected, and recording indignation where their setting has been adversely affected, for example at Stony Stratford where Horn Lane which formerly led to Calverton Mill, had been "illegally obstructed by the grasping landlords and jerry-builders of the town". The causes of the decline of local milling are too complex to be considered in this introduction, but extend back decades before Freese's study and include the importation of foreign grain leading to a shrinkage in the cultivation of home-grown grain, the re-location of large mills near ports, the invention of roller mills and of course the efficient development of other power sources such as electricity.

He outlined his field collecting methods in the preface to *Windmills and Millwrighting* (1957, p. xv) noting that he recorded windmill sites with 'drawings done with a fountain pen … then I turned to photography, and gradually got together hundreds of pictures of interiors and exteriors.' In one instance (Edlesborough watermill) where the owner objected to his property being photographed, he noted that, on developing the film he 'found' that he had an image in his camera. His recording of mill buildings was often less systematic than that of their working parts; for example, he does not always describe the appearance or character of the principal building and certainly often omits to record the presence of ancillary buildings. In one instance, at Stoke Mandeville, he obviously didn't realise that there were mill structures surviving – indeed they still survive today.

He was a prolific photographer and one of us (JHV) is involved with the cataloguing and printing of numerous of his negatives on a range of subjects. Copies of many of these have been deposited in the Centre for Buckinghamshire Studies. The photographs which have been included in this text are a selection from about 300 watermill photographs that Freese deposited at the County Museum at about the same time as he deposited his manuscript. These have since been transferred to the Centre for Buckinghamshire Studies. The great majority are of the exterior of mills and surprisingly few are of internal machinery. About 50 have been included here; the remainder can be seen on the County Council's website by searching under 'parish' at ww.buckscc.gov.uk/photo_database/index.htm The opportunity has been taken to include here a sample drawing from one of his eight sketch books which survive (Fig. 3), currently in the care of one of us (JHV).

Freese was deeply attached to mills and antagonistic, even occasionally vitriolic towards those who caused their disuse. He regarded their neglect as wasteful, particularly in the wartime years he was experiencing, and thought that mills – which were generally falling into disuse, should be given a new life and put to good economic use. His, perhaps prescient, vision of the future expressed in his only published novel *The Ten-Year Plan: A Dream of 1940* (published 1932, see earlier), included windmills as generators (Fig. 4). He often had harsh words for those with no sympathy or understanding of the needs of watermills. Those in his sights included Drainage Boards, Buckinghamshire County Council – in their role as road builders, developers and contractors, and those who defaced the countryside with advertisements. Some of the material scored through in his original text, and hence not reproduced here, contains strong criticism but sufficient remains undeleted to give a feeling for his viewpoint. A few examples will suffice.

Of Three Bridge Mill/Cowley Mill, Preston Bissett he writes; 'Before this book sees the light of day, Three Bridge Mill will probably have been flooded for the first time in a hundred years. The explanation is simple; a new and totally unnecessary road bridge has been erected across the stream, immediately below the Mill with arches about a foot wider than

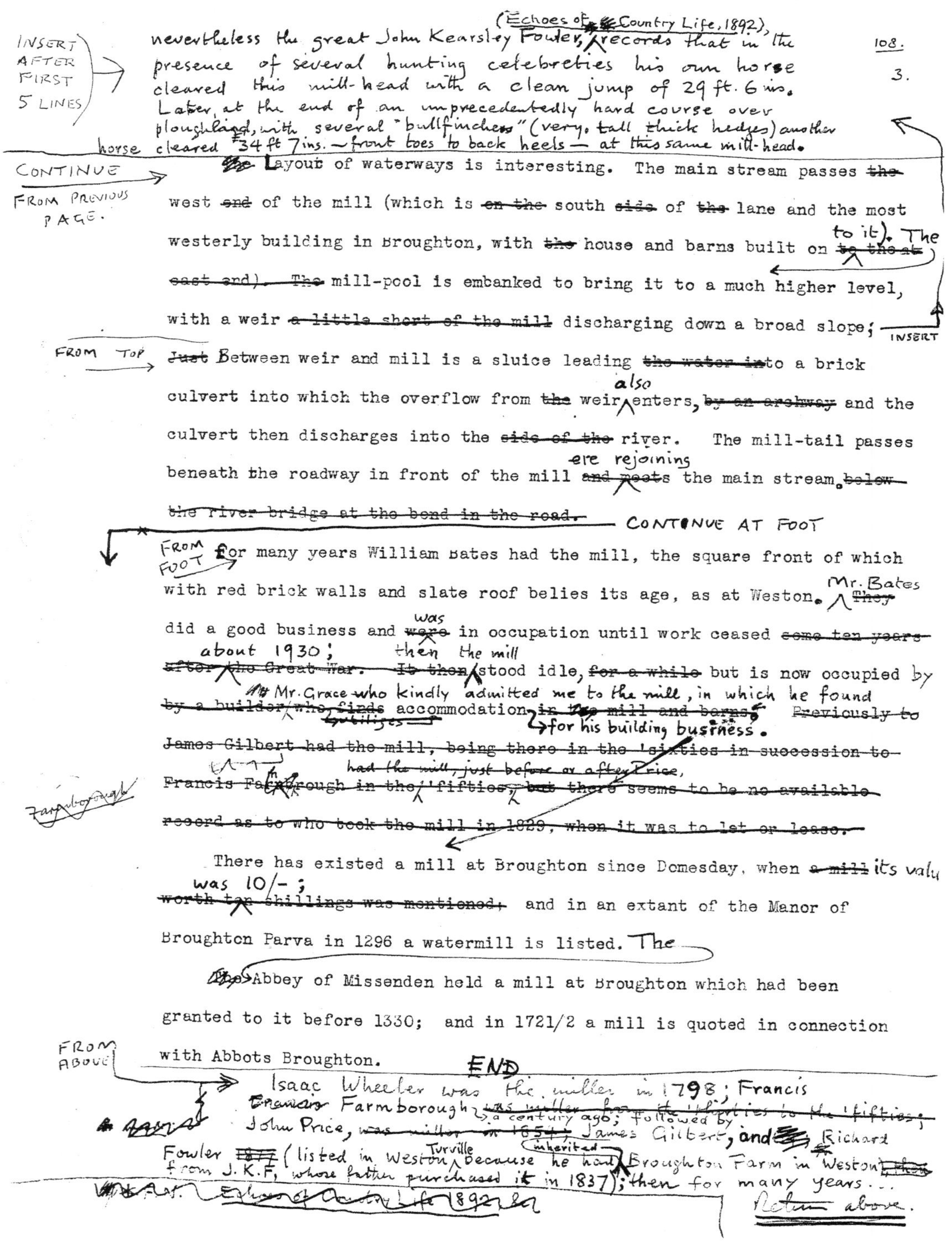

INSERT AFTER FIRST 5 LINES → nevertheless the great John Kearsley Fowler (Echoes of Country Life, 1892), records that in the presence of several hunting celebrities his own horse cleared this mill-head with a clean jump of 29 ft. 6 ins. Later, at the end of an unprecedentedly hard course over ploughland, with several "bullfinches" (very tall ~~thick~~ hedges) another horse cleared 34 ft 7 ins. – front toes to back heels – at this same mill-head.

108.

3.

CONTINUE FROM PREVIOUS PAGE. → ~~The~~ Layout of waterways is interesting. The main stream passes ~~the~~ west ~~end~~ of the mill (which is ~~on the~~ south ~~side~~ of ~~the~~ lane and the most westerly building in Broughton, with ~~the~~ house and barns built on ~~to the at east end)~~ to it). ~~The~~ The mill-pool is embanked to bring it to a much higher level, with a weir ~~a little short of the mill~~ discharging down a broad slope; INSERT

FROM TOP → ~~Just~~ Between weir and mill is a sluice leading ~~the water in~~to a brick culvert into which the overflow from ~~the~~ weir also enters, ~~by an archway~~ and the culvert then discharges into the ~~side of the~~ river. The mill-tail passes beneath the roadway in front of the mill ~~and meets~~ ere rejoining the main stream. ~~below the river bridge at the bend in the road.~~ CONTINUE AT FOOT

FROM FOOT → For many years William Bates had the mill, the square front of which with red brick walls and slate roof belies its age, as at Weston. ~~They~~ Mr. Bates did a good business and ~~were~~ was in occupation until work ceased ~~some ten years after the Great War~~ about 1930; ~~It then~~ then the mill stood idle, ~~for a while~~ but is now occupied by ~~by a builder, who, finds~~ Mr. Grace who kindly admitted me to the mill, in which he found ~~utilises~~ accommodation ~~in the mill and barns~~ for his building business. ~~Previously to James Gilbert had the mill, being there in the 'sixties in succession to Francis Farbrough in the 'fifties, but there seems to be no available record as to who took the mill in 1829, when it was to let or lease.~~ had the mill, just before or after Price,

Farmborough

There has existed a mill at Broughton since Domesday, when ~~a mill~~ its value was 10/-; ~~worth ten shillings was mentioned;~~ and in an extant of the Manor of Broughton Parva in 1296 a watermill is listed. The ~~The~~ Abbey of Missenden held a mill at Broughton which had been granted to it before 1330; and in 1721/2 a mill is quoted in connection with Abbots Broughton. END

FROM ABOVE → Isaac Wheeler was the miller in 1798; Francis ~~Francis~~ Farmborough, ~~was miller from the 'thirties to the 'fifties;~~ a century ago; followed by John Price, ~~was miller in 1854,~~ James Gilbert, and Richard Fowler ~~1877~~ (listed in Weston Turville because he had inherited Broughton Farm in Weston from J.K.F, whose father purchased it in 1837); then for many years... Return above.

~~Echoes of Country Life 1892~~

FIGURE 2 A page from the manuscript describing Broughton Mill, Bierton with Broughton.

FIGURE 3 A drawing from one of Freese's sketchbooks showing Jackson's Mill, Wooburn. Drawn in the Autumn of 1930.

the original railway arch two miles upstream at Godington, which had to be widened on account of floods it caused ...'

At an early mill site at Simpson he notes flooding every time there is a heavy rainstorm. 'It's because a new by-pass (sic) has been built across the river near the old mill site ... it doesn't by-pass anything and it leads nowhere, but the amount of concrete must have done the contractors a lot of good. The villagers warned the 'experts' ...'

At Marlow Mills he records that pollution arising from this mill was 'practically nil' but '... the county authorities have before now prosecuted for as little pollution as this, but they have not objected to the Bucks Water Board choking completely the Misbourne with ... 10% chalk sludge whilst boring for water and subsequently pumping the springs dry so that the river has ceased to flow.'

Old Wolverton Mill, 'one of the most unprepossessing corn mills in the county', was approached by a drive 'on the north side of the new ugly road from Stony Stratford which was unnecessarily reconstructed for the benefit of the contractors and to get rid of the roadside railway – somewhat antediluvian in appearance with long chimneyed locomotives and huge double-decked "tramcar" carriages which at least conveyed its passengers with every safety to themselves and other road users. Since its demolition the death toll, as on every reconstructed road in Bucks, has gone up by leaps and bounds and but for the leaps and bounds of pedestrians it would be higher still!' Later in his description of this same mill, having itemised the repairs proposed for the mill in the early years of the war, he notes 'everything was going well when the mill was unfortunately inspected by a pessimistic official who had no authority to view: and his ridiculous pronouncements that it was unsafe was accepted ...'.

At Little Missenden he notes of the Misbourne which flows 'behind the village and through the

FIGURE 4 An illustration by Freese from his *The Ten-Year Plan. A Dream of 1940*, published in 1932. Caption: 'The omnibuses could be near the top of the cutting, with the street cars upon a shelf-road; and on the hilltop one of the great wind-driven power stations.'

beautiful Abbey grounds' that it is 'now to be carved up and destroyed by Bucks County Council for the benefit of road hogs …'

Finally at Chetwode, he notes difficulty in finding the name of a stream. Such names were commonly recorded where roads crossed bridges by the 'Automobile Association so fond of plastering the countryside with its bilious advertisements …', but not in this instance '…so some good has come out of even this dilemma!'

Since the manuscript was completed a number of other studies of Buckinghamshire watermills have been published and a selection are listed below. Reid's book, for instance, covering part of the south of the county, has a number of pencil drawings done in the same decade as Freese (Reid 1987 and 1989). A published gazetteer of watermills and mill sites extends Freese's list by making greater use of e.g. field names (BCMAG 1982). Buckinghamshire's Domesday mills are examined in more detail by Bailey (1997). There have also been individual studies of mills which include excavated evidence for example at Caldecotte, Bow Brickhill (Petchey 1983), Pann Mill, High Wycombe (Cauvain 1997) and the Oxford Road Mill, Aylesbury (Humphrey 2004). Holmes (1993) takes a detailed look at the products of Marlow Mill, Mary Farnell (1982) draws attention to a nineteenth-century millwrights account book, Mead writes in depth on Glory Mill, Wooburn, and Legg (2005) on Water Eaton.

Bibliography for this section

Bailey K 1997 Mills in Domesday Buckinghamshire. *Recs Bucks* 39, 67–72

Cauvain S and P 1997 Investigations at Pann Mill, High Wycombe. *Recs Bucks* 39, 18–44

BCMAG 1982 Buckinghamshire Watermills, *Recs Bucks* 24, 34–45

Farnell M 1982 Account books of William Cooper, Millwright of Aylesbury. *Recs Bucks* 24, 118–124

Holmes EF 1993 A forgotten Buckinghamshire industry: thimble making at Marlow. *Recs Bucks* 35, 1–10

Humphrey R 2004 The Oxford Road Watermill, Aylesbury, *Recs Bucks* 44, 67–103

Legg E 2005 Water Eaton Mill, *Recs Bucks* 45, 161–8

Mead Alan F 1999 *Days of Glory. The story of Glory Mill, Wooburn Green, Bucks.* Farr Out Publications, no address given.

Petchey M 1983 The excavation of a late seventeenth century watermill at Caldecotte, Bow Brickhill, Bucks *Post Med Archaeol* 17 , 65–94

Reid, Kenneth C 1987/ 1989 *Watermills of the London Countryside; their place in English landscape and life.* Charles Skilton Ltd.(Vol I , 1987; Vol 2, 1989)

The working parts of a watermill

Martin Watts

Ford End Mill, Ivinghoe, the only working watermill in Buckinghamshire, can be used to illustrate the terms applied to parts of a mill and how they are linked together (Fig. 5). Ford End is an overshot mill, that is to say the water is fed onto the wheel from above.

The iron overshot waterwheel, **A**, is mounted on a horizontal iron wheelshaft, **B**. At its inner end this shaft carries the pitwheel, **C**. The pitwheel is a cast-iron mortise gear with wooden cogs, which in turn mesh with the wallower, **D**, a cast iron bevel gear. Both the wallower and the great spur wheel, **E**, are fixed to a vertical timber shaft, **F**. The great spur wheel meshes with the two gears called stone nuts, **G**, mounted on vertical iron spindles, **H**, through which the millstones are driven. Near the top of the upright shaft **F** is the crown wheel, **I**. This is a cast-iron gear with wooden cogs which drives an iron cog or bevel pinion, **J**, mounted on the end of a layshaft, **K**. A belt drive is taken from a belt wheel or pulley **L** on the layshaft to the sack hoist, **M**, in the roof space above.

Sacks of grain are lifted up through the mill on the sack chain, **N**. The grain is emptied into one or other of the bins, **O**, on the top floor and is fed by gravity down a spout to the milling hopper, **P**. The hopper is supported by a wooden frame called the horse, **Q**. Grain is fed steadily into the eye of the upper, runner, stone, **R**, by the shoe, **S**, an inclined wooden trough, which is shaken from side to side by the damsel, **T**. Each pair of millstones is contained in a circular case, called a tun or vat, **U**. The grain is milled between the faces of the rotating runner stone, **R**, and the stationary bedstone, **V**. The ground grain, called meal or wholemeal, falls down a spout to be collected in the meal ark or bin, **W**, on the ground floor.

The fineness of the meal can be controlled by the miller adjusting the tentering screw, **X**, which raises or lowers the bridge tree, **Y**, and thus the stone spindle, **H**, and the runner stone, **R**, while the mill is at work. Each pair of millstones can be disengaged by raising the stone nut, **G**, out of mesh with the great spur wheel, **E**, by using the jack ring, **Z**. If finer flour is required, the meal or wholemeal is refined by passing it through a sieve or flour dresser, by which the coarser particles and bran are removed.

The diagram is based on the layout of Ford End Mill, Ivinghoe, and prepared by the author with kind permission of the Pitstone Local History Society.

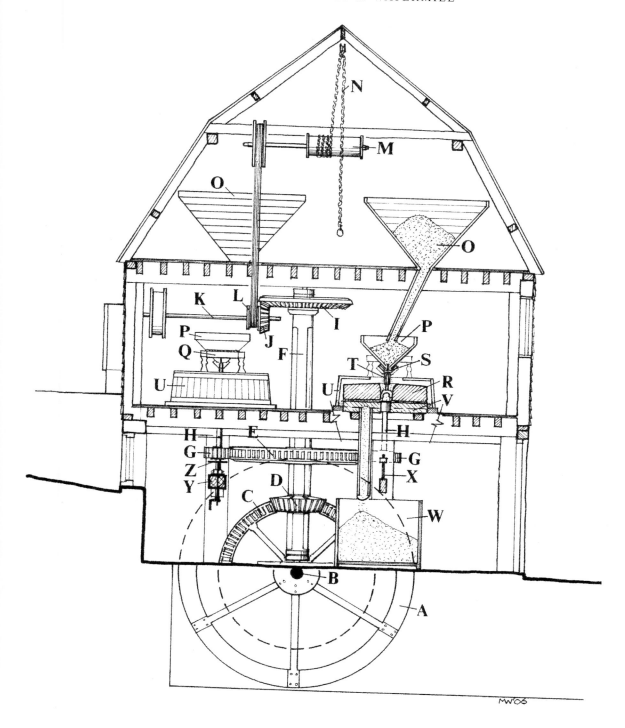

FIGURE 5 The working parts of a watermill, based on Ford End, Ivinghoe. Drawing by Martin Watts.

Finding a particular mill in this book

The easiest way to locate a specific mill is to check the index which follows. If the layout of the book itself at first appears far from obvious, it is because it is based on watercourses respectively, Chapter 1, The Ouse: Chapter 2, The tributaries of the Ouse: Chapter 3, The Thames: Chapter 4, The Thames' tributaries draining northwards from the Chilterns, and Chapter 5, The Thames' tributaries draining the Chilterns dip slope to the south. Mills at the head of the river or tributary stream are described first, then mills downstream, noting the parish or town within which each lies.

There are occasions where Freese was unsure of the local name for a stream. In describing Culverton Mill, Princes Risborough, for example, he notes that he had adopted the name 'Risborough Stream' in the absence of a recognised local name. Occasionally he gives no indication of a river or stream name; some-times this may be an oversight but sometimes it is because the mill has long gone and he is not sure where the mill was sited. In these instances the editors have supplied a best-guess in square brackets to assist in a mill's approximate location. Figure 6 shows the waterways of the historic county and the principal river names, but the scale is too small to show the location of individual mills.

In the entries, following each parish name, the parish's distance from the nearest town is given and then each mill name or names. As sometimes there is more than one river or stream in a parish, parish names may occur in more than one place. Where the author has evidence only from documentation for an early mill, he notes this with words such as 'early mill' or 'Domesday Mill' and occasionally suggests a potential site. Mills or their sites are located by distance from the parish church expressed in miles or occasionally in furlongs (f). It is noted whether the mill is working or used for some other purpose and then a list of dates of maps that the writer has referred to is given. Two common dates 1768 and 1824, refer respectively to the County maps of Jefferys and Bryant. These maps were republished in 2000 by the Buckinghamshire Archaeological Society (*Buckinghamshire in the 1760s and 1820s; the County Maps of Jefferys and Bryant.*)

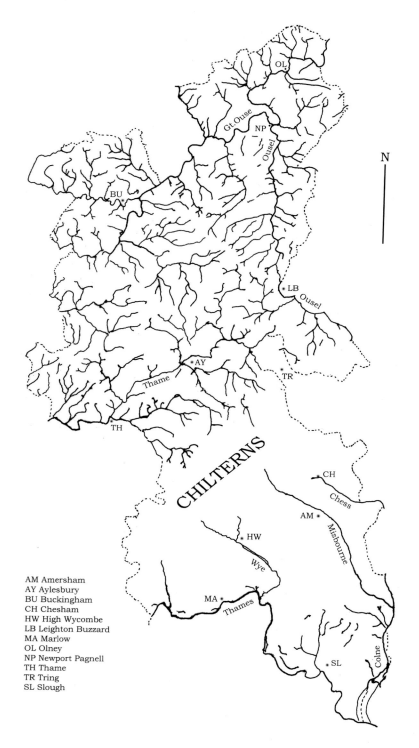

FIGURE 6 Waterways of Buckinghamshire, based on a map by Margaret Gornall.

Index to Parishes and Watermill Names in the Manuscript

Compiled by Diana Gulland

In many cases the parish name is also the name of the mill/mills e.g. Turweston Mill or Chesham Mills. When the mill has a name other than the parish an entry has been made under that name followed by the parish.

The state of Buckinghamshire's watermills in 2006: the Mill Check project

Michael Farley

In order to assess how Freese's watermills have fared since he visited them, the Buckinghamshire Archaeological Society thought it would be worthwhile to re-visit those sites where he had noted above-ground remains, principally mill buildings or mill houses. During 2006 nineteen volunteers visited all of these places and completed a simple presence/absence recording form, largely viewing from publicly accessible places such as footpaths. Where circumstances permitted note was made of current use, ownership, etc and several were also photographed. The survey showed, not surprisingly, that a considerable number have in the intervening decades been demolished.

Freese noted 93 standing mill buildings, of which only 47 (50.5%) remain in any form. This figure includes Pann Mill, High Wycombe, where the wheel has been preserved and a new building constructed adjacent to it houses mill machinery used for demonstration purposes. The figure excludes Stoke Mandeville Mill which still stands today but which Freese missed. Of the remaining mills, Ford End at Ivinghoe has been completely preserved (see Fig .5) and is publicly accessible and restored to working order. A handful of others are known still to have some internal machinery (most significantly at Preston Bissett), or occasionally just an external wheel preserved but it was not the principal intention of this rapid survey to seek access to the interior of buildings. A number of the standing mill buildings that do remain are used for industrial or commercial uses and it is likely that little if any machinery remains within them. A few have been converted to flats.

Mill houses, not surprisingly, have fared a little better. Freese was not particularly interested in mill houses and noted far fewer of them than mills, often, only noting their existence as evidence of the former location of a mill. Altogether he noted 63 mill houses; the survey recorded 45, some of them not noted by Freese. Mill houses commonly remain as domestic accommodation and a number are listed buildings. Overall, where particulars were available considering each mill complex as one unit – either mill or mill house or both together on one site – 47 examples of domestic use were found and 12 of commercial use. It is evident that domestic use gives a better chance of survival to either kind of structure in Buckinghamshire. In conclusion it may be worth noting that the much modified Taplow Mill has recently closed.

Information from the survey has been passed to the relevant Sites and Monuments Records and to local Conservation Officers; the original record forms etc. are deposited with the Society.

Editors' Acknowledgements

The Society is indebted to the Francis Coales Charitable Foundation for a grant towards the cost of publishing this book. The County Museum and the County Archaeological Service provided access to the manuscript and answered a number of queries, and the Centre for Buckinghamshire Studies kindly gave access to all of the photographs. The book cover was designed by Lee Upton. Many volunteers assisted with the Mill Check project and thanks are due to them for their efforts and to several mill owners for providing information.

The Watermills of
Buckinghamshire

Stanley Freese

Preface

A man without a hobby is dead! So, in the writer's view is a countryside without windmills: and the least one hopes to find in the course of a tour around any agricultural county is a disused windmill or two – either derelict or, better still, preserved for posterity. I say posterity because I hope and believe a few of our Bucks windmills will enjoy lasting preservation, also because an antiquarian acquaintance has remarked with a certain amount of truth that to preserve windmills for the present shallow speed-loving generation is like casting pearls before swine!

Among Buckinghamshire millers, interest in Windmills is limited generally to a sort of reminiscent atmosphere – something that used to be of interest when their great sails were gaily working in the breeze, serving a useful purpose, and producing a comfortable living for the miller.

Reduced to idleness the windmill loses its attraction for such practical folk, who have sometimes observed to me of a derelict mill, "she might as well be down – she's doing no good" But there are exceptions – the old time millers, and farmers and ploughmen too, who lament the passing of these giants of the countryside, retaining an affectionate thought not only for the derelict but for the bygone mill. Especially do such men regret the idleness of the mills; and the late Mr. Ben Burton – of whom we shall hear much – wrote to me in 1937, at the age of 83:-

"I well remember riding in the miller's cart when I was working at Aylesbury Mills for Mr. George Hill in 1872; I used to go around Haddenham and remember seeing Haddenham Mill at work, also Cuddington Mill was worked by people named Boddington, who also worked the Cuddington water-mill, while one of my uncles was working Lower Winchendon Watermill. Also I saw Stone Windmill in work; and some years later I went to Crendon and could see the two windmills, and I delivered flour at Brill and saw the two mills at work there. Now one has to say *how are the mighty fallen!* I remember seeing one at work near Thame, by the station; also a little later when I returned to North Marston, and worked the mill until 1876 or 1877, I would often, when I had time take a walk over the hills to Quainton, and when I stood on the hill and saw Mursley and North Marston, and Stone and Waddesdon mills all swinging along. Then a little farther on I used to stand and watch the old post mill near Quainton station, worked at that time under the name of Curtis, then the present mill now standing. It was a delightful sight to watch the sails of all these old mills working away.

Great Horwood was hidden from our view, but many a time I have seen it at work near at hand; and I felt I must pass these few remembrances on"

Mr. Burton who had a particularly accurate memory for date, went to no small amount of trouble in spite of failing health to inform me of every item he could recall in connection with wind and water-mills and milling generally, in numerous long letters, besides sending me such photographs, books and press cuttings as came to his notice bearing upon our local windmills; and for this invaluable assistance I and all students of milling history cannot be too grateful.

The late Mr William Cripps, of Cuddington, also made me welcome on numerous occasions at his little cottage, where he discoursed at great length on wind and watermilling, telling me of his varied experiences at the many mills with which he was associated in his long career; and to him I am very specially indebted. Even at the age of 90, Mr. Cripps propounded his theories about the possible future of windmills, suggesting that six-sailers should be built on the farms to generate electricity, which would drive caterpillar tractors with cable operated machinery, as in steam-ploughing practice. Current would be collected by trolley-arm from wires above the headlands.

Both Mr. Cripps and Mr. Burton – born respectively in 1851 and 1854 – were octogenarians when I first made their acquaintance; and the trouble they each took to place all their information and experiences at my disposal at their advanced ages is the more appreciated.

Innumerable other millers and owners to whom acknowledgements are made in the text, also have obliged me with historical and other particulars of their own and, very often, of neighbouring mills; their co-operation, and willingness to allow me to scramble about their mills – some not generally open to inspection owing to their dangerous condition – has been extremely helpful, and the following account I trust will give satisfaction to all concerned. Several paper manufacturers also have been extremely obliging and informative; and are entitled to special thanks in view of the secret nature of their trade.

Much useful information I have gleaned from the monumental *Victoria County History of Bucks*; from early maps, books and papers in the British Museum; and the maps, *Records of Bucks*, parish histories and other documents too numerous to mention at the Bucks Museum at both of which places one's enquiries have met with the most courteous and obliging attention, especially from the late Mr. Edwin Hollis, Curator of the Bucks Museum, whose memory will long be cherished by every antiquarian student in our County, and from Miss Cecily Baker who must long since have christened me "ITMA".

Most of our local newspapers, directories and Ordnance maps originate in the early 1820's just after a series of especially interesting events – the removal of a number of windmills from one site to another – had taken place; consequently much that would be of interest is irretrievably lost, although Mr Cripp's life-long enthusiasm and remarkable memory have done much to fill the gap.

Inevitably in this mass of facts collected from innumerable sources there will be a sprinkling of errors, political prejudice behind it, is based upon some far distant fact or event and is often distorted by the passage of time. If I have failed to glean all the facts that could have been wished for, I must console the reader and myself with the observation of the worthy Thomas Wright of Olney; – "In research work, the most satisfactory result, next to the discovery of where something is, is the discovery of where it isn't!"

Other County surveys are in progress, touching only upon windmills however; a voluminous history of the four hundred odd Kentish windmills past and present has already been published by Mr. W. Coles-Finch. In Sussex, my friend, Mr. H.E.S. Simmons, to whom I am greatly indebted for enlarging most of my photographs, has undertaken an extremely comprehensive survey; in Suffolk too Mr Simmons was assisting me with a less comprehensive enquiry before the war; and so on.

Let us not rest content until the whole country has been well and truly combed for windmill and watermill history! The task is full of interest; but it needs careful organising, and should not lightly be undertaken without determining to publish the result, for to dabble with the subject and then drop it, as some have is to queer the pitch for other, and is unfair to the millers.

Let us tilt our pens at the decaying mills and ply the worthy Old Inhabitants with questions whilst the tit-bits of windmill lore are yet stored amongst the treasured memories of their youth! Time marches on, and with it the interest and appreciation of fine craftsmanship and the desire to know and understand the life of our countryfolk in the Olden Days.

Chapter 1
Buckinghamshire Watermills
on the River Ouse

"From Brackley breaking forth, through soiles most heauenly sweet,
By Buckingham makes on, and crossing Watling Street,
Shee with the lesser Ouze at Newport doth twin,
Which from proud Chiltern neere comes eas'ly ambling in,
The Brooke which on her Banke doth boast that earth alone:
(Which noted) of this Ile, converteth wood to stone.
That little Aspleyes earth we anciently instile,
Mongst sundry other things, A wonder of the Ile:
Of which the lesser Ouze oft boasteth in her way,
As shee her selfe with Flowers doth gorgeously array".

Michael Drayton's *Poly Olbion 1622*

BIDDLESDEN – 3½ m. N.E. from Brackley

River Ouse

Domesday Mills
Evershaw Mill

All Gone
Site unknown

Rising in the great Northamptonshire hills north of Brackley, the Ouse – reputed boundary of the "Danelaw" a thousand years ago – is formed of two streams coming from Halse Copse and Wappenham respectively, and meeting just below the picturesque lakes in Biddlesden Park. At any rate this is the source anyone would assume from a perusal of the Ordnance maps: but the late Rev. C.E. Farrar, a noted authority on the Ouse, claimed to have found its source about 1000 yards south-east of Farthinghoe Church, *because this is its most westerly point* – a quite irrelevant fact in the present writer's opinion.

The Reverend did, however, establish the fact that the Biddlesden and Turweston branch is locally called the Mill Brook: and the western branch, the Ouse Brook, but it is difficult to know why *the Farthinghoe tributary* is the Ouse Brook, and it would seem more reasonable that the main stream from Gretworth (which it joins) should enjoy the distinction. This however is not an isolated problem, for even the source of Father Thames is disputed.

Domesday Mills

Probably the Domesday Mills were upon the Wappenham stream, which links up with the Biddlesden lakes; and an obvious possibility is the south end of the westerly lake.

Valued at 28 pence, the two Domesday Mills belonged to Biddlesden Manor; and in Henry III's day (1202–1272) the Abbey released a mill to Gilbert de Finmere, which *Victoria County* implies was at Blackgrove near Waddesdon in a somewhat vague passage. In 1278–9 the Biddlesden mills stood one within and one without the Abbey; and in the 16th century, the term Walkermyll is recorded in the parish.

Evershaw Mill

Meanwhile Biddlesden held its portion of Evershaw Manor, including a mill of some kind until the Dissolution 400 years ago. Evershaw Farm and Copse are upon the hilltop towards Shalstone, with only the small Shalstone stream nearby; and it is possible that this was a wind or horsemill although these usually are described as such. Biddlesden Abbey also held quite a few mills outside the county, e.g. Houghton, Charwelton and Helmingham, Northants.; and Boycote, Gloucester.

Below Biddlesden on the Northants bank of the stream, is Whitfield Watermill, after which we come to Turweston.

TURWESTON – 1m. N.E. from Brackley

River Ouse or *Mill Brook*

Turweston Mill   1½ f. N. of Church   Standing disused   1768, (1809), (1847), 1875, 1914

Since the recent alterations to Padbury Mill, none of the old-world thatched watermills survive in Bucks.; but the farmstead to which Turweston mill is attached is a stone-walled, thatched structure, approached by a picturesque ford beneath overhanging trees. This little watery lane is on our right at the foot of the descent from village to boundary bridge upon the Brackley road.

The river follows the county boundary all the way down here, but the mill is built upon the loopway which is wholly in Bucks. Of stone and slate it contains the usual three floors, including attic floor; the latter about two feet below the eaves, accommodating the customary stepped hoppers on either side.

At the east end is the wheel-room, which is divided in two, the outer half accommodating the by-pass with a sluice and a brick flight of steps against the outer walls; inside are the remains of a substantially built all-wooden eight spoked breast-wheel, of 10ft. diameter, unventilated. The "flash" is screw operated from within the mill proper; and mill stream and by-pass combine as they leave the building.

An eight-armed four-piece iron pit-wheel remains, engaging iron to iron with a wallower upon the upright shaft of the same material. Between wallower and first floor is the morticed iron great spur which drove iron stonenuts upon jack-rings; all gear is within the customary cupboard-like enclosure.

Actually one stone-nut is missing, but interesting

Turweston Mill

items lying about are a pair of centrifugal governors and a wooden belt-drum and steelyard, the means of mounting which are not apparent. Governors are extremely rare in watermills, especially where no steam-power was used; and it is possible the set in question belonged to Turweston Windmill which was in the same ownership.

On first floor of the watermill were two pairs of stones; and above them, in middle of room, a large crown-wheel, newly enclosed in a wooden case, drove from its upper periphery an iron bevel upon a layshaft lowered into gear by a lever, and carrying one wooden and two iron drums. Doubtless one of these drove the sack hoist, now missing.

In 1798, John Bliss was the miller of Turweston, followed by George Bliss, probably holding both water and windmills, as did the Course family later. This family were gentlemen millers, leaving employees to tend the mills; and the last proprietor of Turweston Watermill was Thomas Course. The Mill

ceased work near the close of the century, although William Seaton since used the mill in connection with his threshing business for a while down to the Great War. Now it is derelict, floors weak and the waterwheel rotted and part washed away, but the farmhouse is intact.

Perhaps a watermill has stood here since Domesday, when there was in Turweston a mill worth 7/6d. for which, with half a virgate of land, William the Miller paid 14/- in 1278. "William le Muney (Meunier?)" says *V.C.H. Vol IV* "brought an action in 1302–3 against William Maunsell for having by night, out of malice aforethought, thrown a great quantity of quicksilver in the mill pond at Turweston, causing damage to the amount of £100!". Afterwards the mill was held on lease from the Dean and Chapter of Westminster; and removal of a plank bridge leading thereto was the subject of a lawsuit in 1680. Another 17th century document refers to arable land called Upper and Lower Wakes Mill and to a windmill; but this name seems to be forgotten locally. *Victoria County* also mentions Wakes Mill under Waddesdon, and one wonders whether the name links up with the Wakes family who held other mills – e.g. Lower Winchendon – 500 years ago.

Brackley Mill, on a loop-stream against the railway viaduct, in Northants, is next down stream – a roomy mill by steam and water with four pairs of stones; and below, after Mill Brook joins the Ouse Brook, is Westbury Mill.

WESTBURY – 2½ m. E.S.E. from Brackley

Westbury Watermill – 3 f. W of Church

River Ouse

Used as factory
1768, (1809), (1847), 1875, 1887, 1914

Westbury Mill as it now stands is large, four-storeyed, chiefly of stone with some red brick facings, situate at the bottom of Mill Lane, a little steep track leading from the village and formerly flanked by several cottages which were demolished because uninhabitable. Tall and flat-fronted, with two long parallel roofs reaching across the stream, it has a newer wing at right-angles at the west end: and a red brick chimney shaft.

The stream, approaching almost from the south, passes beneath the main wing, where it turned an all-iron closed breast-wheel about 10ft. tread and 14ft. diameter with three sets of 6 arms, situated within the north wall and driving the usual upright shaft and four pairs of stones, the gears being enclosed in a "cupboard".

Formerly the stream, embanked to form a long mill race, drove an old wooden wheel: and the by-pass discharges into a loopway along the county boundary (the mill race being within Bucks by a hundred yards). Mill Close and Mill Meadow adjoin the mill, up the front of which is a wooden sack loft reaching from first floor to roof and providing shelter for loaders in the yard. The older parts of the present structure were erected about 1860 by Mr. Chapman, uncle of the last miller, to replace an ancient little grist mill which John Treadwell father or grandfather of the Radclive miller had in 1798; and the latest portion dates from 1890; the latter housed a condensing engine with roller plant on the ground floor. A line-shaft ran along the west wall, driving up to third floor by belt, to operate cleaners and smutters, etc., aided by other line-shafting, and upright conveyors were provided throughout. A shaft also ran from engine-room to upright shaft so that a belt could be coupled to drive anything that might be required from waterwheel and engine together. During the Great War, the iron axle of the last wheel broke and

six months elapsed before a new one could be obtained. The pit-wheel all iron and a morticed iron great spur, drove four iron stone-nuts.

For several years prior to 1939 only the barley stones were worked, chiefly for grist, engine and rollers being idle. Two pairs of stones were removed when the roller gear was installed; and the mill was entirely cleared out in September 1939, just when it might well have embarked on a new and more useful sphere of life as a water-mill, all gear being in good condition. Manufacture of paint commenced, entailing unnecessary transport, only justifiable if water-power were utilized; the owner's explanation being that he could purchase flour in the market cheaper than grain.

For about a century the mill had run in the name of Chapman, and a miller named Inson worked there all his life, generally doing the day turn one week and the night turn the next; his son assisted for a while some 40 years ago, but did not care for milling. Mr. Collins, the last foreman, aged 75 in 1938, also spent his life at the mill, and in his time six or seven men were kept busy day and night, but trade became very slow in this out-of-the-way spot.

Westbury Mill does not seem to have existed at Domesday, the only mill recorded being, it is thought, at the Huntsmill site. In 1278/9 Hogshaw Preceptory owned land and a watermill (for which Gordon Bastard paid a yearly rent of 30/-) which may have been at Westbury village; and a watermill other than Huntsmill is noted in 1608, when Thomas Slye died seised of hereditaments later described as "a water-mill and lands held of Sir Lestrange Mordaunt, Bart., as of his manor of Westbury by a rent of 13½ d., 2 lbs. of wax and a pair of spurs;" and *V.C.H. Vol. IV* says "this probably is the one standing in the west end of the parish today".

WESTBURY – 2½ m. E.S.E. from Brackley

River Ouse

Hunt Mill or *Huntsmill*   1⅛ m. E.S.E. of Church

Slight foundations
Named on 1768, (1809), 1833, (1847), 1887, 1914

The name of Hunt Mill, recorded as far back as the 13th century, survives to this day; indeed, the old mill cottage was standing until the outbreak of the Great War, for a Westbury man told me his last job before joining up was to help demolish it; and Hunt Mill Field, Huntsmill Ground, Close, Knoll and Meadow, flank the site.

A public footpath from Shalstone Hill Farm is now the best means of access to the site, about half a mile below the farmstead, between fields 1 and 4 in Westbury parish although the above farmhouse in Shalstone parish is sometimes called Hill and Huntsmill Farm.

The mill building appears from slight foundations to have stood chiefly on the north bank of the stream, whilst an open lean-to was behind the building (the stone supports for its front pillars being still there). The stream is walled up by stonework on both banks where it apparently passed beneath the wheelhouse, with a fall just below; and the by-pass is south of the river, sometimes called Huntsmill Mill stream, upon the county boundary.

V.C.H. Vol.IV, (prepared before the Great War) says the mill is standing, but everyone locally agrees that the actual mill disappeared long ago; it adds that one mill is mentioned in Westbury at Domesday "and it was known in the 13th century as Hunt Mill. It remained attached to the honour of Wallingford, though separated from the Manor, and in the 15th century is found in the ownership of the lords of Shalstone Manor. Philip Purefoy died seised of the mill in 1468 and further mention of it in this family occurs during the following two centuries".

Records of Bucks, Vol. XII, quotes the "will of John Purefoy of Shaldeston in the county of Buck, Esquire, in the yeare of Our Lorde God one thousand five hundred threescore and nineteene. "Item to my nephewe Edwarde Purefoye a splayed yearlinge mare colte, A millstone, the mill Pikes and all the furniture of the mill and all the sawen ash and elme aboute the house."

WATER STRATFORD – 2¾ m. W. from Buckingham

River Ouse

Early Watermill   Approx. 1 f. E of Church

Gone
No map reference

Water Stratford is locally claimed to be the earliest Stratford or Street-ford in England; certainly it is a settlement with very early associations and the Roman road from Bicester to Towcester is driven straight through the village, although now deviating near the Church.

Traditional site of the watermill is south-east of the village, probably at the east end of the loop in the river which causes the Tingewick road to cross two little stone bridges as it spans the green below the railway embankment. Many years – perhaps several centuries – before Huntsmill disappeared, Stratford Mill had gone; and an affable farmhand who indicated the alleged site, drew my attention also to the ancient trackway running from behind the Manor House eastwards across the fields, now only a grassy ridge but still capable, he said, of supporting a threshing tackle in any weather and still a public right-of- way. Once upon a time it was much favoured by carters for avoiding the Radclive Toll-gate – a common use for medieval trackways in turnpike days!

At Domesday a mill worth 8/- held by Turstin of Robert Doyley; and there was a watermill on the demesne at the Inquisition of 1278/9; whilst a mill amongst the appurtenances of the Manor, was destroyed by Isobel de Stratford about 1349 – possibly the last watermill in the parish.

TINGEWICK – 2½ m. W.S.W. from Buckingham

Tingewick Mill – 5½ f. N.N.E. of Church

Occasionally used
1768, (1809), 1833, 1875, 1887, 1914, 1926

Most romantically situated is Tingewick Watermill; only a quarter of a mile distant was a Roman settlement on the hillside and nearby was an ancient stone-bottomed ford, perhaps pre-Roman, on the river, whilst across the valley in the Water Stratford direction, ran the old Roman high road and the medieval cartway. Roman remains were found in the field called "Stollidge" at the settlement, where strong clear springs provide good water; but since Roman times no-one has dwelt upon this site.

The old stone and brick-built mill, tile-roofed with hip-gable, and more or less cemented over – its walls tapering a little towards the top in a way suggestive of great strength and containing a few 16th. century bricks – is approached by a very rough and steep lane beneath giant elms, first passing through a gated

farmyard and across a paddock in which cows inquisitively inspect the stranger.

Mr. G.E. Pym the farmer-miller, who kindly showed me round, volunteered an assortment of most interesting information, although pointing out that so far as folklore and stories of past millers were concerned, it is all hearsay, to be taken for what it is worth.

Taking the machinery in order as driven from the stream, we find a new waterwheel in the north end of the mill, almost unique in being of a clasp-arm design although of all-iron construction. The four arms each side of the wheel are of channel section, one pair bolted back-to-back with each other. Believed to have been supplied by Messrs. Joseph Armfield, the Ringwood (Hants) millwrights and

Tingewick Mill

agricultural engineers, 12ft. diameter over the curved and ventilated buckets; and Mr. Pym thinks it develops about 5-7 H.P. Curiously enough although itself all iron, the wheel is mounted upon a very massive, square wooden axle-tree, notwithstanding that it is a new axle, not an old relic.

A good photograph of the previous wheel is fortunately preserved in one of the albums at the Bucks Museum, with dimensions appended. Of similar clasp-arm type and same diameter, it measured 5ft. 4ins. across the tread and had a 16ins. square axle of wood with winged steel gudgeons, the axle ends being secured by iron hoops. There were 32 wooden "buckets" and two sets of spokes; and a good head of water behind this wheel drove one pair of stones at a rate that ground one sack of barley per hour.

An eight-arm, iron pitwheel, in two parts bolted together, drives a small wallower iron-to-iron, upon a wooden upright shaft; and just over the wallower is an eight-spoked *one piece* cast-iron great spur with cogs of foreign wood – not apple – pinned through the shanks. Iron stone-nuts on jack-rings drive two pairs of stones placed abreast on the first floor where, near the ceiling, the upright shaft is carried in a massive framework held together entirely by wedges, without nails or bolts, and within this frame a morticed iron crown-wheel drives an iron cog upon a layshaft with belt-drums. One belt drove the brush and wire wheat cleaner; another the winnowing fan in an old wooden case near the top of a spout, where it blew dirt and dust out of the grain as it passed from cleaner to ground floor.

Only one pair of stones remain, but the wheel also drives a lighting dynamo by belt from the layshaft. Formerly the feeder shoe had a bone tip running against the four-pronged damsel, to secure silent running, but an iron tip is now fitted; and a willow spring and cord hold the shoe up to the damsel.

There had been a flour sifter or cleaner for separating bran, on the first floor; and also a spare bolter. The sack hoist in the roof loft is somewhat similar to those at Thornborough and Three Bridge, the other side of Buckingham; one end of the bollard rests on a pivoted bar, the free end of which is raised by the tip of a longer lever coming from the opposite direction; and the latter lever has a rope suspended from its far end, and runs between two uprights to one of which an iron ratchet is secured. Whilst in the loft I noticed that the tiles are mortared in and cannot slip in the event of the pegs giving way; and Mr. Pym mentioned that years ago some baker rented a bin in the loft so that their grain could be stored there to be ground as required.

There is accommodation for 50 or 60 tons of grain in the bins which are as usual, in aisles either side of a gallery.

At some time the mill has been fired, many of the timbers being burnt on the surface; they are neatly morticed and tenoned but there are various new timbers and throughout the mill are signs of alteration and rebuilding. One wall is cracked, through centuries of vibration and the north-east corner consequently is buttressed. The mill stands across a fine built-up race a quarter of a mile long, beginning just below an elegantly finished railway bridge, the dressed stone facings of which are carved with designs and are thought to have been intended for a road bridge perhaps elsewhere, for there is normally no-one but the cows to admire this artistic masonry.

To check flooding, a short by-pass or cut is placed just above the mill from millrace to the main stream, which passes north of the mill; and a large pair of flood gates are provided, the worms and ratchets of which originally belonged to an old hand-feed saw bench. Below the gate is an eel-trap covered by a wooden bridge with trap-doors; and from the trap a short tunnel leads to an eel tank at one side; whilst in the mill-tail is a sheep-dip to which thousands of sheep were brought in days when a wash in running water was considered sufficient.

On the bank of the mill-tail are remains of a lime-kiln and several clear springs; and another spring is situated in the wheel-pit, probably coming from 20ft. below the river bed. So much have the banks been eaten away by the river, which is quite slow running, falling about one foot per mile, that the ten rods of ground between river, mill-tail and flood cut, are charged at a quarter of an acre under the old rating.

The Mill House, at the south end of mill is of more recent date, but between the two structures some parts of the original mill cottage are incorporated.

On the marsh below the Roman settlement, bog lights – Jack o' Lanterns – may be seen some nights hence the existence a century ago of Jack o' Lantern Farm hereabouts; and many fanciful explanations have been applied to these lights by superstitious villagers some of whom would not spend a night at the mill if you paid them! Indeed the mill itself is supposed to be haunted, although Mr. Pym's practical outlook seems to have discouraged the eerie visitors, who have not presented themselves before him. The valley is exceptionally cold and subject to heavy frosts, so that fruit blossom is usually nipped in the bud; and it is liable to flooding, the water coming up to the mill door on occasion, but not in the house as it does at Radclive Mill downsteam.

All the surrounding country, formerly ploughland was grass in 1939, consequently business had dwindled to nothing; but fifty years ago Mr. Pym's predecessors worked one night a week to avoid having to work on Sunday to cope with the business. The regular practice at that time was to keep back one sack of meal per cartload in payment for the grinding; and outsiders were never allowed within the mill, perhaps because business was business, or perhaps because the millers had many little tricks for diddling the customers in olden days!

Alnod, a man of Edward the Confessor had the Manor of Tingewick in Saxon times; and Ilbert de Lacei held it of the Bishop of Bayeux in 1086, with a mill valued at 4 shillings. In 1291 a capital messuage

and other houses, in bad condition, went with a dovecot and a windmill; and exactly a century later the Manor passed to the Bishop of Winchester, for the use of Winchester College, Oxford (now known as New College), which still holds the mill and surrounding land.

We read of John Bateman, miller and farmer in 1798, and "Late of Tingewick" in 1821; in 1830 Joseph Coles was the miller, and William Neal of Tingewick Mills was in 1835 attacked by three men near Buckingham, and robbed of £10 and his watch etc. The Pollard family, who preceded Mr. Pym, had the mill about three-quarters of a century, William Pollard first, and Mrs. Elizabeth Pollard and Sons till about 1915, when they were given only as steam millers, although the new wheel was installed since then.

RADCLIVE – 1m.W. from Buckingham

Ratley or *Radclive Mill*   1 f. E.S.E. of Church

River Ouse

Standing disused
1768, (1809), 1825, 1833, 1875, 1926

One of the largest and most interesting great spur wheels in the county is in Radclive Watermill; its diameter is, as near as I could measure owing to the difficulty of getting at it, 10 feet; and it is interesting for the shape of its eight spokes which are curved so that the wheel is like a giant saucer inverted. Its 170 teeth engage with four stone-nuts, two one side and two the other, on jack rings, the whole being enclosed whilst the stones, on the first floor, are in pairs spaced apart, so that extra stones could be added if desired to drive six pairs from one spur (with 12ins. nuts six pairs of 5ft. stones might be ranged round a 10ft. wheel at a pinch, but these are under 5ft.

Upon the upright shaft is a small wallower lying in about the same plane as the periphery of the great spur, owing to the domed construction of the latter; and driven by an eight armed pit-wheel of some 10ft. diameter, mounted in 4ins. journals. All machinery is of iron, including cogs.

The fine old 11ft breast-shot wheel, built entirely of wood, has three sets of eight spokes with 40 ventilated buckets; and attached to its outer shroud is an iron cog-ring of about 180 teeth for coupling by shaft and belt to a steam engine in the adjoining field, to drive with or without water power.

On the first floor a six armed morticed crown-wheel drove a line-shaft with solid wooden drums, one being coupled by belt to a dresser in a large case.

In the roof are the bins alongside a central deck; and from this loft was an entry into the south gable of the mill house, so that it could be used for additional storage of grain.

Built of un-dressed stone with slate roof, the mill bestrides the stream with by-pass farther south; and the homely Mill House has plastered wall and tiled roof. The mill floors are weak, however; the wheel is falling to pieces, having stood idle for over thirty years; and the mill building, older than the house, dates partly from the 16th. century judging by the west windows. It is no doubt upon the site of the Domesday mill, value 5 shillings in 1086 and belonging to Radclive Manor, (as does the present mill) and later for some reason called West Mill; and as such it was bestowed by Ralph Hareng in 1243, on St. Michael's Chapel. From time to time the mill is mentioned in later extants; John Course was the miller in 1798 but few details have come to light until late 1823, when the estate including the "Valuable Water Corn Mill, with Dwelling House, etc." was for sale, held on lease by the Warden and Fellows of New College, Oxford. His Grace the Duke of Buckingham purchased the estate in 1824 for £12, 480.

John Treadwell junior was the tenant for the second half of the last century following upon a sale of the Buckingham Estate, including this mill; and

Ratley or *Radclive Mill*

the latter was next taken by the late Alfred Charles Rogers of Buckingham Castle and Town Mills, more to stop competition than to use it, although he is listed at Radclive as late as 1911 in *Kelly's*, the mill being worked by a manager – Thomas Neal. For kind permission to explore the premises I am indebted to Major Leeming, a recent occupier.

THE BOROUGH OF BUCKINGHAM

River Ouse

Early Mills – Sites doubtful

Gone

The Borough of Buckingham, first Mayor of which was Thomas Hillsdon – a name to conjure with in milling circles in Bucks – dates from 1684; and incorporates Prebend End, the hamlet of Bourton and Bourtonhold, and the ecclesiastical parishes of Gawcott and Lenborough. Of the several craft guilds, the Butcher's Guild included Butchers, Bakers Brewers, Cooks and Millers.

Early Mills
Two sites not definitely accounted for occur amongst a large property called Barton's in West Street, purchased from William Godde in 1385; and about 1600 the Lamberts held "the tenement called Castle House. . . an orchard near Podd's lane (the Maids Moreton road), two watermills, a dovehouse and various lands and tenements in Buckingham and Gawcott" Probably these were Castle Mill on the

14

Bicester road and the Fulling Mill on the site of the United Dairies Works, midway between the present church and the railway station; they were the only known mills in Buckingham town, for Wharf Mill (W.H. Smith & Sons) was never water-driven, as erroneously indicated in some directories.

BUCKINGHAM

Castle Mill – 150 yards W.S.W. of Church

River Ouse

Used as factory
1610, 1768, (1809), 1824, 1833, (1847), 1875, 1926

Buckingham was one of the pioneer towns in the construction of progressive agricultural machinery, for the Castle Iron Foundry – named after the same long-lost castle as the above mill – was founded in 1857; and a machine called the Locomotive Steam Cultivator for ploughing and threshing was here put into production. Excellent steam carriages were also made but Buckingham had already refused to accept a main line railway and is no longer the County town;

Gibbs quoted a comment of 1834 "Foolish prejudice still exists against railways. Most assuredly places that have no railroads will be left behind in the march of improvement".

Meanwhile millwrights were established in the town – Robert A'Church in Cowfair and Edmunds & Poynter at Ford Street. On their doorpost flood levels were marked from 1875–94; and they are progressively lower, the oldest being 3ft 7 ins and the latest

Castle Mill

6 ins, – an interesting sidelight on the gradual depletion of our rivers by neglect of field drainage and increased pumping for main water.

Curiously enough no written record exists of the castle after which Castle Mill is named; nor do many particulars of the Castle Mill seem to be recorded, although there was a mill – quite possibly attached to the Castle – at Domesday; and we have to turn to Speed's illuminated county map of 1610, incorporating an enlarged plan of Buckingham, for first evidence of the Castle Mill. He clearly depicts it at the present site on the corner of Nelson Street and Tingewick Road; and Jefferys indicates it in 1768.

George Sackville's estate incorporated Castle Mill until 1803, when the Coles family purchased it, Samuel Coles senior, whose name is amongst the Buckingham Millers in 1791, having apparently rented it for some years. With other property, the Mill was sold to the Marquis of Buckingham in 1804; twenty years later James Coles was the miller; but John Kirby advertised the premises in 1838 (although remaining till 1842) or later, describing same as: "a substantial brick-built and tiled corner premises in full trade, machinery in excellent repair, 2 pair of stones, dressing and smut machines, sack apparatus, meal chambers, garners for upwards of 200 quarters of corn, offal room, large granary, water-wheel house and room adjoining admirably adapted as an engine house for power by steam, Mill buildings are sufficiently spacious for several more pairs of stones; supply of water is abundant, new flood gates, eel traps; mill-head of great length and property includes whole of back brook, strongly built flash and ford with entrance from the street to meadow". A glowing account, especially as the Reverend T. Silvester says that the fall was 4 feet, as against 5 feet at the Fulling Mill close by!

In 1846 the bridge parapet against Castle Mill is supposed to have been smashed by the first locomotive of the Buckingham Railway, (coming by road from Wolverton) which stuck at the awkward corner; but this is an error; the Act for building the Railway was passed that year and the line opened on May 1st. 1850 which brought Buckingham in direct rail contact with Wolverton; and the engine brought by road more probably belonged to a contractor about to construct part of the railway.

In 1845 John King owned "Castle Mill in Bourtonhold" but Kirby was still a miller in Red Lion Street in 1854, and next year the mill was again for sale with 3 pairs of stones. The same year Buckingham Workhouse offered "a corn mill for sale with dressing apparatus", possibly steam powered.

Thomas Gough was next listed at "The Mill",

meaning Castle Mill, but he declined the business owing to ill-health. and in 1879 the great A.C. Rogers – Mayor of Buckingham 1902–3–4 – entirely rebuilt the premises having already established in 1864 the Station Steam Mill with 5 pairs of stones on the site of the steam plough works. (A 20h.p. steam corn-mill also existed at North End, near the Ship Inn, as early as 1841, driving one pair, probably on the site of Wharf Mill). There followed Castle Mill's most prosperous days with the Buckingham Agricultural & Trading Association as the last millers; but in 1936 when the exors. of the late Mrs. S.A. Rogers endeavoured to dispose of the property, the mill itself did not find a tenant.

An unprepossessing structure of red brick with yellow facings and slate roof, three-storeyed, with five windows abreast, it has a loading floor doorway in the centre, and at the far end a drive in for loading under cover. At the other end, on the street corner, a two-storeyed tiled wing contained until about 1940 a surprisingly old wooden clasp-arm breast wheel of 10ft. diameter with three sets of arms – a curious relic in so large a mill. Thirty-two wooden buckets were wedged in place and the wheel was upon an iron axle, the wedges of which seemed to be cemented in to prevent slipping; and it was probably of the same date as the present building – 1879, as set in big letters in the brickwork.

The pit-wheel drove an iron shaft supporting a morticed iron great spur beneath the first floor, driving 3 pairs with iron nuts and bridge-trees between the usual timber uprights. Three bins received grain from the respective stones via wooden spouts with screw-controlled spattles and the west half of the ground floor was for storage. Steam engine room and chimney-shaft are behind the wheel-house; and there is a large wing at the rear which almost certainly contained roller-milling equipment; but the mill was locked up for several years until F & M Richardson Ltd. fitted it out as a paint factory.

Following a tortuous course through the town, the Ouse approaches Castle Mill from the north, thence beneath wheel room and Tingewick Road, and behind the houses of Hunter Street; the by-pass sluice just above the mill, leads away beneath Castle Bridge to rejoin the mill-tail at once, and Speed's and Jefferys' maps clearly show that neither this nor the Fulling Mill layout of water have altered since their day.

In 1830, when "surplus" labourers of Buckingham were forced to march 2 miles to a stone-pit and return with a great stone, twice a day, a local miller proposed that they ladle water from his mill-tail to the mill-head, "which would at all events save shoe leather"!

BUCKINGHAM

River Ouse

Fulling Mill, Parsonage Mill, Prebend End Mill or *Town Mill*
– 1½ f. S. of Church

Incorporated in factory.
1610, 1768, (1809), 1824, 1833, (1847), 1875

At the Domesday Survey, Prebend End Manor (*alias* Buckingham with Gawcott Manor), part of the endowment of Buckingham Church, included a mill worth 10 shillings; and it seems probable this was upon the site of the Prebend End Mill of last century, where the United Dairies factory stands.

Speed indicates a Fulling Mill at this spot in 1610, together with a piece of the Town Wall immediately west of it; and Jefferys' accurately marks it but he has the Parish Church about midway between Castle Mill and Fulling Mill near the bottom of the present Church Street. This old church was ruined in 1776 when the tower collapsed upon the building; and my mill locations are from the present Church.

Bargaining for the Fulling Mills is recorded in 1613 when William Lambert appears to have bought them from Sir Robert Brett for £625.

"All those 2 watermills under one roof considered and called the Parsonage mills or the Prebend Mills in Buckingham, with the mill yard, dams banks, watercourses, streams, floodgates and fisheries thereto belonging, etc.; adjoining Lord's Bridge or the Parsonage unto the Sherriff Bridge and the 2 banks or cobbs standing unto the mill dam and the pond adjoining unto the Parsonage yard, near unto Lord's Bridge and all the Dovehouse near unto the said Mills being within the Court-yard of the Prebend or Parsonage House of Buckingham also Mill Meadow 2 acres".

William King, junior, miller and baker in 1791 sold them to P. Bootlett in 1830, advertising them as "a most substantial WATER CORN MILL with two powerful waterwheels driving three pairs of stones and machinery; a dwelling house, baking house, gardens, tenements and land; situate on the river Ouse in the Prebend End of the borough and parish of Buckingham, in the occupation of the proprietor William King".

The Reverend Thomas Silvester (M/s History of Buckingham, Vol. 2 1826/30) adds that £2500 was the price; the fall was 5ft; and King's father made "a Fuller's mill of it" from which one gathers that the mill led a shuttle-cock sort of life. At that period, says Silvester, every farmhouse spun their own linen, and King had work for himself and a man and two apprentices; the mill, he thought, was erected by the Prebend for the use of his tenants.

A decade later, William Turner the vacating occupier and joint owner stated, that Prebend End Mills were "in full trade and excellent working order, with two waterwheels driving 5 pairs of stones, flour smut, winnowing machine, bolting mill and large store rooms (the whole under a tiled and slated roof) large yard, wagon hovel, garden and tenements" Edward Atkins was the yearly tenant in 1854, when this freehold mill was once more for sale with a steam engine by the great Fairbain of Manchester, driving 3 pairs; the business being "the largest of any mill in the neighbourhood".

Robert Rogers became the miller; then the ambitious Alfred Charles Rogers appeared on the scene, inaugurating the Buckingham Electric Light Works at the Town Mills in 1888, though he seems to have retained a milling business here, being listed as a steam and water miller at these premises as well as at Castle Mills in 1903 and 1911.

On the mill wall, as at several other watermills, is an Ordnance "bench-mark", the altitude being 260 feet.

BUCKINGHAM (BOURTON)

River Ouse

Bourton Mill – ¾ m. E.S.E. of Buckingham Church

Standing empty.
1695, 1768, 1793, (1809), 1833, 1875, 1887, 1914, 1926

Bourton Mill, occupying a Domesday site, stands at the most southerly point of the Bedfordshire Ouse where it makes a sudden double bend just east of the former County Town; the mill is close by the Bletchley turnpike, half a mile beyond the new rash which has broken out on the hillside under the name of Bourtonville.

The Domesday Mill attached to Buckingham and Bourton, was valued at 14 shillings; in 1473 when it or a successor, was devised to John Wadward, who

Bourton Mill

kept it in repair for £7 6. 8, rent of assize included 20/- from various tenants, a pepper rent from Thomas More and sixpence from John Helwell representing the value of a pair of gilt spurs to pay for the right of way to the mill in the lord's demesne of Bourton Manor, which belonged to Humphrey, Duke of Buckingham. Eventually the mill passed to Katherine Atkyns who claimed interest in two water-mills in Bourton in the 16th century; later three watermills were attached to the Manor – probably at least two wheels (counted as two mills) in one building, or again, not all the mills need have been in the parish.

Michael Dover, who succeeded his father or uncle, was miller in 1798 and 1842; followed by Thomas Roper; Turner and White, owners of Prebend End Mill; G. Humphreys; Lane and Sons; W. Powell; R. Mossman (steam and water); T. Hawes, before the Great War; and H. Fricker of White House till around 1925.

The present building – probably refitted in 1886, in which year Mr. J.T. Harrison states that the Flower Show Fireworks concluded with a real fire at Bourton Mill – is of stone and brick with tiled roof, projecting wooden sack-loft and tall chimney shaft. The river passes beneath the north end with by-pass running around same, whilst the Mill House stands separately against the roadway.

An old miller employed at Messrs. W.H.Smith's power mill said that an all wooden compass-arm breast wheel was used; with the usual pit-wheel and upright shaft etc., driving four pairs on first floor by morticed iron spur. An iron cog-ring attached to the waterwheel, as at Radclive, was driven by a hori-zontal engine in its own room in the mill, with Cornish boiler in separate room.

Soon after the mill ceased work, Mr. Gilbert of Leighton Buzzard told me, someone took out the brasses and other metal work, and apparently thinking that a reasonably distant millwright would be a safe customer, brought the materials to Mr. Gilbert's people; but having done some work on the mill, they had more than a suspicion where the "Booty" came from and, not being satisfied that it was paid for, they declined it and the would-be vendor retired in disorder!

A dispute later arose as to the value of the mill; which stands idle with all its equipment cleared out, except for a few oddments such as the long screw-conveyors removed from their cases. The Mill Farm is occupied but as the parties in charge in 1939 did not speak English and I do not speak German, our meeting was short and sweet and my information had to be culled elsewhere.

MAIDS' MORETON – 1¼ m. N.E. from Buckingham

River Ouse

Maids' Moreton Mill – ¾ m. S.E. of Church

Standing empty
1768, (1809), 1832, 1833, (1847), 1875, 1887, 1914

Amongst a long list of field names in Maids' Moreton quoted in *Records of Bucks Vol. VI* are Mill Meadows, Winner Hill Close and Winemer Hill, which might be contractions of Windmill Hill, though no proof of the existence of a windmill in the parish has come to my notice.

Lenin of Nuneham held a mill worth 10/- with his manor in 1086, probably the watermill held by John Pever in 1279; and the Brend or Brent Mill was held by All Souls College in 1483, and leased by them subsequently. Probably these mills were upon the present site, in the absence of any other; and the

Maids' Moreton Mill

19

following notes relating to Brent Mill are in *V.C.H. Vol.IV*. Walter de Moreton occupied Greenhams Manor, on which the mill stood, in 1274, but in 1442 the Manor was granted by Henry VI to All Souls College, Oxford, who still hold it; in 1493 it was leased to Robert Woodward; and in 1535 John Harris was paying rent of £7.6.8. for the Manor of Moreton (Greenhams) with a mill called "Brent Myll"

In 1798 William Brittain was the miller; James Coles sold up his farm business at the mill, which belonged to Thomas Holt in 1832 and James Osborn and his widow ran the mill for many years, followed by John Robert Gough, from Buckingham, probably related to Thomas Gough of Castle Mill. He remained until the Great War using water only, as they all did

apparently; but the mill now stands empty and deserted, alongside a primitive gallows pattern draw-bridge. Approached by a cartway south of the Stony Stratford turnpike the mill is of local stone with tiled roof with brick cottage one end and a barn the other; and a few yards away is "The Old Mill House"

A wooden breast wheel driving two pairs was centrally placed in the mill which stands across a feeder from the Canal (opened in 1821) with main river passing south on the parish boundary, whilst a canal weir and overflow are provided just above the feeder. Usual pitwheel and upright shaft were employed, but the gear has long since been disman-tled; and a serviceable mill-stone went to Thornborough Mill.

THORNBOROUGH – 3 m. E. from Buckingham

River Ouse

Thornborough Mill – 1⅛ m. N.N.W. of Church

Working
1695, 1768, 1793, (1809), 1824, 1833,
(1847), 1870, 1875, 1887, 1914

In the Harleian Library two charters of Hugh de Dunster relate to the conveyance of his Thornborough lands to the abbot and Monks of Biddlesden in connection with founding a Chauntry Chapel at Littlecote; and the first charter, A.D. 1266, conveys to the monks "2 carucates of land and a meadow in the Holme near Stekeford Mill in Thornborough". *V.C.H.*, quoting the Charters says that a mill in Thornborough was granted in 1244 to the Hospital of St. John in Oxford and "probably this was identical with the mill of Stakforde mentioned as a boundary mark at about that date".

No site other than the present one is known; and it is interesting that a mill, with a virgate of land, was given towards the establishment of Magdalen College Manor in 1243 by Robert son of Alan; for the existing mill belonged to the College. The Place Name Society notes the term "Milnedoneslade" (myln-dun-slaed) at Thornborough in 1247, meaning the Mill-hill-valley, and remarks that the present mill is in a small valley or slade opening on to the Ouse. Actually, Thornborough Mill is at the bottom of a lane leading off the Leckhampstead road, just short of the river bridge, and is west of the old tower-mill base. Although unusually well situated as regards flood prevention, with a long by-pass loop north-wards, a weir leading to a small south loop, and the usual sluice – a large one – leading to a short mill by-pass just north of the mill, there is much trouble

owing to the "tailing up" in wet seasons, as the result of a high artificial weir being illegally put across the river in contravention of milling rights, at Thornton Hall, a mile downstream. This weir did not exist in the days of Thornton Mill, as the owners pretend, for this annoyance would not have been tolerated for hundreds of years whilst elaborate laws were in force to prevent it; besides which, anyone can see that the layout at Thornton is not as it was in milling days and the original Ordnance map proves it. The weir has been heightened to increase the ornamental water in the grounds, and this nuisance has hampered the working of Thornborough Mill by water and has damaged the wheel, as a result of which it now runs by engine only.

The present mill, probably upon a Domesday site – for the latter is sure to have been a watermill, at the unusually high value of 20 shillings – is built of stone with some black brick inserted, a tiled roof and an adjoining mill cottage of similar materials, with a newer wing of brick. It stands across the stream, with the cottage on the north bank separated from the wheel-room in the mill by a narrow passage.

An unusually interesting wooden wheel, upon an iron axle, was last used, the three sets of arms being of clasp-arm design, diameter 10ft; and tread 7 or 8ft. An eight-armed pit wheel, dated 1879, engages a small wallower iron-to-iron, above which is a fine big eight-spoked morticed great spur. This drives four

Thornborough Mill

pairs of stones placed around a semi-circle – none of them are located over the pit-wheel, which is in fact impracticable unless the wheel is in the middle of the room. Two pairs are missing, one pair removed many years ago and one pair for wheat more recently; the others are for barley and grist.

The large wooden upright shaft is jointed, a new piece having been inserted by Messrs. Gilbert of Leighton Buzzard, and from a morticed iron crown wheel on first floor a countershaft running along the ceiling drives the oat crushers, etc., and a sack-bollard in the false floor between the grain bins. The bollard lever can be notched down by a ratchet fixed to the uprights between which it works. Another countershaft also driven from beneath the crown-wheel but at right angles to the first, is engaged by a lever with a chain passing under a pulley on a beam which lifts the shaft; and the latter is now coupled by belt to another shaft for driving a lighting dynamo.

Although pig-food was chiefly ground here whilst the tower-mill produced flour, a bolter and wire machine for flour dressing were provided, driven by shaft and pinion; but now only a kibbler is used. About 1937 an oil engine was installed, the wheel being past further use, and it is doubtful whether a new one will be fitted. Fish were extremely plentiful her in 1920, when the Rev: C.F. Farrar reported a "very perfectly constructed eel-trap".

Ownership was the same as Thornborough Towermill – the mill was omitted from the 1798 census; but John Lines had it many years, followed by George Taylor of Waddesdon and Three Bridge, and his son, grandson (William J Taylor, present proprietor) and great grandson. One of the Burton Family is thought to have had it before Lines; and back in 1833, Robert Seabrook advertised that the "excellent and improved fittings-up of the interior are of the best description . . . commands Powerful head of Water supplied by an uninterrupted length of upwards of 7 miles, driving three pairs of French Stones, and possessing Extra Local Advantages to any Mill in the neighbourhood" – a somewhat wild claim as 7 miles would include Maids' Moreton, Buckingham and Radclive Mills!

A story is told of the late Mr. Cripps' brother Tom and one "Stiffy" King who put new boards in the waterwheel before the Tailors moved in; someone inadvertently turned on the water whilst they were on the job and, although they escaped being drawn under the wheel, which has happened before now with fatal results, their tools were all washed away and lost!

THORNTON – 3¾ m. E.N.E. from Buckingham

River Ouse

Thornton Mill – 1 f. N.W. of Church

Gone
1768, (1809), 1825, 1870

On the Manor of Thornton in 1086 was a mill worth 10 ores and described in 1278/9 as a watermill. Ellis, son of Edmund the Miller is mentioned in 1219; and in the 16th century, a considerable dispute was caused by the lord of the manor and owner of the mill, Humphrey Tyrell, who repeatedly destroyed all the common furze and blackthorn which the commoners were entitled for firing, enclosed with a hedge a part of the common on which they were entitled to graze their beasts, and picked a quarrel with the priests and his excuse was that the commoners' wives had "damaged the stone wall around this mill by washing clothes there" (presumably climbing over it to reach the stream) and by allowing their kine to damage it; and he also asserted that one of his servants had been thrown into the water!

Robert Ingleton, Chancellor of the Exchequer to Edward IV, had previously held the Manor of Thornton: but the Tyrells remained until the 18th century, and they claimed to be the direct descendants of Sir Walter Tyrell, supposed assassin of William Rufus in the New Forest.

By 1606 two watermills are recorded, and throughout the 18th century there were three, all corn mills on the Tyrell estate; but probably one was at Leckhamstead, and one possibly Mount Mill – next mill downstream – but located on the Northamptonshire bank.

Thornton Mill stood on the main stream west of the road from the Hall and Church to the Buckingham Turnpike and Thomas Sheppard was the owner in 1798, when the mill was workable but not let; it seems to have been demolished around 1850 when the following appeared:-

"THORNTON WATER MILL; the complete machinery and gears of the above Corn Mill, working 2 pairs of stones, in good condition, for sale in consequence of the mill being discontinued. Apply Thomas Frost at Thornton Hall". Observe that the mill could have remained in commission but it is obvious from a study of the original Ordnance Survey (1825) that the real object of demolition was to alter and obstruct the waterways for decorative purposes, without reference to other peoples' interests*.

*Since penning the above, I find that the Rev. C.F. Farrar describes this obstruction as "an act of sheer wanton selfishness" adding that "we see the destructive nature of this barrier by the wreckage of the river for some miles below . . . when the floods come in winter the upper river pours over the barrage with frightful force" He recommends the Ouse Drainage Board to remove it, which of course they have not done, for such Boards are not noted for fair play to the small miller.

BEACHAMPTON – 2½ m. S.W. from Stony Stratford

River Ouse

Beachampton Mill – 5 f. N.N.W. of Church

Mill farm exists
1768, Name only on (1809), 1824, 1834,
(1847), 1870, 1875, 1914

As early as 1086 a watermill stood on the Manor and was valued at 10 shillings; in 1285, two watermills in Beachampton were conveyed to Ellis de Tingewick by the lord of the second manor (which seems to have been called Whityngham's) in Beachampton; but in 1324 Ellis de Tingewick's widow petitioned the lords of both manors for her dower in the two mills.

They were among the appurtenances of the united manors in 1593, and the "watermill called Upper Milne", was conveyed to Sir Thomas Bennett with the manor in 1609. Anthony Backhouse was the miller in 1798, perhaps the last one, for Beachampton Mill, has undoubtedly been extinct for a very long time, although Bryant (1824) rather curiously names the farmstead *New* Mill Farm. Possibly the old mill and farm had been lately demolished or burnt down; but this is conjecture. Mr. A.G. Rogers of the noted Buckingham milling family occupies the farmstead; and next downstream is Passenham Mill a pretty little building on the Northants bank of stream.

STONY STRATFORD

River Ouse

Calverton or *Stony Stratford Mill*   – ¼ m. almost W. of Church

Used as Laundry
1768, (1809), 1824, 1832, 1834,
1870, 1875, 1887, 1914

Writing a visitation of the Archdeacons in 1756, the Rev: Browne Willis observed:-

"They *would* come to Stony Stratford, where the waters were so out that several were drowned, especially the two churchwardens of Stoke Hammond parish, four miles off here and several places, houses and mills were laid under water, insomuch that several persons were forced to live in chambers and a neighbouring miller was obliged to carry his sow and piggs into the same room with himself and family".

Stony Stratford was not a parish until after the Calverton Enclosure Act of 1782, which embraced the open fields of Stony; and the forerunner of the present mill was consequently in Calverton parish. Indeed Stony Stratford parish embraced only one-third of the town, and is once more defunct since 1934.

A mill worth 13/4d was on Calverton Manor at Domesday, when Hugh de Bolbec held it; and there is mention of two mills there in 1331, and three in 1586. A century later, a Mrs. Bennett was not only enclosing the Common Fields and converting them to pasture for her own use, but was also having to be sued for the tithes on them; and some hundreds of acres of the peoples' land, which she had appropriated, were "untilled so that the parish is almost depopulated and the fields look like a wildernesse little being mowed and that which was (mowed) generally so late and so long till it was spoyled". A typical enclosure result, which explains the local decline of milling; and it is recorded that, being by herself and supposed to have a great hoard of money in the house the premises were entered by a butcher of Stony Stratford, who murdered her in 1694!

Meanwhile a corn mill appears to have been purchased by John Penn in 1581 from Thomas Piggott; and Penn bequeathed it to his son, but the history of Calverton Mills is somewhat disjointed, although the parish is of considerable historic importance and interest. The Manor was often called Calverton (or Calverston) with Stony Stratford, and in its hey-day Stony was a busy market town through which passed eighty stage coaches per day, and at which royalty often rested – King John, Henry IV, Edward V, Queen Margaret of Scotland, Henry VIII and probably Edward IV.

Thomas and John Adkins were the millers in 1711; and writing to the late William Bradbrooke in 1907, Mr. W.C. Pierce said "In 1760 my grandfather lived at Stony Stratford Mill, my mother was born there, also myself in 1828. At that time the river was very sluggish, the bridge over the river not being able to carry the water off, so the Mill House used to flood and they were compelled to live upstairs the greater part of the winter; but a few years before the railway was made a Birmingham firm was conveying a large boiler to London by road with nine horses; the weight broke the bridge in, a temporary wooden structure was thrown over, and a new bridge built much larger with one span, at that time thought to be the finest in England, a sixpenny toll-gate was erected on it . . . After the new bridge was built the old Mill was sold (owing to the death of my grandfather) and a new House built and a Mr. Seabrook erected sawmills which did not answer very well as the river altered its course . . ."

This probably refers to the building advertised as a corn-mill in 1832 – "that valuable and powerful water corn mill lately rebuilt with house and buildings".* Its austere red brick walls rise to a considerable height from the green fields, presenting an imposing but not exactly pleasing vista to the many who walk across

---

* The new bridge was erected in 1835, therefore Mr. Pierce seems to be in error as to the mill being reconstructed *afterwards*.

the adjoining meads at weekends. The roofs are of slate and somewhat shallow, and nothing relieves the aggressiveness of the great red walls except a few willow trees and a narrow iron wheel about 8ft. by 12 or 14ins. driven by a side stream at the corner of the mill. Said to have driven an electric generator, it is of breast type with very numerous rod spokes and curved buckets; and on the axle is a cog which conveyed an external chain drive to the upper floor.

Mr. Gilbert of Leighton Buzzard believed his firm built the mill, or entirely reconstructed it; but Messrs. Roberts of Deanshanger had a hand in it for the tie-rod bosses in the walls bear their name. The main waterwheel almost certainly was Gilbert's and is said not to have required repairs for the first 60 years of its existence. Of large dimensions, it was probably inside the west corner of the building; but the mill, said to have been in counter gear with millstones – not rollers, has been clear of machinery for some years.

The mill-stream comes in from the south-east whilst the main river passes round Mill Field on the west (Milnmede of the 15th century?) and the cut, which drove the dynamo wheel, leaves the mill stream in a brick culvert beneath the public footpath.

In the parish registers we read" 1662, Ye Old Miller, Buried" – proper names being immaterial for we later find "1665 Old Knockstoan ye pavier buried"! Wm. Ashby was miller in 1791 and 1830; Edward Johnson 1842; and Ben Barton was proprietor of this and Wolverton Mills for many years, but for 20 years up to the Great War, James Rogers, relative of the Buckingham family worked the mill by water and steam, at one time working Passenham Mill also, in conjunction with his son. Frederick J Ryland, water and steam 1928, was the last corn miller; and Mr. A.E.Catt, the owner, converted the building to a factory, which was called Swann Works; it is said to have served as a leather factory, and some say the millstones last ground face-powder, but it has now been refitted by the Passenham Model Laundry Co. In 1937 the premises was advertised as having four floors of 6700ft. floor space.

From the High Street the mill is easily reached *via* York Road and Mill Lane; Horn Lane formerly led to it, but is one of several illegally obstructed by the grasping landlords and jerry-builders of the town

Finally a fascinating story of Stony Stratford Mill by Mr. R.E. Barley in *Romance Around Stony Stratford* (1928). Long ago, the ghost of one Nancy Webb haunted the midnight scene once a year. She 'tis said, lost her husband in the Crimea; and returning from his grave in Passenham churchyard on the night of Deanshanger Feast, rushed screaming into the mill-race with her baby where the great wheel caught her up with fatal results. On an anniversary night years later the Curate elected to await her ghost, in company with one Tom Bird and was duly rewarded in no uncertain manner! Stony Stratford clock boomed out the midnight hour. 'Tom! Tom! What's that?' cried the Curate, 'Stand still man, that's it here it comes! ... In the chilly silence a heart-rending shriek rent the midnight air . . . from the Church swept a woman in white . . . her eyes like balls of fire . . . a piercing shriek . . . into the mill-head she plunged . . . an awful groan and gurgling mingled with the cry of an infant . . . The great mill-wheel creaked . . . another shriek and then there was silence but for the ceaseless owls". The Curate was silent too – he had passed out Mr. Barley tells plenty more blood – curdling stories, some of which were retailed in the now defunct Windmill Inn.

WOLVERTON

Old Wolverton Mill – ½ m. W. of Church

River Ouse

Standing idle
1768, 1793, (1809), 1824, 1834, 1875, 1887, 1914, 1926

Old Wolverton Mill is one of the most unprepossessing corn mills in the county and its bare walls of red brick might show to better advantage were it isolated upon the marsh, instead of being accompanied by a belt of pine trees out of keeping with the surroundings. Compare this with the tall, flat-walled Olney Mill as seen from the Causeway, flanked by willow and other spreading trees.

Wolverton Mill is approached by a right-of-way up a drive on the north side of the new ugly road from Stony Stratford which was unnecessarily reconstructed for the benefit of the contractors and to get rid of the roadside railway – somewhat antediluvian in appearance with long chimneyed locomotives and huge double-decked "tramcar" carriages which at least conveyed its passengers with every safety to themselves and other road users. Since its demolition the death roll, as on every reconstructed road in

Old Wolverton Mill

Bucks, has gone up by leaps and bounds and, but for the leaps and bounds of pedestrians it would be higher still! Perhaps it is appropriate that Old Wolverton, served by the only steam tramway in Bucks, was graced by the residence of the eminent Locomotive Superintendent, James Edward Mc Connell of the L.N.W.R.

In 1086, two mills were valued at 32/8d; one of them called, in the 13th century, West Mill; and probably this occupied the present site west of the village. West Mill belonged to the lords of the manor, and in 1342 there were two mills on the manor, only one of which would grind. A terrier of 1639 mentions "the Holmes belonging to the 2 mills", and these, again mentioned in 1689, were probably Mead Mill and West Mill according *V.C.H. Vol.IV*: Mead Mill being located farther eastward; and the same source states that "Mills in Wolverton were sold by Richard son of John, to John son of Alan shortly before 1252, but it is uncertain which mills". John incidentally had to prevent 'John de Kana of Wulfreton' from holding up

the water in the mill-ponds under cover of an obsolete grant.

Wolverton mill was specifically mentioned in a rental of Bradwell Priory (which really had no connection with Bradwell parish) in 1458, but "the whole possessions of the Priory of Wolverton, except the church and rectory were given to Sir John Longville just before the Dissolution in exchange for a farm which he held within its precincts" says *V.C.H.* adding that, it was probably in error that it was included among Cardinal Wolsey's possessions late of Bradwell Priory in 1530".

The present mill, standing on a long mill-race south of the main river, is clearly of no great age – probably much the same as Stony Stratford. It is L-shaped with a chimney shaft at the corner, which served the original boiler (probably Cornish pattern) later replaced by a portable engine standing in a galvanised engine-house between the mill and main stream. The wheel, apparently a 15ft "breastshot" within the building, near the engine-house, was probably there in 1939 but the premises were locked and unoccupied; it drove a 15ft morticed iron pit wheel, geared to a very substantial and long counter-shaft running down the south wing on the ground floor. On this shaft were five large morticed iron spurs driving five pairs in line on first floor. The nuts were large and were lifted on the usual screw rings; and on the countershaft, close to the wheel-house was a 12ft. iron belt wheel, apparently coupled to a line shaft on first floor for driving screw conveyors and auxiliary machinery. Another belt, from an extension of the main countershaft, in the engine-house led up to the second floor to the sack gear, etc.

Richard Besant was the miller in 1830; William Goodman 1842; followed by Ben Barton, as already noted; J.G.V. Field Johnson, 1877; and then Frank Wood, probably the last to make flour, until the present century – hence it is sometimes called Wood's Mill. H.G. Norman ran it for a time and finally T.C.Turney & Son 1928, Mr. Turney being a retired farmer. In the recent war, the Bucks War Agricultural Committee took over the mill, in which another farmer who temporarily ground his corn there, had broken the wheel. The appropriate Officer, Mr. Paget was entrusted with the task of repairing wheel and gear, for the purpose of utilizing the conveyor mechanism under water power in conjunction with a grain drier, to the following specification.

> Rebuild parts of broken main drive gear wheel.
> Refit and rebuild wheel by welding.
> Supply 150 Hornbeam Gear Teeth and ditto Wedges
> 80 elevator buckets 4" × 3". 160 Bolts
> 80ft.6ins rawhide belting 4½" × 4 ply.
> 1 Gib head key machined up specially for sluice gear.
> Fitting approx: 180 gear teeth.
> Rough labour, sundry expences and carriage of material.

Everything was going well when the mill was unfortunately inspected by a pessimistic official who had no authority to view; and his ridiculous pronouncement that it was unsafe was accepted, although Mr. Paget pointed out that it was a far better structure than the well-known Hertingfordbury Mill (Herts), which is in full swing. So Wolverton Mill – a practically new building as watermills go, remains idle.

WOLVERTON

River Ouse

Early Mill – About ½ m.N.E. of Church

Gone

Near the modernised Manor House of Wolverton, is a field called "the Grange" which was in Sheahan's day distinguished by the presence of some remains of an old dove-cote; and upon a small stream adjoining were formerly traces of a building supposed to have been a watermill.

Taken as it stands, this implies a mill site half-a-mile N.N.E. or N.E. of the Parish Church – definitely not Old Wolverton Mill, nor apparently Meads Mill – and a possibility is that West Mill was upon this site, but no confirmation seems to be available.

WOLVERTON

River Ouse

Meads Mill – 1m. almost N.E. of Church

Gone
1768, 1834

Meads Mill stood exactly one mile from the Parish Church and 1200 yards from New Wolverton Church (built 1841 but inserted on the original O.S. reprint) east of the Wolverton Viaduct, just south of the parish boundary (which follows the former course of the river and has a boundary post at this point), and west of the new Haversham causeway, on a loopstream now filled in: but the coming of the London and Birmingham Railway probably put an end to Meads Mill owing to the diversion of the mill-stream

At the same time Mr. Robert Adams of Bradwell told me, the Company erected a pumping engine alongside the viaduct to supply their Carriage Works and this, he believed, stood by the former mill stream.

Very soon the millers downstream realised the river was being tapped and leaving them short of water which the Company denied! The millers did not waste a lot of money at law, they just dropped a large quantity of reddle (red chalk) into the river above the viaduct one night and subsequently ascertained from some friendly workmen in the shops that the offending "bait" was coming through and playing havoc in the machinery where clear water was required. Apparently the chalk or some other trouble caused the engine to cease work, for it is said to have been eventually tipped over into the river, where it is believed to recline to this day!

The priory of Bradwell held Mead Mill; it leased "two Mead Mills in 1491", probably in one mill-house and one Mead Mill is mentioned in connection with Bradwell at the dissolution according to *V.C.H. Vol.IV.* which adds, probably relying on Sheahan, "A branch of the Ouse just north of the Manor Farm seems to have formed a mill race, perhaps for that Mead Mill which belonged to the Priors of Bradwell; and John son of Alan in the 13th. century granted to Bradwell all the fishery between its mill, called Mead Mill, and Stonebridge; the second of these landmarks being represented by the bridge on the eastern boundary opposite the station close, to which is Stonebridge House Farm".

Another reference to Bradwell says that in Henry VI's reign, Maids Milne, East Milne and New Milne occur in a rental of the Priory, whose property became the manor of Bradwell; but there being no water near the Priory it seems to the writer that "Maide Milne" is an earlier spelling of Mead Mill; and even East Milne and New Milne might be merely other wheel under the same roof. Maide Milne "worth by the year iiij li. vj s. viij d." was still among the Priory Appurtenances in 1524/31 and Wolsey who had already acquired the property bestowed it upon his Cardinal College (Oxford); thence it passed to the Crown.

Although Mill Mead survived about another three centuries, no further details seem to be available; but we may sit by the great century-old Wolverton Viaduct and meditate upon the contrast between this old-time piece of engineering, and the slick performances of the modern "experts" as exemplified by the Haversham causeway with its inadequate culverts – a feature of the Three Bridge, Simpson and other Bucks by-passes – which caused the L.M.S. main line to Scotland to be dangerously flooded, whilst only the timely bursting of the concrete causeway saved some 600 square miles of valuable farmlands from inundation!

STANTONBURY – 1¾ mile N.E. from Wolverton

River Ouse

Medieval Watermill – Probably 100yds. S.W. of Church

Gone
No map reference

At Domesday a mill in the parish was worth 10/8d and fifty eels – probably a watermill, the value being fairly high; and in 1326 the Manor which began to be called Stanton Barry, included a dovecote, a broken-down watermill, and 3 acres of wood which provided no pannage because it was composed of ash trees. Three watercorn mills were said to be in the parish in 1653 and 1695 and four in 1721 – a fact difficult to credit when one looks at Stantonbury today, although William Perry was miller at Stantonbury in 1702, and the village was largely depopulated in the 18th. century.

The Reverend A.N. Guest. M.A. (*Stantonbury*

Tales 1924) assumes that Lord Hugo Barre, one of William's barons' built the mill alongside the great Norman castle on a site known as the "Grange" which was a low-lying thatched building of one storey fronting the Ouse. This he is supposed to have done after reconstructing the little Norman church, which would date the mill around 1080, for Hugo arrived at Stanton in 1076.

Not a trace of a watermill can now be found; the only indication of the site being a diversion like a mill-stream by the little church, which lies in an isolated and lonely spot across water meadows.

HAVERSHAM – 3 m. W. from Newport Pagnell

River Ouse

Haversham Mill – ¾ m. N.E. of Church

Standing empty
1768, 1793, (1809), 1824, 1833,
(1847), 1870, 1875, 1887, 1926

No one would suspect, as they stood on the rickety old bridge against Haversham Mill, they were within walking distance of the insalubrious neighbourhood of Wolverton unless they happened to observe distant chimney shafts. Approached by a steep gated track, the mill stands forlorn beside the renovated mill cottage; and beyond is the great marsh stretching away to the hills on which old Bradwell Windmill is perched – cattle and a cowman with his dog are about the only signs of life if one continues along the stony, grass-grown track and through more gates; but the cries of gulls and lapwings and the wild musical whistle of the redshank, will give place to wailing factory sirens and locomotive whistles ere a hard road is reached.

V.C.H. Vol. IV records that the mill amongst the appurtenances of the Manor of Haversham in 1086, was worth 8 shillings and 75 eels; and rentals of the Manor in the 15th. century show that Haversham Mill was then worth 66/8d per annum to the lord. At this time there was a second watermill called Helwoll Mill or the New Mill where the Priory of Bradwell had a fishery, this being, possibly the New Mill already mentioned under my Mead Mill heading. In 1619 two grist-mills existed here, but only one is mentioned in 1764.

Haversham Mill

William Peverel had the Manor in 1086; and we later read that "Galf'r Molindar holds 18 acres with the mill from Matilda, daughter of Nicholas of Haversham and pays 113/4d per annum". Sir Thomas Lucy, Kt, associated with the Manor in the late 16th century, is noted for his alleged prosecution of Shakespeare about 1585 for deer-stealing in his Warwickshire park, which resulted in Shakespeare immortalising his enemy in the character of Mr. Justice Shallow!

In 1729 the Manor sold for £24, 500 to Lucy Knightley, a descendant of the Lucys; and the mill portion of the estate was assigned to Roger Ratcliffe for £600 in 1806. Meanwhile Mary Holman was the tenant in 1798; and William Carr who later had the mill also occupied Castlethorpe Mill in 1864, probably concentrating his attention upon it, for he left Haversham Mill in a bad state. In fact, after it had stood idle for some while, a sum of £400 had to be spent on new floodgates, belts and equipment of all sorts before Mr. Robert Adams from Bradwell Windmill, was able to set to work there in 1871. An unexpected financial hitch arose over this expenditure, as a result of which Mr. Adams eventually left the mill in 1877 and turned to farming: he was succeeded by W.G. Perry from Salford Watermill (Beds); and very shortly by John Carr from Mursley Windmill and Woolstone Watermill, with his two sons – no relation of William Carr, although he in the past had bought a little corn from his namesake to grind. The coincidence was completed when John's son William, became proprietor, and was followed by another Mr. Perry, probably related to the Perrys of Olney and Lavendon Mills in former years, at about the outbreak of the Great War; but he soon vacated and the machinery has since been entirely removed

In Mr. Adam's time a large breast wheel with only a slight lip to the buckets, drove the mill in spur gear; but John Carr had a smaller one installed with curved buckets, and also had a false floor built over the original to raise it, Both wheels were chiefly of wood. Except for the wheel-room which is over the stream, the mill stands on the left bank with brick cottage adjoining, and is by-passed southwards via a large weir; it is of stone with shallow slate roof, wooden sack-loft, now broken, projecting over the bridge; and usual three floors, including attic. Water was admitted to the wheel by a curved worm-geared "flash" the worm being on the end of a long crank handle projected into the mill.

Three pairs of stones were eventually located in line on the first floor, underdriven from a heavy horizontal shaft as at Wolverton, the shaft being at axle level of the watermill with pinion geared to inner face of the peripheral cog-ring on the wheel, which was 15ft. quartershot, of 7ft. tread: and plummer block for mainshaft is still *in situ* in the wall.

On the ground floor, beneath each pair of stones, is a shallow iron trough to accommodate each spur on the mainshaft, this being necessitated by the raising of the floor and the consequent reduced clearance; and adjoining the cottage is an engine room, now empty like the mill proper.

In 1869 a man and his horse were drowned on the mill track in a tremendous flood, just after Mr, N.T.Cole, author of *I Remember* had scrambled through with his father on their baker's cart. Again on "Black Tuesday", 1881 their greatest difficulties were at the mill, where they had to unhitch the two horses they had attached to the cart and leave then at Hill Farm, having only progressed thus far after much digging of snow.

It is worthy of memory that the Reverend E.Cooke (1773–1824) whose monumental history Lipscomb edited and published, was Rector of Haversham.

LITTLE LINFORD – 2m. W. from Newport Pagnell
River Ouse

Medieval Watermill – Site unknown
Gone

The property of Tickford Abbey in Newport Pagnell parish, listed in a deed of Edward II's reign (1307–27) included "the Mill of Caldecote's Chapel of Little Linford and the Mill there, and the title to all the Mills in Newport", and *V.C.H. Vol. IV*, says "the mill on the estate of Little Linford Manor in 1086 was probably identical with the watermill attached to the Manor in the 14th century, when mention occurs also of a fishpond". Confirming the existence of a mill value 8/8d at Domesday, Oliver Ratcliff added that in the survey of 1534 "it was recited that Tickford Convent should enjoy . . . the tithes and eels of Linford Mill".

Various loop streams in the parish offer several possibilities for a mill-site; and history is silent as to the fate of the mill.

GREAT LINFORD – 2m. S.W. from Newport Pagnell

River Ouse

Medieval Watermill – Site unknown

Gone

It is conjectured, from the fact that Little and Great Linford stand respectively north and south of the Ouse, that at some time or other the river was known as the Lin. The only reference to a mill at Great Linford, however, is inconclusive, since *V.C.H. Vol.IV*, merely records that in 1303 William le Waleys and Cecilia his wife owned a messuage, a mill and 120 acres in Great Linford.

GAYHURST – 2½ m. N.W. from Newport Pagnell

River Ouse

Mill Farm and *Mill Cottages* Approx. ¾ m S.E. of Church

Gone
Mill Farm on 1768, 1793, (1809),
1875, 1887, 1926

Gayhurst Mill site incorporates a little by-pass stream below the copse on the riverbank, and some timbers in the bank on the far side of the plank bridge are believed to be the remains of a mill sluice; and the Parish Boundary Survey of the Manor of Newport in 1609 refers to Goathurst Mill (an old spelling).

Early history records a watermill in the following extract from *V.C.H. Vol IV*. "There was a mill (value 13/4d) on the Manor in 1086 and references to a watermill are found from 1279 to the 17th century. At a Court Baron of April, 1628, the tenants were ordered to grind their corn at the mill of the lady of the manor; the watermill and two houses adjoining, then leased to George Backhouse, were in disrepair and one of the mill houses had been converted into a cottage by 1654." The lady of the manor at that date was Mary, Lady Digby widow of Sir Everard Digby, who was hanged in 1606 for conspiracy in the Guy Fawkes plot and Lady Mary being herself as a Papist exposed to suspicion on the rumour of a conspiracy at Gayhurst in 1633, her estates were temporarily sequestered under the Commonwealth.

The big old stone-built, slate-roofed Mill Farm is approached by a rough track from the Gayhurst-Little Linford road, whilst the tiled Spring Mill Cottages stand lower down and eastward of the mill site.

NEWPORT PAGNELL

River Ouse

North Mill, *Town Mill* or *Newport Pagnell Mill* and the *Fulling Mill* – 3 f. N.W. of Church

Foundations remain (and Mill House 1926)
1768, (1809), 1824, 1875,

Looking from the long stone bridge upon the Northampton road towards the culverts of the former mill, we see the ford where the earliest stage coaches crossed the Ouse before the old bridge was built, The gap between the houses where the coach came down from the town is there still, 'tis said because it is to this day a right of way and cannot be closed – and only the galloping and prancing horses and the trumpet call are needed to complete an old world country-town scene.

But watching for the phantom coach at the ford will not unravel the history of the mill. From *Victoria County History* it appears that Newport possessed two mills (probably under one roof) at Domesday, worth 40 shillings, and held by William, Son of Ansculf, who held also the mill in Caldecote hamlet and several others elsewhere. His daughter married Sir Fulke Paganell from whose family the town takes its name and whose son founded Tickford Priory at about the end of William Rufus' reign, and gave it Caldecote Mill and other property,

In 1254 Hugh, son of Walter "molendinarius" is mentioned at Newport Paynel; and North Mill (the Town Mill) is quoted twenty years later when it seems the miller was tenant of Edward I, the mill then being worth 10 marks. King Edward II, about A.D.

North Mill

1400 confirmed that the mill belonged to Tickford Priory; although in 1311 only a *tithe* of the mills apparently were claimed by it.

A Bailliff's Account of 1479 runs as follows:-

"The farm of the mill
And of ix *li* rent of the mill and of the fishery there, in this year devised to Robert Milleward Total ix *li*

Repair of Mills
And in divers repairs this year done to the mill there as well in woodwork and in masonry as in various operations in the work upon the ground-work of the mill also in buying burnt lime likewise with the purchase of the timber with the carriage of the same, and in purchase of planks and nails and likewise in buying a pair of millstones and also in divers other necessities to the same bought as by the particulars in the bills upon this compotus appears and is filed in among the memoranda of this year – Total: xvj *li* iiij s"

V.C.H. Vol IV states that in 1480, there were two water mills at Newport, North Mill and Gayhurst Mill, and two fulling mills; North Mill was the manorial mill on the present site, which could be reached *via* Mill Street from the northern end of the High Street and Gayhurst Mill was on the Ouse "opposite Gayhurst House", i.e. the mill already dealt with and one wonders from this whether it stood across the stream, half in each parish. Edward VI granted "the watermill of Newport" to Lady Elizabeth (afterwards Queen) in 1541; and some thirty years later a dispute arose *re* the spoliation of Northe Mills by James Annesley and others, when John Conye gave evidence of seeing Annesley (whose family held them of the Queen) removing fittings and machinery. Robert Annesley seems to have been the landlord succeeded by Wm. Worthington, holding the mills for £7 per annum, and leasing them to William Cocks; and the Annesleys apparently were sneaking anything they could lay hands on when quitting.

Rather strangely they were termed the grist, or Greist Mills, in 1622, and "the grain mills" when granted to Dr. Henry Atkins the year following: and during another dispute in the former year the presence of a fulling mill was quaintly explained. Thomas Richardson deposed that he

"doth know the three water corne milles in Newport Pannell, and that aboute threescore years sithence when he knew them, there were but twoe mills, and he saith that about ffiftie years sithence there was a third wheele added to that parte of one of the said Milles wch is next to the meadow called the Monkes Holmes and he saith that the said three milles are called Newport Milles, and he hath alwaies taken them to be within the parishe of Newport. And he saith that Mrs. Weston caused the saide thirde wheel to be added, and thereof made a fulling mille, at the desire of ould John Harley, her bayliff, whose sonne was a fuller and occupied the same as a ffullinge myll, and hathe ever when men came to wash them in the place where the ffulling mill was after erected, but he knoweth not that any man ever paid ought therefor or asked leave therefor of any man".

Mr. F.W. Bull (*History of Newport Pagnell, 1900*) adds that Mrs. Weston was Elizabeth Weston of Chicheley, who willed all her interest in "the Three water grain mills under one roof called the North Mills" to her sons-in-law; and that the intention was to prove the fulling mill an encroachment, but it remained standing.

The Court Rolls of 1670 record that John Johnson was ordered to "scour the wattercourse at ye stille in Bury Field next ye mill" – this is the great Bury Field stretching out towards Gayhurst, and un-built on to this day although under the plough in 1944; and quite possibly some more scouring of the "wattercourse" will be required to secure best results from cultivation. Richard Cox was a miller of Newport Pagnell in 1697.

One of the most curious circumstances connected with Bucks watermill history concerns the water supply system operated over a century and a half ago from one of the Newport Mill wheels.

"To be sold a desirable freehold estate situate in Newport Pagnell comprising a Water Corn Mill with 3 water-wheels, gears and stones; etc . . . Also a new erected water engine worked by one of the millwheels, conveying the water by iron pipes into a reservoir of 20ft. by 10ft, and 3½ft. deep, cased with brick and lined with lead, on oak pillars, standing on an eminence in the town of Newport

aforesaid, from which the houses in North St. High St. Bridge St. and Marsh End are supplied with water to the number of 102, the inhabitants of which paying very easy rents for the same. The whole of the premises, with the rents and profits of the water, are rented to Joseph Warner, tenant at will, at the yearly rent of £75, but capable of very considerable improvements". (*Northampton Mercury 29 dec. 1787*, quoted by F.W. Bull.)

This water supply existed till 1820 or later and was remembered by Mr. N.T. Coles father who also recollected the fords on the Lovat and Ouse before the Iron and North Bridges were built.

A reference to an hydraulic machine situated in the market place, is thought to mean that this was the site of the reservoir. In 1789 complaints were made that Robert Williatt who laid the wooden pipes (some now preserved in the Bucks Museum) did not keep them in repair and in 1791, when Williatt was listed as miller and laceman, and Thomas Warner a miller – perhaps sharing portions of the mill – it

"was presented that Williatt had frequently broken up the highways and causeways for the purpose of amending the water pipes laid for the conveyance of water from his mill to different parts of the borough, and that he had not sufficiently amended the ground broken up by him, but suffered the same to remain in a very bad state, which was a nuisance to the inhabitants, and therefore he was amerced for the same £5".

Being upon so strong a stream, floods had to be contended with; and in 1823 a tremendous wind and rain "beyond all precedent" caused the lower parts of the town to be inundated to a depth of 4 feet.

William Swannell succeeded Williatt around 1800; and in 1839 the mills, in good repair, with brick house, counting house, etc; driving 4 pairs, were offered at the expiration of Charles Eve's tenancy; but he remained in occupation; and a steam engine had been installed as early as 1851, when the grinder's son, named Griffin, screwing a nut on the engine so injured his hand that it had to be amputated. William Whitworth & Sons became proprietors about 1870, Whitworth & Rowlatt followed and then Rowlatt & Co. Ltd. when it was finally burnt down on Feb: 9, 1899.

Prior to this disaster, fire broke out in the mill on July 26 1858 and in the rear of the mills Sep.11 1875, when a fireman injured himself with an axe, but the building was saved; then, on Nov: 15, 1880, a great conflagation entirely destroyed the mills, which the enterprising Whitworths rebuilt. Fires were very prevalent however, 126 being dealt with (some incendiary) by the Newport Brigade in 45 years, 1855–99.

Two important prints fortunately are preserved at the Bucks Museum, one showing Newport Mill in the early 19th century, a long low building with unbroken roof devoid of embellishments, the other about 1880, depicting the mill shortly before the first fire, from which it is seen to be heightened at the west end, with projecting sack-loft in the old roof and a tall chimney shaft for steam working. This building, I am told was of white stone; the final structure was a fine building with all the latest conveyors, elevators, cleaners, sifters and silk dressers; and the wheat was said to travel a mile up and down the mill ere it emerged as the finest quality white flour. The Mill House survives; and from the North Bridge the arches for the two big waterwheels, together with by-pass tunnels, remind one of the glorious milling days.

SHERINGTON– 1¾ m. N.N.E. from Newport Pagnell

River Ouse

Early Watermill – Site doubtful

Gone

In 1240–1 Robert de Cockfield and William de Sherington owed arrears of rent in respect of strengthening a mill pond at "Syrinton" to Robert le Blund and his wife, who renounced their claim to this and all future rent. De Cockfield had a right to the mills of Sherington in 1260 and had come into possession of the property, with de Sherington, from Sherington Manor. The Bishop of Coutances himself had the Manor and a mill worth 26 shillings at Domesday, but his lands were eventually forfeited by William Rufus. Later ownership of the mills was considerably divided; and although in 1257, mills in Shyrington were mentioned, no record seems to exist after 1260.

Immediately below the fine stone-built Sherington Bridge, is an ideal loop for laying out a mill and, being on the main stream, this seems the most probable site. At this very spot the Rev C.F. Farrar was moved to pay a well-deserved tribute to the River Ouse. "I know nothing on the Thames which surpasses this stretch of the Ouse" he wrote; "It flows in perfect solitude, unspoilt by river parties . . . My pen can do no justice to this part of the river, nor a photograph give idea of its beauty".

RAVENSTONE – 2½ m. W. from Olney

River Ouse

Ravenstone Mill – Approx. 1½ m. S. of Church

Mill house remains
1768, 1793, (1809), 1824, 1835, (1847), 1887, 1926

Two centuries ago the remains of Filgrave Church stood in a churchyard which is still preserved; but by 1766 the church had disappeared. The Reverend William Cole stated that Mrs. Backwell of Tyringham House gave the order for the "utter pulling down of its tower, what remained of the tower and the side walls of Filgrave church in order to repair a mill". This almost certainly was Ravenstone Mill – the only one in which she was interested; and the desecration was postponed for a short time by the intervention of Mr. Wright of Gothurst, from whose parlour windows the church tower made a pleasant landmark. He offered to supply the necessary quantity of stones from his estate, but the steward a boorish disreputable man contended that old weathered stone would have a longer duration; so the Church was demolished. Mrs. Backwell's son, who was at Eton School, intervened with an impudent demand that the mill should always be repaired with stone from the Gothurst quarries of Mr. Wright who should sign an undertaking committing his family to the scheme!

"Ravenstone Mill was attached to Bolebec Manor in 1086" says *V.C.H. Vol. IV*, "and subsequently belonged to Ravenstone Priory". Valued at 25/-, it may have been granted to the priory by the sub-tenants of the Earl of Oxford.

In the late 13th. century, there were "three water mills" (wheels?) on the Tyringham-with-Filgrave estate, one of which was a fulling mill; and from time to time they continue to be mentioned until the 17th. century, the site undoubtedly being that of Ravenstone

Mill, which was always on the Tyringham estate.

In 1525 it was found by inquisition that nearly everything in Ravenstone, including the watermill, belonged to Cardinal Wolsey; but Edward VI granted the mill to Sir Francis Bryan, Kt. in 1549.

The name of Grace Perry of Ravenstone Mill occurs on a tombstone in Olney churchyard, stated May 4th, 1777; and the Adkins family had it before 1800 and until the fifties. A curious incident was reported in 1821, when William Tame was charged with stealing wheat flour from his master William Adkins, the miller, at night. The mill was separated from the house by a path, near which Mr. Adkins hid, in order to waylay the culprit, and he chased him into a barn, where Tame had a candle-stick in a lantern. Tame lived in the building, and had been slipping out after dark and removing the flour to the barn, disposing of it when opportunity arose.

Alfred and William Scrivener may have been the last millers, for Mr. O Ratcliff mentions a fire "at Scriveners, Ravenstone" on July 25, 1872 – about the time when some local persons believe the mill disappeared. Another suggestion is that the date 1867 on

the Mill House wall records the demolition of the mill and reconstruction of the house. In 1906 the Tyringham Estate Sale Book, stated that "the mill stream could be, at comparatively trifling expense, made to use water power for electricity;" the suggestion was acted upon, and above the mill loop are some outsized iron sluices with tall counter-balance weights, known to local inhabitants as "the black posts", situated in Tyringham parish, and regulating the water supply for a turbine-generator for lighting, sawing and chaff-cutting etc. at Tyringham Hall. The mill site is at the end of a short approach lane off the Gayhurst – Olney road; and the mill stream is probably an artificial loop dating back many centuries; the main river, passing behind the buildings to the south, constitutes the parish boundary.

An old inhabitant recollected the demolition of the mill, which he thought was in working order, but the possibility that it was gutted should not be ruled out. Foundations of the old wall of the mill stream are said to run beneath the garden, between the much-restored house and the little old sluice which regulates the water when released by the big sluice.

EMBERTON – 1m. S from Olney *River Ouse*

Early Mill – Site unknown Gone

In 1276, one third of two mills in Emberton, held by Thomas de Marleberg and his wife, were granted to Roger de Turkelby; but it is not clear which Manor they held; nor is a mill listed here at Domesday, although the Ouse on the northern parish boundary, offers excellent opportunities for laying out a watermill. The Tan Mill next described may supersede an Emberton mill at the approximate site.

OLNEY *River Ouse*

The Tan Mill – Approx.: 1f. W.N.W. of Church Tanyard exists
No map references

"Tannery at Olney. Two large barns capable of holding 230 tons of bark, stables, granary, hay loft, 138 tan vats, 3 water pits, 4 lime pits and 3 drench pits, 2 large bark mills, 4 sheds, 1 stove and 3 store rooms. 3 cottages and a close, and a stone built genteel residence. On the River Ouse, 5 miles from Grand Junction Canal. The Close is in Emberton, 6 acres near the Tan Yard. Newport Pagnell 5 miles, Northampton 12 miles: etc."

June 16 1821

Thomas Babbington of the Tanyard was mentioned at Olney in 1808; and the above advert has to fill a gap thence until we come to Mr. Oliver Ratcliff's recollections in his local guidebook.

Prior to the 'nineties the Tanyard had long been derelict, after Mr. Joseph Palmer, who lived to be well over ninety, had conducted a flourishing oak bark tannery for many years, apparently inheriting the business from Mary Palmer (1830). Now once more (1907) it was in service, Messrs W.E. & J. Pebody Ltd. of Northampton having purchased and re-equipped the premises in 1898, styling them the Cowper Tannery. New pits and commodious workshops containing latest improved machinery were installed, together with 50 h.p. steam-engine and boiler. Chrome leather was almost at once adopted as a speciality – a bold move, chrome tanning being then in the experimental stage; but results soon justified the enterprise. Output grew, necessitating a 140 h.p. gas engine with producer plant – "monster engine started at Tanyard; Dec. 3. 1907" says Ratcliff's diary!

Mr. Sam. Odell, foreman of Olney Corn-mills informs me he has ascertained that the Tan Mill stood close to where the tan-yard is today; where the bark-pits used to be is a lawn and the fine stone-built residence exists, and is occupied by Mr. W. E. Pebody.

Tan-mills beat the bark with a giant cam-operated hammer as used in the "hammer-pond" iron mills of Surrey and Cumberland, etc.; where a cam shaped directly on the water-shaft, raised the hammer arm. General Ulysses Grant was brought up at his father's tan-mill, and as a boy he stood by the horse who went round in a circle, presumably grinding the bark, whilst another boy stood by the hopper with a hammer and broke up the bark, which arrived in 3ft. lengths, and fed it into the mill. Later Ulysses was promoted to breaking the bark, which was less interesting because the horse didn't come into it!

OLNEY

Olney or *Cowper Mills* – 200 yards S.E. of Church

River Ouse

Working
1768, 1824, (1847), 1875, 1887, 1926

The "Domesday" mill at Olney existed before the "invasion" and is described as "One mill of 40 shillings and 200 eels." This rent it provided to Geoffrey, Bishop of Coutances, who ironically styled himself "lord of the soil". He was found to be leaning the wrong way in the disputes between William Rufus and Robert, Duke of Normandy, however, and consequently had to leave the soil to someone else!

One of his predecessors in A.D. 979, seems to have been King Ethelred, who owned some if not all of the Manor property; Borret or Borgret, a Northamptonshire thegn and descendant of the ancient kings of Mercia, held it in Edward the Confessor's time, but the King (Richard I) again had the property at the close of the 12th century. Ranulph, Earl of Chester, a chief supporter of King John and Henry III, gave to "God and the monks of St. Peter at Gloucester" 40 shillings a year charged on the mill at Olney, he having received the mill from his cousin Richard who was lost at sea.

Two mills were appurtenant to the Manor in 1343–4 but only one in 1411–2. The estate passed to the Earl of Warwick's son Henry who married at the age of ten, became King of the Isle of Wight at nineteen, and died at twenty! The property passed to Richard III, killed on Bosworth Field, 1485; Henry VIII demised Olney Mills to "certain tenants" in 1520; and royalty continued to hold the property for a century or more.

Most of the foregoing, and the details to follow of the mill fire, are from *"Olney Past and Present"* by O. Ratcliff and H. Brown – a book worth reading if only for its unusually interesting and amusing folk-lore stories.

Mesrs Harrold & Gee were corn millers at Olney Mills, oldest recorded business premises in the town in 1823, in succession to Joseph Harrold; James Sampson followed for 20 years, then John S. Perry came from Lavendon Mill; but his successor was the victim of the disastrous fire which was probably the most outstanding event in Olney since the incendiary fires of the early 'fifties. Says the report:-

About ten o'clock on Thursday night, January 3, 1878, an alarm of fire was raised in the town . . . and flames were seen bursting through the roof of the mill. It had been purchased two years previously by Charles Henry Whitworth, who had greatly improved it and fitted it with new and costly machinery at a total outlay of several thousand pound. Mr. Whitworth being a very enterprising man, had been carrying on a very extensive trade since the Mill had been renovated. It was with great regret therefore that his friends and fellow-tradesmen saw the nature of the catastrophe – small hopes being entertained from the first that it would be saved.

"The Olney engine arrived at the fire very promptly and worked well, but was totally inadequate to cope with the fury of the flames, which caught the contents of the top floors and burst up so that the fire could be seen at a distance of

Olney or *Cowper Mill*

several mile . . . The wooden lift caught fire and the burning rafters falling down set fire to the contents below, so that the flames poured though every crack and crevice. The appearance of the building at this time, although very terrible, was grand; and the reflection of the fire upon the church showed up the stone spire against the dark sky. The men of the Olney Brigade played on the house (which adjoins the Mill) to keep it damp, for it was thought it must be burnt as well.

At 11.20 the Newport Brigade, whose panting steeds betokened the rate at which they had travelled, arrived upon the scene and at once commenced work. After many hours of labour the flames were got under and the engines left the scene of the fire at half-past-eight on Friday morning. The appearance of the mill was deplorable – a black and charred mass containing half-burnt sacks of wheat".

The present mill, which sprang up from the half-burnt ruins, a fine broad-fronted building of local stone, stands across the river and faces downstream, like most of our Bucks mills, and works entirely by water, although for some years a 45 h.p. suction gas engine drove a roller mill. Ratcliff says she was "entirely remodelled and improved" in 1906.

As a water corn-mill she is quite the best and most powerful in the county except perhaps Hambleden Mill on the Thames; two big all-iron breast wheels some 12ft diameter, one within each end of the building with usual "flash" mechanism, are each designed to drive five pairs of stones, spaced around their respective upright shafts in an arc on the first floor. The south wheel is notable for having no less than five sets of eight arms; it has 48 open buckets and is thought to develop 40/50 h.p. All-iron gears – pitwheel, upright shaft and great spur, etc., are installed whilst the stone-nuts, in the usual enclosure have wooden cogs and are on screw rings. The other wheel, estimated at 12 h.p. has three sets of spokes and, but for its somewhat narrower tread, is generally similar; but only one of its pairs of the stones is now *in situ*. The present stones are of composition material; and Mr. Sam Odell who kindly showed me round, said one pair has ground 1000 sacks of flour since dressing and is good for more.

Most of the other machinery is belt-driven from line shafting; there is a one-ton vertical mixer in which the grain is carried up the centre of the drum by a spiral scoop and is mixed as it descends again to the hopper-shaped bottom. Also a washing machine to which water is conveyed by a belt-driven pump, so that it washes the grain in a sieve-like tank; an oat crusher consisting of a short wheat roller-mill and a cracker for peas and beans, etc.

Grain and meal are handled mostly by scoop conveyors and Archimedean screw; and there is a horizontal dresser in which the meal passes over sieves to separate good stuff from offals; also the usual brush machines, all conveniently arranged in the roomy four floors, with storage in very extensive roof bins, the largest of which, says Ratcliff, holds 700 sacks of corn. He adds that "The first floor is devoted to meal rolls and reduction plant which are placed in the bay; extensive and up-to-date wheat cleaning plant, erected by Simon, Ltd. of Manchester, is at the north end of this floor. The second floor is taken up with purifiers, hanging sieves, etc. The third contains the various centrifugals for dressing the different products". (See *Olney Almanack* 1907 in which amusing pictures of the steam wagon and Mr. Gudgin will be found!)

An externally arranged hoist is operated by the usual sack-gear; and an iron crane raises and turns the stones for dressing, a task which took more than a day in the case of some of the burr-stones.

A very big broad weir and a flood-gate are above the main road bridge, which in the words of Cowper "with its wearisome but needful length bestrides the wintry flood". There was a bridge out of repair in 1334, and has been a bridge of some kind continuously since 1619, when the impossibility of fording the river in winter became an increasing drawback. It may be mentioned the reason for the abnormal width of the long and neat main street is that in days gone by a stream bordered by trees, ran down its length; tramlines were laid about 70 years ago – the only instance in Bucks except at Wolverton – but the project fell through and the cars never ran.

Mr. Odell employed at Lavendon Mill before the Great War, has been at Olney ever since his return from the "front"; and he recalled the days when six men were employed night and day roller-milling here – now only two or three are employed inside, and two or three on the lorries. They are able to run all day under water-power, being upon an exceptionally fine stretch of water.

Mesrs. Hipwell & Co, brewers, wine and spirit merchants and millers, ran under steam and water 50 years ago, followed by A. Gudgin & Co (steam and water, Cowper Mills) but since the death of Mr. Gudgin some years back the mill has been let to Mr. Coales of Bedford Mills.

CLIFTON REYNES – ¾ m. E. from Olney

River Ouse

Early Watermill – 3 f. S.S.W. of Church

Gone, 1768

Fulling Mill – ¾ m. N of Church

Gone

Early Watermill

"The music of its familiar clack and splashing waters has long ceased but the site is still very beautiful, especially in summer time, when the shallow streams that surround it are yellow with irises, and bristle with reeds and rushes, and wax-like umbels of butomus". – Cowper, speaking of Clifton Reynes Mill in the fifth book of "*The Task*" (Winter Morning walk). W.P. Storer, drawing attention to the above in *Some Notes Concerning Olney* says the foundations could be traced with difficulty in 1890; and a further reference states that the mill was "demolished at the close of the 18th. century". It stood at the foot of the

hill south of the village, at the spot called Clifton Plank, reached by a rough track from the village, or by a delightful footpath walk from Olney Mills.

Cowper pictures the stream "quietly flowing under the ice till, scornful of a check, it leaps the mill dam, dashes on the restless wheel, and wantons on the pebbly shore below". Originally a mill was held by Edward's thane, Alli on the Bishop of Coutances' land at Clifton, and there was a moiety of a mill worth 11 shillings and 125 eels from a fishery on Countess Judith's holding. Two mills were on the Manor in 1544 and 1627; and three corn-mills in 1673 when the Lowes sold out to Sir John Maynard – a politician who seems to have lived up to the reputation of his kind in the estimation of Pepys, who called him a "turncoat".

John Medbury was the miller in 1710; and the indefatigable Mr. Ratcliff who states that Olney Mill worked in conjunction with the old Clifton Mill which stood "at the foot of Clifton Hill", has preserved for us an important advert from the *Northampton Mercury* Oct. 21 and 28, 1771:-

"To be sold at Clifton Mill in Olney, in the County of Bucks, Two Pairs of French Mill-stones, with Ironwork and Brailes; a Shaft, Cog-wheel and Heads; Wallows, Counter and Geer Wheel; and Heads; Trow, Flats and Hopper and one ditto; Water-Wheel and Shaft, and Cog ditto; Wallows, Counter, Geer Wheel, Axle and Heads; and Flour-Mill, three Hoppers, Spouts and Flour Tackle all in good Repair. Enquire of John Barnard at Olney Mill".

All in good repair! Another good mill dismantled to stop competition; so it's no new idea.

Fulling Mill

The location and details of other mills in the parish are very uncertain, so I though it well to confine them generally to one heading. A suggestion is made to me, however that a fulling mill, stood at the west end of the Lavendon Mill loop, a bare ¾ mile north of Clifton church, not for fulling cloth, but for grinding fuller's earth (found at one or two places in north Bucks.) but I can find no corroboration, and record this suggestion for what it is worth.

LAVENDON – 2 m. N.E. from Olney

River Ouse

Lavendon Mills – 1 m. S.W. of Church Standing

Disused
1768, 1793, 1824, 1835, (1847), 1875, 1887, 1926

At the disposal of Lavendon Abbey after the Dissolution, Queen Elizabeth granted to Roland Heywood and his wife, a waste or Common called Pickmead in Warrington, with "three watermills at Lavendon", and another record says they were "under one roof". Within recent years there were two mills under the one roof; but only one, in the centre of the building now retains its wheel and machinery.

The date of a reconstruction, with initials, is on a tablet over the mill door:-

JSP . . . Y
1852

and beneath this is affixed the Sun Insurance Company's sign. The partially obliterated initials refer to John Sculthorpe Perry, whose family are said to have held the mill for hundreds of years until they moved to Olney Mill in the 'sixties. F Parsons followed and then Albert E. Skevington, who was found drowned in July 1893. W. Osborn, J Howson, and J.M. Cony were subsequent millers; and at present Mr. A.J.Cony and his son who have been most obliging and helpful, carry on the farm and mill. Built chiefly of stone, the latter joins the house at right-angles; and the by-pass runs through the wheel room alongside the wheel.

This remaining wheel is entirely of wood, with 3 sets of six radial spokes, although most of the wooden buckets are missing. An all-iron pit wheel drove the wallower iron to iron, on a wooden upright shaft; and a fine clasp-arm spur wheel, also of wood drove iron stone-nuts, on jack rings, one pair each side; beneath the spur an iron-bevelled cog-ring was secured to receive a steam drive. On first floor, over the stones, is a four-spoke morticed iron crown wheel for driving one shaft running towards the house, to operate the sack hoist by belt, and one across the mill to the chaff-cutters, etc.

Instead of the bins being in the roof aisles, they have a floor to themselves, whilst the roof is rather shallow. The other mill in the south end, seems to have been arranged much the same as at present – especially the wheel, which shared the wheel-house with its by-pass stream; and the mill timbers are not oak, as in the old mills, but chiefly poplar.

A mill, probably on the present site, was held by Hunfrid, or Humphrey, of the Count of Mortmain, in 1086 at 10/- and 50 eels rent. "One mill in Lauenden" is noted several times in mid 13th. century; and in 1534 it was the scene of a quarrel between the Throckmortons of the neighbouring parish of Weston

Lavendon Mill

Underwood and Thomas Hill who had obtained leave from the Abbot to wash 400 sheep in the mill-dam. At the Dissolution it was valued at £4 yearly; and in the sale of the Manor in 1671 the mills were included.

In her book *On the banks of the Ouse* (1887) Emma Marshall includes an illustration of the mill, which appears exactly as at present; and Chapter III, "The Lace Maker" is a story of Katherine Perry, the miller's daughter, who with other Lavendon personalities is dramatised under her real name, in the true local setting. The mill, Miss Marshall states, went with the Grange, whilst the monks had the fishing. Thomas Wright records that a favourite resort of the

Reverend John Newton, celebrated composer of Hymn tunes and Rector at Olney, 1764–1780, was Lavendon Mill, where he would take tea with his friend Mr. Perry; and afterwards preach to the people who would assemble in a large barn to hear him.

There is nearby a Mill Field, believed to be the meadow running up to the sluice, between the two mill streams. Lavendon Mill, which stands alongside a very ancient track leading from the Olney road to Clifton Reynes, named on the 1835 Ordnance; and a Toll-bar was indicated a century ago near the junction of the trackway with the turnpike.

NEWTON BLOSSOMVILLE – 2¼ m. E. from Olney

River Ouse

Early Watermill – 200 yards N.E. of Church

Gone
No map references

Doubtful Site. 3f. N.N.W. of Church

Gone

"On Sunday, 14 March 1378, at Newton Blossom-ville Isabel Wanter, of Stoke Goldington found William Wanter her husband lying dead in the Ouse. An inquest was held before Wm. Barton on 16 March, and the jury found that Wm. Wanter fell in the mill called the Fulling Mill which belonged to the prior of Ravenstone, and situate over the Ouse. They found that he died through the agency of the mill and fell into the water. The cost of moving the mill was 3s., with which Ravenstone is charged. The prior secured Thos. Stowe and John Clerc as pledges" Extract from Coroner's roll for the years 1–13 of Richard II, published in the *Records of Bucks.*, *Vol. XIII.*

This is one of several note concerning watermills of Newenton, or as styled for many centuries, Newton Blossomville, although at Domesday under the de Blossomvilles, there appear to have been no mills; the above is the earliest reference that has come to light. About 1679 the Farrers, who had held the Manor, were involved in a dispute about the mill waters. "The course for boats coming down from Lavendon Mills" says *V.C.H. Vol. IV.* "was through Costoe Water, into the lake water, out of that into the Loonde Water and so to Newton Mills, but Thomas Bodington and others made a dam of timber, earth, gravel and stones 300 feet long and ten feet wide to

stop the passage from Costoe water. In September 1676 Thomas Farrer cut through the dam and brought an action to prove the right of way for all renting the waters for fishing and other purposes".

Two flour and three fulling mills were mentioned in Newton in the 17th. century, but probably there were not more than two separate mill buildings all told. Last watermill in the parish is thought to have stood close by the footbridge below the churchyard, and since it probably existed at least till the 18th. century, the chances are it was a corn mill.

The *Old Mill Inn* survives in the quiet stone-built village street; and it seems a sheep dip existed on the stream, behind the building, for in January 1824, it is recorded that some horses were drowned near the *Old Mill* (Inn?) by "plunging into a pit in the river" whilst hunting. There is incidentally a local belief that the mill was not approached by the present cartway west of the church but *via* an old track by the east side of the church and through a ford.

Doubtful Site
Another site pointed out to me, is a quarter of a mile or more up-stream, at the diverging of the main river and the loop stream, but like the Clifton Fulling site this seems to be conjectural and no foundations or sluices are remembered: whilst the *Mill Inn* site is accepted throughout the village.

LAVENDON

River Ouse

Snelston Manor Mill – Site uncertain

Gone

Snelston is a Manor partly in Lavendon, and partly in Bedfordshire; and the county boundary being upon the Bucks river bank, Snelston Mill, valued with a moiety at 27 shillings and 250 eels in the manor of the Bishop of Coutances was possibly beyond our terri-tory. Snelson Farm (Snellson on Bryant's map) is in

the north-east corner of Lavendon, but the watermill, existing in Edward the first's time, is long since gone.

The site would have been below Newton Blossom-ville, not next down steam to Lavendon Mill; and only just above where the Ouse leaves our county to pursue its long trek through the Fens to the Wash.

Chapter 2
Buckinghamshire Watermills on the Ouse Tributaries

STOWE – 2½ m. N.W. from Buckingham

Cuttle Brook

Home Farm Saw Mill – ½ m W.N.W. of Church

Working
No map reference

Somewhat difficult to locate are the estate watermills employed in private grounds for timber sawing and sundry other purposes, since they do not appear in the Directories, nor usually on maps; but a sale catalogue brought the Home Farm Mill to my notice.

Situated south of the picturesque and secluded Dadford hamlet, in a spinney O.S.228, it is driven by the Cuttle Brook, which gives its name to a plot called Great Cuttle Brook Piece farther down stream, where the brook divides Water Stratford and Radclive parishes. The sawmill is approached by a drive beneath some fine trees from the Dadford road; and the loop stream is spanned by the drive at a bridge with a wide grill between stone pillars and a curved parapet wall. Upstream is a beautiful lake bedecked with water lilies and forming an exceptionally fine

and picturesque mill-pond in parklike surroundings.

Originally a waterwheel was installed, but a turbine is now employed, and the feed is *via* a large iron pipe coming from a stop valve against the drive between by-pass and farmstead. By the turbine room is a small saw bench, and in the main two-storied building of pink brick, with corrugated iron roofing, is a Westinghouse electric motor. Projecting from the building is a large circular- saw bench, for reducing logs to planks and scantlings, built by the well-known but recently defunct firm of Roberts of Deanshanger. The saw is about 3ft. diameter; and the travelling table of very massive timbers running upon the usual rollers.

The late Duke of Buckingham is believed to have had the mill erected, for its present purpose; it never was a corn mill, and is of no great age.

Paper Mill Wood – ¼ m. S.W. of Church

Remains of Sluice

No Map reference

Paper Mill Wood or Spinney, a 15 acre plot east of the Dadford-Chackmore, and south of its crossing with the Roman road from Bicester to Towcester, lies about a mile below the Home Farm Mill.

Immediately inside the Wood, alongside a little road bridge are remains of a stone and brick culvert through which the mill stream passed; and above this some pieces of the sluice gates, whilst twin wooden channels lead down towards the culvert from the sluice.

Above the sluice is a very fine broad mill-race, reaching up to and beyond the Roman road, and named "Oxford Water" on the maps, but now it is dry.

An early mill on Boycott Manor, on which this site is situated, belonged to the Abbot of Cirencester in the 1240's, eventually passing to the Abbot of Biddlesden; and a recital in 1226 of the boundaries of an area excluding Chackemor Common Pasture (*Feet of Fines 10 Henry III*) quotes the "mill of Stowe" somewhat obscurely:-

"the line along which the royal road called Kingstrete runs from the vill of Langeport (i.e.

Lamport, east of Stowe House) to the royal road called Buggilderoade (the Roman way to Bicester?) and the line along which the latter road runs to the bridge of Boicote (Boycott, probably where the present bridge spans Oxford Water) and from that bridge going down by the course of the stream to the stream which runs from the mill of Stowe and by that stream to the same mill and from the mill along the line of the road to Langeport as far as Kingstrete" (No punctuation. My parenthesis).

Something must have happened to the foregoing roads in the intervening centuries, for it is almost impossible today to locate either the "mill at Stowe" or "Melpethelmill" (Melpeth Hill Mill?) of similar date. As one would infer an 18th century structure cashing in on the paper boom, and discarded when the trade localised itself around Wycombe, etc.

Finally Paper Mill Spinney figured in 1823, in an exciting encounter between a gamekeeper of the Duke of Buckingham, and two men with a dog, bludgeons and a pistol! Seven Years transportation!

CHETWODE – 4¾ m. S.W. of Buckingham

Chetwode Old Mill – 1m. S.S.E. of Church

River Lovatt

Mill Cottage remains
Maps (name only) 1768, (1809),
1870, 1875, 1887, 1914, 1926

A mill valued at 30 pence in 1086 was in the appurtenances of Chetwode Manor in 1223, but no record thence until the 16th century occurs; and it may be that the latter mill is a later structure. Indeed the small value of the former suggests a horse-mill, unless the watermill had been destroyed by William on his march of pillage.

Robert Harris and James Bradshaw were successive millers here in the 16th century, when references are found to what proved to be the last mill of Chetwode; and Bradshaw distinguished himself by his implication in an intended rising of the Oxfordshire people in 1596, when they proposed to attack Lord Norrey's house owing to the high price of wheat. But the plot was discovered, and Bradshaw was "sent for examination", pinioned beneath a horse and forbidden to speak on the journey, it being alleged that he instigated the intended riot. According to the charge he was "a miller travelling the country" by which was probably meant that he wandered as far afield as possible in order to combine propaganda with business.

The mill was still held by the lord of the Manor in 1641; and 70 years later John Sleamaker, miller and his wife had for some reason been "removed from "Chittwood". Mention of the mill occurs in 1785, and Solomon Harris was the miller – perhaps the last – in 1798; for the building seems to have disappeared by about 1850. By a deed of 1654, John Chetwode purchased the watermill from his nephews, their father having bought it from Thomas Packer of Derbyshire.

A thatched cottage of brick and stone remains alongside the by-pass, across a couple of fields from the Claydon road; and from the cottage to Godington Church the other side of the railway viaduct is a prolonged duck-board, marking the site of an ancient cartway, and leading over the main river at the county boundary. A walled mill-race remains, but the lifelong tenant of the cottage never saw the mill foundations; nor could he verify the name of the river, (which comes from Somerton, north Oxon, *via* Fringford), for this is one of the mysteries of Bucks! Is it a second arm of the Ouse; is it the Lovatt (a name more often associated with the Edlesborough and Newport Stream), is it the Little Ousel; or hasn't it a name at all? The Automobile Association, so fond of plastering the countryside with its bilious advertisements, neatly evades the question by omitting to attach its mark to Padbury Bridge upon the main Buckingham road, so some good has come even out of this dilemma! Years ago this stream was known as The Brook, whilst the Claydon Brook was The Burn; and the Reverend C.F. Farrar assumes the Padbury and Thornborough portion is a continuation of the Claydon Brook, but discredits his authority by implying that the latter comes down from Fringford – an obvious absurdity. Lt. Col. J.P. Wyness (*Little Brickhill*) says Thornborough Bridge spans the Claydon Brook, but is possibly relying upon the Rector.

Last we hear of Chetwode Mill is in 1823, when auctioned with Chetwode Mill House, and meadows, called Great and Little Duck Stools, the tenant being John Hiron. "A most desirable purchase" said the advertisement "for any person wishing to re-establish the Mealing Concern, the Mill having been discontinued for a few years, may at a comparatively trifling expense be resumed, the head of water being attached exclusively to this property." Probably about as "desirable" as some desirable property is nowadays, for a good mill would hardly have stood idle for several years a century ago!

TWYFORD – 5 m. S.S.W. from Buckingham

??

Twyford Watermill – 5f. W.N.W. of Church

Used occasionally
Maps 1768, 1793, (1809), 1824, 1832,
1833, 1847, 1875, 1887, 1914, 1926

Twyford Watermill marks one of the "ends of civilisation" in Bucks. The village street terminates at the Church and the only outlet unless we retrace our steps, is a rough lane just short of the Church, leading to a gated field road. Down this we proceed, to emerge eventually in front of Twyford Watermill with a choice of three ways – one, a gated road to Marsh Gibbon; two, a quite invisible track to the windmill, and three the "water road" to Preston Bissett. Number three is the worst, a permanent and thickly vegetated river, which could not be negotiated by a horse and cart, much less any other vehicle; so the only way to Preston Bissett is by a plank over the river and through some fields by a gated footpath, although it is recorded that in 1644 on Friday June 21, King Charles' whole army divided near Twyford Mill and half went *via* the "water gate" to Chetwode!

The watermill, or rather its predecessor, was settled upon Nicholas, son of Henry de Twyford, and his wife in 1321, and corresponds to the Nicholas Mill held by the Dayrells of Lillingstone Dayrell in the 15th and 16th centuries; and it belonged to Twyford Manor.

The present building, a combined farmhouse and mill, of red brick and stone with a tiled hip-gable roof is of pleasing appearance as it stands reflected in the broad silvery stream. Fitted with old but serviceable machinery, it is solely water-driven, doing a little grist work for the farmstead. The wheel is a fine 12ft. clasp-arm breast type, the axle-tree being a very large square oak shaft and the arms of 6ins. square section elm. Shrouds, stays and buckets are of

wood also the last having sole-plates bolted to the stays, making a fairly efficient type of wheel. As usual a flash is controlled by rack-and-pinion, with a sluice upstream. A 12ft compass arm pit-wheel engages iron to iron with the wallower upon an iron upright shaft; and a large new morticed gear drives iron stone-nuts on screw rings, but with tapered spindles as used with lever and yoke. The peak stones remain, and a small crown wheel drives a layshaft for chaff cutter and sack hoist on second, or top, floor. Mr. T.H. King the present occupier, had the iron machinery put in, and removed the wheat stones.

Jame Aris had this, and one of the windmills in 1798. The miller in the forties and fifties was Robert Hughes and for the next 20 years John Treadwell of Radclive was owner-occupier; but the celebrated Tom Bolton had the mill for many years, followed by Mr. Clark, Mr. Smith, whose sons rented Three Bridge and Islip (Oxon) respectively, and Alfred Walker.

Mr. Henry Allen, who worked the windmill, also handled the watermill; and he said that with wheat stones in use they could generally work the flour dresser simultaneously, but barley-grinding was harder going. The neighbourhood is very liable to flooding, causing interference with the mill; and logs and all kinds of debris were lodged in the river, which had not been cleaned for fifty years, in 1939.

The name Twyford is derived from "the two fords", because there were two parallel streams, each with a ford.

PRESTON BISSETT – 3¼ m. S.W. from Buckingham)

[*?Padbury Brook*]

Bridge Mill, Cowley Mill or *Three Bridge Mill* – 2⅛ m. S.S.E. of Church

Working
Maps 1768, 1793, (1809), 1824, 1832,

Before this book sees the light of day, Three Bridge Mill will probably have been flooded for the first time in a hundred years. The explanation is simple; a new and totally unnecessary road bridge has been erected across the stream, immediately below the Mill with arches about a foot wider than the original railway

arch two miles upstream at Godington, which had to be widened on account of the floods it caused; and this despite the fact that there is a greater volume of water and a swifter stream at Three Bridges. The old bridge, built by a man named Woodfield, less than a century ago, is perfectly sound, but such stupidity and negligence are typical, for almost any new bridge in the county causes floods and damage in the first heavy rainstorm.

Three Bridge Mill has witnessed some unusual occurrences, for in addition to its association with the Rhyne Toll of Chetwode, described in several local histories, it was in 1861 the meeting place of the Duke of Buckingham's spectacular funeral cortege for the final stage of its journey to Wotton Underwood. Exactly 40 years previously a less digni-fied event occurred, when the Hillesden and Cowley Association met in the mill, and did themselves so well that many remained till next morning, and some until the morning after that!

Cowley Mill appears to have belonged to Preston Bissett Manor at Domesday and in 1252 a moiety of a mill in "Coueleg" was involved in litigation; in 1469 the watermill was held of John Major by Thomas Giffard.

Early references generally speak of Bridge Mill or Cowley Mill, although the present name of Three Bridge occurs in the press over a century ago. The owner Mr. R.C. Taylor, tells me that a former name – mentioned in deeds – was Tunbridge Mill, a title which was dropped owing to postal confusion. Bryant and *Kelly's* sometimes use the term Three Bridges Mill but this seems to be a misnomer.

Situated in the south-east of the parish, some way back from the Edgcott road (by-passed by the new bridge) near the *Seven Stars* cross-roads, the mill is of brick and stone, slate roofed and built onto the mill-house. An eight spoked iron breast wheel 13 or 14ft. diameter by 6ft., within the mill at the south end (not in the new annexe) has 32 L-shaped well-venti-lated sheet steel buckets bent to shape and bolted to wooden stays. Tom Busby of Messrs. Gilbert's who designed and built it, stuck to his plans although Mr. Taylor thought, and still thinks, the buckets are insuf-ficiently canted to "lift" cleanly out of the water. I noticed also that an excessive quantity of water rushes into the middle of the wheel owing to the large vents, resulting in waste and obstruction. The flash is conventional and the by-pass stream, on the parish boundary, is south of the mill.

The 10ft. eight-spoked mortice gear pit-wheel, iron wallower, and upright shaft, in a wood, built pit-room, drive screw-controlled nuts by a 6ft. morticed gear. The stones are peaks, one pair for maize and one for barley; above them a crown-wheel drives a line shaft with several iron and wooden belt drums, one driving a sack bollard concealed in a dummy floor between roof bins, the chain being carried up to and along the roof-ridge to the sack trap. The sack bollard is controlled as at Thornborough; and the line-shaft is geared to a parallel one which drives the oat crusher belt, engagement being by an elaborately arranged crank in a frame, operating a vertical rod attached to a wooden bridge piece on which the spindle rests.

In 1875 there was a steam engine which Jabez Burton was told was no good, but he soon found that a little matter of a completely choked steam – pipe was preventing any steam from reaching the cylinder! He quickly put this right and, as the motorist says when his empty petrol tank has been replenished, "she will probably go better now". The mill, still in good condition, is in regular use by water only and in 1939 a modern mixer was added in the annex.

John Foster was the miller in 1798; and Henry Foster in the 'forties and 'fifties, "Squire" Perkins probably being the owner; he put it up for auction eventually and a man named Butler, looking like a tramp, proceeded to bid. "Do you know what you're bidding for?" the auctioneer enquired at last, surveying the bidder's attire very hard. "You mind your business and I'll mind mine" retorted Butler. Bidding passed the thousand mark and stopped with Butler in the lead; and producing the cash from his pockets, he put down the price in golden sovereigns! The mill shortly passed on to Charlie Meehan who is thought to have been related to Butler.

A fire occurred in the house in 1868, but did not touch the mill and, as a result, a stone over the back door, bearing date of mill is now built into the foun-dations and partly concealed in the ground. Either Meehan or a Mr. Marshall was in charge, and all the brick-laying for the reconstruction was done by an uncle of Mr. Allen of Twyford Mill, and the carpentry by his father.

A man called Sandeland took over; and in 1875 Jabez Burton came from North Marston Windmill, joined presently by our friend Mr. Ben Burton (his nephew) but they left in 1878 – the latter going to Slough steam-mills and his uncle to Padbury Watermill. Unfortunately a tragedy occurred around the mill when a relative, Will Burton, was acciden-tally shot during a rat or duck shoot. George Taylor, grandfather of the present owner, followed but soon went to Thornborough, leaving his sons Joseph and Frank at Three Bridge Mill which they let to S.Walker & Son, and W.T. Smith & Son of Twyford, for periods. Walker's son Alf, also was at Twyford Mills, and Jabez had milling brothers – Charles, of Wendover Towermill etc. and Ben of Lower Winchendon Watermill. An old jobbing millwright, called Tom Hall, ended his days stone-dressing at Three Bridge Mill where his son is still employed.

STEEPLE CLAYDON – 4¾ m. W. from Winslow

[Claydon Brook]

Medieval Watermill – Site Unknown

Gone

A watermill is mentioned in the parish in mid 13th. century and in 1536, together with a windmill, probably on Steeple Claydon Manor which was held successively by the Crown, the Giffords and the Chaloners.

A mill site suggests itself near Claydon Plank Farm, where a loop stream, deviates into Hillesden parish; and since selecting this spot, I have been assured that this *is* the site, and that foundations are believed to exist in the ground. An earlier waterwheel, apparently in Steeple Claydon, and a windmill were possessed by the Doilys of Oseney Abbey (Oseney Charters 1150–1281); but *V.C.H. Vol. IV* states very briefly that "Claydon Mill appears to have stood in Botolph Claydon" on the authority it seems of a document dated 1313. No indication whether this was a watermill, although one assumes this is meant; but Botolph Claydon Manor is in East Claydon parish, where the only stream of any size is the upper portion of Claydon Brook, on the eastern boundary, which has no loop stream.

PADBURY – 2½ m. S.E. from Buckingham)

[Padbury Brook]

Padbury Watermill – 1m. S.W. of Church

Standing disused
Maps 1695, 1768, 1793, (1809), 1824, 1833, (1847), 1870, 1875, 1887, 1914, 1926

In very early times a bridge on the boundary river between Buckingham and Padbury was known as Padbury Mylle Brydge, a name surviving to this day; and mill and bridge are believed to mark a Roman Camp site. Padbury Mill was the last old-world thatched watermill in Bucks; but it has now been botched up in an unsightly manner with galvanised iron, so that it presents more the appearance of a large pig sty than a mill!

The "good old days" are not so far behind in this part of the country, for a man told me of the exciting scenes his father had witnessed in this vicinity. The great eight and ten-horse carrier waggons travelling between the provinces and London detoured down Featherbed Lane over White Bridge and Padbury Mill Bridge to avoid the Toll-houses on the Buckingham turnpike, and more than once were stranded or overturned in the flood waters by Padbury Mill. Probably they were negotiating the ford alongside the bridge, which latter perhaps was not in a fit state to bear the tremendous weight of these old-time vehicles, far heavier and more cumbersome than any horse driven dray now existing.

V.C.H. asserts quite clearly that the stream at Padbury Mill is the Lovatt, and not Claydon Brook as one would imagine from the maps and as assumed by the Rev: C.F.Farrar and Lt.Col: J.P. Wyness: for it says the parish is bounded north and west by the Lovatt and south by Claydon Brook formerly called the "Burn"

At Domesday there was only one manor – Padbury Overbury – but a manor called Padbury Millbury, in which the watermill is located, was separated later, the term Millbury first occurring in 1379.

A moiety of the mill was held of Simon de Etchingham, afterwards Sheriff of Sussex, in 1227, when it fell to the King for a year and a day on account of the conviction of Hugh de Kingsbridge, son and heir of Walter the Miller, for robbery. Simon de Etchingham was later granted the whole mill with its meadow and pond; but the manor eventually passed to the Crown for the endowment of All Souls, Oxford, which still holds the property.

A long list of early grants are quoted by Lambert B. Larking in *The Knights Hospitallers of England*, 1857 from the days of Edward I onwards:- 5 Ed. I, to Simon de Achingham of Padbury mill; 13 Ed. II, to Walter the Miller: 6 Ed. IV, to John and Wm. Bodynton; 9 Hy VII farm and mill to John Sonell for 20 years at rent of 100/-; 9 Hy. VIII, to Wm. Cokman; 45 Eliz: to Thomas Harris; 1781 messuage to John Whitehall, miller; 1793, the mill to Thos. Shillingford; 1802 leased to Thomas Bates.

Till recently Padbury Mill was mainly of roughly cut timber and ancient thatch, just as one might imagine it centuries ago; and was built on to the end of a nice solidly built brick farmhouse with mullioned windows. Standing back 200 yards from the lane, above Padbury Mill Bridge, the mill was disused some time before alteration. The wheel

Padbury Mill

within the end of the building was a fine old 12ft. clasp -arm type with 4ft. tread, entirely of wood, and built and installed by old Tom Hall of Cowley.

Equipment included an all-iron pit-wheel and wallower, wooden upright shaft, two iron nuts on rings and all wooden great spur; but as a dog was chained on the first floor and the occupier departed after giving permission to view, it seemed best not to hurt the animal's feelings by examining the upstair's machinery!

Main by-pass is outside the mill, with a narrow relief way between the wheel and the end wall of the mill. A spindle passes through this wall, with belt drum outside and a pinion inside near the shroud of the watermill, as though to engage a cog ring (of which no sign) on the wheel for driving an external engine drive, or for driving an outdoor saw bench from the wheel.

Richard Taylor had this and the windmill in 1798; and in 1829 Padbury Mill with 60 acres was advertised – Thomas Bates, tenant; nine years later "this water corn mill in full trade, 2 pairs French stones, gearing and machinery in good order – a great part recently new, and abundant head of water, residence and eel traps – occupier T. Holt". William Kirby was the next miller, followed by James Baldwin; and remaining many years until the present century, when succeeded by Arthur Crook, who undoubtedly worked the mill, although listed only as a farmer in *Kelly's;* and Mr. C.J. Crook is the present farmer.

In 1827 Mr. Thomas Nelson, a Padbury farmer, advertised "a Malt Mill and Wheel", but it seems not to have been water-driven.

Downstream at the turnpike is Padbury Bridge, built 1828 or 9, where Joe Burton a relative of Jabez, but not a miller, was thrown into the river and killed when his dog-cart ran into the parapet. No mills are encountered in the next 3½ miles down to the meeting of the Ouse at the spot called "The Twins" – a name probably responsible for the contention of some that the Padbury stream is the Ouse as well as the Buckingham stream.

HILLESDEN – 3m. S.S.W. from Buckingham

Hillesden Brook (?)

Early Mill – Site unknown

Gone

One mill belonged to Hillesden Manor in 1086; and in 1279/80 Roger de Martinall quitclaimed two mills in Hillesden to John Giffard, but whether they were watermills is not stated. A 17th century deed also records an unclassified mill in the parish, where there is admittedly only a limited flow of water.

A possible site is a quarter of a mile due west of the church, where, on the west of the little streamlet, a suggestion of a gulley about 200 yards long is emphasised by clumps of rushes in its bed; this might be the by-pass loop to a small mill although there are no significant field names. The foundation of a brick wall in the river bed nearby is merely the remains of a little cart bridge demolished because its culvert impeded the water in flood time. The stream joins the Lovett just below Three Bridge Mill.

WINSLOW

Claydon Brook

Early Watermill – Site unknown

Gone

"The Manor of Wynslow, with the Market, Rents, and a Mill for 100 Marks yearly rent, and 100 Marks in hand" are mentioned by the late Mr. A.J. Clear in his *History of Winslow*, but it is uncertain whether this mill of 1326 was waterdriven, although the value suggests so. During Wat Tyler's rebellion, the inhabitants of Wyncelow and Greneberge broke into St. Alban's Abbey and took possession of handmills which the Abbott had confiscated to compel them to have their corn ground at the lord's mill on Winslow Manor and this is almost sure to have had water power. In the Court Roll of 1516, also land belonging to Will Perkins "by the watermill" is mentioned, and the mill may have stood on one of the arms of Claydon Brook which rise in the Swanbourne and Whitchurch hills, and almost encircle the parish; but in view of the close connection between the Manors of Winslow and Granborough, it might have been the Biggin Mill, to be dealt with under a Granborough heading.

MURSLEY – 3m. E.N.E. from Winslow

Clack Brook

Mill Holme – ½ m. S.W. of Church

Gone
No map reference

Down a green lane beneath big old trees leading off the rough track to Church Farm is "Mill Holme" a triangular plot O.S. 239, alongside the footpath to Swanbourne. Old men used to tell the present inhabitants this was a watermill site, but there has been no mill for over a century: in 1824 the "pasture called Mill Holmes" a freehold close of 2 acres, 2 rods and 11 perches, was advertised for sale, but there seems to be no printed reference to a watermill in Mursley.

Clack Brook flows towards Swanbourne to join the Biggin stream; and the name suggests an interesting speculation – is it related to the "clack-clack" of the shuttle in weaving mills; or is it perchance connected with the Bucks term, "cherry -clack", a bird scarer in the orchard?

LITTLE HORWOOD – 2¼ m. N.E. from Winslow

Branch of Claydon Brook

Early Mill – Site uncertain

Gone

Little Horwood finds no mention in Domesday, but in A.D. 795, a wood called Horwudu was granted by King Offa of Mercia to St Alban's Abbey, together probably with the Manor.

An ancient mill – presumably water – was on the estate in the 13th century; and the late Miss Clear, daughter of Mr. A.J. Clear, believed that her father pointed out a mill site at Little Horwood near the moat east of the church, although he does not seem to mention this in his writings. The site would be near the head of the Horwood Stream; and confirmation is found in William Selby's claim to an "unfinished" watermill in the *Posse Comitatus* survey of 1798. Probably the this new mill, which is likely to have been on the earlier site, was never completed.

GRANBOROUGH – 1½ m. S. from Winslow

[Branch of Claydon Brook]

Biggin Mill – Site uncertain

Gone

Probably a watermill stood at Biggin from an early date, said the late Mr. A.J. Clear referring to the well-known Byggyng or Biggin Field on the Winslow road below the old bridge and ford. This seems to be the only mention of Biggin Mill, but the "Mill of Greneburgh" in 1431, recorded under Mill Knob, might have been the same .

Called the "Maneria de Byggyng-cum Grenesborw in Hundred de Wodesdon" in 1340, the Biggin Manor was probably given by Egelwinus to the Abbey of St Albans in Edward the Confessor's day. The Grange and Chapel were near the ford, where some irregularities in the ground may still be seen; and probably the mill was near at hand. Bigend or Biggin Farm, surviving the Grange, existed a century ago.

LILLINGSTONE DAYRELL – 3¾ m. N. from Buckingham

River Leck

Early Mill – Site uncertain

Gone

Appurtenant to Dayrell's Manor at Lillingstone Dayrel was a mill in 1602; eight years later there were two mills, one – called the old mill – being in use as a cottage. A watermill is again mentioned in 1706, which appears to be the last evidence of its existence.

As *V.C.H. Vol. IV.* makes it clear the watermill was not in that part of the parish adjoining the Northants boundary, it was presumably below the lake or mill pond, 200 yds. north of the church, but seemingly unknown locally.

LECKHAMPSTEAD – 3 m. N.E. from Buckingham

[River Leck]

Great Leckhampstead Mill – 1f W. of Church

Gone
No Map Reference

A mill went with the Manor of Great Leckhamstead in 1205: and in 1279 the freeholders included John the Miller who rented a watermill for 20/-. Probably this was the same that Hugh held under Walter de Giffard at Domesday; and it stood on the River Leck, or Lake Brook, which rises in Whittlebury Forest and joins the Ouse between Thornborough and Thornton. Mill Field still exists below the ancient encampment just beyond the church as we leave the village; and probably a mill survived in the 17th and 18th centuries, when three or four mills existed on Tyrell's Thornton and Leckhamstead estates. Perhaps this last mill was of the style and period of the picturesque thatched cottages across the road in front of O.S. 214, which were demolished in 1939

Little Leckhampstead Mill – Site uncertain

Gone

One third of a mill in Leckhamstede village is mentioned in 1206; and in 1279 the freeholders of Little Leckhamstead included Robert the Miller, renting a watermill at 26/8d yearly; and this mill listed amongst the appurtenances of Lymes End Manor in 1360, would be another of Tyrell's three or four water-mills, and would probably be situated near the river bridge at Lymes End on the Wicken road, although I have found no corroboration. In medieval times Leckhampstead was divided into Great and Little, whilst the middle part was known as Tween Towns.

CASTLETHORPE – 2¼ m. N.N.W. from Wolverton

River Tove

Hanslope or Castle Thorpe Mill – 5 f. W. of Church

Working
Maps 1793, (1809), 1824, 1834,
(1847), 1870, 1875, 1887

In the Charter of the foundation of the Abbey of Lavendon, dedicated to the Premonstratensian Order in 1154, John de Biden grants a site for the Abbey of St. John the Baptist near Warrington, and his property in the mill called Hanslapemilne, amongst other grants: and the wife of Bertram Mallore also had property in her "mill at Hanslope".

It seems certain Hanslope Mill and Castle Thorpe Mill or Thorpe Mill as Bryant called it, are synonymous terms; and the site has always been as at present, in the fields half a mile north of the Stratford road from Castlethorpe, with a rough cartway leading to it.

V.C.H. Vol. IV. states that a mill on Hanslope Manor in 1086, worth 12/- yearly, was included in the grant of Henry I to William Manduit. Overlordship rights in the mill passed to Sir John de Wedon before 1279 (at which date Roger Birchmore was tenant of Hanslope Mill and other property) and Tothall Manor held mesne rights in the mill the same century; but these were released in 1292 to William Beauchamp, Earl of Warwick. Hanslope Mills at that date were amongst about four mills sometimes mentioned together, two of which were Bosenho Mill in Ashton (no doubt at the present Bozenham Mill site – next mill above Castlethorpe) and Cosgrove Mill, both in Northants, next lower down. Hanslope Mills, included in the grant of the Manor to Princess (later Queen) Elizabeth in 1550, were two watermills under one roof, leased in 1555 to Robert Matthews, and later demised to Wm. Crowne. "The mills *with a water-malt mill in Church Street*,"* which had been included in the Crown leases, were granted in February 1609–10 (i.e. year ending March 24th. to Edward Ferrers and Francis Phillips; and thus alienated from the Manor. The corn-mills appear to have passed afterwards with the property of the Lanes in Hanslope; Hanslope or Castle Thorpe Mill being situated in the parish of Castlethorpe

V.C.H. adds it was called Hanslope Mill in 1608 in a survey of the Manor bounds. The Tyrells had it in the 17th century but conveyed the estate in 1726 to Matthew Skinner and others. Castle Thorpe Mill surrounded by oceans of buttercups in a peace-time summer stands across the River Tove, which follows a lengthy course through Northants from near Sulgrave Windmill, passing through Towcester (Tove-cester) on its way. The mill itself is in the western half of the building, with a fine 12ft. all-iron breast wheel amidships, carried on a small diameter axle and having three sets of *nine* thin flat spokes – a most unusual feature – and 36 large buckets, spaced apart, with rounded lips. Another curious feature is that the wooden "flash" is curved to follow the periphery of the wheel and guided by iron channels set in the walls as at Haversham – a bollard and two chains being provided to pull the flash up and down instead of the customary racks and pinions. A mortice gear pit-wheel drives a large iron wallower on a massive octagonal upright shaft; with a big wooden spur over the wallower and three iron nuts on screw rings, in a wooden enclosure. Stones are on three sides of the compass; and a shaft from the crown wheel projects through the wall with a belt drive for a saw-bench in the yard; another layshaft drives chaff cutter and dresser by belts – the inclined

---

* This is almost certainly an error, and the malt mill will be dealt with in the Appendix on Horse-mills. [not printed, Ed.]

Hanslope or Castle Thorpe Mill

spindle of the dresser being bevel-geared to a counter-shaft. A belt is carried up to the dummy floor, to the all-wooden sack gear with similar controls to Thornborough and Three Bridge Mills.

A double by-pass is provided, one half passing westwards through the usual sluice whilst one is just inside the mill with a flash admitting water to a large inclined wire mesh eel-trap.

The whole mill of plastered stone with tiled roof, has the appearance of age and is fed by a long built-up mill pond, above which is Milfordleys Farm (variation of the earlier name of Milfordholmes). The mill is actually on a loop stream half-a-mile long with main stream following the Northants boundary as it does for the last five miles down to the Ouse at Wolverton.

Records of Bucks Vol. XI. states that in an account book of Easter offerings and small tythes for Castle Thrupp, 1616, John Banks was levied Xs. for his mill tithe, the largest tithe listed, as the others were for swine and sheep, etc. These mill tythes, personal levies known as "Lammas Tythinges", could be levied by the Statute of Articuli Cleri upon all grist mills erected since 1315. They were based on the actual value of work performed by the miller, so that he had to declare the quantity that he had ground, not the price at which he may have sold it; but under the "enclosure" Act this tithe arrangement ceased in 1788.

William Tooth was the miller in 1798; and William Carr of Haversham in the 'fifties and 'sixties, followed by George Whiting whose descendants farm the surrounding land; and the mill cottage is let to Mr. Scripps, who works the mill for private grist work.

Hanslope or Castle Thorpe Mill

LOUGHTON – 3½ m. S.E. from Stony Stratford

Shenley Brook

Early Mill – Site unknown

Gone

With some trepidation the above brook is mentioned, because of the uncertainty whether it ever turned a mill wheel; but an unspecified type of mill which seems to have been on the original Loughton Manor in 1497, would if water-driven, have been on this Brook, which passes Shenley, Loughton, Bradwell and Stantonbury on its way to the Ouse.

Of local millers mentioned in directories, John Morris of Shenley had a little power-driven maltmill; the Co-op: and Mr. Ready (Bradwell) successively occupied the big power-mill, now demolished in High Street and others have already been dealt with.

EDLESBOROUGH – 5m. S.E. from Leighton Buzzard

River Ouzel

Edlesborough Mill – ¾ m. E. of Church

Standing disused

Maps 1768, 1793, (1809), 1824, 1832, 1834, (1847), 1870, 1875, 1926

At Domesday two mills worth 15/4d were held by Gilbert of Ghent in the parish; one probably occupied the present site, but whether the other was on this stream (perhaps near Bellows mill, on the Bedfordshire bank) or on the Wash Brook to be noted later it is impossible to say. In 1212 one mill is mentioned at Eduluesbir when Hervey "molendinarius" was apparently the tenant.

The Lovat, now generally called the Ouzel – a revival of the name Ousel which seems to have been used in the 16th century (although "Lovat" is derived from the de Lovants of Norman times) – rises in Dunstable Downs and follows the Bedfordshire County boundary down to Grange Mill, below Leighton Buzzard when it swings into Bucks; and a curious contention was once advanced by a columnist that it is the Ousel down to Leighton, and the Lovatt thence to Newport.

Simmons' Mill, at Edlesborough, probably has always been first on the stream, which is a few yards within the boundary at this point; but Mr. Simmons does not allow it to be photographed because the cameraman might be a burglar who wants to study the best means of breaking in. However, I found the accompanying picture on my film when it was developed! Built of brick of non-descript colour, with two floors, sackloft and slate roof, the mill faces north, with mill-house of yellow brick (rebuilt 1871 by William Hawkins, who became the miller) at one end; and beyond this the windmill. The chimney in background bears silent testimony to more prosperous days when steam power was employed; but not even the big long mill-pond, parallel to which is a lengthy by-pass, is now used.

Obliging me with particulars of the interior, Mr. Simmons said the iron waterwheel, broken up some years ago, drove the usual pit-wheel, upright shaft, underdriven stones and silk flour dressers; and Mr. Fred Simmons, his father, employed three millers here and two in the windmill. But trade dwindled and the business did not appeal to Mr. Will Simmons; – "I don't like millering, I like pigs", he said, explaining why he abandoned the mill, now derelict, and concentrated on farming.

Joseph Anstee was the miller in 1798, but the windmill was not mentioned: Joseph Barnard left the mill, removing to Houghton Regis in 1829; and John Buckmaster followed. His relatives, who include members of the Simmons' family, had neighbouring Bedfordshire mills; and Fred Simmons came to Edlesborough as a steam and water miller about 1890.

A curious predicament arose when some sheep were drowned in the boundary stream; the Bedfordshire constable called and made notes; then the Bucks. constable had a look, but neither would note anything that happened on the opposite bank! Linnet catching with nets was permissible in Beds, but not in Bucks. and the fellows sometimes followed the birds across the stream, but the police waited around the mill, where the orchards attract the birds, and caught the offenders! About a century ago, an interesting custom called "Stephening" believed to date from 1597, was observed in Edlesborough; forty-nine bushels of wheat were yearly sent by Lady Bridgewater to the mill, which almost certainly would be Edlesborough Watermill to be ground, and the flour was made into 4 lb. loaves for distribution to the poor of the parish.

Next downstream are Bellows Mill, Two Counties Power Mill, and Moor End Mill, all in Beds; and within a mile of Edlesborough Mill.

SLAPTON – 3 m. S.S.E. from Leighton Buzzard

[River Ousel]

Slapton Mills or *Staptonbury Mill* – ½ m. N. of Church

Standing derelict

Maps 1768, 1793, (1809), 1824, 1834,
(1847), 1870, 1875, 1887, 1914

Early existence of a watermill and the occurrence of such names in the 16th century as Mereditch, Northlake and Broadwater indicate the low-lying nature of the land, although there is now no lake or "broad water" except during winter floods. At Domesday there seems to have been no mill, but in 1291 the Abbess of Barking held a mill or mills here; two watermills were on the Manor in 1669, probably in one building, for after 1724 there were a pair of water-cornmills under one roof called Slapton Mills; and under this title they were offered for sale in 1808.

Today the mill stands derelict in the fields near the bend in the Leighton road from the village; windows are missing and all machinery gone, and the squarish yellow brick mill, standing away from the Mill House, presents a desolate appearance amidst flat surroundings, with Dunstable Downs forming a distant background. Roofs are of slate, and interior framework of good pitch pine. The waterwheel, chiefly of wood, was outside the north wall, apparently a small and broad undershot or low breast shot, for the fall is slight. An upright shaft drove four pairs on the first floor from the usual spur-wheel and in the roof were roomy bins. The stone floor is supported by four iron pillars; and a tall brick-built addition to the mill is divided into engine room against the stream, and coal and stokehole in front; beyond is a lower wing which accommodated the horizontal boiler.

Mr. Gilbert dismantled the gear, and he recalled that an argument arose as to whether the oaken axle-shaft of the wheel would float or sink, so they tipped it into the river and it sank! The next flood water washed it up and they retrieved it.

In 1798 Jnᵒ Buckmaster was the tenant; James Horn rented the mill from James Price of Smewnes Grange a century ago; and Thomas Ginger, David Lee Ginger, and Alexander Maclean Ginger (steam only) followed in succession; whilst Frank Warren – steam and water – held it thence until about 1912, Later the farm was used for fattening stock by Mr. Grace, who kindly conducted me over the empty mill, but he has vacated it. Mr. Ginger's family resided not at the mill but at a genteel residence, as Sheahan calls it, erected in the centre of the village in 1820, and apparently the most distinguished house there. They employed a true miller of the old-fashioned type named Lawrence, but he died before the steam engine was installed and I am told that, had he seen an engine being taken into his mill, he would have dropped dead! Mr. R Richmond (*Leighton Buzzard and its Hamlets, 1928*) says this was about 1885; and he states the fall of water from the Billington – Northall road bridge to the mill is 3ft. 7 ins; to Leighton is 16ft. 7 ins; and to the county bridge near Grange Mill (Beds), 29 feet.

At busy times there was so much to do that sacks of grain were thrown into the upper doorway from the ground by strong men instead of using the hoisting gear. Fine views are obtainable from the upper floors, which formed a vantage point for the races which used to be run over the adjoining fields, one of which is called Mill Ground.

GROVE – 2 m. S. from Leighton Buzzard

[River Ousel]

Grove Mill – 1 m. N.E. of Church

Gone

In 1197 a watermill in dispute is mentioned for the first time, on the De Brok or Broks Manor of Grove, when a fine passed between Cecilia de Brok and Osbert de la Grava, no mill being listed at Domesday. Later the mill of la Grave was stated to be near Hamfurlang (Home Furlong?): Two mills were in Le Brook and La Grave in 1251; and it may be mentioned the term "La Grava" is believed to apply to Grovebury (Bedfordshire side of stream) as well as to Grove. In 1318, two watermills in one building were on the Manor, one wheat and one barley, and a windmill; and John Boughton left a watermill and other property to Toddington Hospital in 1489; after which it passed to the Dormers, against whom Sir Henry Cheyne brought an action to recover it.

Joseph Symons was milling by wind and water in 1798; and at an 1833 sale, James Symons was the vacating tenant; thereafter, George Draper, miller and farmer, was there till the last, and it may be he decided not to repair the great damage wrought by the memorable thunderstorm of Aug 2–3, 1879. The mill – an old barn-like place – had about three pairs of stones, with water wheel and gears of wood; but

round about 1890 Mr. Gilbert knocked out the wheel and machinery, since when farm and mill have entirely disappeared and are almost forgotten. The site, apparently more readily discernible in 1928 than now, is at the end of a loop-stream just east of the quaint little church and canal lock, not far above Tiddingford (Yttinga-ford) in Linslade.

Leighton Buzzard and Grange Mills (Beds) follow, then come the Soulbury mill sites.

SOULBURY – 2 m. N.W. from Linslade

[*River Ousel*]

Fulling Mill – About 1½ m. E.N.E. of Church?

Gone
No map reference

An ancient roadway, 1¼ m. east of Soulbury village, could be traced in Sheahan's time from Chelmscott Manor Farm to a ford where the fulling mill stood upon the Ouzel or Lovatt. The mill was down long

ago but fields in the vicinity are known as Fulling Fields; the cartway is no longer visible, nor does it appear on the original Ordnance map, and exact site is difficult to identify.

Stapleford or *Red Bridge Mill* – 1¼ m. N.E. of Church

Remains of sluices
Maps 1768, (1809), 1824,
1832, (1847), 1870, 1875, 1887

John Michel, bearing witness to Geoffrey Lucy's age, said he remembered the year of birth at Chelmscott because he sold Geoffrey's father a mill six months before, and never received any money for it! Whether this was a watermill is not stated, but in 1550 Stapleford Mill was declared to be part of the Manor of Chelmscott, Francis Temple being a lessee; and a mill of this name existed until recent years. The site, traceable by the wheel-pit and broken sluice gates is behind Stableford or Stapleford Farm east of the canal bridge from which a fine view of Three Locks is obtained.

Very interesting events took place at the mill in the 17th century, when Henry Keach was miller, for he was a brother of Benjamin Keach who established Keach's Baptist Meeting House in Winslow in 1625. Baptist meetings were held in Stableford Mill for many years until about 1669; and at one such meeting about the year 1666, John Griffiths and Jonathan Jennings, well-known Baptists were arrested and committed to Aylesbury Gaol, (said the late Mr. A. J. Clear in his *History of Winslow*) where Benjamin Keach was then in prison for his religious beliefs.

In 1798, John Horn was corn-milling at Stapleford; and Sheahan stated in 1862 the mill was

"very ancient" and mentioned that Gabriel Bull was occupying it. Bull was eventually succeeded by Frederick James Newens; and either he or Robert Bliss was the last miller, at the end of the century.

The mill appears to have stood across the main stream or on the left bank, just north of the square yellow brick farmhouse (built 1855 and still inhabited); and the wheel was a wooden breast-shot, either outside the mill or in a "lean-to". A sluice gate was on the right bank, only a few yards above the wheel and it led down a fall to a semi-circular wall on which a grid or eel-trap might have been mounted, thence to the main by-pass. Lower downstream is Red Bridge on the Bragenham lane, from which the mill is sometimes named. Some of the old red bricks from the mill were used for building barns in front of the Mill House, whilst remains of the *old* mill house of brick and tile are built into a kitchen wing on the present house.

It seems the mill was of moderate size, always used for corn; and Mr. Gilbert said it was a good mill, not in bad condition and only requiring a new axle-shaft when demolished about 30 years ago; but Rothschild, the landlord, who was responsible for the disappearance of several mills, would not repair it. Three pairs of stones and a dressing machine were installed. Under the name of Stapleford Mill it was offered for auction in 1850 amongst the stock of the late John Horne, *including machinery and gears of the mill*, but it was not then dismantled, and great damage was sustained by it in the disastrous storm of 1879.

GREAT BRICKHILL (2½ m. S.S.E. from Fenny Stratford) [River Ousel]

Paper Mill Farm – 1m. S.W. of Church

Slight foundations
Maps 1768, 1793, (1809), 1834, (1847), 1870, 1875. Also 1887 and 1926 as Paper Mill Farm

Last surviving paper mill in the Ouse Watershed in Bucks was probably at Great Brickhill, against the Stoke Hammond Boundary. The site is not very far east of Stoke village on the north side of the Brickhill lane apparently, the little farmhouse being on the south side. Beyond the farm is the by-pass, then the main stream across which the paper mill apparently stood. The corner stones still stand in the stream together with some stones chiselled out to make steps; and brickwork has been dug up in the adjoining field, but this might have been the remnants of lime kilns. Some flood gates were in the by-pass just below the Mill Farm, but were washed away about 1935 in a storm, which suited Mr. Bone, the present occupier, for they caused too much obstruction in flood time.

General opinion is that the mill was not there within living memory; everything points to it being a paper mill to the last, as described on the 1834 map and on Cruchley's. *V.C.H. Vol. IV* records two mills in Great Brickhill at Domesday, one probably on the paper mill site, its successor being known as Smewnes mill in 1251, for the corner of the parish where it adjoins Soulbury comprised the Grange, although sometimes called the Brickhill Grange. The mill was "associated with the water of Novente" (error for Lovente?) in the 17th century, when described as two mills under one roof and "it reappears in the 18th century as a paper mill, giving its name to Paper Mill Farm, the name of Smewnes itself having disappeared from modern maps". Meanwhile,

Anthony Holton, paper-maker of Great Brickhill was mentioned in 1695.

Bryant (1824) marks "Grange Farm and Paper Mill", apparently indicating this site; and ten years later appeared an advert:-

"To Paper Makers and Millers – To be let on a building lease a SITE whereon a PAPER MILL formerly stood, possessing a powerful head of water, in a good neighbourhood adjoining the Grand Junction Canal, and near the line of the London and Birmingham railroad. There is a dwelling house and about 20 acres rich meadow land attached".

A somewhat similar advert of 1840 of "Premises suitable for Paper or Corn Mill" gave the site as *2 Miles from Leighton Buzzard* which is the position of Grange Mill on the Bedfordshire bank; and the similarity of wording may be only a coincidence.

The grant of Smewnes Milne and land in Great Brickhill made by Nicholas de Sunford to Woburn Abbey in 1251 was followed by other gifts before 1337; and these probably formed Smewnes Grange, the mansion itself being built within a moat near the Ouzel. The abbots, in consideration of a grant, agreed henceforth to cause no obstruction in the river to the detriment of the free fishery or the meadow of Nicholas – a somewhat high price for Nicholas to pay to ward off illegal interference with his rights!

STOKE HAMMOND – 3 m. S. from Fenny Stratford [River Ousel]

Domesday Mill – Site unknown

Gone

"A mill at Stoke Hammond worth 8/- in 1086 descended with the Manor to Sir John Williams and was included in his lease of the site of the Manor, but excepted from Crown leases"; says *V.C.H. Vol. IV* and

"the mill-house with some 70 acres of land was held in chief of the crown by William Turvey at his death in 1610, when it passed to his son John"; but subsequent references to Orchard Mill, which is just outside parish, in Great Brickhill, indicate that *V.C.H.* is confused between Orchard Mill and the Stoke Hammond site, and it is very doubtful whether there has been a mill in Stoke Hammond since the Domesday one, nor is it certain to have been a watermill.

GREAT BRICKHILL – 2½ m. S.S.E. from Fenny Stratford

[*River Ousel*]

Orchard Mill – 7 f. W. of Church

Working
Maps 1768, 1793, (1809), 1824, 1832, 1834, 1870, 1875, 1887, 1926

Orchard Mill

In the north west of the parish, Orchard, or as Jefferys has it, Orchard's Mill, preserves a name handed down from the 16th century; it is probably on the site of one of the two mills valued at 30/- in 1086, in Great Brickhill; and *V.C.H. Vol. IV* implies that two mills under one roof in 1574 might have occupied the same site.

The present mill is on the south side of Mill Lane, and going back to 1709 we read of William Stevens, surveyor of Great Brickhill, being indicted for collecting 80 cart loads of stones in Mill Lane . . . for repairing the highway, thus preventing Mill Lane from being repaired! Tall and square, of light-coloured brick, with a shallow slate roof, the mill stands across the stream with by-pass eastwards and overflow from the weir on the other side. The wheel-house, built on the east end of the mill, contains a fine *all steel* 12ft. breast wheel with 7ft. tread, constructed in halves with three sets of spokes. The buckets are slightly rounded with good ventilation; and in addition to the 'flash' there is a smaller sluice at the side, so that too great a rush of water in the wheel-house could be released. Mr. A. Jacobs, the miller, apprenticed at a Canterbury watermill and with experience at several others in Kent and at the well-known Barham Downs Windmill, considers it a very good wheel and prefers it to overshots, which he says will

choke and stop dead under a heavy rush of water if poorly designed.

An iron pit-wheel of some 10ft. diameter with oak cogs drives an iron wallower and upright shaft, a very large morticed gear and three nuts on screw-rings, with iron bridge-beams and fixed bridges, all enclosed. Burr stones are placed either side, and a peak bedstone with composite runner in the middle of the mill. An iron crown wheel with applewood teeth formerly drove a dynamo by belt from a very large suspension type wheel on a shaft; and another shaft drives the sack hoist, and also a long belt leading to a big shaft across the end of the mill for the oat-crusher, maize-cutter with sifter, and fan-blower, etc.

The second floor contains closed-in bins; and the usual open bins with central deck are in the roof. Flour is delivered to the various sacks on ground floor by belt-driven archimedean screws, with hand spattles. Well equipped and in good condition, the mill may remain in service indefinitely and will possibly be turbine-driven, like Water Eaton mill in the same ownership, but the millstones would be retained.

Richard Thornton was miller in 1798; followed by William Thornton till the 'sixties, J. Perkins, David Heath, and F. Allen, but about 1910 Mr. James Smith took possession, the business now being run from Water Eaton.

BLETCHLEY – ¾ m. S.S.W. from Fenny Stratford

[*River Ousel*]

Water Eaton Mill – 1⅜ E.S.E. of Church

Working
Maps – 1768, (1809), 1824, 1875, 1887, 1926

Bletchley (the Bleak Leys) is a parish of particular interest to historians – the living came to Dr. Browne-Willis, noted Buckinghamshire antiquarian and historian, who presented it to the Reverend William Cole, the Cambridge antiquarian and recorder of much valuable information concerning our county; secondly several early documents relating to the hiring and repair of the mill in the hamlet of Water Eaton over 500 years ago are preserved in the County Museum.

A document of 1371 records that John Hore, miller, was fined the sum of 8d. for taking illegal toll; whilst Stephen Milewarde and William Schendon were mentioned as millers taking toll unjustly and paying fines of 3d. or 6d.; and in 1384 Schendon was fined 12d., a large sum in those days, as will be seen from the repair accounts. Hiring of the mill in 1372, is recorded in the following words :(*Records of Bucks. Vol. IX) :-*

"At the Court of Etone;
To this Court comes Stephen Smith, miller and takes of the lord his two watermills of Etone for term of his life under condition that the lord shall provide timber, straw and wattles for repair, and said Stephen for the whole time shall keep up all utensils pertaining to the said mills, paying to the lord yearly thirty-four quarters of corn at the four usual terms of the year".

Covering a period of twelve months from Michaelmas, 1394, is a farm account containing the following details under the heading, *Costs of the mill:*

"To John Jakeman carpenter hired for 14 days, John Janne hired for 11 days and to William Beawings and Robert Pye, carpenters, hired at the same time for 3 days, to make one new mill wheel, with water gate and the ... of the same, as are made in woodwork each taking by the task 4d per day.

10s. 4d.

And for 500 large spikyngs bought for the above work at 6d per 100

2s. 6d.

And to John Deye hired for fourteen days and John Thomas hired for twelve days to cover, fill and strengthen sundry breakages about the said mill each taking by the task as above

8s. 8d.

And for 12 men performing their lovebenes (odd moments) filling in and strengthening flint work round the said mill and in bread bought to feed them

1½ d.

And for 3 flagons of beer bought

3d.

And for cheese bought

3d.

Total   23s. 1½ d.

The farm in question belonged to the Manor of Water Eaton which was held by the family of Greys from the 13th century until 1603; and the accounts include the following:

Toll corn grinding at the Mill.
"And for 21 quarters of corn, straked measure, received from farm of the mill, and no more, because it stood empty for 6 weeks this year.

Total   21 qrs."

Before the advent of William I, Eaton Manor (principal Manor in Bletchley) belonged to Queen Edith whose thegns also held considerable property in Bucks. (The name *Water* Eaton was not originated, according to the late Rev. F.W.Bennitt, until 1431: Eton, he said derived from Eyot, an island; although Cole said it meant "a town of water"). The Bishop of Coutance was in possession in 1086, when a mill worth 20/- was on his demesne; and Sir John Grey, later enfeoffed Herman de Eaton and his heirs of the water-mill of Eaton "with the whole suit to the mill of the tenants of the honour of Gifford", because the Bishop's land had been seized by Rufus and given to Walter Giffard in about 1092.

One water-mill was upon the Manor in 1308, two in 1324 and 1370; and Eaton Mill is mentioned in 1596. Meanwhile, in 1314 Cuttedemulne was mentioned in Little Brickhill parish, (*V.C.H. Vol. IV*) and in the 17th century the name occurred in a document which spoke of Cuttmilles and Upper Bushy, Furzin and *Wheaton* Cutmills; from which one is inclined to think Water Eaton was meant. Little Brickhill parish reaches almost within a stone's throw of Eaton Mill; and although the term Cutmills is now unknown locally a field name "Cutnalls" appears on an early map, just north of Little Brickhill village in Bow Brickhill parish, and half a mile east of the Magiovinium crossroads.

From 1572 to 1674 Water Eaton followed the descent of Giffard's manor in Whaddon but the Duke of Buckingham sold it to Thomas Willis M.D., in 1674, and before long it was in the hands of the famous antiquarian Browne Willis.

Indeed, floods were very persistent hereabouts in the 18th century; Cole records great snows and floods throughout February 1767; again in March; and "an even greater flood and great wind" in June, after 18 days heavy rain – real Bucks weather! Vast flood in October; and prodigious floods in November.

In 1825 Thomas Lake Harris was born at Water Eaton Mill and he later became celebrated in America as a Poet and Mystic, and died in 1906.

Matthew Goodman was the miller in 1798, followed by John Hitchcock and his descendants until well into the present century. Following a period of disuse, Messrs James F Smith of Great Brickhill took over in 1923, installed a turbine (a 12ft. iron breast wheel having previously been employed), cleaned out and extended the mill-head, and made other improvements. Their carter at Water Eaton – Mr. Woolhead – has a beautiful set of horse brasses, illustrated in the Rev; F.W. Bennitt's *Bletchley 100 Years Ago.*

Of renovated brick, with shallow slate roof, the mill, which the Rector said was built just after 1800, stands across the stream; and the iron wheel of that date, described as an undershot capable of grinding about a quarter of wheat or barley an hour, was enclosed within the west end of the building. The 11–15 h.p. turbine which grinds three sacks an hour, doing barley meal, coarse wheat, peas and rolling oats, etc. – no flour – is beneath a new floor in the old wheel room a pendulum governor being provided to control the aperture of the vanes. To stop the mill the governor is disengaged and the vanes opened by a hand-wheel; and there is, of course, the usual "flash" in addition to a sluice for leading water away to a by-

Water Eaton Mill

pass which is fed by a broad weir for maintaining the water level in this floodable country.

"Dreadnought" roller mills in place of millstones are driven from the turbine by shafting; and the space in the former pit-room provides extra storage. The turbine is claimed to give plenty of power; it is easy to control and maintain and only freezes up in exceptional conditions; and it drives a dynamo to light the mill; but in the drought of 1935, when water failed owing to neglect to clear the river, an engine was installed for emergency use only. At one time a second wheel – a large wooden breast-shot was outside the east end of the building, which would bring it under the heading of "two mills" in medieval parlance. The landlord unfortunately seems to have filled in the waterways instead of repairing them, and allowed a bridge in front of the mill to become derelict, hence the layout of waterways has been somewhat modified in recent times.

In the floodgate pool are a good variety of fish –

pike, perch, roach, bream, dace, gudgeon and eels; but no fly-fishing and no trout. The field south of the mill, between river and canal, is Mill Meadow; and the trackway called Mill Lane or Horse-mill Lane over the above mentioned bridge, is the probable site of a pre-Norman strategic road from the administrative centre of Buckingham to Danesborough Camp, where an arm of King Alfred's territory jutted out into the Danelaw, beyond Watling Street.

John ye miller is mentioned in 1599, and a fuller in the 17th century; the water grist mill is noted in 1705 and two watermills in 1735; and there were two millers, perhaps sharing the mill from 1747 to 1766. In 1725 the following quaint entry occurs in Bletchley Parish Registers:-

"June 6th Day. Thare Was A Great flood at Water Eaton River that was so Big that the Like Hath not Bin seen by all Mens knolidge not this fore Hundren year before. it was in 1725".

BOW BRICKHILL – 1½ m. E. from Fenny Stratford [*River Ousel*]

Caldecotte Watermill – Approx 1½ m. W.N.W. of Church) Gone
Map –1768

An unusually picturesque farmstead is the former Caldecotte Manor (occupied by Mr. W. E. Garrett, to whom I am indebted for some of the following details), a long, low, half-timbered and thatched building opposite the ancient and now disused road to Simpson. Much land around here was open common last century; also the extensive hill-top behind the parish church; so a considerable change has taken place in the local husbandry. In 1830 a millwright, Joseph Clarke was established in the village; now there are no local mills to repair. Half-a-mile west of the old Manor Farm were a moated house and numerous cottages, forming quite a little community where now neither building nor road exists, but the moat survives close by a watermill site.

In 1695 John Bishop of Caldecott in Bow Brickhill, was mentioned, and an important reference, helping to verify the site indistinctly marked on Jeffery's map but overlooked by Andrews and Dury, is found in Gibbs' *Local Occurrences*:-

"1754, 25th May – a few days ago, as a man was washing some sheep at Caldecot Mill, near Fenny Stratford, one of them drew him into the mill-pit, where he was drowned; and when taken out he had a large fleece of wool in his hands"

This sheep-dip is known to have existed a little west of the moat, marked upon some Ordnance maps; and nearby are Mill Ground and Mill Close. Foundations of the mill are also remembered by old inhabitants, although no longer visible; and another mill unauthenticated is vaguely thought to have stood probably lower downstream.

V.C.H. Vol. IV., says "colour is lent to the supposition that the small manor of Caldecott was comprised within the larger Bow Brickhill Manor at the Domesday Survey, by the fact that the Chaunceys, lords of Bow Brickhill, were also lords of Caldecott", and adds "The mill of Caldecott, probably on the site of the mill valued at 10/- on the smaller of Walter Giffard's manors in 1086, was granted with some land in 1208 by Geoffrey Chauncey to Robert de Braybrook . . . In 1307 John Grey settled lands, a mill and rent in Bow Brickhill and Caldecott on himself and his sons; and in Queen Elizabeth's time Caldecott Mill was deemed appurtenant to the Manor of Brogborough in Ridgemont (Beds), held by the same family. The miller, Humphrey Blackshaw, paid a rent of £4 13. 4."

Caldecotte is a modern spelling, the earlier name being Caldecote or Caldecot, from Ceald-cot, the cold cottages; and in 1291, when Delapré Abbey near Northampton, held the mill the locality was called South Caldecott to distinguish it from Caldecote in Newport Pagnell.

SIMPSON – 1¼ m. N. from Fenny Stratford [*River Ousel*]

Early Watermill – Approx 200 yds. S.E. of Church Gone
Maps – 1768, (1809)

It might surprise strangers to know that Sympson, or Simpson, is lately liable to extensive and sustained floods every time there is a heavy rainstorm, where it had never, since the highway was raised 3½ feet a century ago, experienced more than an hour or two's temporary flooding. Its because a new by-pass (*sic*) has been built across the river near the old mill site; it doesn't by-pass anything and it leads nowhere, but the amount of concrete must have done the contractors a lot of good! The villagers warned the "experts" as soon as work commenced that the poky culverts in the new bridge were inadequate; but they went ahead*

The watermill site is just south of the old bridge, by a ford on the main stream and a slight fall of water adjoining has always been known to old inhabitants

* Since the above was written, Simpson has been isolated in the greatest flood of the century, caused by this and other new bridges in the district, after the notably dry summer of 1939. Were the villagers right?

as "the Waterfall". They never heard of the watermill, nor is there any mill field, but the cartographers corroborate the site, which is apparently in field O.S. 120, marked The Ambush or The Butts on an early parish map.

Evidence is forthcoming in *Vol. IV* of *V.C.H.* which records that Queen Edith held a mill before the Invasion; the Bishop of Coutances held it, at a value of 10/- with the Manor in 1086; the Cauz family in the 13th century after forfeiture of the Bishop's lands, and the Grey's later; ownership thus being the same as at Water Eaton, assuming the name of Cauz is synonymous with de Caux. Two watermills under one roof, with the Mill House, Millholmesmeadows, fisheries and ferries, were held by the Hatch family in the 17th century, and are probably identical with the watermill attached to the manor in the 18th and 19th centuries.

John Atwood, miller of Staple Hall in Simpson parish, a century ago, erected this building himself in 1840 – a large warehouse for a corn merchant's and woolstapler's business (hence the name) on the Watling Street; but he had no mill, nor is any miller named in the 1791 and 1823 directories.

LITTLE WOOLSTONE – 2¾ m. S. from Newport Pagnell

[*River Ousel*]

The New Mill [South Mill, ed.] – 150 yds, N.E. of Church

Standing idle
Map –1926

The New Mill

The little pink brick mill standing a few yards nearer the church than the older one next to be described is said never to have done a stroke of work; and this is borne out by the spur gears, which disclose only the slightest frictional contact as though the mill had just been turned over for test purposes.

Believed to have been erected for Squire Smith, by Messrs. Gilbert of Leighton 60 or 70 years ago, the new structure failed to get under way owing to some snag in design or construction and apparently was never adjusted to make it serviceable.

Driven by a little loopway striking off from the main stream at right angles, the mill is not very happily situated; the turn in the water seems too sudden to allow of much power being obtained, and the water-wheel is small and of not very convincing design. With a diameter of 7ft. 6ins. over the framework and a tread of 4ft. it carries 24 straight floats 15ins. in depth, with little provision for preventing the water shooting directly into the middle of the wheel, since it is a low breast-shot with no sole plate

at all, and no shrouds. Bolted together in two pieces and entirely iron built, it possesses three rings of eight arms, making it unnecessarily heavy and is mounted upon 5ins. journals, outside the mill on the south side. The mill-tail passes into a tunnel beneath the cartway rejoining the stream below the other mill.

As seen from my photograph, the pit wheel is unenclosed in the mill; it is 7ft. 9ins. diameter, in 2 pieces with cogs 7ins. broad; a one-piece wallower or counter bevel is secured to a counter shaft supported in a standard, the wallower, like the pit-wheel being unsupported by a terminal bearing. A drum on the shaft was meant to drive a sack-bollard mounted in posts on the upper floor but whilst the bollard appears to have been used, it was probably hand-operated for grain storage only. The six-armed spur engaged a stone-nut sliding between upright timbers; but the bridge-tree, and in fact every bit of machinery (except spur and pit wheel cogs) are of iron; also the "flash" control wheel within the mill; and an old set of sack scales. Only one pair of stones was installed; and the

The New Mill

64

stone-floor is timber-walled and tarred, with a shallow slate roof. (In the recent war, I am told, the iron-work from both Woolstone mills has been removed).

The mill, indicated only on recent maps, is approached by a little grassy track from the *Barge Inn*, passing by a fine old brick dovecot, then the Church, then the ancient thatched miller's cottage – a real gem of old-time architecture.

Probably the last corn watermill to be erected upon a new site in Bucks, it is about the smallest and simplest in the county. Its first owner, Squire Smith, who deserves a place in any book of Bucks Worthies, came of a family who occupied the beautiful house with the clustered chimneys near the river since 1637. Eccentric in dress, he always sported a plaid shawl instead of an overcoat; he achieved fame by inventing and patenting a steam ploughing system worked by one engine (not two as generally seen today) and known as the Woolstone System, the machinery being built by Hayes of Watling Street Works, Stony Stratford, and copied by other firms. Smith said he reaped a fine crop of old coins by deep cultivation with his machine; but J.K. Fowler said he grew more weeds than with horse ploughing! The great Trade Unionist, Joseph Arch visited the district and got the Squire's men into his union; and Mr. Smith became alarmed, curtailed agricultural activities; but entered into litigation with the L&NWR over their interference with his water rights, having traced the trouble to a spot nr Bletchley […] which has ever since been known as "New Found Out".

The Old Mill [North Mill, ed.] – 200 yds N.E. of church

Standing disused
Maps 1768, (1809), 1824, 1870, 1876, 1887, 1926

The Old Mill

James Sheahan recording this ancient watermill and the 17th century dwelling house in 1862, considered there were faint traces of a moat around the mill, also indications of fish ponds, tending to show that the little parish had been of some importance in olden times.

"A mill worth 10/- was held by Walter Giffard with his manor in 1086" said *V.C.H. Vol IV* and remained among the appurtenances, being settled by Thomas de Coudray upon his daughter in 1316, and leased in 1564 by Sir William Paulet and his wife to Richard Banes of Woolstone".

John Perry, a petty constable, was the miller in 1692; John Rudkins 1798; and William Warr occupied the mill on a tenancy expiring 1843, when the land and mill were advertised; "machinery for working 2 pairs, flour and smut machines, sack tackle and every requisite for grinding flour, ample storage, well divided for wheat, flour and meal". Only one mill described, although the heading said "Water Corn Mills". James Perkins took the mill; then came E. Hollis, who went to Orchard Mill; John Carr from Mursley Windmill and later at Haversham Mill; and Goodman who is thought to have gone to the Co-op. steam mill at Bradwell. He was followed by Mr. Ready who certainly took the Co-op. mill and may also have had Harris's power-mill by the canal in Fenny Stratford, which Alf Harris had in conjunction with a watermill (possibly Woolstone) about 1840. William Hands, miller at Fenny in 1877, probably had the power mill too. William Casey took Woolstone Mill for some years at the turn of the century; and Ralph Underwood, the last miller, left about 1920 when Messrs. Coales

The Old Mill

the power millers of Newport are said to have bought it in.

Of similar general appearance to the new mill but a little larger, the old building stands on the west bank of the stream with quite a good all-iron breast wheel outside; whilst the by-pass runs a little father round. The wheel, by B Anstee of Kempston, had three sets of six arms each bolted into a large boss, with thirty L shaped buckets, a little curved at the lip, and well ventilated and was upon 8ins. journals – an unusually generous dimension for Bucks. Diameter over the felloes was 11ft. and width 7ft. 6ins.; and a large twin "flash" with the customary rack and pinion was provided.

An eight armed 2 piece pit-wheel 8ft. 6ins. diameter with 128 seven-inch cogs, secured by wood wedges to a 2ft. square bosses which in turn was keyed to the hollow axle shaft, drove three pairs of stones by a single unit 8 spoke spur of 112 cogs, engaging with morticed iron nuts, the jacks controlling which were of exceptional length (especially the middle one which resembled a stirrup nearly reaching to the ground). Bridges guided the long rods of these rings; and from one end of the bridge the respective bridge-tree was suspended, whilst a return rod passed up through the other end, where it was geared to a short horizontal shaft and tentering screw. A 48 cog 2–piece wallower and upright shaft were provided both of iron, like all the foregoing machinery; and on the upper floor a morticed gear crown wheel drove layshafts beneath the ceiling, belt-coupled to one another, with wooden and iron drums. Remains of a dresser and shaker were in the mill, and on the ground floor was a ratchet controlled "flash" wheel.

The Old Mill

WILLEN – 1½ m. S. from Newport Pagnell

[River Ousel]

Lower Mill – Approx 3f. S.E. of Church

Gone
Maps – 1768, 1793, (1809), 1870

Another paper-mill upon the Ouzel is believed to have been this almost forgotten structure at Willen or Willien; although another suggestion made to me was that it was a leather or tan mill. Within living memory a beam believed to be the remains of a sluice existed, upon which children could scramble across the stream at the upper end of the loop-way south of the church; and the mill is thought to have been upon the main stream between O.S. 74 and 79, with the by-pass detouring round the adjoining field. Some brickwork exists about midway from sluice to road, but it is uncertain whether this is part of the mill foundations.

The present railed and duck-boarded road to Milton Keynes was non-existent in olden days; and the old lane may still be discerned bearing away into the bushes and shrubbery to the north, following the stream bed for 100 yards to emerge beyond the more recent bridges. This was a "water road" similar to that at Twyford; and an old man told me it was negotiable in his time and he once drove a cart containing some water tanks into it and proceeded to fill them from the stream. When he had finished, the cart was so firmly stuck in the mud, he had to empty all the tanks before the horse could pull him out!

Willen is not listed in Domesday but can be identified with the four hides and one virgate assessed under Caldecote in Newport Pagnell parish; and the more important part, assessed at two hides, including the Domesday mill, the Crown having overlordship rights. One mill was held with the manor in 1499 and two watermills are mentioned in 1641, after which no record seems to be available.

NEWPORT PAGNELL

[River Ousel]

Caldecote Mill – 7 f. S.S.E. of church

Sluices remain
1695, 1768, (1809), 1834, (1847),
1870, 1926(name only)

In its closing days, Caldecote Mill was described by Sheahan as a "very ancient mill"; although Mr. William Anstee had found it more serviceable than his windmill at North Crawley, which he abandoned about the time of Sheahan's writing, in the early 'sixties. The Reverend William Cole's favourite man, "my Tom" enjoyed many a happy hour's fishing by the mill a century previously. The sluices of Caldecote Mill remain; and the little bridge crossing the stream, which has been called Caldecote Mill Bridge for quite four centuries, also exists, the mill site being at the north corner of Mill Dam Meadow (O.S. no. 48) whilst the plot north of the bridge is Mill Leys.

Mentioned in Domesday Survey when William, Son of Ansculf apparently held it for 8/-, the mill became an important possession of Tickford Priory. William's daughter married Sir Fulk Pagenell or Paynell who founded the priory and gave it to the Church of Newport with other property, including the Mill at Caldecote and the meadow belonging to the mill, the latter items being appurtenant to Caldecote Priory. *[sic]*

In 1187 a Confirmatory Charter included the mill, as did an inventory of 1293, when Caldecote Mill was valued at 66/8d; another Charter next century, after the Priory had been burnt, included the mill although the extent of the Priory possessions in 1324 recorded only "a broken watermill which is worth nothing until it be repaired; then it will be worth 8/4d per annum and they say it can be repaired for 40/-".

Several times in the 14th century the miller of the Priory of Tykeford is mentioned – possibly the Caldecott miller, failing proof of a Tickford mill – John atte Ok of Haversham in 1349; and again when the miller "hath gone away this year by reason of the dryness of the summer". (Tickford Field enclosed 1806–8, east of the London Road, included some 13 acres called Mill Field, but owing to 'jerry building and so forth', no 13 acre field remains there).

Another inquisition, in 1526, showed "one water-mill in Caldecote at £6. 3. 4", which is a little odd, because at the Dissolution the mill was" greatly in decay". Still more curious, in 1534 the rental of Cardinal (King's) College, Oxford included "Firmer

68

molendini Caldecote £6. 13. 4." Queen Elizabeth granted the "Manor or late Priory of Tickford and the Manor of Caldecote with "the two mills called Calcott Mills" to Dr Henry Atkins, for £1534. 6. 0. in A.D. 1600 and in 1630 "the mill at Caldecot; and the two grain mills and Rectory of Newport Pagnell" were mentioned. Possibly the reference to *grain* mills was to indicate that only these, and not the fulling mill of Newport were included. In 1707 William Backwell, banker who held the rest of the Manor, required from the trustees of Sir Richard Adkins, the mill and land in Caldecote; and he left the property to William Harwood, who assumed the name of Backwell, and remained till 1815. His tenant in 1798 was John Hooton, who was the miller for 40 years; in 1839 the "Valuable freehold water-corn mills of Caldecott" driving 3 pairs and other necessary

machinery, with horse and stables, etc. were for sale.

Edward White took the mills followed very shortly by William Anstee, who had them for some time before leaving Crawley Windmill. He is believed to have rented both from Mr. Eve of Newport Mill, but eventually went to Cranfield, Beds. and built (or rebuilt) the present towermill and the adjoining steam mill, afterwards removing to a Lincolnshire water-mill. Finally Caldecott Mill was completely burnt some time before the first serious fire at Newport Mills in 1880; but the "Old Mill House" – really a modern enlargement – still exists in well vegetated grounds alongside the gated road from Tickford End to Willen.

Caldecote Mill is sometimes referred to locally as Newport Mill, but the latter name properly belonged to Rowlatt's Mill (Mr. Eve's) as already indicated.

"Calcott Fulling Mill" – Site doubtful   Gone

At Newport Pagnell, states *V.C.H. Vol. IV*, a fulling mill was converted to grist before 1623, a curious assertion since weaving was still a trade of the town, and more especially as both Newport and Caldecote fulling mills are reported in existence just about that date. A grant in 1627 mentions "all the water called Lovens which extends itself from the Bridge of Calcott Mill into the common water which leads to the Mill called a Fulling Mill . . ."

Joseph Staines records in his *History of Newport Pagnell, 1842*, that the Hon. Arthur Annesley of Newport granted to James Annesley, a tanner, residing in Marsh End (Newport), a lease of the fulling mill holme, now called Annesley Holme; and he adds that the mill was on the stream of the Lovatt "and there are still some remains of it in existence". (1842). Probably the mill stood near The Green, on the Bletchley road, where there is a by-pass loop; indeed since this paragraph was written I have learned that a plot now occupied by the gasworks between road and stream at this point was Mill Close.

The grant preceded another lease made in 1672 demising to Matthew Annesley, tanner, all that Fulling Mill Holme which he possessed since 1642.

Apparently the mill remained the property of the Annesleys until a political drive was made against them in the 18th century, as a result of which the romantic career of James Annesley, on whom Scott's Character, Guy Mannering, is said to be based, was interrupted by a framed-up trial against him at the Old Bailey for killing a man although it was quite obvious that this was due to the purely accidental discharge of a gun. Later when one Lord Anglesey had a clear right to the property, the vendetta continued, a protracted dispute being engineered against him, so that he was deprived of his right to the title of Baron Annesley of Newport by the House of Lords in 1770 and had to sell his estate to a man called Hardy. Probably this was about the time the mill disappeared.

The Lovat or Ouzel joins the Ouse just below Tickford Bridge, in the town; and of the Ouse at this point is written:-

"Shee with the lesser Ouse at Newport doth twin
Which from proud Chiltern neere, comes eas'ly ambling in".

Michael Drayton (1622)

PITSTONE – 2½ m. N.N.E. from Tring

Whistle Brook

Pitstone Watermill – ¾ m. N. of Church

Used as house
Maps 1768, (1809), 1825, 1832, 1875

Two mills of some kind are mentioned at "Pichelestorn" in 1231, when Ralph de Boneville quitclaimed them to William, son of Herbert, in exchange for other land, but even if water-driven they were probably beneath the same roof. In 1306 Henry Spigurnal received pardon for acquiring without licence a watermill in Pitstone from John de la Bere, yeoman of Master Ralph of Ivinghoe, the latter having held it of the King for 20/-. Thomas Spigurnel succeeded his father; and in 1346 the mill was included in the Neyrnut's property. Anne Kirkham died seised of the site of a watermill called Ivinghoe Mill in 1427, having held it as heir of Sir Henry Spugurnel Kt: but whether this was in Ivinghoe parish or on the Pitstone site, which is contiguous to Ivinghoe village is not indicated. In 1520 William Cowper had custody of the Pitstone mill for a twenty-year period.

No later history seems to be recorded; but in a little cul-de-sac against the *Bell Inn*, the pink walled, slate-roofed Pitstone mill will be found today. Square and double-fronted, it is not at all prepossessing and has a general air of newness; but interiorly it is of considerable age with one or two latticed windows at the back, and low ceilings. A fine 15ft. iron overshot wheel, 5ft. wide with broad buckets and small mouths, is within the east end, driving the standard arrangements of spur gearing for three pairs, all machinery being of iron except pit and spur wheel cogs, and bridge-trees.

Stone nuts, now missing, were engaged by screw rings, and one pair of governors are in the pit-room over the great spur, probably for steam control, the spur being rather low, owing to the water wheel being slung low down with a smallish pit wheel. A good mill-head is secured with concrete and brick retaining walls; and a sluice in the right bank discharges *via* a tunnel beneath mill and road. Possibly the whole building was reconstructed by Messrs. Gilbert at the same period as some of the Risborough mills to be described. Westwards are extensive detached storage rooms, etc; and eastwards the neat Mill House looks upon a walled garden which Mr. Beesley said he enclosed "to keep the devils out".

James Burt had this and the windmill in 1798; and in 1842 Pitstone Water Corn Mills were for sale, driving 2 pairs by a 12ft. iron wheel and "other improved iron Machinery", together with capital modern dwelling house and Land and the Windmill. Probably Arthur Meacher, a miller of Ivinghoe in the current directory had worked them. Francis Beesley was the miller for many years, until succeeded by his son Francis, who employed the late Thomas Robinson before that gentleman – then a young lad – went to Hawridge Windmill; and in those days an old beam engine was used in the annex adjoining the wheel house. The present tenant, Mr. Horne, who kindly showed me over the mill, worked for 4d. a day as a boy, for Beesley, who died about 1890; and Mrs. Beesley retained the mill until a miller named Saunders took over, followed by Mark Sharratt. Finally James Wright (steam and water) carried on until the Great War when Mr. Jellis, whose brother has Ivinghoe Mill, moved in without using the mill, which even now could be made workable.

The Beasleys for a time also had Pitstone Green Windmill; and it may be mentioned Bryant (1824) marks Pightlesthorn Watermill – the old name of the village.

IVINGHOE – 3½ N.N.E. from Tring

[*Whistle Brook*]

Ivinghoe Mill – (3 f. N.W. of Church

Working
Maps – 1824, 1832, (1847)

Whistle Brook rises near Pitstone Green, to flow northwards by Pitstone Mill, passing under the Leighton road at Ford End, where in olden days there was clearly a ford; and so to join the Ouzel just above Slaptonbury Mill.

In an orchard west of the road is Ivinghoe or Ford End Mill – a small Mansard-roofed structure with yellow brick lower floor, and heavily tarred wooden upper walls and galvanised roofing; it is fed by a good built-up mill-pond of considerable length. The all-iron

Ivinghoe Mill

overshot wheel has six arms of flat section rivetted to the shrouds, with a total of only eighteen buckets; and the sole plates form a complete ring without ventilation. Housed in a brick lean-to at the north end of the mill, it replaced a wooden wheel within the last 50 years, and is fed by a wooden pentrough.

Arrangement of machinery is orthodox, with eight-armed pit wheel, wooden upright shaft, and two stone nuts on screw jacks all enclosed; the wheelwork being all iron, except pit-wheel, great spur and crown wheel cogs. Most unusual is the by-pass lay-out, for the water is discharged over a weir on the right bank into a funnel-like cavity, brick lined, descending into a tunnel to pass beneath the mill; and a sluice with single rack and pinion is alongside the weir.

Henry Heley was the miller in 1791, and William Heley 1798; William Tompkins had the mill for 50 years from 1842 or earlier, and he was great uncle of John Tompkins, who worked for him for 30 years from boyhood onwards and whose father, John, had the Old Pitstone Windmill near the new cement works, in the 'fifties. Moses Tompkins William's son followed him and, early this century, Mr. Charles Jellis took the mill, which goes with the adjoining farm; and it is even now in daily use, water driven only.

Curiously enough neither this nor Pitstone Mill usually appear on the maps; they are the only mills on the Whistle Brook; which Sheahan said was a corruption of Muscle Brook.

IVINGHOE

Old Mill – 1¾ m. N.N.E. of Church

Wash Brook or *Aston Brook*

Gone
Maps –1768, 1800, (1809)

Jeffreys, 1768, and Andrews & Dury, have this early site to themselves, except for a large parish map 345/29 at the Bucks Museum, apparently dating from about 1800, which marks "Old Mill" and a mill-pond; authenticity is also suggested by the fact that a resident recalls that when the Wash Brook was in full flow in days gone by, there were indications of a ford adjoining the supposed site; whilst a track running by the south wall of Edlesborough churchyard continues directly towards the mill site for a quarter of a mile or more, afterwards almost petering out. A little disused bridge stands where track meets brook, and the mill

is marked 1½ furlongs north-west, but no visible indication of a mill can be found, nor is there a by-pass; but on so small a stream, with little risk of flooding, the wheel might be mounted alongside a sluice, with a party wall in the river bed.

The Wash Brook, so named because it served as the local sheep wash, (although a field near the site is called Aston Brook Field), rises in the Comb, or Coombe Bottom – the great natural cul-de-sac which is said to have been a Roman Cow-pen – below Gallows Hill on the Icknield Way, and joins the Whistle Brook just above Slapton Lane.

WING – 3 m. S. W. from Linslade

Wing Mill – 5f. S.S.W. of Church

Wing Brook

Gone
Maps 1824, 1832, 1834, 1875
Name only on 1870, 1887, 1914, 1926

A long time back Wing Mill or Wingmill, stood by the north side of the Aylesbury turnpike on the west loop of the stream, where there are some red brick cottages at the bottom of a longish dip in the road. A dovehouse, watermill, windmill and horsemill were on Wing Manor, which was in the King's hands, in 1484 (first year of Richard III). Four years later an Act of Parliament confirmed the Manor to William Berkeley, Earl of Nottingham, by whose will it passed to the Earl of Derby in 1492; the Manor (with mills presumably) having belonged to various other Earls in the Past.

Little seems to be recorded or known about Wing Mill; one or two old people claim to have seen it but cannot describe it, others say it has not existed for a century. Mr. Kirby who worked Mursley Windmill for a time, believed it was a small mill, and some stones were transferred to Mursley from it when

dismantled – this was some time before he worked the windmill but probably not before 1850.

Henry Howes had the watermill and the windmill (to be taken down) in 1798; Wm. Heley was a malt-ster at Wing in 1831; and for the next 30 years Richard Harris had Wing Mill but this might apply to the steam mill in the village, which is also styled Wing Mill, and which had a beam engine at one time. An old inhabitant believed a man named Manning occupied the farm on which the watermill stood, when it was demolished. Bryant named it Way Mill, probably in error; and Heley's descendants incidentally occupied the steam mill.

Wing Brook, rising near the most northerly corner of the parish, flows south and then eastwards by Ledburn to discharge *into the Grand Union Canal* by Grove Lock, although obviously it originally joined the Ouzel.

LINSLADE – ½ m. W. from Leighton Buzzard

Southcott Mill – 1½ m. S.S.W. of church

Southcott Mill Pond

Working
Maps – 1887, 1926

The Manor of Linslade in 1086 included a mill worth 20/- which, if it existed a century previously (A.D. 975) will have been held by Queen Aelfgyfu; and later by Alwin, a man of Queen Edith (wife of Edward the Confessor). Southcott, first mentioned in 1241, descended with Linslade, being held by Woburn Abbey from 1291 until the Dissolution; and in 1553 Edward VI granted to George Wright the grange of Linslade and two watermills in this parish and that of Leighton Buzzard, Beds.

G. Richardson of Linslade (possibly a bailiff) advertised in 1858 for a young man to manage a watermill with two pairs of stones; and previously – 1845 – a most interesting offer was made of a 4 h.p. *high pressure steam engine* at Linslade which had

driven all the usual gear connected with one pair of French stones, dressing cylinder with case, sack tackle, with shafting, bins, etc. William Poole, near the *Bedford Arms*, Chelsea New Town advertised it; "Chelsea" being the present Linslade village, as distinct from the old village around the disused Parish Church (from which my location is given).

The Rothschilds acquired Southcote or Southcott – the south cottages – upon establishing themselves in Bucks, their residence being Ascott Park in the adjoining parish of Wing. They always used for private purposes this very interesting mill, which is in the west end of a huge old tarred wooden barn upon an ancient buttressed brick-walled ground floor, with roof of slate; it is approached by a short "blind" lane

Linslade Mill

facing the *Hare Inn*, the mill being the last old building on the right, whilst the mill pond lies up in the meadow west of the mill and is fed from springs in the fields.

A very long galvanised trough mounted on tall wooden posts, serves as an aqueduct to the wheel, receiving its supply *via* a stop valve in a brick tank against the pond, from which the field falls away so that the pentrough at the mill is 25ft. above ground. An exceptional all-iron overshot wheel 23 or 24ft. in diameter by 2ft. 6ins. is designed with large centres, to each of which are secured twelve T-section arms; the shrouds are in twelve segments and the 72 unventilated buckets have inlets of about 3ins. depth. The axle, supported by the outer wall and by a brick retaining wall inside, is at first floor level, with the wheel reaching up into the roof; and it carries a small spur of 56 teeth. This drives a pinion iron to iron, upon a countershaft at floor level, and on this shaft is a morticed gear turning a layshaft under the floor, which drives belts for the chaff cutter on upper floor, and the countershaft beneath a hurst-frame on the ground floor. Bevel gears turn the millstone upon the hurst; and the bridge-tree and all other mechanical equipment is, of iron.

Other belts operate an oat crusher on ground floor and two screw conveyors at the top corner of the mill, where they meet, the first leading up from the oat crusher and the other travelling along the roof to a storage cupboard near the waterwheel. The crusher is gravity fed from a large bin on the upper floor, which is supplied *via* a sack-loft facing over the roadway; near the water-wheel are a spout delivering meal down from the store, and a countershaft formerly conveying power by belts from a portable engine outside to the millwork within. The upper floor is open to the roof; and the whole mill is very clean and tidy, and is in charge of the stud-groom and stable hands, one being the general barn for the hunting stables. Most of the equipment is fairly new; and Mr. Gilbert, whose people did the repairs, said at least one new water-wheel had been installed in his time.

Not always is sufficient water available to start the mill, but conditions permitting, it is in regular use for grist. The mill-tail formerly emerged through a little arch, visible but bricked up, in the lower wall of the mill, and ran down the side of the lane; but it now descends into a tunnel beneath the lane to emerge inside the garden wall of a house called "The Cottage", south of *The Hare*, thence under the railway goods yard, finally discharging into the grand union 200 yds. north of the branch railway, total length of stream being a bare mile.

Sheahan states in his *History and Topography*: "There is an old mill at Ascott, said to have been built by the Dormers," and Gibbs has a similar statement probably copied from Sheahan; but I can find no authentication for a mill at Ascott, and it is almost certain he meant the mill belonging to the Ascott estate but situate at Southcott.

MILTON KEYNES – 3¼ m. S.S.E. from Newport Pagnell — *Salford Brook* or *Crawley Brook*

Medieval Watermill (Fox Milne) – Site unknown   Gone

For many generations the only mill on Salford Brook has been Salford Mill, just over the Beds border, but probably Milton Keynes Mill of bygone days was upon this same brook.

Of this mill *V.C.H. Vol. IV.* says:- "A mill was held with the Manor in 1086; and one-third of a watermill was claimed in 1313 by Philip Aylesbury in right of his wife Margaret. In 1349 this was held by grant of the Earl of Oxford; it was called Foxmilne in 1418, when a fishery in the stream and pond was also included in the appurtenances of the Manor. This was the chief manor, which is now the only one, originally called Middleton Keynes Manor". The Domesday value differed from all others in Bucks being 6/8d.

Old inhabitants are sure there is no Mill Field or other indication as to the location of the medieval mill; no loopways exist on the stream hereabouts, but it has always enjoyed a decent flow of water, and Salford Mill will work all day in winter and half a day in summer, as a general rule. The big meadow on the west side of the parish, adjoining the Woolstone Mills and known as Mill Close, is doubtless so named after the latter mills.

Salford Brook rises in Bedfordshire at Husbourne Crawley, hence the alternative name of Crawley Brook* and forms the eastern parish boundary of

---

* Crawley Brook is named on the original "O.S." as Salford; and there is an old saw (associated by some authors with North Crawley) "as crooked as Crawley Brook".

Milton, joining the Lovat below Willen Mill site. It is just possible Milton Mill was upon the Lovat, near Woughton-on-the-Green, but a mill on so good a stream would be unlikely to disappear in early times.

BROUGHTON – 2½ m. S.S.E. from Newport Pagnell

??

Early Watermill – Site unknown

Gone

A mill was held with the principal manor at the Domesday Survey; and there was a watermill in 1623, but the overlordship of the manor at that date happens to be unknown. Salford Brook forms the Broughton parish boundary down to a spot near Broughton Bridge; but there is also a little tributary from Broughtonlodge Farm, which might have driven a small mill. Here again, as at Milton, nothing seems to be known of a mill.

CHICHELEY – 2¼ m. N.E. from Newport Pagnell

Chicheley Brook

Early Watermill – Site unknown

Gone

V.C.H. Vol. IV, states that a watermill is mentioned on Thickthorn's Manor belonging to Tickford Priory in the 16th century, but no other information concerning this has come to light. The late Mr. Wooding of North Crawley, and other inhabitants, agreed that there is now no mill field, nor any tradition about a watermill: and it seems probable this was a small mill of comparatively temporary nature. The Chicheley Brook which forms the southern parish boundary for several miles, seems to be known as Swansriver at one point, and eventually joins the River Ouse between Newport and Sherington sites.

STOKE GOLDINGTON – 4m. N.W. from Newport Pagnell

Goldington Stream

Medieval Mill – Site unknown

Gone

"In 1235, on the death of Robert Saucey, Robert son of Hugh surrendered all claims to the manor, park and mill of Eakley to his heirs – four nephews and two sisters; but no reference to the mill or the park has been found after 1279, by which time Sir John Wolf was in possession." (*V.C.H.* Vol IV). Another account says that in 1236 the manor of Ickele (Yckeleye or Hikelega) the park and mill of the vill, are mentioned in an action in which Peter de Goldinton was concerned.

No evidence seems to exist that this was a water-mill; and in view of the solitary reference and the fact that no mill is recorded here at Domesday, there is quite a possibility of its being a horse-mill. A small stream rises in the hamlet of Eakley however, and forms the eastern parish boundary until it joins the Ouse just above Ravenstone Mill.

On this somewhat unsatisfactory note, we come to the end of our watermills survey on the Ouse and its tributaries; and we turn to south Bucks with its wide assortment of corn and paper mills upon the Thames watershed.

Chapter 3
Buckinghamshire Watermills on the Thames

"The art of printing has changed the mind of man and the face
of society . . . Printing in fact generated a sixth sense, and
raised man and society above half, in the scale of intellect . . .
It was a new power conferred on human nature, to check the
insolence of kingcraft and priestcraft. Popes took alarm and
printed lists of forbidden works . . . but what has been done
has filled every head with more knowledge than was possessed
by whole colleges of learning 4 or 500 years ago.

Sir Richard Phillips
in *Million of Facts.* 1841

HAMBLEDEN – 4 m. W. from Marlow

River Thames

Hambleden Mill – 1m. S. of Church

Working
Maps 1768, 1824, 1870, 1875, 1887, 1914

It is appropriate that Hambleden Mill happens to be the first to come under notice in this chapter sharing the honours as it does with Olney Mill on the Ouse for pride of place amongst Buckinghamshire watermills.

In 1086 the rent of Hambleden Mill was worth £1 yearly; and it was granted before 1236 to Keynsham Abbey, Somerset; and the Abbot's successor in 1396 claimed the rent worth £1.6.8 from Sir Richard Scrope. In 1338 says *V.C.H. Vol. III*, two watermills were named, and again in the 17th and 18th centuries; and part of the present mill is said to date from the 17th century. Probably both mills were beneath one

roof, and certainly only one building appears to have existed in 1789, when the *Topographer* stated that "there is one mill in the parish, on the Thames and it belongs to Sir Kenrick Clayton". Meanwhile a laughable incident occurred in 1695, when justices were appointed to visit Hambleden and Marlow Locks and mark the level of water below which the mills were not to be worked. Half the justices went to each lock, owing to a misunderstanding; those at Hambleden knocked spikes into the weir, and whilst waiting 7 hours for the Marlow party, disagreed about the level and knocked each other's spikes out again, finally dispersing with frayed tempers!

Richard Fisher was the miller in 1798; Jethro

Hambleden Mill

Lailey occupied Hambleden Mill in 1843; followed by John Henry House, then Messrs. Barnetts acquired the business for many years as Mrs. Augusta Barnett; Messrs. Barnett & Smith and later as C. Barnett & Sons; but they now have been superseded by Messrs. James Donaldson & Sons (Oxon) Ltd, with a resident foreman. Smith and his father probably were associated with Barnett many years before the partnership, for the marriage is recorded at Medmenham in Jun 1869, of Stephen Smith (25) miller, of Hambleden, son of Stephen, miller, and Mary Hobbs.

Remarkable in these days is the fact that this white boarded three storey mill was until 1939 worked solely by a single waterwheel, notwithstanding that it does a big business and is almost entirely a roller-mill.

Against the roadway is the attractive tile-roofed Mill House and beyond this, on the loopway of the river, is the fine wooden mill upon a brickwork foundation. The great undershot wheel some 22ft. diameter by 6ft. tread was of iron except for the two sets of eight radiating wooden spokes placed with their greatest thickness parallel with the axle (the section being in the proportion of about four to one) and the radial floats were very massive and of the most unusual depth of nearly 4ft. This enabled a strong head of water to enter almost breast high without surging into the middle of the open wheel, which was housed in a tarred lean-to with galvanised roof, and was claimed to develop no less than 70 to 75 h.p. Owing to its excellent situation upon the Thames the wheel was never unable to run except in time of heavy flood; and there is an extensive and elaborate series of sluices mounted over an immense 250 yds long weir upstream (where the river curves away) giving maximum control of the plentiful water supply. In the "bad old days" very severe floods were occasionally experienced, the worst – in 1894 – being recorded upon an enamelled plate on the wall only a couple of inches below the mill floor, and bearing the legend "Flood Mark November 1894".

Beyond repair of the floats the big wheel required no attention for many years and the curiously designed spokes proved entirely satisfactory. The usual inclined "flash" was worked from within the mill, where a morticed pit gear wheel of about 15ft. is accommodated in an open pit (no wheel room) on the edge of which are the large socket and beam for a former upright shaft. Now the mill is in "counter-gear" with all-iron shafting; belts drive the machines and convey the power from floor to floor; and from a countershaft, an iron upright shaft drives direct a pair of little-used barley stones enclosed in a modern circular iron case, on the first floor.

Five or six pairs of rollers grind English wheat brought, largely by road, for a maker of quality biscuits – an industry that occupies several Thames watermills – whilst some water borne foreign wheat is unloaded via the tall sack loft on the waterside. Not only is this a well-placed building for river transport, but it is considered the best mill on the Thames* and is provided with excellent storage in the white-boarded west wing which stands on stone slab piers with small brick piers between, and has a massive brickwork and concrete foundation floor at ground level. Something like a thousand tons of grain are generally stored in this fine slate-roofed building which in common with the mill is always cool to work in; and the mill windows can be entirely removed from their sashes in summer time, allowing a nice breeze to float in from across the beautiful expanse of water that stretches away pleasantly along the broad wooded valley.

In the event of trouble with the mill wheel, I was informed water turbines would be installed – the mill being favourably situated for this purpose – the probable cost being some £2000; and since my visit this plan has been carried out.

The age of the present mill is doubtful, but the appearance of the interior seems to corroborate the statement in *Victoria County* as to a part of the mill being of 17th century vintage.

Tradition says that Queen Maud (wife of Stephen) marched upon Hambleden Mill from a stronghold at Warborough in 1147 "in the course of her affray with Stephen's enemy Matilda, who had confined him in a dungeon at Bristol Castle." One likes to think that these stories of remote times are true and to picture the medieval scene in ones mind; and in substantiation, we can at least record that at Domesday the mill belonged to Matilda, daughter of King Malcolm and Queen Margaret of Scotland, who married Henry I after his accession in 1100. Henry intended his daughter Matilda to follow him to the throne, owing to his son being drowned, but Stephen, grandson of William I was pushed into the Chair, although not a direct descendant since he was the son of William I's daughter. Now it seems that the mill must have come into the hands of Henry's daughter, the direct lineal descendant, and thus the mill became an object of attack in the conflict.

---

* Mapledurham (Oxon) is a good mill, but is or was liable to flooding.

MEDMENHAM – 3 m. W.S.W. from Marlow

River Thames

The Manor Mill (Frog Mill?) – 5 f. S.E. of Church

Gone
No map reference

Frogmill Farm is upon the Berkshire bank, but possibly the name is derived as the Reverend A. H. Plaisted claims, from the Manor Mill which stood immediately opposite, on the Buckinghamshire side, although in a fanciful map in his *English Architecture in a Country Village*. 1927, the Parson appears to have Frogg Mill or Frogmill in Berkshire.

An Inquisition in Henry III's reign showed the Manor Mill to be in ruins and not worth more than 2 shillings. Speaking of the weir at the mill site, Mr.

Plaisted mentions that the Saxon *wera* was a screen of stakes and bundles set across stream to catch fish, but shipping and milling jointly established the demand for the modern weir. Of the mill itself, he says, very little is known; there were no Domesday mills at Medmenham and Frogg Mill was not apparently restored after the above mentioned Inquisition.

Millgrove Wood and Millpond Hill were mentioned in 1787, but these may have been near the village mill on a tributary.

MARLOW

[*River Thames*]

Marlow Mills Nos. 274, 276 and 277 – ¼ m. S.E. of Church)

Standing disused
Maps – 1768, (1809), 1824, (1847), 1875, 1887, 1926

To preserve the continuity of a long extract from *V.C.H. Vol. II*. it will be convenient to take an early reference to Harleyford Mill, together with the Marlow Mills with which it was from time to time connected as regards ownership. It says;

"The most important item of the (Southwark) Hospital's estate in Great Marlow consisted of three mills called Gosenham Mills, one of which, however, is sometimes spoken of as Harleyford Mill. This was probably situated further west, near the present Harleyford Mill, while the other two would lie towards the east where there are now two mills, adjoining which on the east is meadow land called Gosmer, probably the modern form of Gosenham. Two of these were bestowed in the middle of the 13th century by Geoffrey de Marlow, clerk, in return for several bushels of grain.

Geoffrey's ancestor, Matthew de Marlow, had received them at the beginning of the century from the Earl of Gloucester. Fresh arrangements concerning payment of grain were made in 1269 and 1277 at which latter date Geoffrey, son of John de Marlow took 12 quarters of the best corn yearly. John obtained in addition the remission of toll for grinding his corn and right of fishing near the land, for which 6 silver marks and 1d. were paid. The sum was still owing in 1298 when John's widow

Alice was ordered to pay 40/- a year until the debt was paid.

The third mill was given to Southwark Hospital by Richard de Clare, Earl of Hertford and Gloucester, who at the same time confirmed Geoffrey de Marlow's gift but in 1315 Gilbert de Clare, the then earl, acquired the three mills from the Hospital in exchange for land elsewhere.
Matthew Miller obtained a lease from the earl at 14 marks yearly, of which one was to go to the Canons of Missenden, but the hospital evidently recovered the two mills given by Geoffrey de Marlow, as only one was included in Great Missenden Manor in 1416 and a lease of the other two was made in 1362 to Thomas Pynell by the prior of St. Thomas's.

Thomas was to pay 5/- for life and his heirs 10/- This later rent probably accounts for the 10/- in Gosenham credited to the hospital at the valuation of 1535, other property there being assessed at 6/8d.

In 1560 John Brinkhurst received a lease of a mill here, but by 1609 these two mills with Gosenham Meadow and plots of osiers were in possession of Thomas Farmer, at whose death in that year they descended to his son John. On account of his recusancy, however, they were granted for 41 years to Sir Richard Conningsby.

Marlow Mills

John Farmer died in 1631 and the watermills said to be three, passed to his son John, whose estate in Marlow, as that of a Papist, was returned in 1647 at £124.

Four mills in Great Marlow were in possession of John and Mary Ferrers in 1723; and by 1797 there were corn and paper mills on the river, which exist at the present day.

Leland, writing in the early 16th century, speaks of two mills at Marlow, one for making linseed oil and the other 'erected for the machinery of thimbils'. The thimble mill was afterwards the property of John Loftung, a manufacturer and inventor of fire engines, who settled here in the early 18th century. One of his seven sons founded the charity now called Loftin's charity."

An important item however, is that the *United British Directory of Trade and Commerce 1791 and 2* specifically stated that these mills – one copper, one thimble and one pressing oil from rape and flax seed, were the *Temple Mills*, which are on the Berkshire side of the boundary line; and it lists Temple Mills as "brass and wire mills". A "cotton-wire" factory was however sold at Gt. Marlow in 1822 – apparently *not* water-driven.

Jonathan Jones was a miller of Great Marlow in 1694, and George Phelps 1696. An article on paper milling, quoted in the previous chapter but one mentions that good paper was being made at Marlow in 1725; and in 1791/2 Thomas Rickett was a paper maker here, and Edward and Jnº Wright 1798. By 1823 the paper mills were being conducted by Mr. Francis Pepper in conjunction with the Wrights and their sons, whilst John Jacques described himself as a "corn miller and paper maker". A disastrous fire broke out three years later, on April 19th; it involved the whole of Messrs. Wright's portion of the premises and was described in the following words in the local press:

"On the evening of Wednesday se'ennight the paper mills in Marlow belonging to Messrs. William and Jos. Wright Jun. were consumed by fire. The outbreak commenced at 9 o'clock at the two extremities of the building at the same instant and the whole premises soon exhibited a heap of burning ruins. By great exertions the paper mills of Mr. Pepper and his residence, and the flour mill of Mr. Jacques were preserved but, due to the confusion, some diabolical miscreant cut the pipes of the engines in several places and this, coupled with the discovery of a chain of combustible materials found in the mills, with the circumstance of the fire having commenced at two extremities at the same instant and in a part where no fire had been used for months before, are evidence that the whole was an infernal act of some incendiary."

The account goes on to explain that Harleyford and Marlow engines were both in poor condition. The mill was fortunately insured; and the stock was very heavy because Messrs Wright had kept workpeople on when there was little demand for paper owing to big mill competition. It was difficult to account for this "villainous act" as the Wrights were young men of the most humane and benevolent disposition; and the use of machinery in the mills was supposed to be the only cause, and a very weak one, for such a transaction. At a subsequent enquiry to assess the amount of damage, it transpired that 4297 lbs. (320 reams) of paper were destroyed. The late Mr. A.H. Cocks, who did so much for the Bucks. Archaeological Society, had in his possession a "View of Great Marlow, Bucks c. 1810" which, he said, showed the old mill buildings timbered perpendicularly, and it is probable these were the ones destroyed in the fire; picturesque old cottages adjoined the buildings, but these also are now no more.

Mr. Francis Pepper died in 1832 and his Executors advertised his portion of the mill in the following terms:-

"Freehold Paper mill. Every necessary appendage, all its valuable fittings, engines, chests, boilers, machines, cylinders, presses, in one lot; very powerful head of water, every convenience for

Marlow Mills

loading boats. Also new Dwelling house. Fine opportunity for manufacturer, or mill might be converted for any purpose where steam or water is required."

A few months later John Brooks, a miller of Great Marlow, was mentioned when a landlord prosecuted someone for using a public road which he pretended was private, but Brooks was doubtless an employed miller. The following year a brief advertisement offered to sell by private contract "a net rent charge of £60 per annum secured on the above well-known and valuable property (Marlow Mills) payable half yearly for ever"; and a sale announcement of 1858 stated that Mr. Jacques held the water corn-mill under lease from 1803 at £105. William Jacques was the miller until about 1875.

This exhausts the printed references to this interesting group of mills, and we can conveniently pick up the thread of the story from information collected at the site, chiefly from Mr. Taylor of Marlow, whose long association with the mills continued until the recent war, although they had ceased to serve their original purposes and were partially derelict. For the general arrangement of this unusually interesting and representative group of corn and paper mills I will refer the reader to the accompanying diagram. [diagram missing]

The three storeyed red-tiled corn mill is wooden boarded, partly tarred and part white-painted with sack lofts either end; and on the west side is a fine old undershot wheel some 18ft. diameter by 14ft. tread with shrouds of iron and six iron spokes either side, the radial floats and their staves being of wood and of good depth. The axletree is a very massive old wooden one, octagonal in section carrying the usual pit wheel, with upright shaft and great spur, nearly all of wood, enclosed, and driving four pairs. Some of the machinery was removed some 30 years ago, including iron belt drums, which had replaced the original wooden ones in the sack hoist and machine gears, and utilised in the paper mills, the equipment being all very good stuff.

West of the corn mill is the slate-roofed paper mill No. 277, of two brick floors, inscribed "W.W. 1800" and a top floor of white painted woodwork with adjustable louvres for air dried paper- a very good line, the process being superior to steam or electric heat drying. Against Mill Lane, eastwards is another very large louvred drying house with a brickwork lower floor.

The drying room over No 277 Mill has been disused some fifty years, but the machinery worked until a few years ago and consists of breaking machines or "rag engines" for tearing and cutting rags and sacks; and pulp beaters, etc. These were driven by a very large undershot wheel some 20ft. by 3ft. with iron arms and shrouds, but mounted upon a much smaller wooden axle than the corn mill wheel, the radial floats being of deep-section wood. The outer end of the axle rests upon the same supporting wall as that of the corn mill, but not directly in line with it; the two wheels are separated by a wooden fence, whilst galvanised iron sheeting provides protection from the elements.

In a single floor brick and wood-work building with slate roof at the north west corner – the drainer house – are large wooden sieves for draining off the main body of moisture, after which the pulp was passed to large vertical drying cylinders (in No. 277 building) about 8ft. high and 4 or 5ft. diameter, in which pulp was dried out by steam heat at 20 lbs pressure from a boiler in the far corner. Thence to the "chest" from which it was fed into the continuous paper machine, of which a fine example can be seen in working order in No. 276 Mill – a low brick and white- painted wooden structure – in the other group of buildings across the yard.

Facing the house – a converted miller's cottage now designated "The Gables" is a small building of brick with two tiled ridges and a galvanised iron bay, in which are more beaters driven by a third undershot wheel broader than the others, diameter being about 12ft. and width 6ft, with three sets of eight iron arms carrying iron shrouds whilst the axle is of wood; and this wheel also is sheltered by galvanised iron.

Turning again to No. 276 Mill, the machine installed could be photographed through the window; and the rollers carrying the wire shaker may be seen, also the suction boxes beneath; even the paper sheet is still *in situ* arrested in the process of manufacture. The pulp is fed on to a felt band which carries it through the adjustable "press rolls" determining the thickness of paper; thence to the wire shaker which vibrates the paper whilst it passes over the suction device and the latter helps to draw off the remaining dampness, so that on reaching the end of the machine the paper is dry and ready to feed on to the rolls for storing.

At the north end of this building is an upright vat with revolving agitator, and beneath the southern end a good 40 h.p. water turbine – said to have been repaired only once in 35 years -which drives the agitator and a spherical revolving copper. The latter, of iron, is mounted so that it is turned very slowly about a horizontal axis by a shaft and gearing. Steam at 20 lbs. is fed into the copper with a suitable alkaline solution, for boiling out colouring matter and so forth; for all kinds of rags, within certain limits, are used, silk and woollen being inadmissible if white paper is to be made, because the bleach fails to act upon animal substances.

Adjoining the mill on the east side is a room containing a small furnace by Poulton's of Reading with chimney shaft, for supplying the steam to the copper and to a small modern engine installed by the Dexter Foundry of High Wycombe for driving the paper machine in flood time; although as the boiler should "blow off" at 20 lbs. whilst about 80 lbs. were required to keep the "machine" going, it was normally found inadvisable to use the engine.

In the same room, fenced off with galvanised, is a smaller undershot wheel some 14ft. diameter by 3ft. all of iron except the radial floats, coupled by line shafting and belts to circular saws and lathes in an adjoining building. This and the furnace room flank the third paper mill building No. 274, of brick with pyramidal roof of slate, from which the "machine" was removed many years ago. Just outside, in the mill-tail, is a felt-washing drum of 6ft. diameter and similar width, constructed with solid wood end plates and an open-work periphery – (see photograph) with iron fulcra, in lieu of axle, mounted in posts; it is raised and lowered into the stream by a crank wheel and rack and pinion and a series of paddle-boards cause the drum to revolve when in the water. The felts from the "machine" become matted with pulp and residue, etc., and are first beaten upon a large table, then placed in this washer to complete the cleaning process whilst another felt is in use.

Against the roadway, beside the big drying shed, is a paper finishing room or "salle", one of several French terms reflecting the influence of French inventors on our paper industry. (There is also the term "guillotine" or as the men generally pronounce it "Gull-en-tine", for cutting the paper, and the French naturally know all about the manufacture of these handy instruments! The white wooden and tiled cart-shed formerly housing the old wagons that carried the "small-hand" paper – a hand made speciality and typewriter papers, etc; stands at one side of the yard; and between cart shed and saw mill are the brick-lined settling bays for freeing the water of sludge and impurities before discharging into river; pollution from the Marlow Mills was practically nil and only on one exceptional occasion was a measurable pollution found – namely .006! The county authorities have before now prosecuted for as little pollution as this, but they have not objected to the Bucks Water Board choking completely the Misbourne with about 10% chalk sludge whilst boring for water, and subsequently pumping the springs dry so that the river has ceased to flow.

The various mill streams are really loop-ways regulated by the weir and sluice-gates upstream; a certain amount of flooding occurs now and again, which is unavoidable on a reach which inundates the adjoining countryside.

From earliest days of newspapers the Wright family and Mr. Pepper had an interest in the paper mills; the corn mill being worked, partly by steam, by William Jacques whose connection if any with the Hawridge and Datchet Jacques, I am unable to trace. F. Headington became the corn-miller later, followed by Stephen Smith, whose manager was Mr. Partridge, later of Hills and Partridge. Smith went into partnership with Mr. Barnett, and they had some quarrel with the Wright's over alleged waste of water in the summer months by not working the wheel as economically as possible; and round about 1900, S.J. Smith became sole and last user of the corn mill. Messrs. Wright and Sons continued for many years, finally ceasing paper-making in about 1935; and in 1911 a Paper Trades Directory shows that they had 3 machines and were making fine Small-hands and "Biscuit-caps".

TAPLOW – 1½ m. from Maidenhead

Fulling, Corn and *Cotton Mills* – ½ m. W. of Church

River Thames

Now pumping water, etc.
Maps – 1768, (1809), 1822, 1824, 1875, 1887, 1926

Many references to watermills occur in Taplow and two were on William Turville's estate in 1194. They passed to Merton Priory (Surrey) which in 1213 granted Stephen de Clyveden and de Tappelaw the tenant, wood to repair them. (Another account says Robert "molendinarius" held them that year.) In 1304 William de Cliveden received a licence to alienate in mortmain to the Priory three mills in Taplow; and eleven years later it leased to John the Dyer a fulling mill in Taplow with two islands, for £40 a year, which his father had before him. The Fulling mill was demised to John Holderness in 1523 for 21 years at a rent of £8 10 0 and farmed out by Upton Rectory in 1535/8 at a similar rent; and in 1544 to John Rye for 21 years at £11 with barges and islands (from which there seems little doubt this mill was on the present Taplow Mill site alongside the Thames).

Some time during Henry VIII's reign (1509–1547) the mills of Taplow were rebuilt and certain old fulling mill stock was found. In 1609 the lease of mill and islands passed to Francis Phillipps and Edward Ferrers; and four years later when Henry Mansfield (who seems to have held Amerden Manor for a time) attempted to set up an overshot mill, the damage to the fulling mill was estimated at £10 per annum. A suggestion was made in 1613, during an inquisition regarding these mills, that the name of an eyot in the Thames called Tenter Eight acquired its title from the tentering of cloth. In 1621/2 Widow Phipp (Phillipps?) was summoned to repair the mill gate and fence bordering the mill lane.

William Tatham was a miller of Taplow in 1693 and a cornmill was leased 5 years later to Joseph Darnell at £60 a year and the site of mill and orchard at £20; in 1709 Mr. Morris obtained a 50–year lease of the mill at £40 rent. Towards the end of the century mills were held by two tenants, one of whom paid £8 6.6. in rates for his share. Two corn millers were at Taplow in 1798 – Joseph Spencer and William Cook. The mills were constantly mentioned during the 17th century and three mills are recorded thence to the 19th, (of which at least two were in one group of buildings). A 21 year lease of Mill Place and the old mill at Taplow – the cotton manufactory – was made in 1803 to Joseph Wise, the cotton works being let at £77 yearly; and it is on record that cotton mills existed at Taplow and at Amerden from 1802 to 1825, but Amerden Manor Ray Mill was on the Berkshire side, below Boulter's Lock, although a large part of Amerden estate lies in Taplow parish.

Still standing on the east bank of a loop-stream is the long slate-roofed corn-mill building, brick one end and wooden at the other; and it is marked separately from the Paper Mills on Jeffery's and Bryant's maps; but is said to have ceased work before the last miller – Weston – died in about 1870. George Norrington was the previous corn miller for some 30 years.

Weston's family were brought up in two unbelievably primitive rooms the like of which it would be difficult to find outside of Dicken's books, almost like cupboards in the upper floor, which is plastered right up to the roof-ridge, without a flat ceiling, like some of the oldest farmhouses in very remote parts of East Anglia. Access to this floor was by a sort of hatchway, but the ladder obstructed the entrance downstairs, and so was hinged and coupled to a rope and lever, to be swung up and down as required! Indeed it is difficult to know which are the older – the rooms or the cobwebs, which latter must have been the forerunners of the wartime black-out curtains, and must I think have been contemporary with an inscription upon a floor joist "Eltham 1632".

Probably the water-wheel was the largest all-wooden breast-wheel in Bucks in its day – 25ft. diameter by 9ft.- but on King Edward's Coronation Day, (August 9, 1902) while some sports were in progress near Boulter's Lock, flames were seen rising from the mill; and a party of helpers hastening to the scene were in time to save the building but not the wheel. The fire seemed to have started in the wheel-room near the south end of the building, the wheel which was at that time used for pumping water to Taplow Court, probably having run hot. Now a turbine drives the pump, with a nice horizontal steam engine in reserve, and the whole of Taplow is supplied, both the corn-mill and paper-mill and all the houses being on Lord Desborough's estate.

"Old Joe the Boatman" who builds and repairs the estate boats, is in charge; in 1939 he had worked there 51 years and was 77, and he has taken out Queen Victoria, Edward VII, the King of Siam, Queen Mary before her marriage, and the Duke of Windsor amongst others, and has taught several generations to swim and row.

To conclude the windmill depicted on the 1 inch O.S. map 1898 on the notable Anglo-Saxon tumulus in Taplow Court grounds is an error. No mill ever stood on it, and certainly not at that date, which is of course within Old Joe's memory.

Taplow Paper Mills or *Cleifden Mills No 282* – ½ m. W. of Church

Working
Maps – 1768, (1809), 1822, 1824,
(1847), 1875, 1887, 1926

Taplow Mills, only a short way above Maidenhead Bridge upon an island within the Buckinghamshire boundary, are best reached by way of Mill Lane, which follows the river bank from the Bath Road and then turns sharply away up the hill into Taplow village. At this turn is the entrance-way to the mills, which stand on a little loop-way from the main stream, close alongside the old corn-mill building.

Established as a paper manufactory, it is said in 1790, Taplow Mills were inspected in 1820 by the Williams family who with Mr. Grenfell, M.P. had closed the Wraysbury Mills, but the proposed transfer of business was abandoned; and the Venables family of Soho mills in the Wooburn Valley who also had Cookham Mills (Berks) for some time, were in possession by 1843, the mills running under the name of Charles Venables & Co. Ltd until 1933 (by which time the family had died out) and being at one time known as Cliefden Mills (1853). Mr. Charles Venables used to tell how as a boy he often walked with young Disraeli, and one day asked what he was thinking about. "Dizzy" at once said very deliberately "I mean to get myself talked about . . . I shall write a book; then I'll make some speeches and get into Parliament – and I won't rest till I'm made a Privy Councillor". C.V. told him not to talk such nonsense!

Mears Nicholson's, the Maidenhead brewers and Captain Mullins carried on the business for a period, and twenty years ago the mills were generally known as Taplow Brown Paper Works. After standing vacant for a while the premises were opened and refitted in 193 [?] by the New Taplow Paper Mills Co. Ltd; who still have them and to whom I am indebted for many particulars, and for kind permission to inspect everything of interest, (a greatly esteemed favour in a paper-mill owing to the secrecy of some paper-trade processes).

Previously 25 tons of brown paper per week had been made; but the new Company was making around 120 tons in 1939, having considerably enlarged the premises with brick and slate buildings; and modern steam exhaust cowls now project from the roofs.

Always two mills have been incorporated in the premises – No 1 standing east and west over one loop stream; No. 2 just north-west of No. 1, reaching north and south over the other loop. Five water turbines (vertical spindles) were installed about 1895 – three in No. 2 of which a small one is at the far end for pumping water for the paper, and two large ones *working in tandem* with coupled "flashes" in the middle of the building; the water now comes in from the west – formerly it seems to have entered diagonally judging by the position of a water-wheel pit at the south end of the building.

No.1 has a pair of turbines as in No. 2, driven by a stream passing south under centre of building; at the west end there was, until about 1904, an old beam engine for one of the two small paper machines, but even then it was considered old-fashioned and regarded as a joke! At the other end are remnants of a good 14ft. all-iron quarter-shot wheel, 8 spoked with 24 curved buckets 3ft. by 3ft. with big stay-bolts but no sole-plates. This was used until 1937 for pumping and for driving a "rag devil" or rag chopper which tore and cut sacks and ropes etc. for brown paper. Previously there had been in all, four wheels, but location of the other two is lost; they had flat paddles or floats of elm – no sole plates- and were wider than the iron wheel but probably smaller diameter. On the site of one turbine there formerly stood a rope chopper driven by a steam-engine out of a ship.

A big diesel engine is now installed in the old corn-mill, in the south end, is smartly done up and goes with the papermills. Only one big continuous – roll machine is at present employed, producing mostly one class of paper, in place of the two very small old machines; and there are all the usual beaters and chests, etc. The old machines making high – class "Browns" and "Krafts" could be controlled it is said by one man, with time to sit down!

Formerly a lock was situated between paper and corn mills, where now a footbridge exists. From the bridge in front of the office (west side of buildings) one could previously see right across the Thames – not a tree in sight, and river much wider, with barges coming upstream to the mills – but today all we see is a ravine completely filled with trees.

ETON

Thames

Mill at College Eyot – Approx ½ m. W. of Church

Gone
No map reference

Apart from the inclusion of two mills in "Domesday" valued at 20 shillings – probably equal to £30 in modern money – and held by Walter son of Other, first mention of a mill at Eton seems to occur in 1224 when William de Bovenay was tenant of two-thirds of the mill in Etton, and his mother one third of the same mill. Eton mill is again mentioned in 1443, when the College obtained from Merton Priory, property in Upton now known as Upper and Middle Clubs It included "all those lands, meadows and feeding grounds and 'pastures with torrents' called Mychelmylwardeshay, Millepond *alias* Milledam,

and cowpenning lying by Eton between the Thames and the road from Windsor to Slough, and between le Werde on the south and Spitelbrigge leading to Datchet on the north". The foregoing location seems to tally with the College site, 300 yds. north of Tangier Mill which bears out the contention of the Reverend John Shephard M.A. that the latter is a comparatively new site. He gives few details, but makes it clear, with a map, that the Eyot site is some 200 yds. north of the School Cloister, saying it stood, "in what is now the Playing Fields perhaps near the gate which now opens into the College Eyot".

Mill at Cuckoo Weir – Nearly 3f. N.E. of Church

Gone
No map reference

Of this site the Rector said, "one mill is supposed to have stood at Cuckoo Weir; and what is known as Deadman's Hole may have been caused by the washing of the mill-stream". His map, based on an earlier one, of Eton-cum-Stockdale and Colenorton has every field delineated, and most of them named. The mill site is seen to be one furlong west of the

railway viaduct, almost beneath which (north of South Field Lane) is Mill Furlong, with Mill Piece the next plot westwards; the latter is due north of Deadman's Hole and the former north of Cuckoo Weir, which can be approached by the public footpath across a 25 acre field O.S. 91.

Tangier Mill – 1½ f. N.E. of Church

Gone
Maps 1824, (1847), 1870, 1875, 188[?]

Little seems to be recorded concerning Tangier Mill, most of the local Bucks historians being entirely preoccupied with the School and even Windsor Castle, notwithstanding that it is outside the county; but the Reverend J. Shephard said "Tangier Mill, built probably at the beginning of this same (19th.) century, close to the present water-works site, stood alone, and gave its name to Mill Fields". A man who did not actually see the mill said he believed it had an outside wheel; and it may be added the Windsor Corporation Waterworks are now at the bottom of Tangier Lane.

In 1829 a printed notice invited all persons having a claim upon Mr. Thomas S. Alger late of Tangier Mill, a bankrupt, to enter particulars of their claims; and the following year the exors. of W.H.Cutler

informed his friends and customers that the business of Tangier Corn and Flour Mill would be carried on by them (John Cutler and William Stephenson). Formerly Edward Feldwick was the miller, and later Henry Drye; John Cleave, who wanted a "good stone man" in 1854; and William Mitchell, who was College baker and probably the last miller, around 1860. Mr. Ben. Burton thought the mill was not standing when he went to Slough in 1878, and certainly not in use.

It stood at the bottom of Tangier Lane (a turning nearly opposite the parish church in High Street) across a short loop called Mill Stream, whilst another loop, forming a by-pass, ran beneath the lane and between the mill and High Street, the two loops meeting at their confluence with the Thames. On the

6 inch Ordnance 1875, the building is marked Flour Mill; it appears on Taunt's strip map of the Thames about 1850; and Bryant calls it Tangiers Mill probably in error.

For many years there was a *Jolly Miller Inn* named after this mill – a typical Victorian public house of yellow brick, still standing on the far corner of Sunbury Road (off Tangier Lane) but de-licenced in 1910.

The Thames, which rises at Thames Head Bridge, on the Cirencester-Malmesbury road, follows the Bucks boundary from just below Henley, past Eton, and almost to Staines, where the southermost point of Bucks is reached.

Chapter 4
Buckinghamshire Watermills on Thames Tributaries North of the Chilterns

WADDESDON* – 5 m. W.N.W. from Aylesbury

Branch of River Ray

Colwick and Shipton Mills – Sites doubtful

Gone

The late Reverend C. Oscar Moreton, Curate of Waddesdon, made a number of interesting references to obscure mill sites within his parish in his *History of Waddesdon and Over Winchendon* (1929). Some are definitely water mill sites and the first to concern us is that of Colwick Mills on Collett or Colwick Grange – originally a hide (120 acres) of land in Beachendon Manor. This does not appear to be the Beachendon site to be mentioned later, since the latter was probably on the River Thame.

Colwick is situated a little west of Akeman Street Station in the hamlet of Woodham, where the railway crosses the Roman Road, and it incorporates Binwell Lane Farm, about a mile north-east, past which a very ancient bridle road used to run from Waddesdon to Grendon Underwood.

Just west of the farmstead on an Elizabethan map reproduced in the above-mentioned work is an indefinite mark like a cross which might represent a windmill, but it is scarcely distinct enough to warrant a

heading in my Windmill section in the absence of other evidence, especially as Lipscomb says "Benwell Lane Farm, of which about 37 acres are in the parish of Wadddesdon, is described in ancient writings as locally situated on the verge of a small stream near the old Roman Road called Akeman Street, where once was a mill, on the border of Wotton". The stream is that which skirts Doddershall House and follows the railway down to the main road to meet another rivulet from Quainton station, afterwards again crossing Akeman Street at Gallows Bridge to join the River Ray at Three Points.

Victoria County History vol. IV. implies there was another mill site at Colwick and this might have been nearer to Shipton Lee, by Doddershall House since *V.C.H.* says "The mill and court of Shipton Lee are both named as pertaining to Thame Abbey in 1291" but in view of the uncertainty, it is impracticable to attribute these mills to individual streamlets.

Ham Mill – Site uncertain

Gone

On the Manor of Fieldham or Ham-cum-Wotton – subsequently Wotton Manor – William de la Rokele was holding Ham Mill of the Knight Templars in 1185; and eventually this Manor followed the descent of the Manor of Ham in Waddesdon said *V.C.H. Vol. IV.*; but no later reference occurs, except that in 1521 a pasture called "the mill" was leased to Christopher Wren. To this day Ham Farm survives a little north-west of

Akeman Street Station and it seems possible the site of Ham Mill is near to the Roman road, a little below the supposed Colwick site. This farm with Ham Green and Ham Wood is now in the hamlet of Woodham, in Waddesdon; although Moat Farm formerly Ham or Hame House where Dean Collett held his Courts of Hamme-cum-Wotton is in Wotton Parish; Shipton Lee is in Quainton, but this is a very doubtful site.

BRILL – 10 m W. from Aylesbury

Another branch of River Ray

Sawmill – 7½ f. N.W. of Church

Derelict
Map 1922

A mill appears in the Manor of Brill in 1086 at a rent of 10/-; but no early site is known, nor is a watermill recorded until recent times, and a horse or cow mill might be assumed but for the high rent.

Adjoining the beautiful 38 acre artificial lake in

Wotton Park, on the west side of the water and close to Edgcott and Brill road there is now a disused water-sawmill superseded by a small steam outfit with portable engine. A sluice in the wall of the lake fed the mill, below which is a little streamlet eventu-

---

* Vague references to supposed mills at Waddesdon are also noted under Biddlesden and Turweston.

ally passing beneath the road, through a well constructed but nevertheless broken sluice at Sheepwash thence to Tittershall Wood to join the Colwick stream about a mile below the lake, and a little cut at the end of the latter relieves the sluice when the mill is disused, as at present.

Standing upon the parish boundary, the mill is a little pinkish building with red galvanised iron barrel roof and a wing forming a little wheelhouse over the stream. Lattice windows in keeping with those of the cottages on the estate give a countrified touch to the structure, which is thought to have been built between 1800 and 1810 by the first Duke of Buckingham in the present line.

Mr. Fenemore of Moat Farm, believes it formerly had an overshot wheel with small cup-like buckets, driven at an angle by the stream, and consequently ineffective; but latterly an eight-armed wooden breast-wheel upon an iron axle and measuring 15ft. diameter by 4ft. drove a cross-shaft near the top of the wheel-house by means of a peripheral iron cog ring, upon the shroud of the wheel, farthest from the building. This might have been to make the ring more accessible for renewal than if it were against the mill wall, or possibly to facilitate receiving a shaft drive from a

portable engine if required, or because a rigid bearing could not readily be fitted above the inner periphery; and the wheel is incidentally in Wotton parish

All internal machinery is dismantled, but some of it was recently lying in a heap in the yard, including iron rollers from the old travelling bench, brackets with half-brasses to carry shafting, long arms to swing the belts over, shafts with belt-drums and bevels, a large centrifugal governor of two lead balls, and two long iron rollers. Mr. Fenemore however, states that about 3 vertical reciprocating saws side by side, made by a very clever blacksmith at Wotton Row (smithy now done away with) were formerly used; then a circular saw was installed, but the mill was insufficiently strong to handle really heavy timber, and so fell into disuse about the end of the Great War.

At peak times the mill employed as many as six or eight men, but in 1939 it housed the best timber from the adjoining steam mill. This has a portable engine in a wooden shed, with a long timber-frame travelling bench which is now also in no more than occasional use. The little stream is un-named and the parent River Ray which V.C.H. suggests was the Yhyst, meets the Cherwell at Islip, the latter in turn joining Father Thames at Oxford.

CAVERSFIELD – 2 m N. of Bicester

Another branch of River Ray

Medieval Watermill – Site unknown

Gone

Another tributary of the Ray, watering the parish of Caversfield, which formed a detached portion of Bucks. until 1844, but is now Oxon, evidently turned a water-wheel in the Middle Ages for *V.C.H. Vol. IV* says:

"John de Wynncote succeeded to the Manor of Caverfield in 1312 by arrangement with Simon de Wynncote, whereby the latter was to hold 19 messuages, 2 carucates and 7 virgates of land, 10/- rent and half a mill in Caversfield, of John for life at

a rose rent, with reversion to John" adding that the property of the Gargates in Caversfield in the 13th century included a windmill and a watermill and the "Capital court of Caversfield".

Most likely site for a watermill in the parish is at the foot of the lake adjoining Caversfield House – quite possibly an enlarged mill pool; and the streamlet joins a larger stream just below Bicester, the Ray being eventually met near Charlton-on-Otmoor.

STEWKLEY – 4 m W from Linslade

River Thame

Littlecote Mill – Site uncertain

Gone

At Domesday, no mill was recorded at Littlecote, but in 1248/9 Robert de Loering or Lovereng conveyed one carucate of land and a mill in Littlecote in the parish of Stivecle to Hugh de Dunster. The probabil-

ities favour a watermill, for windmills were generally named as such; and there is a stream which had the power to drive a small mill in bygone days. Also at a spot 1⅜ miles south of the parish church, are

Millpond Buildings and Millpond Spinney midway between Warren Farm and Steart Farm, and actually against a tiny tributary of the main stream, which is the River Thame; but the tributary is now a mere rivulet. The Thame rises at Stewkley North End, wending its way *via* the delightful Littlecote Ford, amongst the fine isolated hills undisturbed by the three great curses of the age – road building, jerry building and motoring – until eventually it crosses the Aylesbury road at Hardwick, where another ancient ford can still be seen alongside the modern bridge. The late Venerable Archdeacon E. Bickersteth D.D. whose work in getting the Bucks. Archaeological Society established will always be remembered, advanced the curious contention that the Thames itself rises at Stewkley, because this 450ft. height is the most elevated spot at which any of its tributaries are to be found, and because the proper name of the Thames above its junction with the Thame at Dorchester is the Isis; but the archdeacon followed a lone trail with this argument.

WADDESDON – 5 m. W.N.W. from Aylesbury

[River Thame]

Eythrope Mill – Approx. 2¾ m S.E. of Church

Gone
No map reference

More than one watermill stood at Eythrope, possibly upon the same site. The first recorded was held by Wallingford Priory in 1291, and the late Reverend C Oscar Moreton suggested that Mill Ground, on the north bank of the Thame between Beachendon Farm and Eythrope Park was the site. Eythrope watermill was, at the Dissolution, included in the grant of possessions of the Priory to Cardinal Wolsey to his proposed College; the lord of Eythrope Manor was tenant of two-thirds of the mill in the 14th century and finally in 1640 a Thomas East owned a mill of some kind at Eythorpe.

In addition to Mill ground, which is crossed by the old and obviously very ancient road to Winchendon from Stone – at one time illegally closed – there is Mill Close adjoining; and this mill quite probably stood at the meeting of these two fields, against the roadway.

The late Mr. Will. Cripps said that in his time a mill-pond existed with waterfall below it, in the narrow spinney between Mill Ground and the stream, but Miss Alice de Rothschild had the falls and weir moved to the other side of the bridge in order to form a lake in the park. She suggested removing the bridge, which would have isolated Beachendon Farm from Aylesbury, but the Authorities intervened, thus proving there is a right of way. Mr. Cripps also remembered a funeral coming this way from Winchendon and he understood this to be done because of attempts to block the road.

Sir William Stanhope "improved the house and grounds in 1730" (did it include improving the mill by demolishing it?) and possibly altered the name from Eythorp from (eca – þorp = river farm): to Eythrope.

Beachendon Watermill – Site unknown

Gone

In 1198 Carbonel Manor, Addington held a watermill in Beachendon; in 1241, one-third of a mill in Bychendon is mentioned and the Earl of Pembroke had it prior to his death in 1324. Probable position of the mill is west of the Eythrope site on the same loopway of the Thame (the main stream being 100 yards southward), but there is also a Beachendon Brook or Bican broc (the brook of Bica -Saxon) flowing round north of the Farm and discharging into the Thame just above Lower Winchendon Mill.

Medieval Mill – Site unknown   Gone

Miles de Crispin held a mill of some kind in Waddesdon at Domesday, valued at 12/-, and further references occur from the 11th to 15th centuries, but this should be read in conjunction with my previous Waddesdon headings. Again, the medieval site might have been two-thirds of a mile west of Eythrope Mill, assuming it was a watermill; or, on the other hand, there is the now very small Wadds brook known as Wottesbroke in pre-Norman days and the Wade later, flowing from Warmstone Farm near the tower-mill site, down to the Great Western Railway and along the Long Crendon boundary to meet the Thame above Nutley Mill.

LOWER WINCHENDON – 4½ m. N.N.E. from Thame   [*River Thame*]

Lower Winchendon Mill – 3f. E.S.E. of Church   Working

Maps 1824, 1832, (1847), 1875, 1887, 1914

The watermill now standing in the parish probably marks the site of that which is mentioned in 1086. The way of approach is very pleasant, for the village boasts a fine array of half-timbered and herring-bone brick cottages, some thatched; and in front of the medieval church is a little circular letter box of stone upon a piece of green in the centre of the road. Bearing right from here, past the Priory grounds, we stumble down a stony lane beneath tall overhanging trees, until a five-barred gate suddenly opens into a field across which is the stone-built watermill, and the stream emerges from beneath the mill and flows down the field towards the gate and alongside the lane to rejoin the by-pass stream near the Priory.

In Saxon times Eddeda held Nether Winchendon of Queen Edith, wife of Edward the Confessor; but before 1086 the property had been seized by Walter Giffard for a fee of 20/- and four score of eels, and eventually it was granted to Nutley Abbey by Giffard's son who founded the Abbey. By the 16th century the rent for the mill and some land had risen to £12 per annum; and it became a paper-mill, most probably about a century later. But in common with other Buckinghamshire mills, Lower Winchendon reverted from paper to corn milling during the great machinery riots of the 1830's although marked Paper Mill by Lipscomb in 1847 because his map is based on Bryant. It always went with Scotsgrove Mill in paper milling days, making up the paper which had been pulped at Scotsgrove, and in November 1829 both mills were offered for sale by auction.

Equipment of the mills was listed jointly, as follows:

"The whole of the Machinery connected with the manufacture of Paper at Scotsgrove Mill in the parish of Haddenham and the mill at Lower Winchendon, with Stock of rags, paper; horses, wagon, cart, hay, corn, furniture etc. The Machinery comprises complete paper machine with chest, lifter-case, two good engines with new rolls, various pumps, presses, coppers, iron water-wheel, treble stands, ladders, large scales and weights, 10 tons of rags, hay, beans, barley. Stock of paper will be removed to Aylesbury: 206 reams of double small-hand of 12 and 20 lbs. each; 200 couples of 14 lbs. each; 16 reams of brown, 50 reams butter paper and a few lots single small hand. (By direction of the Sheriff of Bucks under an extant)".

Lower Winchendon Mill seems to have found a buyer, but probably it remained a paper mill a little while longer.

Thomas Alcock of Waddesdon and Quainton Windmills had the Winchendon Mill in the 'fifties for corn milling, apparently taking over from Henry Martin; both were related to the Burton Family by marriage; and Thomas Alcock, who was also at Whitchurch Mill under William Burton for a short time afterwards, was succeeded by Benjamin Burton (uncle of our friend Ben Burton of Whitchurch and brother of Jabez and Charles Burton); and his son, Henry, learned milling at Winchendon at an early age, later establishing a corn business in London. Returning in the nineties to Winchendon Mill as a miller and farmer, Henry became a well-known Methodist preacher, lending his support to the building of chapels at Cuddington and Marlow; but in

Lower Winchendon Mill

1904 Henry migrated to Manitoba to take another flour mill. Mr. Ben Burton told me that his Uncle Benjamin once carries a load of 5 cwt – presumably a 20–stone sack under each arm.

Mr. Fred Cox later became the miller, and aroused quite a bit of ill feeling at one time by affixing to the Church gate a note: "No more milling for people owing money, unless paid"!

Since about 1910 the mill has chiefly been engaged in private milling for the Priory to which it belongs Mrs. N. Higgins-Bernard being the owner. It is said that the late Colonel Bernard once found an old Act of Parliament requiring that a parish shall maintain a road to the local mill, and so made the parish repair his road; and the Boddingtons did likewise at Cuddington!

Winchendon Mill is now worked about once a week by the farm hands for grist milling and Mr. Cripps, whose son Bill was stone-dressing there in 1941, believes the population was increasing in this neighbourhood a century ago and this facilitated

conversion to the flour business when the paper millers were afraid of being ransacked and burnt; and Scotsgrove Mill, being worked in conjunction, was simultaneously converted.

The present building, constructed chiefly of local stone with slate roof, stands end on to the stream, with mill house, partly of brick and some barns built on to it, making an imposing old group. A 10ft. undershot wheel entirely of iron (with sluice immediately behind the "flash" providing a local by-pass against flooding), drives two pairs of stones, the eight-armed pit wheel and the wallower being iron, upright shaft wood; and the eight-armed great spur and the crown wheel are mortice gears. Bridges supporting the stone gear are of iron, with wooden bridge trees; tentering hand wheels, and the thumb screws for adjusting the feed-regulating cords project from the gearing enclosure.

A permanently engaged layshaft from the crown wheel drives the dresser, chaff cutter, oat crusher and sack gear through wooden belt drums, that of the dresser being on the inclined spindle and thus in a different plane from the initial drive. The sack bollard drum, quite new but of old-fashioned solid wood construction, is in the roomy top floor which contains unusually ample bins. To drive a dynamo for house –

lighting a baby water-turbine was installed, but wouldn't do the job, so an oil engine was put down.

The word Thame, by the way, is thought by some to mean "the broad water" and to be derived from the broad floods which sometimes inundate the lands from Winchendon to Cuddington and elsewhere.

CUDDINGTON – 4 m. N.E. from Thame)

Cuddington Mill – ½ m. W.S.W. of Church

[*River Thame*]

Standing disused
Maps 1768, (1809), 1824, 1832, 1833, (1847), 1870, 1875, 1887, 1914, 1926

Two mills worth 20 shillings stood in Nedreham – believed to be Cuddington and Haddenham combined – at Domesday; and of these, one probably corresponds to Cuddington Mill and the other to Scotsgrove Mill, which is still in Haddenham parish. A watermill is mentioned in a grant of Cuddington Manor to John Dudley; and in 1588 Cuddington Watermill was sold by Richard Holyman the Younger to Thomas Tyringham, to whom he let it on lease for 21 years, for £650. A century later, the two watermills under one roof called Cuddington Mills, with appurtenances, were sold for £1000; and attached to the mills were rights of free fishery, but the Holymans still retained these after the sale.

To reach the present building we descend the hill on the Crendon road where an accommodation lane will be seen on the left, short of the river bridge, leading to Mill House and farm, and at the far end is the mill itself. The wheel placed within the building, which Mr. Cripps considered a wrong arrangement since it occupies useful space unnecessarily, is a comparatively new iron semi- undershot, (fall only 2ft. 6ins.,) with open floats; and there is an eel trap adjoining. Machinery, arranged practically as at Lower Winchendon, is nearly all iron except for teeth of the great spur. Part of the former wooden axle -tree serves as a gate post at the bottom of the green lane which led from the village to the windmill. It was replaced by a steel one, but so much difficulty was experienced in inducing the keys to remain *in situ* against the steel axle that it had to give place to an iron one. Then one day the mill stopped working all at once and, on investigation, the wheel was found to be running at full speed! The axle had snapped clean in two, so the steel one was again requisitioned with a new arrangement for fixing the keys; and it is still there. Mr. Cripps was not partial to iron axles, having seen several broken a-two. Three pairs of stones were originally used, and a

steam engine extensively employed, the owners being in a favourable position to purchase coal; but eventually one pair was replace by a Bamford steel roller mill for grinding rough pig stuff.

Milling is said to have been carried on at Cuddington for 1000 years, and the Boddington family claimed four hundred years' ownership up to the time it ceased work. They stopped in March 1936, but may have done odd work at intervals for a year or two, although it is probable the mill has now ground its last sack, and the Misses Boddington have vacated the mill. In quite good condition, the present building was erected by a London firm, it is believed in 1844 – the same year as Culverton Mill at Risborough. Years ago, presumably prior to 1844, Cuddington Mill is reputed to have been arranged in counter gear like Notley, the next down stream.

When Aylesbury Mills were dismantled a mixer from there was put into Cuddington Mill; but a man purporting to be a Board of Trade inspector, but suspected of being a paid agent of the milling cartels ordered it not to be used, although the same machine is permitted in the big port mills to which the board extends its benevolent protection.

In succession to John Bodington, William Boddington had the mill from the early 'fifties until about 1910 after which his executors ran it for a time. He was a real old-time miller who made a success of the job; and he employed a first miller named Edward Adkins from about 1853 till his retirement in 1870. Meanwhile George Atkins, second miller, whose job was to tend the windmill, took over the watermill after Adkins; later a man named Edwards was first miller and Mr. Cripps second miller, during the periods he was employed there; and in calm weather his job was to help dress the flour on the broaching machine in the watermill, this being a two-man job. Miller Smith from Quainton took charge for a short

Cuddington Mill

time just before Mr. Cripps, but he was then past it, and did no more milling. Mr. Cripps born October 1851, worked in his father's windmills at Wheatley (Oxon) as a mill boy as early as August 1864; and it is a pleasure to recall that from 1935 to 1940, when he recounted his recollections to me, this true country miller, whose life had been devoted to wind and watermills, whose thoughts were with the mills in leisure hours as well as during the days and nights of toil, and whose interest never flagged to the last, was as hale and hearty as any man of his age, although somewhat troubled with asthma – the bugbear of millers – in winter months. Always he was ready with a fresh fund of information and new and interesting opinions about windmill and watermill design and construction as often as I was able to call on him and when this book sees the light of day, the milling fraternity – by which I mean all those genuinely interested in wind and watermills – will owe the late Mr. Cripps a depth of gratitude.

During the Great War Mr. Cripps worked by steam and water at Cuddington, the windmill being unserviceable, partly owing to neglect from other hands; one of his sons sometimes worked there as did the late Harry Crook of Long Crendon tower mill. Speaking of early days, Mr. Cripps mentioned that during his very first week's work at Wheatley, they had hot calm days with a breeze at night, so he was initiated to night work in the tower-mill; in the ensuing winter, he was promoted to miller in the adjoining post mill (afterwards burnt down) which they used to close down during summer months to save rates. Details of Mr. Cripps' career having been given under Cuddington Windmill; also reference to a deed of 1822 implying that two windmills and two watermills stood at Chearsley – the next parish downstream, (Cerdisesceah, where Cerdis & Cynric defeated the Britons) – but probably referring to Cuddington and Notley Mills in the adjoining parishes.

LONG CRENDON – 2 m. N.N.W. from Thame

[River Thame]

Crendon or Notley Mill – 7 f. almost E.S.E. of Church

Some foundations
Maps 1768, 1793, (1809), 1824, 1833, (1847), 1870, 1875, 1887, 1914

The Foundation Charter of Notley Abbey, about A.D. 1162 says that Walter Giffard* and his wife Ermengarde "gave to God and St. Mary "de Parco" of Crendon in perpetual alms for the health of their souls and the souls of their ancestors and kindred, and of King Henry and Queen Eleanor and their issue, their ancestors and successors, all the land within the Earl's Park" (the only Buckinghamshire park mentioned in Domesday) and between the park and the Thame stream, a meadow for a team and Crendon Mill, for the erection of an Abbey, etc., etc.

As for the name Notley (Noctele), pronounced and sometimes spelled Nutley, was originated by the founders of the Abbey, Crendon Mill is doubtless the one known henceforth as Notley Mill; and in 1542, Sheahan records that King Henry VIII demised to Sir John Williams, Kt. and others, about 250 acres in Crendon and a watermill in Notley; late belonging to the Abbey. Richard Ridge, last Abbot of Notley, surrendered the property to Henry VIII in December 1539 when it was worth £5000 a year in present day money. The watermill was not then let out and he paid £26. 18. 4. rent for the whole property.

Amongst the features of interest around the former Abbey, Sheahan mentions the dovecote of stone containing 1200 pigeon holes; and a little distance westward the very ancient watermill which is "mentioned in the early history of Crendon and occupies the original Domesday site". Lipscomb said the mill was "an interesting object to the antiquarian visitor"; and the same mill appears in the appurtenances of the Manor of Notley in the 17th century.

Henry Taylor was the resident miller in 1828, when he gave evidence in the famous or infamous, Sewell murder case – the murdered man Edden, being waylaid in his cart and found dead in Windmill Road, between Towersey Windmill and the turnpike; and it is interesting that after Sewell was acquitted with no apparent justification, he was re-arrested and received a well-earned, if rather irregular, death sentence.

The miller who had Horton postmill (Oxon) at the time it was blown down, came to Notley Mill, Mr. Cripps said, although he could not recall the name; but he saw him and remembers he had a pair of undamaged sails from the postmill at the time, which he wished to dispose of. He was at Notley until about 1870, working the mill for William Reynolds, whose family owned it from the 18th century until 1930. Mr. Reynolds also owned Abbey Farm, to which the mill always belonged; and he later employed one Somerfield to work it for many years. Henry Reynolds grand nephew of W. Reynolds, became the last owner of the mill which had deteriorated very much when Henry Holyfield, who had worked it for Reynolds finally ran his own milling business there as a tenant under steam and water, and no one being inclined to renovate the structure, probably owing to its very great age and lack of trade, it was demolished just after Reynolds left.

The late Harry Crook often brought corn from his tower mill in calm weather for grinding into flour at Notley Mill which Mr. Cripps recalled as a very old-fashioned whitewashed building with thatch reaching

---

* There were two or three Walter Giffards in succession.

down to about 6 feet from the ground. The floors were rather unsafe; stone floor inconvenient to work in, being only 6ft. high; and at the finish the water-wheel was broken and the engine, mounted on a concrete block on the south bank of the stream, provided the power. Two pair of stones were installed in counter gear, one counter shaft running right and one left, so that stone-spindles and stones were some way apart. The mill stood across the stream between fields O.S. 63 and 65, where the brick-built breast or slipway with a walled by-pass alongside it, may still be seen; and the south front of the mill seems to have

looked on to a cart-bridge spanning the stream and the main by-pass with bricked sluice-way. A mill-race nearly a quarter of a mile long reached down from the Abbey Farm; and the parish boundary stream east-wards was an extra safeguard against almost inevitable flooding. The Thame, sometimes known as the Chearsley Brook at this point, is on the Oxford side of the county boundary at the market town of Thame, but at Shabbington a mill site upon a loop-stream is in Bucks. It has been observed that it is surprising Notley Mill was never utilized by the famous Shrimpton family.

SHABBINGTON – 2½ m W.N.W. from Thame

Early Watermill – 300 yds. S.E. of Church

[*River Thame*]

Gone
Map – 1830

One of the quaint spots of Shabbington is down by the *Old Fisherman P.H.* where the little duck-boarded lane to Thame makes an abrupt turn across the stream. Strenuous work is done here by anglers, whose patience is greater than their catches, although it is surprising what is taken in such quiet backwaters by ignoring the best traditions of the sport and dangling a minnow on a string! (You don't know how to catch minnows? They catch a jarfull in five minutes at Shabbington). All the old-timers speak of the *Fisherman* as "The Mill" and this it is said, is the former name of the establishment, although known as the *Fisherman* over a century ago.

Various references are made to the watermill (value 10/- in 1086) but the site only is named in 1683; the watermill is marked 'Mill' on the 1830 Ordnance; and an old lady in the village believed she saw it in disuse before 1870, but could recollect no details. The water here divides into two rivers for half-a-mile, only the stream nearest the *Old Fisherman* being in Bucks; and in it, facing the inn, is a double arch beneath the road and a buttress beyond. The mill seems to have stood just here, but whether above or below the bridge it is difficult to say. After following the parish boundary the Thame crosses a corner of Oxfordshire to join the Thames at Dorchester.

WHITCHURCH – 4½ m. N.N.W. from Aylesbury

Dunn Mill or *Whitchurch Mill* – 3 f. S.S.W. of church

Chatel Stream

Standing dismantled
Maps 1768, (1809), 1824, (1847), 1875, 1887, 1914

In 1555 Anthony Cave of Chicheley scheduled in his will "the water mylne called the dune mylne at Whitechurch . . . whereof I do appointe into the King and Quene's majesties" etc., etc. John Waterhouse bought the major portion of Whitchurch manor in 1581 from Edward de Vere, 17th Earl of Oxford (who had it from his ancestors back to the 12th century, and who is claimed by some to have written certain plays of Shakespeare); and he left the Manor to his wife and the courts and watermill to his son, Thomas, who in turn settled it on his wife Mary. Her son John inher-ited the mill in 1600, but it changed hands frequently.

Earliest reference to the watermill seems to be in 1263; and in 1667 it is mentioned by its present name of Dunn Mill. A clause guarding the water rights was inserted in the "enclosure act" of 1771, no doubt by the lord of the Manor to protect his own interests, nevertheless the mill eventually ceased to work by water owing to the supply being illegally diverted by a wealthy Doctor in the town who was in a position to make litigation too expensive for the miller.

This person had wells sunk in the hillside above the mill for his own use and although he denied the millstream was affected Messrs Gilbert of Leighton

Dunn Mill or *Whitchurch Mill*

were present at the mill taking water levels daily and were in a position to prove to the contrary. In fact the mill pool, which used to flood round the mill on small provocation and was never dry during the most prolonged drought, has *from that time onward* been dry all the year round, the springs having ceased to flow.

Dunn Mill is situated at the end of the picturesque Weir Lane below the village, passing the ramparts of Bolbec Castle on the way down the hill adjoining which the oldest inhabitants, about a hundred years ago, could just remember the drawbridge which once led to the Castle Keep.

The two springs which fed the mill rose on the site of the Castle in fields called "The Lord's Gardens" one being the Chatel (Chatwell or Cattle Well) Stream at which cattle were watered in olden days, near the summit of the hill, yielding 40 gallons per minute; and the other Whittle (Whitwell or White Well) Hole – probably a chalky well – rising nearer the village and supplying 32 gallons per minute. They turned a wheel claimed to be of the largest diameter in Bucks – 26 feet – although it was narrow across the tread, being no more than 2ft. 3ins.

Of overshot type it was mounted and wedged upon a 20ins. wooden axle-tree and had cast eight-arm centres of 9ft. spaced 3ft. apart on the axle and from these centres the iron shrouds were suspended by 16 radial arms of 2ins. rod 8ft. 6ins. long, with eight similar cross braces from each side. The iron buckets, 64 in number, were some 18ins. broad, separated by very small orifices of only about 1in. although the late Harry Alderman, the last miller said that a sudden rush of water would not stall the wheel but would merely make a great cascade all over the wheelhouse. The latter was added after a fire which occurred about December 7th, 1890, the wheel being previously exposed but partially sunk in a deep pit; it was fed by an 8 ins, round iron pipe from a high oval-shaped mill-pond 40ft. wide with a shallow brick-work wall either side of the sluice or flash that admitted water to the pipe, and a gate at the side discharged to a by-pass east of the mill.

When the adjoining smockmill was removed to Wingrave over a century ago, Dunn mill, or as Bryant calls it Whitchurch Mill, was a low thatched wooden building, with external wheel, but before the fire it was similar to the present structure of red brick with a slate roof; and a good painting in Mr. Alderman's possession showed the windows rather more old-fashioned than at present, with shutters to them. Also a chimney shaft for a Cornish boiler stood at the south-east corner. Until 1890 the mill contained the usual pit-wheel and upright shaft driving two pairs of stones; a separate pair was driven by the beam engine, and the latter probably caused the fire, which began during the night after it had been running, and spread along the roof to the house at the west end.

In the excitement of the fire Mr. Alderman and his brother tore down two of the outer doors of the mill, apparently thinking these the best things to save! They are still in use and bear marks of the fire; and part of the walls of house and mill survive, but a party wall was put in the roof afterwards to confine the flames in the event of another conflagration. P.C. Austin discovered the outbreak and aroused the occupants, but the fire had almost run its course when the Aylesbury fire brigade arrived, the journey being about five miles up hill.

When rebuilding, Mr. Alderman installed a line shaft in place of the upright shaft partly to provide better facilities for driving auxiliary equipment by belts; and he dispensed with beam engine and boiler, he and his brother taking down the chimney shaft. As already indicated in my Introduction he departed from the usual practice with suspension type wheels of driving his line shaft by spur gear from the periphery; preferring to retain a pit-wheel (8-armed all iron) within the main building upon a large timber axle, with iron to iron bevel drive to a short, stout wooden axle laid at right angles. (see diagram) On this was a 7ft. morticed spur gear driving a strong iron main shaft running right along the east wall, in a sort of corridor, not very accessible – in fact he had to crawl under the main shaft and clamber over the intermediate gearing to oil the machinery, which had to be stopped for this purpose!

Projecting through the south wall, the shaft terminated with a flywheel to receive a belt-drive from a portable engine in a new lean-to, so that *all* machinery could be driven by steam or water or both

in tandem, instead of only one pair of stones, as previously. A belt drove up to a wooden sack-bollard mounted low down on the second floor, the sack chain running diagonally to traps in the far corner. Stone spindles passed through iron bridges to rest upon a pivoted iron bar with a long tentering screw with peg and holes and the jack passed down to an iron pot on the floor, with handle and screw beneath main-shaft. Three pairs were driven by a very large morticed bevel gear, and at far end was a belt to first-floor where a line shaft drove a large cloth dresser, etc; and a smaller modern dresser was in opposite corner. Formerly Mr. Alderman ran a thrashing outfit in conjunction with his milling and sometimes dressed iron mill-stones (15 inch rollers); but farmers nowadays do everything themselves, not that they grew much corn hereabouts up to 1939. The engines and the mill-wheel as already mentioned were as good as stolen by the authorities in 1942, when Mr. Alderman was enfeebled and almost penniless.

The death of an early miller – Leonard Sharp – is recorded in 1719; and at the "enclosure" in 1771 it was noted that one of the open fields was called Dunmill Field, comprising all the land down to Hardwick from the watermill and there is still a field called Dunmill Leys or "Dumberleys".

In 1798, John Johnson was the miller; Robert Goodson was selling up and leaving Whitchurch Mill in 1822: and in 1826 boring operations for coal commenced close to the watermill, but rock was struck and the work abandoned. John Holt and William Rose were millers at Whitchurch in 1830, but Mr. Ben Burton's grandfather, William Burton, rented the mill from 1840 or '41, when he left Wingrave Windmill, remaining till his death in 1871; and he it was who installed the engine in order to cope with business in the summer months, making this, it is locally believed, the first steam-mill in Bucks* . In June 1868 he was joined by his grandson aged 14, from North Marston Windmill, who never again lived at home and who went to George Hill of Aylesbury in 1871. Thomas Alcock of Waddesdon and Lower Winchendon Mills was there for as short time while under William Burton but his ideas not being in accord with those of Mr. Burton, who was a very good and greatly respected miller, he shortly migrated to America. Joseph Woods followed selling up in 1878; and William Alderman, who married a Burton, took over and installed a pair of governors,

---

* A steam engine was in use at Buckingham North End in 1841; at Walton (Aylesbury) 1843; and before 1845 at Chelsea New Town, Linslade, all for corn-milling.

not for the steammill, which probably had governors on the engine itself, but for the water-driven wheat stones, because the big wheel was apt to be ice-covered on the half which held water when stopped of a winter's night, so it alternately raced and eased up when started next morning. Messrs. Gilbert are believed to have installed this wheel for William Burton, building it up on the spot, of course; and it seems to have answered very well for half a century or more, only requiring the bolts tightening from time to time.

William Alderman's two sons, of whom only Harry survived in recent years, eventually drove the former and present mills; and Mr. Alderman, who lived alone at the mill after his wife's death told me they often worked practically day and night in winter to prevent the premises being flooded, rather than discharge a lot of water unused. He recollected seeing several beam engines during his journeyings in Bucks years ago, mostly with Cornish boiler in separate shed; and Mr. Ben Burton said the Whitchurch and all other beam engines he saw had overhead beams. Early in 1944, poor Harry was found drowned in a stream, having apparently fallen into it in the 'black-out' – last of a great line of country millers; and the new owner has pulled out the machinery under the impression that he is making "improvements".

Chatel Stream joins the Thame near Upping's Farm south of Hardwick, and has never driven any other mill.

HULCOTT – 2¾ m. N.E. from Aylesbury

Hulcott Mill – Approx. ¼ m. N.E. of Church

Thistle Brook

Gone

Maps – 1768, (1809), 1870

In an ancient book of Memoranda and Institutions in the time of Oliver Sutton, Bishop of Lincoln, is the following account re presentation of Adam de Berington to be ordained for the Vicarage on the 7th Kalends of December (Nov. 25th) 1294:-

"And that in the parish and chapel of Bierton is given certain corn, commonly called "Puttecorne" for the burial of the Parishioners of Hulcote who are buried at Burton, which belongs to the alterage of Burton: And there are there two Mills, the one a Water Mill and the other a Horse Mill . . ."

This seems to imply that corn was to be given to Bierton by the people of Hulcott, in which case Hulcott Mill would be indicated, although there is one at Broughton, in Bierton. First definite mention of a mill at Hulcott is in 1322; whilst in the reign of Queen Elizabeth the Fountains held a watermill here, which is again mentioned while the Neales held the Manor.

In 1652 a windmill is quoted as well as the water-mill and was quitclaimed with the Manor of Thomas Wyan; and in 1686 Robert Maine, gent, and William Smith of Hardwick, were charged with failing to cleanse the brook between Hulcott Mill and Eythropp Mill (a distance of some six miles).

The watermill site is reached by a footpath from the north-east corner of the village green, down two or three fields and along the bank of the stream where there are some remains of old cowhouses; and the mill building stood midway along the loop stream with the main river passing behind it on the parish boundary. Probably it was always a farmer's mill, since there appears never to have been a road to it. An old inhabitant said he recollected the mill, an old disused brick building more or less falling to pieces 60 or 70 years ago and soon done away with; and the only recorded miller seems to be John Munger, 1798, who also had the windmill.

Thistle brook follows the Weedon parish boundary down to Holmans Bridge on the Buckingham road (where at the ford of olden days, one of the last battles in England was fought, 1642), afterwards joining the Thame near Quarrendon's ruined church.

MARSWORTH – 2 m. N. from Tring

Nottimore Brook

De la Hay Mill – Approx ¾ m. N.E. of church

Gone
No map reference

Standing on the big railway bridge near the new cement works and looking towards the winding canal in the north-westerly direction, the remnants of Nottimore brook can be seen following a hedgerow in which are seen some fine old elm trees. Now the brook discharges into the canal and in summer is no more than a trickling stream, but for centuries it drove a mill which in 1571 was the subject of a dispute between Michael Seare (heir to De la Haye Manor and probably an ancestor of the present Mr. Sear whose grandfather had the windmill and John

Gery. Mr. Sear never heard of the mill; and but for the record in *V.C.H. Vol. III* it might have escaped notice.

John de la Haye held the property in 1379; and Sheahan says one of the Marsworth Manors – evidently this one – belonged to the Seare family for 300 years – A.D. 1500–1800, the Christian names of the sixteen generations of Seares being alternately Michael and John all the way down.

Apparently Nottimore Brook formerly proceeded toward the "Linces", thence westward to join Thistle Brook below Marstongate ford (now bridged).

MARSWORTH – 2 m. N. from Tring

Branch of Thistle Brook

Paper Mill – 3 f. S. of church

Gone
Maps 1768, 1793, 1809

Although marked upon one or two maps such as Jeffery's as a paper mill, this is entirely forgotten. It occupied a spot now covered by the reservoir bank, or just outside it, and judging by the location of the present stream and from the maps, it stood opposite the lane now leading to Mill House from the Lower Icknield Way. Apparently this was not originally a paper mill for *V.C.H. Vol. III* says it was "later used as a paper mill and it had passed from the possession of the Hospital by 1790" having been granted by an earlier king to the Mayor and Citizens of London for the endowment of St. Thomas' Hospital.

The mill is believed to have been upon the Savoy

Manor and *Victoria County* definitely states in a chapter about Industry, that paper was made at Marsworth and the mill was destroyed in the construction of the Grand Junction Canal, which took away the water of the stream for the reservoir.

The Grand Junction was constructed between 1792 and 1805, the Wendover Cut in 1799 and the Aylesbury cut in 1814; but it is doubtful whether the mill survived the building of the main canal which necessitated the reservoirs. Water was pumped up from these into the canal, the summit of which was higher, by a beam engine, of which good photographs are preserved at the Bucks Museum, and a Cornish boiler.

Wendover Stream

Dyer's Mill or Marsworth Mill – ¼ m. W.S.W. of church

Gone
Maps 1768, 1793, (1809), 1825, 1875

Of the three mills valued at 15 shillings on Marsworth Manor in 1086, one was probably in Tiscot, (Herts.) which had the same Domesday over-lords; and this site, doubtless near Tiscot Farm, 4 miles north-west of Tring, need not concern us much. It would be the watermill called Athelynemulne leased in 1313 by Philip Aylesbury to Walter de

Gubblecote for £3. The lessee in about 1415 was Richard Venour, probably lord of Goldington Manor, to which another watermill, eventually known as Dyer's Mill, was apppurtenant. the latter was valued at 57/4d in 1292 but only 30/- in 1324. Descending with the Manor, it was in Edward West's possession in 1618, but its later history seems obscure. Dyer's

Mill stood south-west of the village, where the Mill House survives on the site marked "Corn-mill" on the 6" Ordnance; and William Dyer was in fact the miller in 1798. According to *V.C.H. Vol. III*, this was "turned into a windmill and called Dyer's mill" which seems quite possible since the construction of the Grand Junction Canal incapacitated all the Marsworth watermills. At any rate there was eventually a windmill, and local opinion differs as to which was used last – the windmill or the old watermill building working under steam only; but the windmill as recorded elsewhere was idle many years before its demolition

In 1700, Mary Bates complained that Thomas Carter, overseer of Marsworth, refused to pay her an allowance because he said her son Joseph had purchased a mill in the parish and could maintain her.

Sixty years ago the Sear family had Dyer's Mill and Sheahan mentioned a steam flour mill "near the canal bank" in 1862, evidently referring to the same. A man named Clarke was probably the last miller, after which Thomas Mead of Little Tring power mills bought up the premises to put the windmill out of business, whilst his son W.N. Mead demolished the Gamnel Windmill at the neighbouring barge building yard in Hertfordshire.

Jefferys (1768) uses the term Dyer's but Bryant in 1824 called it Marsworth Mill and marked Bellows Mill near Edlesborough as Dyer's; perhaps Dyer went to Bellows Mill from Marsworth.

This branch of the Thistle Brook, after meandering through Gubblecote, and Puttenham, joins the parent stream three-quarters of a mile above Hulcott Mill Site.

WENDOVER

Wendover Stream

Early Mills, Fulling Mill, Upper and Poyntz Mills – Sites uncertain

Gone

Domesday Book records two mills attached to Wendover Manor, valued at 10 shillings and known as Upper and Nether Mills. In 1295 says *V.C.H. Vol. III*, they were worth £10 yearly – a good figure, but by 1417 the value had dropped to £1.13.4. In the 16th century they were leased for £6. It is believed Nether Mill was on the present Wendover Mill site; Upper Mill may have been farther up towards the church, where there is now a pool; although the present sluice would have nothing to do with this mill, which has been so long gone that the most painstaking historians of Wendover cannot positively place the site.

Meanwhile exceptionally early fulling mills (molendina Folentia) are mentioned in Wendover in 1223, and again in 1291 and 1414; and one mill granted to Gilbert Spreng is noted in 1223 also. Roger Cheyne, who had the fulling mill until 1414, held rents in Wyvelsgate Manor also, which suggests that this was one of the Poyntz Mills attached to that Manor in the 16th century; and since the latter was held of the Wendover Forrens (part of Wendover Manor divided up) it seems that they were really the Upper and Nether Mills reappearing under the name of the Poyntz family of Wendover.

!n 1411 and again in 1555 a watermill attached to Wendover Manor is mentioned as Clerk's Mill; and

one suspects that the Upper Mill was the fulling mill, since it disappeared centuries ago; and Clerk's the Nether Mill on present site, In 1679 Henry Short was summoned for not having a sufficient way leading from the Town towards the parish church, and ordered to put a sufficient bridge in the "market way" (unidentified) near Mill Mead.

In his *History of Wendover* Sir Leonard West LL.D. records that grants of 1562 quoted one "brest" mill called Upper, and one overshot called Nether, granted for 21 years at "100/- and 2/- increase" and for £6 respectively. Upper Mill was apparently situated near Bucksbridge Farm, or the Sluice; for Millmeade was shown due east of church between road and stream; and Mill Close where the church gate now is, on a 1620 map; with Lower Mill on present site.

Sheahan mentions two flour-mills at Wendover, but evidently includes Shift Mill, farther downstream; and Sir Leonard advances the possibility, which I imagine is the correct one, that Upper Mill was transferred to Shift Mill site, hence the name.

Wendover Stream rising at the springs by the *Well Head P.H.* discharges into the Canal, near the Wharf; but the Canal also taps the stream by a tunnel or pipe from near its source and has thus greatly reduced its flow at Wendover Mill.

Old Mill or *Wendover Watermill* – ¼ m. N. of Church

Used as residence
Maps 1768, (1809), 1825

The supposed early history of Wendover Mill has already been outlined under the foregoing heading. Seldom has the mill appeared on the maps, following the not unusual rule of once omitted, always omitted; but the renovated shell of the last mill-building is preserved in excellent condition, its brightly painted white wooden walls with green doors making a landmark behind the clock tower near the centre of the town.

The southern wall differs from the other three in being of warm red brick and the Mansard roof is tiled and has an attic which formerly contained a little door instead of being glazed. No less than five other "windows" in the south wall were also little doors, but they have now all been reconstructed. Placed with its west end across the stream the mill is low built; and standing on the river bank, one could see under

the first floor door into the upper room before it was repaired. A long mill-pond (considerably larger on the 1620 map, than the present pool which is no more than a widening of the stream) fed an iron-framed wheel of about 12ft. by 5 or 6ft. tread inside the west wall, whilst only a party wall within separated the by-pass.

Gearing was arranged as usual with an upright shaft, and millstones on first floor, these and the broken wheel remaining until the reconstruction about 1931, by Mr. H.H. White, retired builder.

Joseph Hoare was the miller of Old Mill from 1798 onwards, followed by his descendants till the seventies; then Joseph Senior Holland had the business until the Great War, describing himself as "proprietor of the Red Lion Hotel and Posting House, Wendover Brewery and Malthouse and Wendover Water Mill;

Old Mill or *Wendover Mill*

builder and contractor and assurance agent". His son, Jack Holland, last had the mill, employing a miller named Hopcraft, who was unfortunately found drowned downstream with his bowler hat on the bank marking the spot; and the mill ceased work in the 'twenties, without having had steam or other auxiliary power.

The tunnel feeding the Canal from near Well Head is said to be a glazed brick culvert about 30ft. below the open stream, with a well sunk down to it close to the upper pool near the church, and various diversions from the canal are again made beneath the wharf, partly for maintaining a steady level on the Cut.

Next site downstream – Shift Mill – is on an overflow of this description, being fed by a little weir and a pipe beneath the tow-path about north-east of the windmill.

Shift Mill – Approx 1¼ m. N.N.W. of Church

Gone

Maps 1768, 1793, (1809), 1824, (1847), 1870

No-one recollects the actual existence of Shift Mill, although remnants of a roadway that led to it are visible, and some timber belonging probably to the sluices, is said to have lain in the stream until recently. The old roadway ran diagonally across what is now the Recreation Ground, a little north of the light railway crossing, but the present path is along the south and east sides of the Ground until it meets the old track. The mill site will be found on the right of the track facing two cottages in the field; and in front of them can be seen a stone set in the ground to prevent carts from cutting the corner as they turned down towards the mill. The stream, being now an overflow from the Canal, is very small but still has its little by-pass around an island bordered by willows. Incidentally the Recreation Ground after being snatched from the parishioners under the "enclosure" was later "given" to them again "in exchange" for another four acres of their land, so they got one piece of their own land for another. How kind of the benevolent donor!

The name Shift Mill well-known to older folk in Wendover, appears on Bryant's map; but Jefferys and others collectively name this and the next mill, which was in Halton parish, Halton or Haulton Mills. Apparently both existed for some time after construction of the Cut in 1799 when Mr. Lucas was the miller; although the supply of water must have been curtailed, and probably brought about cessation of work and subsequent disappearance of the mills.

An advert. of 1833 seems to imply that the mill had by then disappeared, for it refers to Mill Meadow, half-a-mile from Wendover (an estate agent's half-mile of course!), a convenient distance from the turnpike to Aylesbury; with a shed on it and fruit trees, a right of way to the Grand Junction Canal and a good road to it, but no mention is made of a mill although the meadow evidently adjoined the Shift Mill site.

HALTON – 1½ m. N. from Wendover)

[*?Wendover Stream*]

Halton Mills – Nearly ¾ m S.W. of church

Gone

Maps 1768, 1793, (1809), 1870

The most northerly of the two so-called Halton Mills was situated on the right of the Halton lane from the Aylesbury road, just before the double bend short of the Canal bridge. Now a sort of spinney, the spot bears no sign of having been a mill site; the stream being very small and almost choked by undergrowth, and it gathers itself into a little tunnel beneath the roadway to discharge into Weston Turville Reservoir.

According to Cruchley's map, the cart track to Shift Mill continues northwards to reach the other mill and emerge in the Halton Lane. The former existence of this northerly mill which doubtless disappeared considerably earlier than Shift Mill is unknown locally, but Edward Hill was given as the miller in 1798.

WESTON TURVILLE – 2 m. N.W. from Wendover [*?Wendover Stream*]

Domesday Mills – Sites uncertain   Gone

Four mills worth 33/4d were in Weston Turville in 1086: but the driving power of the present streams is now very small even with the aid of Weston Turville Reservoir (specially built to maintain supply to the mills after opening of the Canal). In the 14th century Walter de Gayton held 4½ carucates of land and a mill and £4 rent in Broughton and Bedgraves, which had been let to Michael of Northampton in 1276; and another mill is mentioned in Weston in 1346/7.

Weston consisted of three manors in olden days – Weston Turville, Weston Molyns and Weston Butters (le Botiller) and one of the early watermills might be identified with Weston Butters Manor, for there was on Mill Farm a meadow called Bullers Mill Field in the old deeds, north of the Halton lane and nearly opposite the Halton Mill site. The meadow, which old men could remember ploughing, has become a spinney and is separated from the lane by the keeper's lodge; and Perch Bridge over the canal is believed to be sometimes called Mill Bridge. This suggests that the old course of the stream, now merged in the Reservoir, was along the north bank of the latter, although the river now resumes its course from the west corner.

Weston Turville Mill – 3 f. N.N.E. of church   Working

Maps 1768, (1809), 1825, (1847), 1870, 1875, 1914, 1926

We may safely assume that the present mill is upon one of the Domesday sites; and the medieval names already mentioned may or may not apply to it.

Weston Turville Mill was purchased in 1716 from the Duke of Buckingham by a Mr. Purssell, of whom Mr. Charles Purssell, the present owner is a direct descendant. Richard Purssell was the miller in 1798; and in 1825 William Purssell of Weston Turville, miller, is mentioned in an unproved charge of assaulting a manservant; and he was the miller when Mr. Charles Purssell's father, William, who lived to be 79, was born at the mill.

Standing at the end of Mill Lane, south of the main thoroughfare of the village near some very picturesque thatched cottages, Weston Mill is of red brick with slate roof, and bears obvious signs of outward renovation, but is actually an old mill with a history. It adjoins a homely Mill House and is well supplied with water, for besides having an unusually large and high-banked mill pond (with by-pass sluice in right bank) it enjoys an almost unlimited supply from the 40–acre Reservoir which Mr. Purssell's ancestors and others had built to supply this and Walton Mills, which may also have been in the family at the time. The Canal Cut had, of course, impoverished the stream and this probably led to the building of the reservoir; but the latter was not tapped, the flow over the top of the sluice being sufficient after Walton Mills were power driven, although Mr. Purssell opened the sluice in time of drought, until 1940 when he found the Canal Co. had got there first and taken the water. This appeared to be illegal but the Company produced a document proving they bought the mill rights when the canal was built.

Water is fed to the wheel housed in the south end of building, by a wooden pentrough; and so high is the mill pond that the flash is immediately beneath the upper floor with the rack carried upwards to a screw with double tommy bars near the millstones – a very handy arrangement. Measuring 11ft. diameter by 4ft. 9ins., the wheel is an eight armed unventilated iron overshot with 3¼ins. orifices to its 36 buckets, the latter being 13ins. deep; and the sole plate is in 18 segments. The square section axle had 4ins. journals; and the wheel is older than it looks, for Mr. Purssell's father could not recollect it being installed. In the event of too great a rush of water, it spills down the back of the wheel, which seems to show that the pentrough is a bit short. Once or twice the wheel has stopped with a head of water behind it, and Mr. Purssell has found it to be due to the stones being choked with a paste formed by wet beans being ground. His remedy is to ease off the stones a bit and put some maize through to clean them.

All the machinery except the upright shaft is of conventional iron pattern; but the teeth of the large six-arm pit wheel are of oak; whilst those of the great spur, with eight arms, are 40 year old beech,

Weston Turville Mill

and are suffering from dry rot. Three pairs of stones are arranged in the usual manner with bridge-trees adjusted by crank handles through bevels; and the iron nuts are on jack-rings. A layshaft from the crown wheel has a belt driving the iron sack bollard in a sub floor, with wooden chain [?] pulley in roof-ridge; another shaft, sliding longitudinally into engagement, runs the other way to drive a kibbler by means of a hollow wooden drum built around an iron centre.

An interesting curiosity in the mill, which speaks for its antiquity, is a secret brew-house – a sort of cupboard containing an oven – only approachable by a little window in the wall of the wheel room, where no-one would find it unless they searched every inch of the mill!

Only a small amount of grist work on odd lots of barley, etc; for the farm is now carried on, but the whole premises retain their old world atmosphere, being surrounded by muddy tracks, lined with ancient elm trees, with a fine example of an old-time thatched cart-hovel; and the place is a happy hunting ground for the artists who visit the village for the picturesqueness of its cottages and fruit orchards and gardens, a painting of the mill itself having been exhibited in the Royal Academy.

BIERTON with BROUGHTON – 1½ n. E. of Aylesbury   ?

Broughton Mill – 1⅛ m. S.E. of Church   Standing Disused

Maps 1768, (1809), 1824, (1847), 1870, 1875, 1887, 1914, 1926

Broughton Mill is unique amongst Buckinghamshire mills, so far as I have discovered, in having what the Bucks millwrights call an "eleven o'clock" wheel; in other words a semi-overshot, or "pitch-back" in which the water is applied by a pentrough stopping a little short of the top of the wheel, so that the water goes down the back instead of over the top.

Constructed entirely of iron with eight-armed centres in two pieces bolted together and 48 buckets, it has continuous sole plates without ventilation; diameter 12ft. and width about 6ft. The axle rests on a bearing immediately inside the pit-room, the pit-wheel being on the end of the axle without further support; it is 10ft. diameter, in two pieces and engages iron to iron with the wallower. The 6ft. great spur, eight armed in one piece with cogs of wood, drives two pairs of stones, controls for which are individually arranged, so that the southern pair, now missing, might have auxiliary drive in dry weather. The stone-nut for this pair was engaged by a long lever and yoke with chains; and the large, round iron spindle extended down to an iron bridge-tree, almost on the floor; with its inner end in the pit room and coupled at its outer by a long rod up to a tentering screw. The iron bevel for receiving a drive from outside the mill is near the bottom of the spindle, with a hand wheel and sliding ring resting on an iron bridge in the small space between bridge-tree and floor. passing across the pit room just below this stone-nut is a long rod controlling the "flash" in the pentrough, with a hand wheel at its free end, in the mill proper.

The other stone-nut is controlled by the customary jack-ring upon an iron bridge-tree which is unusually close beneath the nut, with a little vertical screw set in its free end connected by bevels to a tommy wheel in the mill. The mortice-gear crown wheel, of light construction drives a line-shaft carrying wooden and iron drums for the sack-gear and the other machines, which are missing, the former being in the sub-floor as at Weston. A large wooden bollard with strakes, had a chain running along the roof ridge; and each pair of stones was fed by three spouts leading down from various open bins ranged along the roof aisles.

An advert of 1829 showed the mill to have been entirely refitted with new iron wheel and all new machinery – doubtless the same that is there now; a bolting mill and small dressing machine are mentioned, but not auxiliary power, and one wonders whether the present arrangement of gear for the stone in question is a later alteration. Probably Messrs. Gilbert of Leighton fitted out the mill, for they did the repairs latterly.

Layout of waterways is interesting. The main stream passes west of the mill (which is south of lane and the most westerly building in Broughton, with house and barns built on to it).The mill-pool is embanked to bring it to a much higher level, with a weir discharging down a broad slope; nevertheless the great John Kearsley Fowler (*Echoes of Country Life*, 1892), records that in the presence of several hunting celebrities his own horse cleared this mill-head with a clean jump of 29ft. 6ins. Later, at the end of an unprecedented hard course over ploughland with several "bullfinchers" (very tall thick hedges) another horse cleared 34ft. 7ins. – front toes to back heels – at the same mill-head.

Between weir and mill is a sluice leading to a brick culvert into which the overflow from the weir also enters, and the culvert then discharges into the river. The mill-tail passes beneath the roadway in front of the mill ere rejoining the main stream.

Isaac Wheeler was the miller in 1798; Francis Farmborough a century ago; followed by John Price, James Gilbert, and Richard Fowler (listed in Western Turville because he had inherited Broughton Farm in Weston from J.K.F, whose father purchased it in 1837); then for many years William Bates had the mill, the square front of which with red brick walls and slate roof belies its age, as at Weston. Mr. Bates did a good business and was in occupation until work ceased about 1930; then the mill stood idle, but it is now occupied by Mr. Grace who kindly admitted me to the mill, in which he found accommodation for his building business.

There has existed a mill in Broughton since Domesday, when its value was 10/- and in the extant of the Manor of Broughton Parva in 1296 a watermill is listed. The Abbey of Missenden held a mill at Broughton which had been granted to it before 1330; and in 1721/2 a mill is quoted in connection with Abbots Broughton.

AYLESBURY

[*?Bear Brook*]

Walton Mill – 5 f. E. of Church)

Working
Maps 1768, (1809), 1824, 1875, 1887, 1926

Historians do not seem to have been kind to the watermills of Aylesbury; indeed we have nothing but a few casual references to them until modern times. Nevertheless, two mills existed there at Domesday and very probably Walton Mill is of early date. First mention of it seems to be on December 12th, 1662, when the Parish Register contains the following entry:- "An infante childe of Thomas Parsons died and was buried the 15th of the same; there was a verie great snow and a flood which was the cause they could bringe itt no sooner; they lived at Walton Mill".

On May 18th, 1789, a riot took place along the London road not far from the mill, in the course of one of the corrupt elections for which the borough towns were famous. ("Votes for the Borough of Aylesbury and County of Bucks to be sold by private contract" says an advertisement of 1826)! Supporters of the candidates clashed and the Riot Act was read by a constable, who was rewarded with a black eye; and, arising from the riot, William Purssell, miller, of Walton Mill, and three others were summoned for assault, but no bill was found against them; William Purssell was still the miller in 1798, when he also had Walton Windmill.

A mishap was reported in 1827 when Mr. Purssell, Senior of Walton Mill was being driven in his cart and the horse shied and its driver was thrown out and sustained a broken rib. The following year Mrs. Grace

Walton Mill

Purssell of Walton Mill died, aged 80; and the burial in Castle Street Chapel is recorded of William Purssell, aged 82, in 1838. Meanwhile Joseph Purssell was selling up in 1836, advertising a capital millers wagon and mill implements and tackle. Exceptionally fine and well-known horses "which have bred some of the best horses in the nation" and the water-mill itself was to let by tender the following year.

Probably Joseph is the Walton miller referred to by J.K. Fowler, who says he was a big burly man and overseer of Aylesbury parish during a great wrangle over church rates about 1835. Purssell called on J.K.'s father and was so abusive that J.K.F. seized a hunting crop and gave the miller a good beating up. Perhaps it is as well at this juncture to mention that the Purssells of Wendover and Weston are not aware of any family connection! In 1843 the premises were described as: "this New and well-situated Walton Steam Flour Mill, offered by private contract on 20 years unexpired lease. Machinery new erected, at large expense with first-rate modern engine of 8 h.p. driving 2 pairs stones 4ft; with flour machine and jogging screen complete, of sufficient power to drive saw-mill also. Partnership subsisting for some time between Henry Woodman and James Gilbert is now dissolved". The Gilberts had been millwrights in Walton since 1790 at least, and continued there many years later. By 1850, Thomas Jefferay was the miller but he did not remains so long, and he was followed by Claudius Hill, son of John Hill of Aylesbury Mills, A.P. Scrivener and Henry Gunn, who left in the 'nineties. Scrivener's niece married Raban of Stone Windmill and had the disposal of it eventually. Messrs. Hills & Son followed and the son joined

forces with Mr. Partridge, who had managed Marlow Corn Mill for Smith; and Messrs. Hills & Partridge remain there today.

In years gone by the mill, now incorporated amongst a group of red and yellow brick buildings, mostly slate-roofed with a tall grain tower, south of Park Street, was driven by a broad overshot wheel about 8ft. diameter by 8ft. tread, with the usual pit wheel and upright-shaft arrangement. Two pairs of stones were water-driven, and Scrivener put in three more pairs with an engine; but Messrs. Hills and Partridge had just taken out the wheel and some gear when Mr. Cripps was there for awhile during the Great War. A 3½-sack roller plant was then installed with a gas engine, and the wheel house accommodated pumps for raising water for the wheat-cleaning apparatus. The mill-pond was filled in and nicely planted out as a garden; the wheat stones were replaced by two pairs of composition stones with circular furrows, for pig meal, and one pair composition for barley meal, the old upright-shaft still being used for driving one pair of stones. Later a 5-sack plant with bigger rollers was installed and the spouts and conveyors for the previous plant being now inadequate, they were altered; more recently a 7-sack plant has been set up, gas being employed for power.

Mr. Cripps was engaged at an aircraft hanger factory in 1918, but on visiting Aylesbury Market after the Armistice he found Mr. Partridge looking for him and was asked to do some stone dressing and other work at the mill, but did not resume regular work there.

The river comes in *under* the Canal without making connection with it until below Park Street, where a cross cut maintains the correct levels.

Pumping Mill – 3f. S.E. of church

Working
No map reference

The smallest working water-wheel in Bucks is probably Mr. A. Harvey Taylor's ornamental wheel in his garden adjoining Canal Wharf of which he is the proprietor; and no one passing down Walton Street would suspect the size and beauty of this garden modestly hiding behind a brick wall. Situated south east of the Wharf it contains an excellent bathing pool and, principally to feed this, an overshot wheel entirely of iron and some 3ft. diameter by 9 or 10ins. breadth, is fed by a 4ins. pipe from the canal weir against the tow-path with an extension nozzle which carries the water straight over the top of the wheel when at rest. Thence the tail-water returns to the foot

of the weir, making the apparatus simple and automatic, except for pulling the nozzle off the pipe when power is required.

Having passed beneath the railway, this overflow skirts the Printing Ink Works (enlarged from Hazell's original printing works building which has been described as a "disused silk mill", but appears to have been the damask weaving works erected in 1865). The wing straddling the stream and resembling a wheel-house is an addition placed there to utilize an old cart-bridge for a floor; the looms were probably treadle operated, and the chimney until recently served the fires under the varnish vats.

Brook Mill, Spittle Mill or *Aylesbury Mills* – Nearly ¼ m. S.W. of Church

Disused
Maps 1768, (1809), 1824, 1832,
(1847), 1870, 1875, 1926

The mill stream in Aylesbury, according to Robert Gibb's *History of Aylesbury with its Borough and Hundreds* (1880), is artificial and of comparatively modern construction; and it helps to obliterate the site of Grey Friars Monastery, one of the most notable early institutions of the town. Certainly the section around the railway goods yard is artificial, and it is joined by the canal overflow below the by-pass, which is a short loop between mill and railway line. A water company planned in 1858 to supply Aylesbury town from the Mill Stream, which seems also to have been called Bear Brook or the Common River. Just above Spital Bridge, on the Oxford road, the stream for many years turned the wheel of Aylesbury Mills or, as they seem to have been called until recent times, Spital Mill (probably acquiring the name from an adjoining "Spital" or leper hospital.)

In the fourth part of the Aylesbury Parish Registers, dating from 1701, the name of Impey appears as a miller, without specifying an individual mill. The *Poll of Electors* in 1802 and 1804 etc.; gave various Aylesbury millers, but some seem to have been employees, and the first authenticated proprietor is Thomas Hoar (probably related to the Wendover Hoars) who had Aylesbury Mill in 1791. John Hoar had them for 30 years, and Thomas Turpin until 1840. An assessment for the parish in 1831 quoted Spital Mill at £30. Millers named Moores and Gadsden were followed by John Hill & Son after the half century; and George, the son, was in charge in 1871 when Ben Burton went to work there after his grand-father's death at Whitchurch, in succession to William Rose, who then took Haddenham Old Postmill on his own account. Two other sons of John Hill were Augustus and Claudius, who had Bassetbury Mill, High Wycombe.

The present Aylesbury Mill is approached by Mill way, which is a short cut to the railway bridge on the Oxford road from Green End (bottom of Castle Street), and it is a tall Victorian building of yellow brick, slate-roofed, part three-floored and part four-floored, (1897), with a projecting sack loft; and adjoined by a dormered and tiled mill house. In George Hill's time a 10ft. overshot wheel was in use;

and a very fine sweet running overhead beam engine was installed, four pairs of stones being employed. Driving a single cylinder, the engine worked by a low pressure boiler at 60 lbs, these each have their own buildings separate from the mill proper, and the drive being conveyed by a 9ins. double belt. Work here was very hard and hours very long – 5 a.m. to 8 p.m. and Mr. Burton being small and young, (he was 17) was obliged to leave after nine months. He joined his Uncle Jabez who took North Marston Windmill mainly for Ben's benefit. John Terry, a farmer's son, succeeded George Hill, who retired in 1874 but Joseph Rogers from Park Mill, Risborough shortly took the mills and had a roller plant put in by Henry Simons, driven by steam and water. Later he put in a compound condensing engine by Robinson of Rochdale, who also remodelled the roller plant.

Edward Philip Collier acquired the business early in the present century; and he took out the condensing engine and installed a suction gas engine in conjunction with water power, until about 1917, when he discarded gas and switched to town elec-tricity. In 1907 Mr. A Hervey Taylor, became Collier's foreman for about five years; and one of Mr. Cripp's sons, who had also worked at Walton Mill served under him before going to Cuddington watermill. Mr. Taylor then forsook milling to take the Canal Wharf with its fleet of barges; and in about 1930, after the death of Mr. Collier, much of the machinery was sold, some to Mr. Boddington at Cuddington who resold it at auction and the Hadsphaltic Construction Co. Ltd. now occupy the building.

Two mishaps, which might have proved more serious, may be recounted, one in Mr. Burton's time and one in Mr. Taylor's. One day when the hoppers ran out of grain, a man who went to open the sluice was detained on the way, with the result that the mill-stone, gathering speed and running hot, suddenly burst; but no-one happened to be in the danger zone.

Mr. Taylor's adventure occurred whilst he was looking for a hole in the "silk" with a candle, the electric light having failed at the time. The flour dust being suddenly ignited by the naked light, there was an explosion, but Mr. Taylor fortunately escaped injury.

Spitell Mill – 500 yds. S.W. of Church

Gone
No map reference

Just below the present Aylesbury Mill is the probable site of a very early mill, mentioned *in V.C.H. Vol. III* in connection with "Spitilbrugge" which, the *History* observes is "probably the site of Spitell Mill, a watermill destroyed before 1477".

Later the Aylesbury Silk Mills were established in Oxford Road, steam and treadle operated, in conjunction with Tring Silk Water Mills; and they worked into the eighties. Other branches of this silk weaving concern were at Waddesden and Whitchurch, also steam-driven; and it is interesting that Mr. Nixon erected his Aylesbury looms in 1834 in a building provided by the parish on condition he employed only parishioners, but fires occurred in his mills, probably of a malicious origin.

HARTWELL – 1½ m. S.W. from Aylesbury)

[*Bear Brook*]

Haydon Mill – 1m. N. of church

Standing disused
Maps 1768, 1793, (1809), 1824, 1834, (1847), 1870, 1875, 1887, 1914

Approach to Haydon Mill is *via* Weir Lane or Raban's Lane – a small turning west of the Aylesbury – Bicester road (Akeman Street); and in the lane is a pool at which according to tradition the harts in Hartwell Park used to slake their thirst, although in 1865 complaints were made to the Aylesbury Board of Health about the offensive state of Haydon Mill Stream – fish were poisoned and cattle would not drink the water! From the mill onwards to Hartwell House is a beautiful mile – 150ft. wide double avenue of trees, ash, oak, elm, lime, beach, chestnut, sycamore, walnut and white poplar.

Sir Henry Lee whose family had the estate for a great many years lost a flock of 3,000 sheep and cattle at Quarrendon in a great flood c. 1570, which must have heavily flooded Haydon Mill, this part of the Vale being particularly vulnerable in wet seasons. Another great flood occurred on October 30, 1823 when 70 sheep were drowned close by the mill; and it was said that a greater wind had seldom been known and the fall of snow was immense. On November 20, 1852 says Gibbs who noted the above event, inundations in many parts of the country were unparalleled; no such floods had happened within recollection, and damage was very great.

At Domesday a mill at Hartwell was valued at 8/- and in 1300 Heydun Mill belonged to Hartwell Manor, as it still does. An early Parish Register records that "On the 16th February 1673 William Oviatt, the miler, of Hedon Mill, was buried, who died att the Grayhound, with a blow of a man's elbow, being a quarrilinge coward". Oviatt continued to be a common name in the parish for the next century or two. In 1808 William Watkins of Haydon Mill was convicted of retailing spirit without a licence, to farmers while washing sheep at his mill; the magistrates said this was becoming a common practice amongst millers but was illegal! The building was referred to as Edon Mill in 1823; and the same year Mr. Loosly of Aydon Mill was prosecuted for breaking down the side gate at Stonebridge Gate Toll – Stonebridge or Stannebridge being on the Bicester road, Holman's on Buckingham road and Glasyer's Bridge at Walton. The present name Haydon is probably the correct spelling since it is derived from Scandinavian "Ha" – high, because Haydon Hill overlooks the river. In an 1835 directory it appeared as Heydon Mill.

The Loosly family remained for many years; Richard Loosly died aged 73 in 1867, and William Raban became proprietor. He first went from Stone Windmill to work for Loosly or Loosley, and on the latter's death the executors found Raban on friendly terms with Loosley's daughter, so they moved her to a relative's farm at Princes Risborough, but Raban followed and, in the best story-book manner, he got her out of the bedroom window at dead of night and married her! He then came into Haydon Mill property, working both this and Stone Windmill, but the story book flavour continued to haunt his life, for eventually he fell upon bad times and drowned himself in the millpond.

Joseph Rogers worked the mill by water and steam in the 'nineties; followed by R.S. Norman, W. H. Newman, and Frederick Henley (1928). Mr. Watson, a farmer, is the present occupier, but probably the

Hartwell Mill

mill has not worked since Henley's time for it was, in 1939 in a very dilapidated state.

Haydon Mill is a square neutral-coloured brick and slate building with a brick wheel-house and an engine-house and chimney at one side; and although some fine old machinery remains, the building has not the appearance of age.

A good 11ft. all-iron breast wheel 8ft. 3ins. across the tread, drove the mill. Constructed by Gilbert's of Leighton, it has three sets of eight flat-sectioned arms secured to butt-jointed shrouds of eight segments, and is upon a square axle. The 44 unventilated buckets are more tangential than usual and consequently not curved at the lip; they are bolted to flanges on the shrouds – not rivetted. A conventional all-iron pitwheel drove the wallower upon a heavy old

upright-shaft and below the wallower is a smaller bevel, driven from the engine which is now missing. Below the latter cog, a belt drive was taken direct off the upright shaft itself to a very large, long set of centrifugal governors which appear to have controlled one of the bridge-trees, but some gear and the mill-stones have been missing several years. Close above the wallower is a fine old all-wood clasp-arm wheel of 9 or 10ft. diameter which drove two pairs of stones.

A long by-pass runs north of the mill, whilst the main river joins the Wendover stream in a little over half-a-mile. Although only a mile and a half from the County Town, Haydon Mill, owing to its isolated position, is probably as little known as any in the district.

ASTON CLINTON – 3 m. W. from Tring

Aston Clinton Stream

Early Mill – 1f. S.S.W. of Church

Gone
Maps – 1824, 1834

One mill worth 5 ores of silver (6/8d) was listed in "Domesday"; in the 13th century Robert son of Martin held the mill from William de Paris; whilst a watermill was appurtenant to the Manor when it was later held by the Earl of Salisbury.

In 1501 the mill was in so completely disrepair that no tenant could be found to take it, but by 1520 this had been remedied and a new tenant was in possession. Mark Fenner of St. Leonards in Aston Clinton, was presented in 1699 for "turning the water out of the water-course which feedeth Thomas Kingham's Mill", but the indictment was found "not to lye before the Court". Thomas Kingham was still the miller in 1706, when he was fined ¼d. for trespass; and Richard Slaughter was the miller in 1798. The Manor included a water cornmill and house at a sale in 1836, but there has been for a long time no mill in Aston Clinton because the Rothschilds destroyed the last one 80 or 90 years ago in the course of "beautifying"

the landscape; for with the exception of Miss Alice de Rothschild, the site of a homely mill seems to have been offensive to the family.

Approached by a picturesque green lane skirting the churchyard and bending southwards into the park land, the site is still marked by the remnants of an orchard (adjoining O.S. 259) which probably belonged to the miller; and a bank alongside what is left of the stream called Mill Bank. Two springs, called Well Head and Cold Bath Spring, arose near the present Howard Park Hotel and fed the mill which, with the mill cottages, was remembered, an old inhabitant told me, by his mother in her younger days.

The stream meanders through the village and along towards Broughton Mill, to join the Wendover Stream opposite a row of Victorian cottages called Normill Terrace, on the Aylesbury road. "Normill" is a name of over 100 years standing, the origin of which seems to be unknown.

STOKE MANDEVILLE – 2½ m. N.W. from Wendover

Stoke Mandeville Stream

Stoke Mandeville Mill – Approx. ½ m. S.E. of church

Gone
Maps 1768, (1809)

Although a mill is quoted in Domesday, value 10/-, the moiety of the Manor to whom it was afterwards appurtenant does not appear; but in 1628 Edward Brudenell held the whole manor and the watermill.

In 1798, Archelias Bennen (Benion?) was the miller; and in 1846, household goods were auctioned by Mrs. Bennion, who was leaving the mill; no doubt she was widow of Thomas Bennion, miller in 1830. Mr. Bennett, corn-miller advertised in 1853 –

"Mr. Bennett of Stoke Mandeville, desirous of receiving tenders from persons to contract for the re-building of a water-mill and cottage adjoining,

situated at the above place, and in his own occupation"

– and this probably was the swan-song of Stoke Mandeville Mill. The building in question is just remembered by old inhabitants although they cannot remember its appearance. It belonged to and stood a little westward of Stoke Farm now called Stoke House, where the mill pond yet remains; and the stream which tradition says was diverted from another course in order to serve the mill, joins the Wendover Stream immediately below Haydon Mill.

GREAT AND LITTLE KIMBLE – 2m N.E. from Princes Risborough   *Elmbrook* or *Ford Brook*

Marsh Mill – 2⅛ m. almost N. of Church

Disused
Maps –1768, 1793, (1809), 1824, 1834,
(1847), 1870, 1875, 1887, 1914

Great and Little Kimble parishes were combined in March 1885, the hamlet of Marsh having previously been in Great Kimble, although Little Kimble lies in the direct line between Great Kimble and Marsh Mill.

Domesday Survey records only a mill at Little Kimble (Chenebllle Parva) value 16/-, from which one imagines it would have been a watermill. Absence of further reference and the appearance of a medieval mill at Great Kimble suggests this might be one and the same mill, the discrepancy being perhaps attributable to a change in the parish boundary. Mr. Pick, owner of the present mill tells me the stream has no name and is definitely not Bonny Brook (which is a tributary of it); and I somewhat arbitrarily adopt Elmbrook, the name of a farm just above the mill, or Ford Brook as it is sometimes called at Dinton and Ford.

A pool resembling a mill pond in the grounds of Lady Mead House in Little Kimble, is the chief source of Elmbrook, but it probably never had a supply of water which could drive a mill. The medieval mill mentioned was granted by John, son of Hugh de Kimble in the 13th century to Gilbert Martel, who in turn granted it to the Abbey of Missenden. Martel held the mill in return for homage and service and 1lb. of pepper, paid yearly at Michaelmas; and for all services except the foreign service due to the King from two acres of land. The Abbot held it as a sub-tenant of Martel, paying 6d. a year for the mill, and all the land belonging to it.

Nothing further seems to be recorded of this structure, which is not specifically described as a watermill, although the above particulars suggest a building of some importance; the next item that comes to light, apart from mention of Francis Clark as miller of Great Kimbell in 1690 and John Hussey in 1798, is no less than 500 years later, when John Langston appears as the miller of Marsh in 1835, of Great Kimble in 1852, and of Marsh Green (that part of Marsh nearest the mill) in 1853 all the same mill

of course, but the deeds show that the present mill existed in 1805, when it changed hands from Apsley Manor. Joseph Taylor, who had Waddesdon Steam Mill, later worked Marsh Mill for Joseph Rogers; and the latter sold it to Peter Higgins who remained there for 47 years. Upon his death at the age of 84, in 1831; his son carried on for 18 months then disposed of the mill to Mr. T. S. Pick.

A curious little structure is this mill, the lower floor is of old brick and the upper, which alone projects above the banks of the long mill-dam, is tarred wood, with a shallow hip-gable roof of slate. The wall facing the yard is partially rebuilt to make it more serviceable, the building having fallen into a poor state. Probably the mill pond was heightened when the present wheel was installed in 1870, for the previous wheel, of wood, is believed to have been of breast type, whilst the new one is an 11ft. overshot. Built of iron in six segments it is 3ft. 8ins. wide with 36 closed buckets, which would probably be improved by a little ventilation, for Mr. Pick has noticed a slight sucking when the wheel is running; on the other hand he finds it is practically self-regulating as regards speed, because if running fast the buckets do not fill owing to being carried over into an almost tangential plane (with centre stay-bolts between) thus pointing almost directly at lip of trough; and speed is thus automatically reduced. The six-armed mortice gear pit wheel is small – only about 6ft; the wallower and octagonal upright shaft are iron; the great spur similar in design and size to the pit-wheel; and the two stone nuts, driving wheat and barley stones, are iron.

A lever-operated flash is within the mill, on first floor, as at Weston Turville; and a steam engine drive came in from outside, *via* a belt drum and shaft to the crown wheel. A layshaft from the latter drove the sack-bollard in the roof, cleaner and shaker on first floor and more recently, a 500 rev; dynamo on ground floor for lighting the adjoining dairy. The stream is by-passed on to the Aspley House streamlet.

DINTON – 3 m. S.W. from Aylesbury

[Thame ?]

Domesday Mills – Site unknown

Gone

Dinton (Danitone) Manor had a mill of 4/- value, in possession of Odo. Bishop of Bayeaux (brother of William I), and the mill was held by Helto, probably a native Saxon left undisturbed as a tenant (*Records of Bucks. Vol. IV*). The adjoining parish of Opetone, now Upton on the same parish, a village of Earl Harold's, answered for 18 hides, and also had a mill valued 4/- with a fishery.

Dinton parish extends to the River Thame in the north and is almost cut in two by the Ford Brook which runs from east to west; but the location of Eythrope Mill adjoining the Dinton boundary, with Beachendon Mill probably just below it, renders the chances of another mill on this piece of the Thame rather remote, and so it is possible they were horse-mills.

HADDENHAM – 2½ m. N.E. from Thame

[Branch of Thame]

Scotch Grove or *Stotsgrove Mill* – 1½ m. W.S.W. of Church

Working
Maps –1768, 1793, (1809), 1824, (1847), 1870, 1875, 1887, 1914, 1926

As mentioned under Cuddington, two mills stood in Nedreham at Domesday of which one probably was the predecessor of Scotsgrove Mill, or Scotch Grove as Bryant has it, (in Haddenham parish) at the end of a long winding green lane, off the Aylesbury – Thame road, near the junction with the old direct road from Haddenham; and this was presumably the watermill in Haddenham granted for 40 years to Richard Beake by James I (1603–1625).

Before the Machinery Riots, this was a paper-mill – proprietor John Wetherley – preparing pulp for making up at Lower Winchendon as already mentioned; and details of the machinery in those days are covered to some extent by the advert. quoted under Winchendon. Robert Wells had Scotsgrove Mill in 1798; Thomas Saunder, 1840, then for many years Daniel Freeman worked the mill for corn and flour; Charles Burton went there from Wendover Windmill to work for him in 1855 but left after three years to take Quainton Towermill. Later Charles W. Freeman was the proprietor for a great many years, and his sons Henry and Percy are now in charge.

Steam power was used for a long period, an old local-built beam engine being employed.

The somewhat austere walls of the mill are partly stone and part brick, with engine room and chimney one side, house and store rooms north, and stream passing beneath the other end, split in two only as it passes the building with sluice and grid at the corner.

Other loop streams, providing relief from flooding are across the Oxfordshire border, which follows the Ford Brook from Aston Sandford until the Thame is joined a mile below Scotsgrove Mill, the River Thame then becoming the border.

The wheel is a 14ft. all-iron breast-shot about 7ft. wide of unusually light construction, with eight arms, a square shaft and ventilated buckets; and it is thought to have replaced a wooden breast-wheel some 50 years ago. Formerly the new wheel showed an inclination to "tail-up" and choke, but there was an improvement after the river was cleaned, about 1936, for the first time in living memory. A large mortice gear pit-wheel drives the usual wallower, great spur and two pairs of stones; and crown wheel with layshaft for small machines and the sack-gear. The great spur is unusual in having only the arms of iron, the felloes as well as the cogs being of wood; the stone-nuts are iron, on jack-rings.

The party wall between mill and house is of "witchert" (wattle and daub) and has a curious little "squint" through which the miller can watch flour coming down whilst he is in the house; and the roofs are tiled. Although still operating by water power, little work is done as compared to the "good old days" when one 4 wheeled and three 2 wheeled carts were sent out on delivery every day.

On the far side of the green lane from the mill is Mill Field.

Haddenham Mill

ELLESBOROUGH – 2 m. W.S.W. from Wendover   *Bonny Brook*

Ellesborough Mill – 3 f. N.W. of Church

Gone
Maps –1768, (1809), 1824, 1875, 1926

Of the various little streams in Ellesborough, Bonny Brook, which joins Elmbrook north of Kimble Station turned a mill until 1933 or 4 when a fire unfortunately gutted the building. Bonny Brook House (to which the mill site belongs) stands at the corner of the mill lane; and local opinion is that this is Bonny Brook although the Ordnance has this name at the top of Elmbrook; Mr. Benyon, whose father and grandfather had the mill, consider it is Bonny Brook, and he says that some of their tail water went to Marsh Mill, for Mr. Higgins relied on Ellesborough Mill working and releasing some water. The Brook is fed by five springs, and has three mill ponds one above the other, each with a sluice; consequently the mill wheel would always turn, even if not very fast.

Mr. Benyon who very kindly supplied all the following particulars, believes the wheel was about

20ft. diameter; it was a 3ft. wide overshot of unusual construction – iron arm, elm felloes, steel cups, and an iron axle on brass bearings. It once had the timber work renewed (with oak, he believed) the old cups being re-used. A 2ft. wide wooden pen-trough with sluice mid-way along it, led in the water; and on the axle was a cast iron mortice-gear pit wheel, the cogs of which were stripped about five years before the fire, putting the mill out of action. The wallower, only all-iron wheel in the mill was on an iron upright shaft; the great spur was of wood, with deep cogs engaging with two stone nuts raised up and down by levers and yokes. Peak and burr stones were adjusted by bridge-tree and wheel control (no governors, auxiliary power never being used) but trade appears to have been small, the stones being dressed only about once a year; although the peak stones did all

120

the work, for flour was not made latterly and the power would not usually drive two pairs.

A crown-wheel on the second floor drove the machines and the sack gear, which had the usual belt drive with rope and lever control; but the winnower was on the stone floor. All the meal was delivered to bins – not direct to sacks; and if pressed for time in dry weather, grain was taken to Wendover Windmill.

Built of brick and slate, Ellesborough Mill was 3-storeyed, but small; and was joined to the house, and it bore no date of erection. After the fire, at which time the house was empty, the mill was cleared and used as a garage until the whole premises were demolished.

William Allen seems to have been the miller in 1699: a century later Joseph Johnson was the miller; and William Bray, of the *Bear and Cross P.H.* (Gt. Kimble) in the 'fifties: but thence onwards mill and farm were in the Benion family; William Benion in '64; John Benion later, and Edwin Benyon till the mill ceased work.

There seems to be no very early record of Ellesborough mill the site of which is between fields 227 and 231; and one is somewhat at a loss to know when it came into existence.

PRINCES RISBOROUGH

Risborough Stream

Culverton Mill – 5 f. S.S.W. of Church

Working

Maps –1768, (1809), 1822, 1824, (1847), 1875, 1887, 1914, 1926

Before embarking upon an account of the group of mills around Princes Risborough it should be explained that the term "Risborough Stream" is a purely nominal one which I have adopted for want of a recognised local name. Actually the stream in question is sometimes referred to near its source as the Culverton Stream, but there seems to be no accepted name lower down. Three streams of similar length meet near Longwick, and of these it is generally agreed amongst local millers that the Culverton Stream is the parent – perhaps because it is the strongest of the three – and I therefore place it first.

In 1317 a watermill at Culverton was mentioned in a settlement between Hugh de Culverton and John de Foxle; and in a conveyance of the Manor of Culverton in the 17th century a watermill went with it.

Culverton Mill stands a short distance up the Saunderton lane from Risborough; and the present building, chiefly of pink brick and slate and not particularly prepossessing, dates from 1844, having been built at the same time as Cuddington Mill by the same London firm, whose name seems to be forgotten; but Culverton Mill is the better of the two and is also much more serviceable than Park Mill with which it works in conjunction. The north end of the mill is older, however, and has not the same newness about the brickwork; but the white-boarded upper floor was added to it in 1923, in Cup Final week, for they remember the procession of trains passing whilst work was in progress.

Most of the mill machinery is in this old portion; and the stream passes through the end of it to drive an 18ft. all-iron overshot wheel, about 5ft. wide, with rather wide mouths – 4 or 5ins. – to the buckets. The very heavy 14ft. iron pit-wheel has twelve solid square section arms and a heavy rim; it is in two pieces with wooden cogs. The upright shaft, also very large, is an octagonal piece of timber with a big eight-armed mortice – gear spur driving three pairs, and the nuts are on jack-rings. Machines and sack-hoist are conventionally arranged; and a cog-ring is clamped to the underside of the great spur to receive the drive from a steam engine (since dispensed with) behind the mill, and an oil engine now augments the water power by driving one pair of stones.

Mr. Will Cripps, who did a lot of repair work here and at Park Mill, estimated that in a normal season the flow of water at Culverton was the same almost to a bucket every day; and with a lighter water-wheel than that at Park Mill (now replaced by a turbine) and much simpler and more direct gears, she was a nice mill to work. There were, he believed, about 7 tons of iron gears in Park Mill and it always had 4ft. stones; but at Culverton, when the foot-brass of a stone-spindle settled down so that the shoulder rested on the "pot" and the stones would not run, Mr. Cripps removed these stones, which were 4ft., and put in a pair of 3ft. 8ins. He then ground 24 sacks in 4 hours with 5 or 6 lbs. less head of steam than the 4ft stones required. Under water-power he ground 7 bushels more per day with the smaller stones and, as the water lasts 7 or 8 hours here, this represents about one bushel per hour more.

Culverton Mill

When the oil engine was put in at Culverton it was found possible to grind much more here with 3ft. 6ins. stones than with 4ft. stones oil-driven at Park Mill; and Mr. Cripps also noticed that in driving the large stones hard by steam, the furrows were gone in about four days!

In 1798 Thomas Winslow was the Miller; Robert Winslow was owner occupier a century ago, but he later let the mill to Edward Barnett; and a man named Russell is the first miller Mr. Cripps remembered here. He had a very bad time owing to a drought occurring as he moved in; but in August 1879 the terrific thunderstorm of the 2nd. and 3rd. surrounded Culverton, Saunderton and Park Mills with several feet of swirling waters. John Frost (1875 was miller to Thomas Williams who was established at

Culverton, Bledlow and High Street, Risborough; and Mr. Cripps said Frost was also a baker, and probably ran a shop in High Street for Williams, Frost being the brains of the business).

Later, John and Thomas East were at Culverton and they apparently installed the steam engine. Mr. William Silsby, who had worked the mill for Thomas East, bought it from him early this century and his sons are now working it by water and oil. Meanwhile Mr. Silsby took Monks Risborough Mill, and then Saunderton and Park Mills.

The Culverton or Risborough Stream rises at some good springs near Culverton Pitches – Pyrtle Spring, above the turnpike from Wycombe – and continues east of Risborough Station and beneath the Aylesbury and Birmingham lines to Park Mill.

Park Mill – 3f. W. of Church

Working
Maps –1768, (1809), 1822, 1824,
(1847), 1875, 1887, 1926

In addition to Longwick and Culverton Mills, a third mill is referred to at Princes Risborough in the 17th century; and this no doubt can be identified with Park Mill, which is in a sort of cul-de-sac on the Longwick road from Risborough Station, just west of the two railway bridges. All three mills are named by Bryant and Lipscomb, as are practically all the Aylesbury Vale mills which they depict.

In 1712, a watermill and a windmill are mentioned in the possession of the Dormer family, but particulars in the *County History* re ownership of the Park Manor are rather vague.

Park Mill formerly had a good overshot wheel 23 or 24ft. in diameter and fairly wide, which it is said would do twice the work of the present turbine, although the owners seem fully satisfied with the latter. The wheel was of iron, by Gilbert's of Leighton Buzzard, and had cast-iron arms, not rods as at Whitchurch. Probably it was the best of all Messrs. Gilbert's wheels, being very powerful and altogether satisfactory, except for the space it occupied, which is much less if a comparatively inaccessible vertical-spindle turbine is used; but accessible horizontal-spindle turbines do not save much space. Usually the wheel would run well with only half the water coming over the bar, and most people who had to do with it seem to have been better pleased with it than they were with the turbine or, as the local millers call the new-fangled device, the "churn".

Previously there had been a wooden wheel, but Messrs. Gilbert refitted practically the whole mill, putting in a new pit-wheel of uncommon design with back stays, believed to have been of ebony, behind the arms. The 12ft. great spur drove three pairs placed as usual, the waterwheel being at the east end of the building, stones etc. towards the middle and storage the other end, adjoining the substantial mill house. This is in the Georgian style, covered with ivy, with tiled roofs; and the mill, of warm red brick with iron clamps in the walls, is reputed to be the oldest of the Risborough mills as they stand today.

It seems that Mr. Silsby considered that the big wheel, rather than the 7 tons of gears and shafts, made the mill cumbersome in action, but as the huge great spur and the upright shaft etc., were taken out

as well as the wheel and axle-shaft, when converting to turbine, this is a debatable point. Few millers, I think, would agree that there is anything wrong with a big wheel if there is a head of water for it, but heavy gearing was discredited by Fairburn a century ago! The wheel never drove all three pairs of stones together, nor would any wheel on this little stream; and although it is complained the wheel used too much water, the millers downstream say that when the "churn" is driving even one or two pairs of stones, with light gearing, an abnormal quantity of water comes down, and at Longwick they have a good time with their mill-pond being filled faster than they use it!

Two pairs of stones have been retained, and the stone-nuts are now coupled to a belt-driven counter-shaft parallel with the spindle of the turbine, which is apparently of Pelton type, in the middle of the wheel-room, with an 18 ins feed pipe. From the other end of the countershaft is a belt up to a layshaft on the first floor, for driving the scoop elevator, chaff cutter and sack gear.

Thomas Grace was the miller here in 1798; and in 1850 the following rather quaint advert appeared:-

"The Partnership formerly subsisting between SAUNDERS NASH and ME, the undersigned ROBERT HUTT, as MILLERS, and the business of which Partnership is carried on at PARK MILL in the parish of Princes Risborough was dissolved, on and from 11 May 1849 and from that day the business has been carried on by me on my own private account at Park Mill aforesaid. Robert Hutt".

This partnership dated back some years but in 1858 the mill effects were for sale, Hutt being then deceased. Benjamin Darvill from Saunderton Mill had Park Mill next, before moving to High Wycombe; he was followed by T. & J. Young, Joseph Rogers (steam and water), Gurney Bros, and then Mr. Silsby. Joseph Rogers who went to Aylesbury Mills afterwards was listed at both mills in 1891; and he installed at Park Mill one of the earliest "centrifugals" in the district, for more efficient flour milling.

Long Wick or Longwick Mill – 1m W.N.W. of Church

Two local mills valued in "Domesday" at 14/8d probably were those that stood in Henry III's reign; or their predecessors. Geoffrey Neyrnut held one, of the "King of Almain" (Richard, Earl of Cornwall, lord of the Manor, who also called himself "King of the Romans" although he does not appear to have been king of anything); and the second he held of Richard de la Forde. Richard, Earl of Cornwall, by the way, once distinguished himself by taking refuge in a windmill at Lewes, Sussex, from some pursuers, who ironically hailed him with "Come out, you bad miller you who would have no meaner title than King of the Romans!" and a sarcastic ballad was later composed to commemorate the occasion of the mountebank's distress.

One of the above mills was probably upon the Longwick site; and Longwick Mill is named in the 17th century when William Hampden left it to his cousin, Richard Hampden. It stands back from the Lower Icknield Way on the bend just west of the G.W.R. line to Birmingham, although this bend is scheduled to disappear under "Be-kind to motorists" scheme. The memory of the mill will outlive the memory of the vandals, however, for there is something solid and workmanlike about our old watermills. For what purpose this 17th century Longwick Mill was used does not appear; but the present structure was erected as a paper-mill and used as such until a century or so back; it is marked Paper Mill on the 1768 and 1809 maps.

In May 1823 it was offered for sale by direction of the Devisees in Trust for the late Henry Pegg and it then comprised

"a Two-Vat paper-mill, worked by a powerful stream of 18ft. fall with Sal, Drying House, and Offices, Garden, Paddock and Meadowland, Cottages, etc., and convenient Paper Master's House. The whole of which is let on lease determinable at Lady Day 1823 to Messrs. William Cubbage Senr. and William Cubbage Jnr. at £200 per Annum"

Possibly Mr. Cubbage Jnr. then removed to West Wycombe where a William Cubbage was engaged in paper-making the same year; but Longwick Mill was still in the family when an incendiary fire occurred in an outhouse of the mill in 1829.

Meanwhile a preliminary sale was conducted from Bledlow and Longwick paper-mills in 1828, and two years later the equipment of Longwick Paper Mill was auctioned by direction of the Sheriff of Bucks:

"Machinery, household furniture and effects, valuable and modern paper machine, set of 3 copper drying cylinders in triangle order by Donkin (very superior), steam boiler of 4 h.p. and 7 large presses, large lead retorts and piping, cart, iron furnaces, overshot waterwheel 14ft dia × 8ft 10ins., pitwheel, flywheel, 3 capital beating and breaking engines, large chests, bins, boxes, scales, wts, 12 reams paper, rags, benches, stoves, trebbles stand and hair lines, pumps, cisterns, tubs, boards, planks, piping, etc."

Next item is a passing reference in 1835 to a 3 acre close of arable land at Longwick in Fulling Mill Field, and a century ago there was a Fulling Mill Farm at Risborough; these names were of very early origin for Fulling Mill Lane and Fulling Mill Water existed in 1693, when the inhabitants were indicted for not repairing the road from Chepping Wycombe to Bissester, in Longwick Field.

By 1840 William and Edwin Payne were occupying the building as a corn mill; and Edwin Payne was the proprietor till the present century; but William Silsby worked the mill by steam and water during the Great War. About 1923 Mr. George Gomme bought the mill from Mr. Thompson, the owner, and established himself in business there; and he and his son are still in charge. Edwin Payne did well there and he is believed to be the man who introduced American flour to the district; it came in barrels in sailing ships and was mixed with the English product.

Longwick Mill is considerably more powerful than the others around Risborough, with the advantage of being below the confluence of the three streams; it has a fine mill-pond, as will be seen from my illustration [not included, ed.] which is taken from the railway embankment, but the latter cuts right across the pond, the stream first passing from west to east under the embankment to one half of the pond, from which a conduit returns to the other half.

The all-iron overshot wheel, of similar dimensions to that of 1830 is eight-armed, and is in the east end of the white weather-boarded building, but the latter has been shortened at some time, and formerly reached right down to the by-pass 3 or 4 yards away. Machinery is conventional with mortice-gear pit and spur wheels and three pairs – two barley and one wheat; upright shaft, iron; stone nuts on jack-rings. Belt and cup conveyors are driven from the crown-wheel so that after the meal has descended to the ground floor it is carried up by the cups, thence by screw conveyor from back to front of mill (which is end on to the stream); and a series of spattles regulate discharge of meal into the various sacks. A layshaft drives down to a circular saw on ground floor and is also coupled to the conveyors, with another shaft across the end wall to which the yellow washed and tiled mill-house is attached; and this shaft drives the two large dressers by belt. Formerly a cleaner stood between bins and stones, and another elevator carried

meal up to the store bins.

Upright shaft was previously of deal, bit it rotted owing to water splashing where the gudgeon pin was let in; and Mr. Cripps, who repaired this and Park and Culverton Mills for Mr. Silsby, put strakes and "copses" round it, but five years later it gave way higher up. One of the old conveyors in the upper part of the mill over the mill-wheel, where the walls are formed of sliding louvre frames for paper drying, consists of a round iron shaft with a spiral steel web sprung into a continuous groove cut to receive it.

Longwick has now become an independent parish, because the people grew tired of Princes Risborough raising the rates and spending the money on itself, which is of course the usual practice wherever a town is able to levy rates on outlying hamlets.

SAUNDERTON – 1¼ m. S.W. from Princes Risborough

[*Risborough Stream*]

Lower Saunderton or *Bledlow Lower Mill № 409* – 1¾ m. N.W. of Church

Working
Maps –1768, (1809), 1822, 1824,
(1847), 1875, 1887, 1914

Bledlow Lower Mill or Bledlow Mill (Bryant) stands in the long narrow strip of Saunderton Parish which extended almost up to the parish of Ilmer until the 1934 revision of parishes; it is reached by the Bledlow Station road from Pitch Green, over the railway and right turn in front of a very picturesque timbered and thatched cottage, when the mill is found on our right, beyond the separate Mill House. It is a large cream painted and red brick structure somewhat disfigured by tarred, galvanised ironwork; and continuing along the lane we pass the still waters of the spacious mill pool.

Little early history is recorded of the mills in Saunderton, although several references occur in the 1820's but we may first mention that the tenant of Bledlow Mill in 1784 was Thomas Lovell; and Francis Fleetwood the freeholder; and two water corn-millers, Abraham Eustace and John Jarden operated in 1798. One of these no doubt had the mill, which Langley clearly stated to be a corn mill the previous year.

Early in 1823 there is a reference to a paper mill, not definitely named at Saunderton, when Francis Oliver was indicted for stealing a quantity of indigo bagging the property of William Pegg of Saunderton, paper-maker. Mr. Pegg said he bought the bagging for making paper and was the only person using it, as he bought the whole lot from the Custom House.

Between November and December 1822 he missed about 1 cwt. Of it from the mill. The foreman of Mr. Cubbage, paper-maker of Princes Risboreugh (Longwick Mill) said the prisoner tried to sell it to him. The case was proven and Oliver received 12 months.

In February, 1824, "Bledlow and Saunderton Paper Mills" were offered for sale: "A patent Machine works the stuff prepared by the Engines of both Mills. The Bleaching apparatus has been erected on the best principle and every Department of the extensive Manufactory is in perfect order for a tenant". This suggests that William Pegg operated the Bledlow North and Lower Mills, which generally worked together; and the following year he was described as "late of Bledlow, Paper Maker, an Insolvent Debtor". In 1830 the mills again on the market were described as "The Three Paper Mills of Bledlow and Saunderton, in occupation of James Philps". This means that Philps had Saunderton Mill near the Parish Church, as well as Bledlow North and Lower Mills, as confirmed by *Pigot's* the same year. Equipment included:-

"Complete paper machine, copper drying cylinders. 3 large water-wheels and other wheels attached to rag engines complete, 14 valuable large presses, 4 expansion pumps, 8 iron and copper

Lower Saunderton Mill or *Bledlow Lower Mill*

steam boilers and furnaces. Large quantity lead pipes and taps. Vats, chests, stoves, grates, boards, timber vessels, utensils 8000 bushels of ashes in 7 lots, extensive new shed etc., dwelling house, horses, carts, ricks, scales, wts, bricks, tools, tubs, 8 tons of printing and shop paper 20lb each, 200 reams of demy 15 lb each, 60 reams double crown 21 lbs each, 50 elephant 30 lbs. each. 50 small hand 14 lbs each, small quantity blue and other papers".

The North and Lower Mills were alone offered later in the year; and although it said they were two furlongs apart, the distance is five furlongs as the crow flies!

"Two Valuable Paper-Mills commonly called Bledlow Mills on excellent stream; the lower Mill is in the parish of Saunderton with drying rooms, large soll, rag-houses, stables dwelling, has been in full trade as paper manufactory up to the present time. The other mill, in Bledlow parish, 2 furlongs from the first, on the same stream, called North Mill, ample buildings, labourers' cottages, water sufficient and movement able to drive three pairs of stones. This machinery (except principal movements) may be taken or not by the purchaser. Freehold, with election vote for County of Bucks and Borough of Aylesbury. £300 per annum rent of both. Mr. Gilbert will show the premises and machinery"

Note the hint that the latter mill might be converted for flour milling, although actually it never was. Another advert. offered "Three powerful water-mills near Princes Risborough; would convert to any manufactory for safe tenant. All on same stream." John Stevens & Son were paper makers at Saunderton and Bledlow in 1842; but the following year saw another proposal for letting or selling both mills when rags, half-stuff, carboys of vitriol, and cylinder felts were advertised.

J.J. Sheahan said in 1862 "the North Mill is used in preparing rags, after which they are sent to the other (the more extensive mill in Saunderton parish) to be made into paper. Small Hand, Royal Hand and Elephant paper are made". George Austin, who also had Solesbridge and Mill End Mills, (Rickmansworth) had then been in occupation at Bledlow for some years; and the latter mills apparently became jointly known as No. 409. The business now goes by the name of H.J. Austin Ltd; and Lower Mill is chiefly engaged in making and printing paper bags for tradesmen's use, etc; the North Mill is idle, but there is some very interesting old paper-making equipment in both of them.

The all-iron 10ft. overshot wheel remains in the north end of lower Mill but pit-wheel and upright shaft which conveyed the drive from the former wooden water-wheel and axle to a pair of beaters, have been removed. The present wheel carries a small iron spur engaging with a pinion and shafting, from which a series of belts drive printing machines on the upper floor, where are also some electrically-driven paper-bag making machines.

Towards one end of the mill a continuous-roll paper machine similar to that at Marlow was formerly used; and there is still a very interesting old pulp-mixing vat built like a broad copper, about 8ft. diameter. It contains a central standard around which revolves a four-barred agitator shaped like half a gate or hurdle; and a horizontal shaft over the vat received a gear drive from another shaft now disconnected. From this vat pulp was pumped up through iron pipes to the chest for the machine.

In another department is a massive old Samson press standing 8ft. high; upon its solid base are huge uprights of timber at either end, and an iron upright in the middle, with a great beam across the top. The uprights carry iron channel guides for the two heavy wooden blocks which descend and compress the paper; and over each block is a big ratchet wheel with an iron ball a foot in diameter in which are holes for a very strong tommy-bar or pole. A heavy worm passes up through the top beam; and when 3 or 4 feet of paper is stacked on the base, two or three men screw down the press bit by bit.

Part of the mill where the continuous machine was housed was burnt a little before the Great War, in a fire which was fortunately kept in hand.

BLEDLOW – 1¾ m. S.W. from Princes Risborough)   [*Risborough Stream*]

The North Mill – 1½ m. N.N.W. of Church   Standing disused
Maps –1768, 1793, (1809), 1822, 1824, 1832, (1847), 1875, 1887, 1914

The North Mill, Bledlow, an unprepossessing square building of red brick with shallow roof of slate is situated picturesquely at the end of a winding cart-road, alongside which is the banked-up mill pond on our left. Across the stream, which disappears beneath the mill, is a pretty little half-timbered derelict cottage and a black-boarded barn with hip-gable roof of red galvanised, looking more like a watermill than the mill itself and closely resembling Ivinghoe Ford Mill.

The North Mill prepared rags for the larger mill just described; and most of the early references to the two mills have already been quoted; but a brief note about North Mill, which John Stevens occupied in 1840, is contained in Gibbs' *Local Occurrences Vol. II.* under the date Jan. 21, 1743:-

"North Mill was burnt down last night and a great deal of paper and other effects burnt belonging to

Mrs. Harman, widow; the next house, occupied by T Dorset, was also burnt".

Later tenancy down to the present day is, of course, the same as Lower Mill; and no doubt the present building dates from the year of the fire. The stream drives an all-iron 11 or 12ft. high-breast wheel with closely spaced buckets, which reaches almost up to the first floor, with usual straight rack-and-pinion "flash". From the end of the axle against the mill wall, a belt is taken to a shaft passing through to the black barn, for chaff-cutting, etc; and a two-piece mortice-gear 10 or 11ft, pit-wheel drives a small iron wallower wedged to a large upright shaft with a very massive old wooden great spur immediately *over* the first floor, instead of beneath it; teeth face upwards probably to drive layshafts, but the mill is kept locked. This is a very fine wheel, some 10ft. diameter with twin sets of six arms – *i.e.* one set above the other – and is an unusual piece of equipment. From one side of the pit-wheel a bevel-driven countershaft is carried out through the river bank, which is high against the mill-wall this side, and into a well-head where it drives a submerged pump in a well, sunk down through the river bank against the roadway into the ground below. This lifted water for the pulp vats presumably, through various large iron pipes some of which pass into the upper floor after bending down to form a settling sump. Over the stream as it passes into the building, is a trough for discharging used water back into the mill-stream, so that it then helps to drive the wheel.

The by-pass is behind the black barn, where it forms a pretty little ford at the entrance to the Common Leys fields.

ILMER – 2¾ m. W.N.W. from Princes Risborough [Branch of Thame]

Domesday Mill – Site unknown   Gone

Among the appurtenances of the Manor of Ilmer in 1086 was a mill probably the same water-driven structure that was found to be "broken and valueless" in 1328 and repaired in 1342/3. About this time the Bernard family and Sir John de Molyns held the Manor, but later inquisitions and the surveys of the economic state of the Manor, etc., in the 14th and 15th centuries do not record the mill, nor have my enquiries produce any result.

An obvious site is on a loop-stream which existed a century ago half-a-mile south-west of the Church, near the parish boundary; and the stream was, in those bygone days, followed by a cart road from North Mill to Towersey, which joined an ancient way from Ilmer to Coldharbour. Today (1939) all is engulfed in a wilderness of watery fields with sedges and mire; and not a habitation in sight – no wonder they sometimes spell it Illmire!

KINGSEY – 2¼ m. E. from Thame [Branch of Thame]

Kingsey Mill – ¼ m. S.S.W. of Church   Pumping wheel on site
Maps –1768, 1793, (1809), 1824, 1875

A little iron waterwheel beneath a culvert marks the site of Kingsey Mill, which in its time was in Bucks, (Bryant has both Kingsey and Towersey in Bucks, 1824) although the parish later became part of Oxfordshire but is now once more in Bucks, so that both corn-mill and pump merit a place in these pages. Meanwhile *V.C.H. Vol. IV*, refers vaguely to a water-mill being appurtenant to Kingsey Manor from the 14th to the 18th centuries.

The old cornmill which stood at the end of a stoney track diverging from the turnpike as one leaves the village for Thame, was one of the last three thatched watermills in Bucks, sharing the distinction with Notley and Padbury. A wooden breast-wheel was positioned inside the mill, driving three pairs, either 4ft. 2ins. or 4ft. 4ins., in spur gear, a good comple-ment for a mill which it seems was not very big. All or nearly all machinery was wooden, so the whole building must have been a fair example of old-time millwrighting. It is appropriate, therefore, that Henry Young, millwright and his celebrated uncle, Robert Young, who moved our old Buckinghamshire post-mills from place to place, eventually settled down at Kingsey some time before 1828; (John Winslow being the previous miller); and Henry remained there for 50 years or more being listed as late as 1877. He simultaneously worked Towersey Windmill, which he and his uncle had probably moved and reconstructed; but eventually abandoned this and carried on with the watermill. He lived till 1880 or later, at which time he was very old and must have been the last man able to remember the heydays of Buckinghamshire wind and water milling when it was worth while moving a windmill from one place to another. Henry Young is the man I would like to have seen more than any other miller of the last century, and it is of interest to recall that he was a relative of Mr. William Cripps' mother.

In 1828 it is recorded that Thomas Shepherd, servant of Mr. Young of Kingsey Mill, was charged with "riding in his master's wagon and refusing his name!" For some years till the 'nineties Thomas Way worked the mill, after which it stood idle a year or

Kingsey Mill

two until Squire Wykeham of Tythrop House demolished it. The mill at which flour was made within living memory, stood on the first stream encountered as we enter the fields from the cart lane, at the north corner of O.S. 88, farther southwards, diverging from main stream by a sluice and small tunnel or arch which probably accommodated a cartway.

On the mill site is a little red-brick and slate hutment spanning the stream and sheltering a very small six-armed iron over-shot wheel with 36 curved buckets, fed by an iron pentrough, with rack-operated "flash" at the point of ingress, instead of being over the wheel. This is towards one side of the stream; and on the axle shaft, the other end of which rests upon an iron girder, is a broad iron belt pulley the purpose of

which is not clear, and beside the "flash" is a wooden bollard with chain. The actual machinery, which pumps water to the farm buildings at Tythrop House, beyond the turnpike is in a small locked shed in the field; but the whole apparatus is somewhat of an anticlimax to the watermill of old, and one turns from the site wondering whether memories of the past would not be better served by a few foundation stones without the new pump-box.

The Risborough Stream which diverges into a veritable network of streamlets between Coldharbour and Kingsey, receiving Cuttle Brook from Wainhill Spring, and a rivulet from Longwick, eventually joins the Ford Brook a mile below Kingsey Mill, above Scotsgrove Mill.

SAUNDERTON – 1¼ m. S.W. from Princes Risborough   *Saunderton Stream*

Saunderton Mill – 1 f. N of Church   Slight foundations
                                                Maps –1768, (1809), 1822, 1824, 1875, 1926

Saunderton Mill is one of the few demolished in the county in recent years; it was not very serviceable but could quite well have been improved. The County Council, however, has been particularly active in promoting totally unnecessary road schemes in the Princes Risborough area, and so it had the mill removed to make way for another grandiose plan on the eve of the war when every available mill should have been restored to use.

In 1086 there were three mills in the parish, two valued at 8/- and held by Osbert of Milo Crispin, on the Manor of Saunderton St Mary; and one by the Bishop of Bayeaux at Saunderton St Nicholas. Until about 1457, two churches existed but the manors were combined eventually, and there is now only the Church of St. Mary and St Nicholas. In 1212 Roger de Saunderton and Margery, wife of Ravening, were concerned in an agreement about one-third of a mill; and thirty years later "one watermill at Saunterdon" was mentioned, but nothing further seems to be recorded for some 500 years.

That this was a paper-mill for many years is certain; Langley (*History of the Hundred of Desborough*) mentioned this in 1795, it is marked as such on the 1822 Ordnance and is locally known to have been a paper mill; and the upper wooden walls contained the sliding louvres which always denote a paper drying room. Joseph Philps had Saunderton Mills in 1830, but by 1843 they were almost certainly converted to corn, being then occupied by the Darvell family, who never appear to have been paper makers; indeed Ben Darvell was corn-milling here in 1853 (and is remembered to have been at Park Mill later as already mentioned). Thus we find Saunderton and Lower Mills (Austin's) exchanging duties about the time of the Paper Riots, and adopting trades more suited to the size of their respective streams.

William Gilbert, probably related to James and John Gilbert, the Princes Risborough millwrights in 1830, was the miller for a time, followed by William Bliss; then Ned Britnell from Bledlow Ridge Windmill, turned his hand to watermilling at Saunderton, later going to Lord's Mill at West Wycombe. Finally in 1895 William Silsby took the mill, remaining till it ceased regular work whilst still in good condition, early in the present century.

Mr. Silsby had worked for Thomas East at Culverton Mill, as mentioned, and took Monks Risborough Mill for a time before moving to Saunderton. Then he disposed of the latter mill and took Culverton and Park Mills, both now in his sons' hands. At one time also he rented Longwick Mill, which was bought over his head after the Great War; and he thus handled every mill in the Princes Risborough group. For a short time after Mr. Silsby left another man, whose name seems to be forgotten, worked Saunderton Mill, and installed a crown wheel and part of the upright shaft of Park Mill, which was extensively altered when a turbine was installed.

The old mill, demolished in September 1938, was an imposing weather-worn structure of old brick and white-painted wood, with tiled hip-gable roof. The actual mill was in the west end of the building, near the top of which there were apertures giving access to a dove-cot. A large but fairly narrow iron overshot wheel was fed by a wooden pentrough entering through the south wall; and it turned a fine 10ft. iron pit-wheel of unusual pattern for it had ten deeply webbed arms. The axle was a very large iron one, and a square iron upright shaft carried a mortice bevel gear above the wallower to receive the engine drive, with a conventional morticed gear spur, higher than usual above the bevel, recessed into the wall. Engine and water-wheel could, of course, be run in tandem with this layout, to drive the three pairs of stones. Probably this was very desirable for she was considered a poor mill with no head of water worth having, although the mill-pond is very commodious, of about an acre in extent. Standing on the right-hand side of the Risborough Lane, a little below the Church, and opposite the Three Horseshoes P.H. the mill was next to plot 113 and in front of 120. The millpond is fed by two short streams rising one near the Church and one by the railway line; and in half a mile the Horsenden fish-ponds and moat are met.

HORSENDEN – ¾ m. W.S.W. from Princes Risborough

[*?Saunderton Stream*]

Horsenden Mills – 100 yds. S.E. of church

Gone
No Map Reference

The Domesday Mill at Horsenden held by the Count de Moretain was of no value and possibly was demolished and not replaced for a long time, for no further mention of a mill occurs until the 16th century when the Cotton family of Gloucestershire had a watermill in the parish.

A survey of the Bounds of the Parish in 1620 recorded that they followed a hedge from Little Lane to Horsingdon Mill, "excluding ye mill, over or through a hedge . . . into an angle called Chedg Hill corner . . . and to a gate called Mill Close gate . . . and by a highway into ye end of the village of Ilmer . . ." etc. Land was advertised in Fulling Mill Field in 1792: and thirty years later two watermills were listed in connection with the Manor of Horsenden and Princes Risborough, of which only that of the former

is likely to have been in the parish. *Records of Bucks. Vol IV.* referring to "the Mill-bank" gives a clue to the mill's location, in describing the old road from Risborough to Thame *via* Horsenden as it was in A.D. 1700. The bank, it says, is alongside the terrace opposite the moat by the Church, and is encountered before that edifice is reached; it is therefore south of the church, on the left of what little remains of the present road, for the latter degenerates almost into a swamp and no longer provides a short-cut to Thame. Probably the watercourses were altered along with the roadway so the mill site is now lost. Midway between Park and Longwick mills, the Saunderton stream joins that from Culverton, and the Monks Risborough stream comes in on the other bank a little lower down.

MONKS RISBOROUGH – 5f. N.E. from Princes Risborough

Monks Risborough Stream

Monks Risborough Mill – 1 f. N.W. of Church

Some buildings left
Maps –1768, (1809), 1822, 1824,
(1847), 1875, 1887, 1914, 1926

Upon a small stream flowing from Askett, past Monks Risborough church to Alscott and Longwick (joining the main stream above Longwick mill) is Monks Risborough Mill House; the actual mill-building is demolished

No mention of a mill occurs in Domesday, but in the 14th and 15th centuries a millward was repeatedly presented to the Manor Court for taking excessive tolls from manorial tenants; and at the Dissolution of the Monasteries two mills at Monks Risborough were occupied by leasehold tenants.

Sir Jerome Horsey kept these in his own hands when he settled the Manor on his sons; and towards the end of the 16th century he died seized of a windmill and a watermill, both formerly a parcel of the Manor of Monks Risborough. This Manor belonged to the Bendictine Monks of Canterbury, hence the distinctive name of the parish, which had been called East Risborough until the middle of the 10th century.

Like most mills in the neighbourhood, Monks Risborough had an overshot wheel; in fact it seems possible Messrs. Gilbert of Princes Risborough recon-

structed all this group of mills between a century and a century and a half ago, for they are the only group where overshot wheels were standardized in Bucks. This wheel was 14 or 15ft. diameter, and two countershafts were provided between the pit-wheel and the stone-nut the first shaft having a bevel running off the pit-wheel at axle level, as at Woolstone New Mill; and the second a bevel about twice the size of the stone-nut to engage with the latter. This was to gear up the stone-spindle owing to the slow speed of the water-wheel on so small a stream, and was an almost unique arrangement in Bucks. One pair of stones were 4ft. burrs and the other pair 3ft. 6ins. peaks; but somewhere about 1910 a young man named Joseph Cotching took the mill and removed most of the old gear, except the water-wheel to install a roller plant. Disposing of the peak stones to Mr. Silsby for Culverton Mill, he put in a new 4ft. pair on a portable iron frame with a half-sack midget roller plant. To give this a firm stance, presumably, the wheels were removed and the frame mounted on brick piers; so the authorities raised the rates because the improvement was a "fixture". The water-wheel would not drive the "midget" satisfactorily and it was coupled to a 7h.p. engine, also semi-portable.

Sometimes Mr. Cripps dressed the new stone, but not much work was done, and the mill seems to have been run mainly for a hobby and was vacated early in the Great War. Finally cleared out after the War, the building was shortly demolished but the Mill house remains.

Sarah King was the miller in 1798; and Frank Rogers a little later; he was father of Steve, who worked for Ben Darvell at Millbank; and another of the family, Joseph Rogers, had Monks Risborough Mill in the 'fifties before going to Park and Aylesbury Mills. He sold out to the Pauling brothers, but Mr. William Silsby took over as already mentioned, before opening up at Saunderton and elsewhere; and he was followed byGeorge Pope, Joseph Fletcher and finally Joseph Cotching. In 1920 Mr. Quilter, sausage skin maker, used the building, but he is now at Stoke Mandeville, where there is more room for the refuse.

Monks Risborough Mill stood by the south side of Mill Lane below a curious V-shaped mill-pond fed by three brooks, halfway to the railway "halt" from the Church, and is so indicated on all the maps listed in my heading; but upon a very early chart mentioned in *Old Records of Monks Risborough, Part I, p. 14.* by F.G. Parsons, D.Sc., F.S.A., the road is shown south of this mill, whilst a building marked Cutmill is across the road, closer to the present "halt". On another early map, it seems that Monks Risborough Mill is marked Cutmill; and land at Cutmill was mentioned in 1843, from which the probability is that this was a former name of the recent mill.

Dr. Parsons also mentions that in A.D. 903 the Meadle Brook, running from the hamlet of Meadle to meet the Ford Brook near Aston Mullins, was called Full Brook which he thinks suggests an earlier fulling mill; but only a portion of this brook is in Monks Risborough, and the evidence is too flimsy to warrant a separate heading under any particular parish. Several field names in the document of 903, says Dr. Parsons, survive to this day – a very significant fact in relation to early mill-sites, etc.

BLEDLOW – 1¾ m. S.W. from Princes Risborough

The Lyde Stream

Pitch Green Mill – ½ N. of Church

Standing derelict
Maps –1768, 1793, (1809), 1870, 1875, 1887, 1926

Near the Icknield Way cross-roads at Pitch Green is a very old cornmill set back from the Bledlow station road, with a timber and "herring bone" Mill House notable for its antiquity; whilst the mill is of old red brick, with picturesque tiled roof in which are some dormer windows decrepit to the point of insecurity.

Within the mill are the remains of a very old wooden clasp-arm wheel of 12ft. diameter by 3ft., with unusually thin arms, and now falling to pieces; indeed, in so ruinous a state is the building that visitors are not encouraged to prowl about in it. All the other gear was cleared out somewhere years before the Great War, when the last miller, John Brooks, had finished with it. The Brooks family are the only millers I can trace, except possibly Eustace or Jarden (see Bledlow Lower Mill); James Brooks had it in 1853, Mrs. Deborah Brooks later; and then John Brooks.

There has been a mill at Bledlow from earliest times, however; and it is not improbable the early records refer to this site. At Domesday, a mill there had the singular distinction in Bucks of contributing 24 loads of malt in lieu of the usual coinage or eels; from which one infers that it may have been a malt mill. Simon Hochede held the building in question in 1198, when Hugh de Gurnay excepted it from the grant of Bledlow Manor to the Abbey of Bec Hellouin, Normandy. Simon's widow sued William Neurnuit in regard to the mill in 1240; and in 1285 it seems to have been the only mill on the Manor. At the death of Hugh Bardolf in 1304, the rent of the mill was held by Christina, daughter of Reginald de Hampden.

The Lyde Stream rises on the hillside below Bledlow Cross, and passes beneath the mill building, with by-pass adjoining the school playground and encircling the Mill House garden, afterwards passing beneath the cross-roads to meet the Risborough stream immediately below Bledlow Lower Mill; and from this interesting Risborough group of mills, we shall cross the Chiltern range to another large and compactly grouped series in the industrialized Wycombe valley.

Pitch Green Mill

Chapter 5
Buckinghamshire Watermills
on the Thames Tributaries
South of the Chilterns

MEDMENHAM – 3 m. W.S.W. from Marlow)

Medmenham Stream or *Bulbank's Ditch*

Medmenham Mill (formerly Fulling Mill) – Approx 3 f. E. of Church

Used as pump room
Maps –1768, (1809), 1824,
(1847), 1875, 1887

From now onwards we are south of the Chiltern escarpment, having reviewed all the Thames mills and sites in the Vale of Aylesbury and surrounding country within our county boundary.

The original grant to Woburn Abbey in the reign of King Stephen (1135–1154) includes Medmenham Mill, which was not mentioned in "Domesday". In 1553 the first grant to William Rice included "all mills", and in 1595 two mills stood on the Manor lands (refer back to Medmenham Manor Mill, on the Thames). A fulling mill was mentioned in 1326, and the Reverend A.H. Plaisted state that "the present mill was an old-time fulling mill on the manor

desmesne, driven by water from a spring in the village, on a brook called 'Bulbank's Ditch'", and he adds that the rent of the fulling mill in Henry III's day was 50 shillings, but towards the close of the 14th century the mill was disused, mill pond broken away, and in fact much of the village in ruins. Four centuries later the mill-pond was sold in connection with a scheme to lay a waterpipe to the mansion of Danesfield. Little connected history of the mill seems to exist however; and Mr. Plaisted mentions only that corn was ground within living memory at the present mill, which stood originally north of the road, when the latter detoured down the side of the Church

Medmenham Mill

towards the Thames and through the village. But since the realignment of this road over a century ago, the mill stands immediately south of it, with by-pass stream running round behind the mill; in fact Bryant (1824) shows this layout.

Built of red brick, this is a small compact mill of two floors, one wing of which contained the mill cottage, and the wing next the present road the machinery. An elongated mill pond against the roadway drove a breast-wheel with a 5ft. fall, two pairs of stones – wheat and barley – being worked.

On the new owner taking the estate 30 or 40 years ago, the mill was cleared out; and a pump has been installed for supplying water to the Abbey.

Jasper Jones was the miller of Medmenham in 1702; Robert Grey, 1749 and 1757, William Fisher, 1798; and from the Reverend A. H. Plaisted's *Parsons and Parish Registers of Medmenham* we can trace most interestingly the life history of the Lowe family who held the mill for generations – 1834 a daughter and 1837, a son to Richard Lowe, miller and Elizabeth Lowe; 1841 and (1847), daughters; and 1848, a son, to William Lowe, miller and Elizabeth Lowe; 1188, Elizabeth Lowe (71) of the Mill, buried; 1893, Joseph Albert Lowe, miller, son of William, miller, married Catherine Elizabeth Ollson, widow; and 1896, a son to Joseph Albert Lowe and Catherine Elizabeth.

This is the only mill on this small stream, which discharges into the Thames a mile east of the Church; and it may be added that the old name of Bulbank is derived from Bullbank's or Bolebec's Castle, of Norman times . North of the turnpike, facing the mill, is an extensive plantation called Millbank Wood.

WEST WYCOMBE – 2½ m. W.N.W. from High Wycombe

River Wye or Wyke

Domesday Mills; *Wythditch Mill etc.*: *Pitmill*; *Margery Mill* – Sites unknown

All gone

Medmenham Mill provided an interlude between the Princes Risborough and Wycombe groups of water-mills. Now we come to the Wycombe stream on which Lipscomb counted 39 mills from the west boundary of High Wycombe parish down to the Thames. (Lipscomb's *History of Buckinghamshire (1847), Vol. III p. 633)*.

On this comparatively short stream –10 miles from source to mouth, with a 3 mile loop, it is difficult to say precisely where Lipscomb's mills stood; but since he excluded West Wycombe, he obviously counted two wheels under one roof as two mills (quite a general practice in paper-mill advertisements in his day); and his 39 wheels would be made up *approximately* as follows: Wye stream – Ash, Temple and Millbrook Mills, 1 each. Pann 2, Rye 1 Bassetbury 2, Bowden and Wycombe Marsh, 2 each; King's 1; Loudwater 2; Snakeley 1; Hedge 2; Clapton 3; Glory and Lower Glory, 2 each; Soho 1; Princes and Gunpowder, 2 each; Hedsor Upper 1; Hedsor Lower 2; Bourne End 1; = 34. Back stream – Marsh Green 2; Beech 1; Treadaway 2; Total 39. It is interesting to note that Snakeley and Soho, which seem to have had only one wheel, are now amongst the largest on the stream, which suggests they may have had to resort to steam-power at an early date; indeed they are known to have improvised a horse-mill at Soho owing to water shortage.

Meanwhile the following are the brief particulars of the Domesday and medieval mills on the West Wycombe Manor about which there is nothing further to be said.

In 1086 the Bishop of Winchester's Manor included three mills worth 20/- and a fishery of 1, 000 eels.

A mill called Wythditch or Wytedicke was farmed for 66/8d. in 1251 and 1267 and for £4.6.8. in 1307. Robert, son of Robert the Clerk (possibly the Bishop's bailiff) acknowledged in 1311 the right of Geoffrey le Dusteburgh (Desborough) and Christina his wife, to a messuage and two mills in West Wycombe.

The fishpond of Pitmill is mentioned in 1400.

Margery Mill rented in 1457 by John Pusey for 44/7d was in a very ruinous state; nevertheless it is again mentioned in 1502, 1520 and 1550.

Saw Mill House – ¾ m. E.S.E. of Church

Dismantled
Maps 1822, 1875, (1926 as Sawmill house)

A small and little-known mill stood in the broad stretch of parkland just opposite West Wycombe Station, where the Wye Stream passes the big flint-walled Park Farm.

Sir Francis Dashwood at the end of the 17th century became owner of the West Wycombe Estate; and his son, Lord le Despenser (Chancellor of the Exchequer, etc.) erected temples, grottos and statuary about the grounds christening them with fancy names. Saw Mill House was amongst these embell-ishments; it consisted of "three symmetrical blocks" and was named "The Saw Mill". Combining sawing and corn milling for estate use, it was remembered as a private corn-mill with two pairs of 3ft. 10ins. stones and an undershot wheel, by Mr. Cripps and other old millers who worked on the stream fifty years ago. About this time, however, it was dismantled; and the farmer during the next few years filled his mill-pond over the week-end and opened it Monday morning to oblige Mr. Gillett at the next mill downstream, whilst a weir in the bank of the mill-pond maintained the level.

After the mill ceased to work they are believed to have used a small stream or oil-driven sawing bench for some time. No millers are listed in the directories owing to the private nature of the mill, except John Coltman, occupier of the Saw Mill, 1843 and James Coltman, miller 1854 (descendants of John Coltman, millwright 1792?)

The Wye Stream rises in Lang Meadow, beyond the cress ditch by the Bledlow Ridge road; and several millers 80 or 90 years ago put down £10 each towards the boring of a well in the meadow, to get a good course from a spring, but the local louts during the next twenty years spent their Sunday afternoons throwing stones at the cage over the well and the spring was eventually choked. Consequently the first two or three mills on the stream had then to rely on direct rain water from the hills.

Francis Mill, Gillett's Mill or *Mill End Mill)* – 1¾ m. E.S. E. of Church.)

Gone
Maps –1768, 1793, (1809),
1824, 1875, 1887, 1926

Thomas Darell, miller is mentioned from 1505 until 1540; and the ancestors of Hugh Darrell who died 1667, are stated to have held the Mill End estate for nearly 400 years. This implies that Mill End Mill was in the family, since Fryer's Mill, next downstream, was a paper-making concern in early days and has been in the Fryer family as far back as records can trace.

Jeffery's 1768 map bears the name Francis Mill, and in the *British Directory of Trade and Commerce 1792* is the name of Thomas Francis paper-maker and miller of West Wycombe, who can only have been at Mill End Mill. Thomas Murren and John Beesley were paper-makers in the parish in 1700; and John and Thomas Phelps, 1823, were almost certainly at this mill, but Mr. Cripps believes the paper machines were taken out and destroyed to avoid the mob, just before the Machinery Riots of 1830. In 1842, Joseph Marshall, corn-miller and seedsman of West Wycombe, was most likely here; and in 1856, Alfred Lane, junior, corn-miller, announced that he had let Mill End Mill and moved to High Wycombe.

Probably he was a son of Alf Lane the paper-maker of Bowden Mill (Wycombe Marsh). Abram Gillett then held the mill until the 'nineties, at which time he was about 80, and his son was in charge. another son, James, established a steam-mill in Baker St. High Wycombe. For some years up to the Great War, H. B. Redfearn occupied the Mill End premises as a flock-mill for the manufacture of chair stuffing; and they were marked as such on some maps.

This is one of the many mills at which Mr. Cripps worked; he was here for about five years, after being at Park Mill Risborough, and before his chief period at Cuddington Windmill.

A brick ground floor was surmounted by weather-boarding, but there were no paper-drying louvres in his time, the whole building, which was demolished shortly after the Great War, being somewhat similar in size and style to Fryer's Mill; and Mr. Cripps said the wheel was a wooden overshot of unusual dimen-sions – 7ft. diameter and 14ft. width, upon a wooden axle-tree; the pit, great spur and crown – wheels were iron, and upright shaft wood, driving three pairs.

Whilst here Mr. Cripps persuaded Mr. Gillett to install a "centrifugal" flour dresser, having seen the one at Park Mill and this at once brought in an extra 2/- per sack of 280 lbs., or as it was loosely called a 5-bushel sack. In the 'nineties a good trade was enjoyed at Mill End, and it is possible the family's interest in the Baker Street Mill led to the premature closure of the watermill. Mr. Crochett, who was recently at Bowden Mill went to Gillett's mill from Ash Mill years ago, and in his time they worked six days and three nights one week and six days and two nights the next, because of periodical water shortage. He knew it had been a paper-mill at one period; and recalled a fatality there owing to a young workman attempting to put a belt into gear incorrectly in the foreman's absence; and the man was consequently caught up by it and killed. From here Mr. Crochett

went to Bray Mill, Berks.

Mr. Fryer, whose ancestors had Fryer's Mill, considered Mill End Mill decidedly picturesque, especially in summer time with a pleasant filbert grove at the back; these two mills and the old *Bird-in-Hand* "pub" – lately replaced – were practically the only buildings between High Wycombe town and West Wycombe in his young days. He believed Mr. Redfearn drove tearing machines in the mill to tear up rags for his chair flock.

The site is approached *via* Mill End Road, and along Gillett Lane, which was part of the old Oxford Road until the present turnpike was built in 1752. The mill stood south of Gillett Lane, almost behind the miller's cottage which still exists, with by-pass still farther southward.

Fryer's Mill or *Lower Mill End Mill* – 1½ m. E.S. E. of Church

Derelict
Maps –1768, 1793, (1809), 1822,
1824, 1875, 1887, 1926

A paper mill, mentioned in extants of West Wycombe Manor in 1686 and 1745, can no doubt be identified with Fryer's old-fashioned wooden-boarded structure, which produced paper until the introduction of machinery early last century.

There appears to be no record of anyone but the Fryer family having Fryer's Mill, reputed to have been there from the 16th century, they were there until the mill ceased work. Jefferys marked it Frier's Mill in 1768, and in a fine 16th century building in which the family used to live, facing the mill, are inscriptions cut in the wall – Michael Fryer 1777, James Michael Fryer 1877; leading down to the mill is Fryer's lane and in the little shop called Fryer's Lane Post Office we found Mr. Fryer himself – the last of the Fryers – behind the counter, where he could watch what went on at the old mill which was Fryers's as far back as anyone can trace. (Mr. Fryer unfortunately has now gone, and the little shop has degenerated into an iron-merchant's junk shop.)

This is a big rambling, ramshackle building with a brick lower floor, and weather -boarding partly white and partly tarred above, with tiled roofs irregular in outline from the ravages of time. The mill stands west of the lane just short of a picturesque ford; and years ago the old Oxford road which struck off the present road opposite Hobbs Lane and passed behind Ash Mill, ran immediately north of the building, alongside a little stream which became choked and ceased

to flow after the sluice burst and made havoc around the mill. In the east wing is a 9ft. iron overshot wheel, driving in latter years two pairs of burr stones and one pair peak, but formerly there had been four pairs; the upright shaft is carried up inside a big iron caisson.

Paper was manufactured here in Mr. Fryer's great-grandfather's time, but deciding not to install the new machines which caused so much trouble, he converted to corn. Mr. Fryer's father, last to run the corn-milling business, installed an engine and chimney shaft at his own expense although he was only the tenant; and now Mr. Dean a builder, stores quantities of material and junk in and around the old mill, which still retains some of its discarded machinery.

In 1823 Michael and William Fryer were listed as paper-makers at West Wycombe; Michael Lewis Fryer was both corn-milling and paper-making in the thirties, until the milling trade was established, and James Michael Fryer carried on the business until 1915. Fryer's Mill is one of the few in the Wycombe Valley never known to have been burnt, but the miller's thatched cottage which stood by the old main road was burnt down.

They were gentleman millers on this stream in days gone by; and Alf. Lane at Mill End spent his evenings feeding and watching his trout from a seat on his lawn, which ran down to the water's edge. One day Mr. Fryer's father told his miller to put out a drag net and get some of Alf. Lane's trout, which he did. He secured 20 or 30 brace, and Mr. Fryer sent the miller along to fetch Mr. Lane, the two being on familiar terms, and showed him the trout all nicely laid out. "You've had the pleasure of feeding 'em, and I've had the pleasure of catching 'em" said Mr. Fryer, "now take the pick of 'em for yourself!" Alf.

Lane entirely failed to see the joke, and stamped about and refused to have any, so some of them were given to Mr. Fryer's customers.

Sheahan said the Wye Stream was once celebrated for trout fishing, but owing to the use of chloride of lime by the paper-makers to accelerate bleaching of rag pulp, the fish have ceased to inhabit the waters.

Ball's Mill, Nowne's Mill or *Lord's Mill* – 1⅛ m. E.S.E. of Church.

Used as shop
Maps – 1768, (1809), 1824, 1875, 1887

Lord's Mill seems not to be singled out by name in the early histories, although the title suggests that it belonged to the Lord of the Manor. Jefferys 1768, names it Ball's Mill, and William Ball had two water-mills (under one roof) at West Wycombe in 1798, and there was also James Ball amongst the buyers of corn in 1826; later, millers of this name were at Loudwater.

Edward Spicer was a paper-maker at Chepping Wycombe as early as 1694, when he and other were indicted for rioting and breaking a pipe and sluice belonging to George Clewer, lace weaver, but he was found not guilty. Freeman Spicer was paper-making here in 1791-2 (possibly "going halves" with Ball?); and Wm. Cubbidge papermaker, 1823, had a working arrangement at Lords with Spicer, to whom he was related, but Spicer was listed at Hedge and Glory Mills, downstream in that year, having apparently left Cubbidge.

Mr. Fryer, to whom I am indebted for much information concerning the Wycombe mills, understood that Mr. Spicer was disgusted with the flow of water, or lack of it, at Lord's Mill and he eventually told Mr. Fryer's great grandfather that if he could not find a mill with a better head of water than Lord's he was finished with paper-making. He moved to Kent soon afterward, where he is believed to have founded the present well-known Spicer's mills, but he also acquired interests in the Wooburn district. For years afterwards, the family vault was maintained in West Wycombe churchyard, and the most elaborate funerals came by road from Kent; and Mr. Fryer's father could remember seeing one or two of these processions headed by a hearse with eight fine black horses in charge.

On Bryant's large coloured map of 1824 the building is marked Nownes Mill, for which I can find no explanation, the 1822 Ordnance does not name it. In 1830, Alfred Lane (possibly later at Mill End) was listed as a corn miller and paper-maker "near Canal" (i.e. near the canalised portion of the river), and later at High Street as a paper-maker only.

From the forties to the sixties John Rawlinson of Flint Hall Farm was corn-milling at Lord's Mill, and he was followed by George Darvill who was at Pann Mill, for many years; in 1881/4 when Mr. Cripps had 3 years at Lord's, William Beasley was the miller – whether he was related to the other Beasleys is not known. Finally Ned Britnell, from Bledlow Ridge and Saunderton Mills came here in the 'nineties, but he died in a year or two, and the mill ceased work. Generally speaking, each mill along this stretch had less fall than the one above and here it was about 6ft. For a moderate sized mill – much smaller than Fryer's and Mill End – a large wooden breast-wheel, 14ft. by 14ft., with three sets of arms, drove a wooden pit-wheel, upright shaft, and crown-wheel, only the great-spur – probably new – being of iron; three pairs were employed. The water still traverses the wheel-house within the mill which was largely reconstructed around 1921 to serve as a furniture shop for Mr. G. F. Hunt; but the very large octagon wooden axle-tree was still *in situ* recently. The Mill House, next door, retains its original appearance, neat, double-fronted and yellow-washed, but the roadway is built up so one now descends some steps to the door. Belonging to the Dashwood estate, the mill stand on the right of Oakridge Road facing the *Bird-in-Hand* P.H. formerly *Bird-in-hand-and Two in the Bush*. A loop-stream south of the mill remained until 1940; meanwhile the parish boundary has been altered, bringing Lord's Mill into High Wycombe.

141

HIGH WYCOMBE

[*River Wye*]

Domesday Mills; *Fulling Mills*; *(Early millers)*
Sites uncertain

Gone

Always the mills in High Wycombe have been numerous and important; at Domesday six water-corn mills were attached to Wycombe Manor, worth between them 75 shillings yearly. Five of these reverted to the Crown with the Manor of Wycombe or Bassetbury in 1326, and they can probably be identified with existing mills or mill sites; the sixth possibly was on the site of Rye Mill, since the latter is not accounted for, amongst the others.

The unidentified mill was granted by Mabel daughter of Siward about A.D. 1200 to the Abbess of Godstone, who alienated it to William, son of Hervey, who held the Burne Mills (Bourne End?) here in 1235. In 1797, Langley said the stream turned 15 mills for grinding corn or making paper, in its course through the parish; and these would be the twelve from Ash Mill to Hedge Mill inclusive, and the tree on the Back Stream.

Water-driven fulling mills were also here quite early, in connection with Wycombe's woollen trade of which the last survival is probably the warehouse on the London road near the *White Blackbird* P.H. bearing the legend "FELLMONGERS AND WOOL-STAPLERS".

The principal fulling mill, held of Bassetbury Manor, was sometimes called Robyn Mill from an early 13th century holder; Henry Chesemonger next held it, and in 1250 Sebricht the Carpenter and William the Fuller, and their wives acknowledged the right of Philip Basset to a rent of 3 marks for two parts of their mill. In 1255 Philip Basset transferred the moiety of "the mill that was William Robyn's in Wycombe, with all the watercourse in the the the pool thereto belonging" to Richard, son of John Fuller; and they were fullers in Wycombe during the 14th century. In 1420 the fulling mill was called Hochedes Mille, implying that the family of Hochede, who were settled in Wycombe from about 1300, had farmed the mill.

Another fulling mill at Loudwater, belonging later to the Templars, was in the family of La Lude when first mentioned in 1250. Later this was demised to Philip Bassett with lands, for 21 years; and he granted to Thomas de la Lude permission to build (or rebuild?) a fulling mill. Thomas was to pay 1 mark rent, and at no time were cloths made in Wycombe Borough or delivered to be fulled there, to be received into the said mill. Thomas de la Lude later held two watermills, probably under one roof, leased in 1337 to Richard de Wegeneholt for life, although temporarily confiscated for felony about that date. In the 16th century this mill (the two combined?) was possessed by the Hospitallers, being held of them by Edward Case, clothier, and described as Ludewater Mill, with all walls, banks and water works belonging to it, with free fishing from the King's Highway on the east, to the Over King's Mead. Subsequently it was attached to Temple Manor; and the Hospitallers held a second fulling mill called Gosham or Gosenham, first mentioned in 1403. At the Dissolution this was held by John Carter on a 61 years' lease; and still known as Gosham's Mill, it was fulling cloth in 1625, for the Raunce family.

Early Millers

Since a number of paper-makers' and millers' names occurring around Wycombe defy identification, they may be disposed of here to avoid entering later into speculation as to which mills they occupied. Earliest paper-maker mentioned in High Wycombe Church records is William Harman, 1659. "Jno Kingham for ye fulling mill" is mentioned in the Wycombe accounts 1667–84; Kongheil Moskath, a Dutch widow from the Weir mill (unidentified) was buried apparently in 1690; and three years later Daniel Kingham, miller of Chepping Wycombe, was indicted for substituting mixed wheat and barley for pure wheat brought to him to grind! In 1694, William Russell was a paper-maker, and William Paltrock a miller, at Chepping Wycombe; and in 1740, William East, paper maker, probably of High Wycombe, was being searched for at Marlow and elsewhere; in 1760 Edward Heel was a paper-maker here.

The Universal British Directories of Trade and Commerce 1791/2, list the following paper-makers and millers for whom no addresses are given:- Francis Blackwell, John Goodwin, William Veary, and John Wildman, paper-makers; William Clark and Joseph Stevens, millers. (Thomas Blackwell was a paper-maker of Wooburne in 1696). In later directories some names are difficult to place exactly, but as far as possible passing reference is made to them under individual headings.

On May 13, 1826, an agreement was made stating

that "the undersigned buyers of Corn at Wycombe Market will neither buy nor sell corn after May 19 other than by the Imperial Measure"; I have added in parentheses, the mills with which they were probably associated; but some may only have been dealers:-

Biddle & Wheeler; Thomas Edmonds (Ash Mill); William Payne (Bassetbury) Alfred Lane (Mill End Mill); John Prestage, Jun. (Temple Mill); John Stacey; James Ball (Lord's Mill); Joseph Edmonds (Bowden Mill?); Michael L. Fryer (Fryer's Mill); William G. Edmonds (Ash Mill?); Richard Lucas; William Huntley; William Young; James Moody; Thomas Rayment (Bury Mill, Amersham?); John Prestage, Sen. (Temple Mill?); Henry White; Thomas Edmonds; M Trinder; W. H. Williams; Richard Gellett; George Barnett.

Lane's Mill or *Ash Mill* – 3 f. W.N.W. of Church

Foundations remain
Maps – 1768, (1809), 1824, 1875

Ash Mill appears to be the one at which the famous Machinery Riots of 1830 actually began, so far as the Wycombe paper-mills were concerned, and as it is the first mill on the stream amongst those involved, it will be convenient to include an account of the events under this heading.* The fateful day at Wycombe was Monday November 29, 1830; although various forms of Swing Riots (from the penalty of hanging or "swinging" for arson) occurred both earlier and later. On the previous Wednesday, a meeting of paper-makers and magistrates was convened in a building on the Rye to discuss measures for the protection of property; it will be observed the magistrates took sides before anything happened, and one does not suppose that they would have been perturbed to learn that the paper-makers had laid in some vitriol to pour over the rioters, since the employers were always right! A great multitude got wind of the meeting, however, and gathered on the Rye; and before the meeting was far advanced they broke in and pushed the chairman out, and a loquacious barber addressed the assembly on behalf of the rioters. They then smashed the furniture and proceeded to Lane's Paper-mill (Ash Mill); but the Newport Pagnell Yeomanry** arrived, and the multitude was dispersed.

Next Monday (November 29) they descended upon Lane's Mill again at 9 a.m. from Flackwell Heath (where numerous paper-makers have always lived) assembling first on the Rye as before, at the sound of the horn; and it is interesting that Lane's were here described as "the first paper-makers on the stream," the inference being that Fryer's and Lord's Mills had already abandoned paper-making. The crowd, armed with sledge-hammers, crowbars and pickaxes, tried to force an entrance to the building where the Machine was situated, but they were shot at from inside, and William Bryant, paper-maker of Flackwell Heath, was shot in the arm; and for the moment they could not get in. (Employees were commonly referred to as paper-makers, employers being distinguished when necessary by the term paper-manufacturers).

Then they broke the windows, but several gallons of vitriol were thrown at them from within, and many were burnt by the liquid. At last they got in however, and destroyed the machine completely in fifteen minutes. The man who threw the vitriol was seized and ducked, and they nearly killed him.

Next the mob proceeded to Allnutt's Paper-mill at Marsh Green – presumably Marsh Green Mill, which was a paper-mill in 1823 under Mr. Howard, and the machine was speedily destroyed. Thence to Mr. Haye's mill (Wycombe Marsh Mill) where they broke in, and were opposed by red-hot pokers, but they smashed the machine in spite of promises that it would not be used. At Plaistow's Loudwater (King's Mill?) they also ignored promises not to use the machine, and smashed it; and at Hedge Mill – Spicer's – they destroyed the machine.

Now they were getting tired and drunk, and two or three had been shot; the reporters were also getting tired apparently, for it was only later that news was received that two paper-mills were destroyed near Wooburn in the same riots, one being W.R. Davis's, which was also set on fire.

Prisoners were secured and removed by a brake

---

* For a stirring account of the corresponding cloth-mill riots in Yorkshire the reader could not do better than refer to Charlotte Brontë's *Shirley*, which probably is based on the Leversedge Riots.
** It is clearly established by a long editorial in the *Bucks Chronicle* June 8, 1822 that the Bucks Yeomanry in 1821 in particular were paid several thousand pounds of the ratepayers' money at the instigation of the Lord Lieutenant of the County for *nothing* – under the heading of "suppressing riots" when in fact no riots occurred – the real object being to bribe them into hostility and violence against local workmen and women.

Lane Mill or *Ash Mill*

and stage-coach to Aylesbury; and another account (*Bucks Gazette*) states that the constables came from Beaconsfield to Spicer's (Hedge Mill) implying presumably that this put a check on the riot; and adds that Clapton and Glory Mills were visited also. It states that the Gentlemen of the King's Hunt and the constables, *proceeded to the upper end of King's Mead* where they found the mob had just entered Mr. Davis's mill at Loudwater (this being the only definite evidence I have of the location of Davis's Mill); and it seems to limit the choice to King's Mead or Loudwater Mills, since Mr. Hay was at Wycombe Marsh). The horsemen rushed into the mill and seized some prisoners, but they were a bit too late, for the machine was smashed during the contest; and 24 men were charged on this account in the following January. No progress was made, the mob being now completely dispersed. Eventually it was learned that £12, 000 worth of damage was done; and at a meeting at the *Windmill Inn*, Salthill, the High Sheriff and others congratulated themselves on their intrepidity during the riot at Mr. Davis's mill near Wooburn.

John Lane had Lane's Mill in 1792, and Joseph Lane was at Ash Mill (earliest printed reference I have found to this name) in 1830; and the family must have remained here for over three quarters of a century, for Lanes finally announced in November (1847), that they had "declined paper-making", and the principle part of a paper machine, presses, rollers, engines, rag boilers, etc., were for auction. Six months later another advert offered a mill "at the west end of Wycombe" formerly used for paper, with considerable portion of machinery intact, adding that "As a corn-mill, the situation is exceedingly advantageous ... the working capacity equals 3 pairs of Stones." But Spicer – a relation of the Lord's Mill people – then took the building for a short period, as a paper-mill; and James Edmonds, jun. first used it as a corn-mill in the 'fifties. Doubtless he was related to the Edmonds at Rye, Bassetbury & Bowden etc. who would be the Quaker brothers mentioned by Henry Kingston as having mills in High Wycombe about 1845.

In the 'seventies, Reuben Pearce of Temple Mill was at Ash Mill and in the 'nineties Frederick J.

Mullett was doing a good corn and bread trade there. The Mulletts were corn dealers in Wycombe 60 years previously. Mr. Crochett of Bowden Mill worked under Mullett after being apprenticed at Culverton Mill and before going to Mill End Mill.

Messrs. James Cox & Son then acquired the premises which they cleared out and used as a store for chair seats, but at the death of Mr. George Cox, through falling downstairs in 1938, the property was sold; the old doors, one of which was iron-studded as though to keep out the rioters, were pulled off and the doorways boarded up; and in June 1939 the place was almost completely demolished. Standing on the west corner of Westbourne Street, the red-brick Mill House abutted on the Oxford Road, with the mill, of red brick and cream-painted wood with sliding paper-drying louvres, and tiled roofs, extending down the turning. Behind the building could be seen the wheel-pit which had accommodated a 10ft. low-breastshot wheel, 5 or 6ft. wide, the fall being only 2ft. or so; indeed Mr. Cripps confirming these figures, declared

the mill no good owing to inadequate fall. The mill-tail appears from beneath the roadway, running alongside the main street, in a channel or canal in front of the houses for the next quarter of a mile, and making the street somewhat pleasanter than it is further westwards; the by-pass returns into the road-side stream from between the houses, a hundred yards down.

Incidentally the Globe Insurance Co. seem to have taken their courage in both hands by insuring Ash Mill in olden days, when a fire at a wooden-built mill would have proved a ticklish problem, but their luck held out and their sign remained on the wall almost to the last.

Some directories list "Cox's Mill" (by which name Ash Mill was sometimes known) in Bridge Street, but this was a small steam saw-mill in which Cox and his foreman, Thead, installed some millstones to do some cut-price corn business against legitimate millers, much to the latters' disgust, seeing that the Wycombe Valley was already overburdened with corn-mills.

Temple; St John's or *Bowdrey's Mill* – 330 yds W.N.W. of Church

Foundations and Mill House remain
Maps 1768, (1809), 1875

Temple Mill, situated in the heart of the town, went with Temple Wycombe Manor, which Robert Doyley held in 1086; and is sometimes named after the medieval Hospital of St. Johns. The Knights Templars acquired it in 1227, and the Knights Hospitallers had it in 1307, Michael atte Grene 1310 and the Hospitallers again from 1345 until the Dissolution, the Crown then holding it till 1553.

Victoria County Vol. III continues that, this seems to be the sixth and last Wycombe mill listed in Domesday, and it was granted at the Dissolution to Thomas Keate, then to his son Sebastion and in 1588 to Michael Barker, and to William Martin in 1637. The Bowdrey family had the mill in 1674; Robert Bowdrey was the miller in 1791/2, and a Trade Token; date unreadable, was put out by the family and inscribed SAMVELL BOVDREY, with a king's head. By 1823 the mill was occupied by John Prestage, Jun; and he was succeeded by Job Pearce about 1840, who previously had Wycombe Heath Windmill. In the 'seventies Job retired, and until 1900 or later Reuben Pearce had the mill, which ended its corn-milling days with 3 pairs of stones in use.

Never having been used for other purposes, this was, so to speak, the first 100 per cent corn-mill on the stream – but Messrs. Alec Stacy & Co. Ltd.

acquired it for the manufacture of "wood flour" for conversion into linoleum about the year 1902, and proceeded to grind sawdust in the millstones. They had only been there a few weeks, however, when the mill went up in smoke! Grinding of sawdust was the cause, and it is believed the fire started with an explosion. Later they took Staines Mill (Mddx) which also "went up" and then stored 2,000 bags of woodflour in an electric mill driving 8 pairs of stones under the railway viaduct at Frogmore, Wycombe, and this too ended in flames. At one time they were at Clewer Mill, Windsor with six pairs of stones, but this escaped the usual fate!

The fall was about 5ft. at Temple Mill and the 18ft. wheel with 5ft. tread was, like most on this stream, between breast-shot and undershot – locally they are generally called undershots, but really they are low breastshots, or as some say quarter shots. This distinctive type of wheel is almost standardised here, but little used elsewhere in Bucks.

Situated in a cul-de-sac in Bowdery's Lane (formerly St John's Lane) on south side of Oxford Street, Temple Mill was without the Borough, but adjoined the ancient borough boundary, which came down the backwater from just above the mill, and then up the mill-tail for a few yards into the

Hughenden stream (which joins the mill-tail) and under the *Angel* P.H. The Mill House, double-fronted and yellow washed is now Messrs. W. Worley's office (facing their warehouse) and beyond this was the mill on a site now vacant.

Bridge Mill or *Millbank Mill*; Nº 1. St Mary's St. – 200 yds. S. of Church   Derelict
Maps 1768, (1809), 1875

"The house and water mill at No. 1 St Mary's Street, although of late 16th or early 17th century, contain many timbers of a much earlier date, which probably belonged to the medieval mill and were later used again" Quotation from *V.C.H. Vol. III*, which also observes that this first mentioned of the six Domesday mills at High Wycombe, was known as Bridge Mill, and was attached to Angote's Fee. The name originated from a bridge at the entry to St. Mary St. which in 1848 still retained for its top rail the cross-piece of a very large gallows that had been used on the Rye in 1736. In the late Mr. John Parker's *Early History of Wycombe* it is suggested that Bridge Mill marked the boundary of the "inland" or demesne, constituting the small borough and homestead, or dwelling, of the Saxon chief. The burgesses cultivated the common fields on the hillsides, and depastured cattle on the Rye; and it is added that the Hospital of St. John in Easton St. extended down to the millstream, the present road being cut through the site. Easton Street originally led only to the Hospital and Pann Mill; and around these two buildings a group of houses known as East Town, sprang up.

Bridge Mill is just behind the Market Hall, facing the lower end of Crown Lane; and its row of half-timbered gables at the rear overlook the Public Library and Museum. For some time an old discarded fire escape stood significantly in the mill-yard, now part of a car park – a silent reminder of the innumerable mill fires which distinguished the Wycombe Valley during the last couple of centuries!. Bridge Mill itself finished up with a fire in 1933 or 4 but was not completely gutted; indeed it was afterwards used by a shoeing and general smith and now stands derelict in an odd corner, as though being elbowed out by the adjoining buildings, and it is capped with an assortment of jaunty little hip-gables in the tiled roof. The front walls were partly of wood, with retractable loading stage but they were clumsily botched up with galvanised, after the fire and the mill plastered with adverts, has ceased to be an embellishment to the landscape.

The miller had the advantage of being just without the borough and therefore paid parochial rates – a point which would have enjoyed the unreserved approval of the illustrious William Cobbett, greatest hater of "borough-mongers" – whilst nevertheless situated squarely in the heart of the town!

The wheel immediately inside the building was of breast or low-breast type, driving three pairs, whilst another two pairs were at one period driven by electric motor.

For half a century from the 1820's to the 70's the Thurlow family had Bridge Mill; they were gentlemen millers, and James Thurlow is said to have been the best fly-fisher in the town, and was in the habit of going up to Mr. Fryer's of an evening to throw his line; his grandson, nearly 80 in 1939, became well known as an architect in Wycombe.

Ben Darvill whose stone-dresser was Steve Rogers from Monks Risborough had the mill for many years towards the end of the century, whilst his brother George, with whom he unfortunately had a long dispute about water rights, was at Pann Mill. Ben seems to have had Marsh Green Mill, on the back Stream at an earlier date, retaining an interest in both mills for some time; and until after the Great War he worked Bridge Mill with his son. William Bayliss who then took the premises was the last miller; and it may be added that Mr. Cripps did some repairing and stone dressing here for the Darvills. Like Temple Mill above, and Pann Mill below, this was a corn-mill from earliest times.

Pann Mill, №̱ 44, Easton Street – 3f. E.S.E. of Church

Working
Maps 1768, (1809), (1847), 1870, 1875

Pann Mill

Third of the six Domesday mills at Wycombe was Pannells, or Pann Mill, still standing at the north-west corner of the Rye against the London road (No. 44, Easton Street). Probably it belonged to a family in this parish called Pinel, mentioned in 1185 when the widows of Roger and David Pinel held half a hide in dower in Wycombe. In 1235 Richard of Croyedone held this mill, and in 1344 Adam de Martham granted 2 watermills under one roof called "la Pennell in Wycombe" to Sir Hugh de Neweton. Presumably the mill was attached to Temple Wycombe Manor, for it was among the possessions of the Hospitallers at the Dissolution.

In 1558 it was decreed by the Common Council that the millers of Pann Mill and Christopher Pettifer's Mill (Bridge Mill?) should not be allowed to pasture any horse, gelding or mare on the Rye, but such as they shall serve and load to the town with, upon pain of forfeiting their commonage; for like the Bridge Mill, Pann Mill was outside the borough and as assessed parochially; thus it seems there was no mill within the original borough boundary at all.

Christopher Wase died seised of the mill in 1643, having inherited it from his father.

An advert in 1841 offered a water-corn mill at High Wycombe and dwelling house, two water-wheels in complete repair, 3 pairs French stones, four-mill, bolting mill, etc. carrying trade 15 to 25 loads a week. Stables for 3 horses, carts, right of pannage in meadow adjoining called "the Rye". Thomas Edmunds and Thomas Quartermain, both of Easton St, were probably sharing the mill the following year; but throughout the second half of the century, George Darvell, the elder, held the mill, and the High Court ordered its sale, by auction, George Davill being the tenant "for 3 years from Lady Day, 1857, at yearly rent of £140." Three floors and 4 pairs of stones. Fred Ware senior, from Coleshill Windmill worked it from about 1900, always closing down promptly at midnight Saturday, and holding up as much water as possible till midnight Sunday; and Frederick Lane Ware, his son, worked it two nights a week, after a day's work on Ongar Hill Farm, Coleshill, so anxious were they to make the most of the water. More recently, Mr. Robert Jarvis, whose father had the old Bekesbourne Windmill, Kent, has worked Pann Mill first by electricity and now, once more by water, his miller being Mr. E. G. Simmons, who served 50 years, up to 1937, in the mills of the Thames and its tributaries – 32 years with Hill's and Bassetts at Bassetbury (and at Marsh Green and Treadaway Mills which Basset's also occupied).

Facing up the London road and overlooking the Rye, the mill is largely encased with white weather-boarding, which partially conceals three slat-roofed gables that accommodate a series of bins on either side of central decks; and between the eastern gable and the roadway is a substantially built Mill House of brick, of much later date.

The fine eight spoked all-iron breast wheel, 15ft. diameter by 8ft., has shallow curved buckets; and the axle has been turned up to provide a large bearing upon its shoulder, Mr. Jarvis not being an admirer of the unduly small journals too often provided in our local waterwheels! Placed outside at the rear, near the west corner, it is driven by a diverted stream which formerly flowed straight in beneath the east wing, but now turns southward, along behind the mill to the present wheel, to discharge around the end of the building. Clamped to the wheel and facing the mill wall, is a disused iron cog ring; and within is a large mortice gear pit-wheel, an iron wallower on substantial wooden upright shaft, a fine wooden great spur, and iron stone-nuts.

To disengage the latter, which drive millstones upon the first floor, a block of three teeth, held by two bolts, can be removed from the nut – a somewhat tricky business unless the miller runs upstream to open the sluices, because the closing of the "flash" behind the wheel does not always bring the mill to a dead stand for some time.

The bridge-trees are tentered by bevel gear and screw projecting through the wall of the gear enclo-sure, and a belt from each stone-spindle drives another spindle which is bevel-geared to a horizontal screw conveyor to draw flour from the stone-case and obviate scooping by hand; and this led Mr. Simmons to observe that the first conveyor he ever used was one he made out of a rick-pole with blades set into it, at Bassetbury Mill. On the first floor are two crown wheels driving a short iron sack bollard, both belt and sack chain being guided by pulleys. In the yard is the old wooden axle of a former water wheel.

The east end of the mill is very old indeed – perhaps the oldest watermill equipment in the county; but it has for some years been disused and is now entirely derelict although electrically driven in its time. As already mentioned, the stream flowed straight in here from the rear; and remnants exist of a large wooden pit-wheel and spur which are displaced owing to decay of timbers. Also a small diameter iron breast-wheel upon a square wooden axle; and a shaft projecting through wall, by which the electric drive was conveyed to the nearest stone-spindle after the water-wheel and great spur had fallen out of commission. Years ago, when the water rose and fell frequently owing to the excessive complement of mills on the stream a hinged scoop and pipe were so arranged that the scoop filled and tipped over, ringing a bell, when the water rose, a signal to set the mill to work!

Whether the mill will remain in service for very long is dubious, for Mr. Jarvis is not enthusiastic about decayed watermills; there is a possibility also that an ill-planned by-pass (if indeed the word "planned" can be applied to anything the Ministry of Transport does) may interfere with the mill, which ought by rights to be preserved for posterity. ("Let those who like 'em look after 'em" says Mr. Jarvis!) So we can but hope for the best, meanwhile noting that he has since let the front of the mill for a great eyesore hoarding advertising petrol, and showing little apparent respect for one of the three Buckinghamshire water mills recorded by the Historical Monuments Commission as a pre 17th century structure.

Rye Mill or *New Mill*, *No. 33*, *London Road* – 5f. E.S.E. of Church

Used as workshop
Maps 1768, (1809), 1822, 1824,
(1847), 1875, 1926

Of the numerous paper-mills down the Wye stream, Rye Mill is the first one which was never converted for corn-milling. Perhaps this was appropriate, since Rye Mill always maintained a reputation for the very highest quality product in the paper world. At the end of the 18th century, the mill then existing had been there at least a hundred years, according to the chapter entitled "Industry" in *V.C.H. Vol. I*; and Messrs John Bates, the proprietors, had produced good paper for writing, drawing, ledgers, and banknotes. In 1787 John Bates having brought about improvements in paper suitable for printing mezzo-prints, which placed it in a class with French papers of this description, received the Gold Medal of the Society of Arts & Sciences, London: and in recognition of this, Gibbs included the noted paper manufacturer in his *Buckinghamshire Worthies*.

John Bates was still at Rye Mill in 1792; but seven years later, the mill was burnt out, Edmonds was the occupier. In 1823 Thomas Edmonds is listed as a paper manufacturer of High Wycombe; and a miller of the same name is given in Oxford Street in 1830, in addition to Edmonds & Lucas, High Street. Thomas Harry Saunders was the next proprietor with James Millbourne as manager; Thomas Edmonds having died in 1852, when Rye Mill was described as a "Highly Distinguished Paper Mill, with very superior range of brick and slated buildings, 218ft. long, with dwelling, offices, workmens' cottages, etc. The building has been erected within a few years, expressly as a paper manufactory for fine papers, regardless of expense; a corresponding degree of success and celebrity has been attained, working capabilities equal 3 vats; and adjacent, a natural spring for washing water is available . . . Valuable implements, wire moulds, 35 quires of felts, glazed boards, copper glazing plates, zinc ditto, lattice wire, mahogany and elm layboards, press blocks, planks, 6 cwt. parchment scrolls, vitriol, blue, pearl ash, pump, wheel cogs, rag boxes, sizing troughs, glazing bench, fire engine and paper truck for sale".

Saunders took the mill on a 14 years lease, at £190 per annum; and the following year he was listed at "Marsh", meaning Beech Mill, Wycombe Marsh which he held simultaneously for many years but the business, which became known as T. H. Saunders & Co., and remained at Rye Mill until the end of the Great War, terminated at Beech Mill at the turn of the century.

Situated at the London end of the Rye (from "at ther Eye" – island – or atte reye), the mill is the first building alongside the roadway, and is square-built, of red brick and slate; and the mill stream which separates the Rye from the roadway passes beneath the mill, where it drove a fair-sized wheel 40 or 50 years ago. Steam power was later used and it is doubtful whether the wheel existed in later years. A by-pass ran round the big white-painted, slate-roofed drying room at the rear, and a man named Marchant added the low brick-built warehouses surrounding the drying room, and called the enlarged premises New Mill a name sometimes appended to them in the past, e.g. on Bryant's 1824 map, and in 1847 when a reference makes it clear that New Mill was *on the Rye* (another New Mill being on King's Mead lower down). Messrs. Wilkinson (The National Paper Co.) last used the mill for paper; and they sold the machinery to scrap merchants before 1930.

Now the original mill-building is occupied by a metal worker, the drying room by chair-makers; and the yard and new buildings by a mineral water concern; and the premises are called "Old Rye Mill".

Bassetbury Mill – 6½ f. E.S.E. of Church

Used as antique warehouse
Maps 1768, (1809), 1822, (1847), 1875, 1887, 1926

Basset's Bury Manor seems to have come into existence out of Wycombe Manor in the 15th century; and the fifth mill listed in Domesday Book out of the six belonging to Wycombe Manor was attached to the demesnes of what became Basset Bury Manor.

Thomas Basset held Wycombe Manor from 1171; and his kinsman Alan Basset, one of the barons who signed Magna Carta, received a permanent grant of Basset's Bury in 1203. The Charter of 21 Henry III (1228) recites an agreement between Alan Basset and the burgesses of Wycombe, by which he granted to them all the borough with rents, markets, fairs, etc.; except his demesnes, outlying lands, and mills, etc.; and Bassetbury Mill was thus retained in his own possession. Fulk Basset, Archbishop of London, held the Manor later, the mill being let out to Richard de Sobington; but the Manor reverted to the Crown in 1326 when Hugh le Despencer was executed for high treason; and it was assigned to Katherine; mother of Henry VI in 1422, and began to be called Basset's Bury fifteen years later. In 1483 the Manor was granted to the Dean and Canons of St George's Windsor, who held it for 400 years, the property, including the mill, thenceforth being vested in the Ecclesiastical Commissioners who still hold it.

Like the mills in the town, this was always a cornmill, unless by chance it was the fulling mill mentioned on the Manor centuries ago; and the early millers were John Clark, 1798; Clark and Edmonds, 1830 and 1842; and probably William Paine, of London Rd. 1853. He was listed in White Hart St 1830, where he probably had a corn-chandler's office; and although the mill is not really on the London Road, but some distance down Bassetbury Lane, (first right, going from town) it is sometimes given as London Road in Kelly's. Augustus Hill, son of John

Bassetbury Mill

Hill of Aylesbury Mills, was here in 1864, but he unfortunately hanged himself by a sack chain in the 'eighties, and was succeeded by his brother Claudius, who previously had Walton Mill, Aylesbury, for a short time. Thence forward until after the Great War David Basset of Maidenhead, occupied the mill which was thus by a coincidence in the hands of another Basset after 700 years.

In 1928 the Bassetbury Roller Milling Co. were proprietors; and H.T. Turnbull was the last corn-miller, about five years later. For a short time Lintafelt patent flock, for filling upholstery was made here, the business soon being transferred to an ugly factory building near Loudwater; and since the machinery was cleared out, Frederick Skull, Esq. of the Manor House has established an antique business here. Mr. E. G. Simmons of Pann Mill worked for Augustus and Claudius Hill and David Basset, for 32 years, also working Treadaway and Marsh Green Mills on the Back stream for Basset, who had all three for a time; and Mr. Will Cripps was here with Augustus Hill, for six months before going to Lord's Mill in 1830.

Dating probably from about 1690, the present mill is of old red brick and mellowed tiles, with some plaster on the walls which are clamped with iron and buttressed outside; the miller's Cottage is somewhat lower, but a newer cottage also adjoins the mill. Standing across the stream, on the west side of Bassetbury Lane, the mill was largely reconstructed internally within living memory. Two 8ft. wheels of about 4ft. tread were formerly provided – one inside driving a roller plant latterly, and one which may have been outside, coupled to two pairs of stones.

Two millers, Edmonds, and another, probably William Payne, had the mill in those days of dual ownership, using the water separately if the supply was short – one from 12 midnight Monday morning till midnight Tuesday, and the other until midnight Thursday, and so on. The wheel driving the millstones, in particular, was inefficient and needed to be more or less flooded to get any speed on the stones; and so the mill was rearranged probably when Augustus Hill moved in. About that time. Mr. Cripps said, there was also an overshot wheel of some 18ins. diameter, coupled to a crank which got under weigh and rang a bell when the water reached a certain level, this being for the same purpose as the scoop at Pann Mill!

An impressive-looking all-iron wheel, easily capable of driving two pairs efficiently, was installed at the rear of the mill, outside, and at right-angles to the stream, which turns right to lay on to the wheel. It is a quarter-shot with fall of about 6ft. and well-rounded and ventilated buckets which lift out of the water remarkably clean – only a very little water passes the vents into the centre of the wheel, whilst the water draining off the lips is only like a light rain shower. Consequently she is comparatively silent in running; in fact more noise is heard within the mill from vibration, than outside, although she appeared to be running only at half-speed when this vibration was pointed out to me, and in full swing she might set up a healthy roar! Three sets of eight arms are fitted, and the axle shaft only extends just into the mill wall, where a large spur gear drives a pinion above it, and a counter shaft caries the eight-armed iron pit-wheel, from which two further counter-shafts run in opposite directions – a short one formerly driving a large belt to the roller gears, and the other a little return counter-

shaft, which drives a belt to a lighting dynamo. The latter is 210 volts, 35 amp. and functions satisfactorily at 4 to 5 r.p.m. of the water-wheel and a cut-out switch is compulsorily installed for emergency, in case of any difficulty in stopping the wheel.

Some stones were retained by Augustus Hill, but Basset made it all rollers about 1905, and also installed a 20 h.p. electric motor which could not be used after dark in the Great War as the power was switched off. Stones and rollers were on first floor, machines on the second, sack gear in loft. Traces of the position of one of the old wheels can be seen where the main counter-shaft is now situated; it had a wooden axle and appears to have been overshot. Main by-pass is south of the mill, with a group of four sluices on the right bank, but an extra flood release is also provided by a waterway beneath the mill, in line with the stream, and this is no doubt the former mill-race, with a weir placed in its path under the mill wall.

For the present wheel the "flash" is controlled from inside by a shaft with large double tommy-bar and bevels, the main flash spindle being mounted in a box over the flood-way, and a ratchet on the spindle is operated by a wire from near the "tommy".

Bowden Mill – 1⅓ m. E.S.E. of Church

Working
Maps 1768, (1809), 1822, 1824, (1847), 1875, 1887, 1926

Working as a corn-mill in the good old-fashioned way by water-power and serenely oblivious of the industrialisation of the surrounding valley, is the whitewashed brick and wooden walled Bowden Mill. Remarkable that it should be still at work, for seldom has a miller had a greater struggle to make a "do" of a mill than the late James Edwin Saunders, who came from Stone Windmill in 1865. Taking Bowden Mill in the hope of finding more scope for business than an old post windmill afforded, Mr. Saunders was sadly disillusioned, for his arrival at Wycombe proved to be the opening stage of a long run of hardship and financial stress.

"In the first place" he says, "it was not a good neighbourhood and already over-run by millers. There were ten flour mills in the valley before we started; many of them paper-mills converted into flour mills during the bad spell of papermaking . . . Nearly all the land in the valley was poor and hilly, which meant second-rate farmers; our mill had been shut for four years so that every bit of trade had gone, and the machinery was worn out and permeated with dry rot. The water supply also turned out very ineffi-

cient; the business swallowed up money faster than I could make it, and I was forced to seek overdrafts and loans which were a constant anxiety by day, and a nightmare at night".

Prices were heavily cut all down the stream, for the Quakers who had maintained high prices by agreement, were gone, and the overdraft steadily increased despite every effort to retrieve the situation.

At last in 1873, Mr. Saunders found a way out of Bowden Mill and moved to the new steam-mill at Slough where after initial difficulties, the business grew and grew for the next nine years, as many as 26,000 sacks of corn being ground per year at a comfortable profit, so that he at long last reaped the full fruit of his labours, of his faith and determination in face of years of threatened defeat, so justifying the banker's confidence in him. In 1888, at the age of only 44, he was in the happy position of being able to enter upon a life of comfortable retirement, finally passing away at the ripe age of 91 in 1935. Mr. Saunders left behind him a copious diary, now published in the book *Reflections and Rhymes* edited by W Ridley Chesterton.

Bowden Hill, receiving its name from Buga's Hill – old English Bugan-dun or Bughendune – stands nearly opposite a narrow lane leading up to Totteridge from Upper Marsh, a quarter of a mile east of the Maidenhead line railway bridge over the main road; and it always worked as two mills with separate wheels. Both wheels are of low-breast type 9 or 10ft. diameter and of similar width, with three sets of iron arms, and curved buckets, but the axle-trees are square shafts of wood. The only noticeable difference is that the disused one is ventilated by having buckets spaced slightly apart, and she was, as is to be expected, the better wheel of the two; the present one "lifts" rather a lot of water and runs with considerable splashing and commotion. It is sheltered by a lean-to and drives the usual mortice gear pit-wheel, large round wooden upright shaft on which is a fine old fourspoked great spur with, immediately above it, a six-spoked crown wheel, both entirely of wood. The two stone-nuts are of all-wood construction and, from each three cogs can be removed by withdrawing long iron pins like meat skewers. Gears are in the usual wooden-built enclosure, and there was formerly a third pair of stones. A creeper conveyor is belt-driven from the upright shaft, just above the crown-wheel, which is now disused; and a very large pair of disused governors, which Mr. Saunders is believed to have installed for the barley stones, were more recently coupled to the wheat stones.

Possibly this half of the building was formerly a paper-mill, as the half now burnt and demolished is known to have been. In 1791/2 one part belonged to John Scott, paper miller, but in 1805 this was burnt out, and Barton's mill, presumably the other half of the building was burnt at the same time. Richard Barton was described as a paper manufacturer and farmer in 1791; and corn-miller in 1798 and also in 1823, when a man was charged with selling a lot of stolen rick-cloth to him; the *Gentleman's Magazine* Nov: 23, 1805 stated that "the adjoining flour mills of Mr. Barton were burnt" Bryant (1824) marks two separate mills; and in 1830 Abraham Barton was the miller. James Edmonds was the corn-miller in 1853, at which time Alfred Lane was paper-making at Bowden. Meanwhile in 1874, Lane advertised some paper-mill effects in conjunction with the exors. of Joseph Edmonds – layboards, half-stuff, part of a paper machine including press-rolls, steam cylinders, deckle tackle, agitator, etc; and part of water-wheel; and a man who died aged 92 about 1937 claimed to remember this being a paper-mill in Lane's hands. No doubt there was a family connection between these people and the proprietor of Ash Mill upstream.

About the year 1860, William Gilbert, brother of Mr. T Gilbert of Leighton Buzzard, and nephew of William Gilbert the millwright of Princes Risborough, took the whole establishment. He set up a mill-wrighting yard on the premises, and reconstructed the paper-mill as a corn-mill in counter-gear with belts, putting in three pairs of stones here whilst another three were in the spur-gear mill.

Instead of gearing the counter-shaft directly by spur to the pit-wheel, Mr. Cripps told me with that lucidity of explanation for which he was remarkable, Gilbert drove it by belt from an extension of the axle-shaft, beyond the pit-wheel, possibly because he could not arrange the counter-shaft directly in line with the latter and wished to stagger it to one side.

From the middle of the axle-shaft he drove a wallower and upright shaft for the auxiliaries; the millstones being geared to the counter-shaft. Beyond these came belts for the chaff cutter and layshaft respectively – the latter to drive an oat -crusher; and an old pair of wheatstones served for bean splitting etc. Gilbert vacated the premises in 1861, however, and four years later Mr. Saunders moved in, remaining until 1873. Ben Darvill from Princes Risborough, came in next; after which the Corporation bought up the mill temporarily in connection with making their sewage farm, and Ben and his son settled down at Marsh Green Mill. The Corporation kept Bowden Mill closed for two years, then Fred Ware from Coleshill Windmill opened it up, but soon left for Pann Mill; and William Keen who had worked the latter for George Darvill, came to Bowden Mill, the two thus changing places. William Keen's youngest son, Mr. A.W. Keen, succeeded him after the Great War, and his name and address are now emblazoned in large black letters on the building. Mr. Cripps did a lot of stone dressing and repairs here about 1915, and was invited to work the mill when Mr. Keen's son and his miller were called up, but he had just joined Hills & Partridge of Aylesbury, and decided to remain there.

The foreman in 1939, Mr. Crockett, apprenticed with Thomas East at Culverton in '87 gained further experience at Gillett's Mill, and Eggleton's Mill at Bray where, he was particularly proud to say, he made flour for the Queen's Life Guards at Windsor before he was 21. Leaving there, Mr. Crockett worked Pann Mill for George Darvill, who paid him off along with Mr. Keen, on retiring. He secured a job with Basset of Maidenhead, but Mr. Keen wanted him to work Bowden Mill, so he consented to assist for a fortnight only, but stayed two years until 1896, when he went to Cuxham Watermill, the supposed oldest in

Oxfordshire, remaining there 21 years. In 1917, when Mr. Cripps declined the offer, Mr. Crockett accepted, and has been at Bowden Mill ever since. Up to 1939, he had worked *every day for 52 years*, except Sundays and Bank Holidays, without a holiday or a day's unemployment, surely a notable record!

I hoped to take a photograph of this typical had-working old-time miller, stockily built with reddish face and white clipped moustache, but he said, "No, I have been photographed only twice – once at my wedding and once since"!

Mr. J. E. Saunders once visited Bowden Mill while Mr. Crockett was there; and he pointed to the wheat-stones and said they were the ones he used, and were the finest he ever saw; and it appears that he tried to buy them from Mr. Keen who wouldn't let them go at any price; presumably J.E.S. wanted them for a keep-sake. Mr. Crockett said that Mr. Saunders (whose portrait is in *Reflections and Rhymes*), was a very big tall man, who could "only just stand up in the Mill"; this would make him, I think, at least 6ft. 3ins.

Marsh Mill or *Wycombe Marsh Mill No 414* – Nearly 1⅜ m. E.S.E. of Church

Power driven factory
Maps 1768, (1809), 1822, 1824, (1847), 1870, 1875, 1926

Gynault's fee, an estate on the outskirts of the parish, included the second of the six Domesday mills attached to Wycombe, and this one may be identified with that belonging in the late 19th century to Mr. Henry Wheeler at Wycombe Marsh, and later the property of Messrs. A.E. Reed & Co. Ltd. In 1171 Maud, widow of Ginaut or Ginant of Wycombe, conveyed her life interest in one-third of "Ginand's Mill" in Wycombe, to Walter de Penn. About the same date Ellis Gynaunt granted to Missenden Abbey his mill at Wycombe called Gwnauntes mulne, with appurtenances as "the water divides Frieneth from the corner of Upper Mill Croft down to the bridge below the said mill".

None who pass the present-day premises would suspect this picturesque medieval origin of the mill. Large and extensive, it is a purely utilitarian structure on the west corner of Abbeybarn Road; walls are chiefly pink brick and asbestos board etc; roofs partly corrugated iron, and a large chimney shaft dominates the scene.

Not alone in its aggressiveness is Marsh Mill, for we are approaching a whole group of mills which would find a more fitting place in the pages of a paper trades journal than in this topographical account of whirling windmill sails and rumbling water-wheels. But they have a past history; and Gynault, to be favoured with a Fee in 1086, was presumably one of William's henchmen.

Originally Wycombe Marsh Mill or part of it is believed to have ground corn; but about 1780, J Bates converted it to a vat mill, and the next owner was John Hay, or Hayes, from around 1805 onwards. In Feb. 1830 his mill was auctioned as "a water-corn and paper mill at Wycombe Marsh, on the London –

Oxford Road, 2 miles from High Wycombe" :-

"Vats and machine houses, spacious drying lofts, picking and finishing room, rag house, engine and bleaching house, plenty of water working one vat. Paper machine, drying cylinders.
Adjoining water corn-mill. Two pairs stones dressing, and bolting machines. Capable of grinding 16 loads a week. Dwelling house.
Several 100 reams of paper, in fine post, foolscap, pot, crown, and wrappers, paper-moulds couch planks and layboard, felt, press-blocks, levers treb-bles, trebble-lines, ladders, scales, weights, large strong press-frames and saddle, stuff-chest, iron vat pots, rag dusters, fulling stocks, light wagon, carts and horses".

Mr. Hay retained some interest in the premises, however, for a mill described as his was attacked in the November riots; but another sale was announced in 1837, when the Marsh Paper Mills were stated to include costly and complete machinery, a most powerful fall of water, and a natural spring of fine water in the grounds giving "a plentiful supply equal to six vats". No occupiers name was mentioned, nor was the cornmill offered.

Charles Venables became the proprietor and put in a new machine; but in 1850 Mr. Henry Wheeler – later Henry Wheeler & Co. – acquired the business, which seems to have been confined to paper-making, rags being chiefly dealt with until 1862, when the premises were burnt, and an esparto plant installed. Mr. Wheeler's son took over and the new building which was of wood in the upper floors, with two water-wheels, beam engine and horizontal steam engine, principally for beating and breaking. Blotting paper, drawing, and Government papers were made;

and Hedge Mill downstream and Treadaway, on the Back stream were used for half-stuff.

The premises were demolished in 1898, when Messrs Albert E. Reed & Co. Ltd. a Kentish concern, took possession, Mr. Salmons, whose father managed for Wheeler's being the new manager. They started making paper, with the aid of two gas engines, wood pulp being largely worked, but later reverted to steam. Most of the paper – white and coloured blottings and filterings, etc – was delivered by road to London in horse vans. A new wing was added in 1902, Mr. Will Cripps of Cuddington being employed upon it; and a little later his brother took charge of the three or four steam engines, and three (later four) big double-furnace Lancashire boilers, side by side.

Messrs. G H Wilkinson took charge in 1917, but the Company was shortly reformed as the National Paper and Pulp Co. Ltd.; and in 1937 as the Wycombe Marsh Paper Mills, Ltd. The first two companies used King's Mill Downstream and the present Company retained it out of use, with Loudwater Mill, lower down, in use. Three paper machines – two continuou roll, of which one dates from 1898 and one a modern "lick-up" type – are used at Wycombe Marsh Mill, a steam turbine being employed now, but a water turbine at one time replaced one of the water-wheels. About 1929 a minor fire gutted the old pulp sheds which were separate from the mill.

New Mill, Bryant's Mill or *King's Mill, No. 417* – 2⅜ m. E.S.E. of Church

Derelict
Maps 1768, 1793, (1809), 1822, 1824, (1847), 1870, 1875, 1926

New Mill, Bryant's Mill or *King's Mill*

King's Mill lying back from the London Road, and more or less surrounded by trees, stands almost a quarter of a mile north-west of the better known Loudwater Mills on the corner of the Maidenhead turn. More attractive than some of its neighbours, the fact of its being derelict imparts a little bit of character to King's Mill, which is largely of white-painted woodwork, with shallow slate roofs; the buildings are now grey and weather-beaten – roofs and windows are in holes, and there are several brick out-buildings and a chimney-shaft. Most attractive part of the premises is the red brick and tiled Mill House adjoining. Probably the present buildings date from 1881, when the mills were burnt and reconstructed only 40 years after a previous fire.

Whether the mill is named from its location on King's Mead, or from an "iron merchant and miller" of 1792, Isaac King, is doubtful, but the name King's Mill does not seem to occur in any early reference, Jefferys and Bryant call it New Mill, and the 1822

Ordnance names Bryant's Mill, Mrs. Bryant, paper-manufacturer, being then the owner followed by William Bryant. Mr. Spicer says that "Mrs. Brian", meaning Bryant was the original owner; but by 1830 the mill had probably passed to Plaistows, who occupied a mill hereabouts at the November riot. After the fire of January 5, 1841 it was described as "Bryant's Mill" when Thomas and Richard Plaistow were occupying it as paper-makers; and they appear to have installed a machine when rebuilding. Possibly they left after the next fire, in 1881, for Messrs. Soper & Co. were there at the end of the century, manufacturing blotting paper. Since 1898 the mill has served as an adjunct to Marsh Mills, in the hands of Mr. Albert Reed, the National Paper Co., and the Wycombe Marsh Co., the first two using it for paper making with steam engine and an iron wheel about 16ft. dia. by 8 or 9ft. The new concern dismantled most of the useful equipment, leaving a spherical boiler and water-wheel etc.

Loudwater Mill, No. 430 – 2⅜ m. E.S.E. of Church

Power driven factory
Maps 1768, 1793, (1809), 1824, (1847), 1875, 1926

Three mills were recorded under Lede in Domesday at 14/- and from that place the la Lude family seem to have acquired their name. Lipscomb says that Loudwater arises from "the noise incessantly made by the rapidity of the stream as it rushes with great impetuosity towards Wooburn, and is derived from Lauten Wasser", (although it is difficult to see why not from Loud Water!) but as the stream was formerly the Lude water, it seems to the present writer that the derivation is from la Lude family of medieval times. The river has also been called the Loddon, probably in error, but is generally known as the Wye until it leaves Wycombe parish.

In the 17th century, when the paper industry started in Bucks, various paper-mills were established in Loudwater and surrounding neighbourhood; and in 1638 a paper-mill called Loudwater mill "newe-built", was let for £50, and attached to Basset's Bury. Perhaps this was the forerunner of the present mill, no part of which puts one in mind of the 17th century, nor even the 18th! Generally resembling Wycombe Marsh Mill, it is a tall light-coloured brick building mainly of three floors, with iron window frames and some galvanised iron additional buildings and roofs, a chimney-shaft, and a tall black fence all round; but early in 1945 it was badly gutted by fire.

Mr. Spicer described the mill as "partly built in 1814/5 with 4 vats for book papers": and a machine was installed in 1830/2 for writing, printing, and bag papers. The Ecclesiastical Commissioners were the owners; and they sold it to Plaistowe's who had probably been renting it for a considerable time, but the unfortunate W. R. Davis, whose mill was set on fire and burnt by rioters, seems to have been established here at the date of that event. Various accounts state that Davis was at High Wycombe, Loudwater, and Wooburn, respectively, but we have to accept the evidence of a sale-notice specifying Loudwater, which narrows our choice to Loudwater and King's Mills. Two years prior to the riots, in 1828, the paper – mill of W. R. Davis was broken into and robbed of a quantity of old copper and brass. Davis & Crutch were listed at Loudwater in 1830, and in September that year, Davis's mills were offered for sale, but like Mr. Hays, he was not fortunate enough to dispose of the property before the rioters descended upon it

Equipment of this mill, and another which seems to have been Treadaway, on the Back Stream, comprised:-

Capital two-Vat Paper-mill with excellent machine for making paper, with drying cylinders complete. Also another two-Vat overshot papermill 200 yards distant, for preparing stuff, will be found a great accommodation to the first mill. Adjoining the latter is a convenient dwelling house. The whole situate at Loudwater, 3 miles from High Wycombe, 26 from London. Wm. Rob. Davis to View."

During the Riot, the machine was destroyed, and the premises burnt; and in Jan. 1831, twenty-four men were tried for this offence and 126 the previous day in relation to other mills; nineteen were sentenced to death, but according to Gibbs, the Aylesbury historian, "no one was seriously concerned about these

machines, and a petition for the men's reprieve was successful."

Situated at the west corner of the Maidenhead turn from the London road, Loudwater Mill belonged later to William A Kolle; and Mr. Charles E Ashdown had it from about 1902 to 1915 for making blottings and sterios with a 60 inch machine. Messrs T. B. Ford of Snakley Mill, next down the stream, then used it for a year or two, followed by the National Paper people, who worked it in conjunction with Marsh Mill, until the fire. An average-sized water-wheel served till about 1915, since when steam engines have been employed.

Snakeley Mill, No. 428 – 2⅞ m. E.S.E. of Church

Power-driven factory
Maps 1768, (1809), 1822, 1824, 1875, 1926

Not unnaturally industrial development at Loudwater had an adverse effect upon trout fishing; and it is recorded in 1820 that the steam at Snakeley Mills abounded in these fish, but in 1850, only "a few fine trout" were left; and this notwithstanding elaborate regulations and more elaborate proposals as to prevention of pollution and the preservation of trout. It was a pleasure to learn from a Thames Conservancy official, however, that things have vastly improved lately, with the willing co-operation of present mill owners; and he mentioned that the gas works originally did more damage than the mills.

A chimney-shaft of pink brick, bearing the title; "FORD'S BLOTTING" in great white letters ranged from top to bottom dominates the landscape so that "he who runs may read" but Snakeley Mills as a whole are not as displeasing as one or two others, although the premises are modern and extensive.

Past ownership and history seem rather obscure, but T. B. Ford & Co. Ltd. have been there at least 80 years, the founder being Thomas Birch Ford, who came into the blotting trade through marriage into the

Slade family, who invented blotting paper at Hagbourne Mill, Berkshire, about 1780 or 1790. Only hand-made blotting was produced by Slades, apparently, but Mr. Ford made it by machine.

The only previous recorded tenants are William Crutch & Henry Crutch, Snakeley Mills, 1830. About 30 years later Messrs. Ford rented part of Clapton Mill, second downstream, from Mr. John Unite as a half-stuff mill with beaters, sending the stuff back and forth by horse and cart as other mills did; and towards the close of the century they rented a portion of Treadaway Mill in the same way, in conjunction with James Saunders, corn-miller, and Henry Wheeler. In 1911 Ford's advertised "Finest quality white and coloured blottings and filter papers".

Snakeley Mills with about a 6ft. head of water, are now steam turbine driven and are – in the slight valley between the London and Wooburn roads, due east of Loudwater station. The premises are named Chapel Mill by Bryant, 1824, but on the original Ordnance the titles of Snakely and Hedge Mills are transposed, whilst Bryant also puts Snakeley instead of Hedge.

Hedge Mill, No. 427 – Almost 3 m. E.S.E. of Church

Power-driven factory
Maps 1768, (1809), 1822, 1824,
1875, 1887, 1914, 1926

No one can miss Hedge Mill as they proceed along the Wooburn road from Loudwater, where the Wye becomes known as the Wooburn Stream, although its past history as a watermill might not readily be suspected; its yellow brick walls with red facings flank the left-hand footwalk for some hundred yards,

and the muffled roar of big machinery floats down from the windows at all hours.

Hedge Mill, so named by Jefferys, 1768 and occupied in 1823 by Freeman Gage Spicer from Lord's Mill, was the scene of a big fire in the old wooden-built rag-house in October, 1828, the building and its contents, value about £1,000, being destroyed, but mill and house were saved; and the premises were insured with the Globe Fire Office. Freeman Spicer had recently erected a machine and strong suspicions were entertained of incendiarism, but nothing was proved, although no fire or candles had been used in the rag-house. Spicer also had Glory Mill, next downstream, retaining both mills until the middle 'fifties, and Lower Glory Mill also; all three buildings being used for the manufacture of paper.

Half-stuff was produced at Hedge, until the machine was installed, for making up and finishing at the other two mills; but previous to Spicer's time it had been a vat mill. In 1864, when John F. G. Spicer moved to Kent, Henry Wheeler acquired it for an auxiliary rag-pulping mill, and made half-stuff there until Messrs. Geo. H Hedley Ltd. took over in '95. Water power only was used, with a 6ft. 6ins. fall; and the building had wooden upper walls like King's Mill and the old Marsh Mill, which it supplied.

Small hand-made millboard and leather-board sheets were produced from two vats, by Hedley's, who had also a machine for making newsboards; and in 1903 a folding box machine – the second in England – was installed. This they described in 1911 as a "54 inch machine making box-boards and Duplex Wrappings". The premises were greatly extended meanwhile, alongside the Wooburn road, all the new part being in Wooburn parish; the old portion in Loudwater (High Wycombe) was demolished and replaced with modern brick buildings, a vertical water turbine of 40 h.p. being fitted in place of the wheel, but the turbine in 1938 did not justify repair, although usable. Steam power was also used until 1919, and there is still a big 2–cylinder tandem compound Uniflow steam engine in service. A steam turbine generator has been added, most of the power plant being in the rebuilt Loudwater wing; and a 165ft. brick chimney serves the furnace. Part of the mill-stream passing through the premises marks the parish boundary.

WOOBURN – 4 m. S.E. from High Wycombe

Wooburn Stream

Wire Mill or *Clapton Mills* – Nearly 1⅜ m. N. of Church

Standing empty
Maps 1768, (1809), 1824, (1847), 1875, 1926

Clapton Mill has enjoyed more vicissitudes than most of the Wycombe Valley mills, and that is saying a good deal.

Standing about midway between the upper and lower main roads, near the *Mother Red Cap P.H.* it is in a part of the parish called The Moor, and is now surrounded by beautiful gardens and waterfalls, with lakes and a bathing-pool. The Mill House 100 yards eastwards, was described by *Country Life* as one of the best small Queen Anne houses in England.

Jefferys marks the premises "Wire Mill", wire having been manufactured there 150 years ago. The invention of drawing wire is ascribed to Rodolph of Nuremberg, in about 1410, and mills for that purpose were first set up in that town in 1563; the first wire-mill in England was erected at Mortlake exactly a century later; but there seems to be no other record of the industry being pursued in Bucks. Peter J. Fromow conducted a paper mill here from the 'twenties to the 'forties, giving his address as "late Wire works"; and Bryant, who shows two distinct mill buildings, call them Clapton Mills; Lipscomb following suit, instead of omitting the name as he otherwise does all down the valley.

Later G. H. and F.E. Venables were paper – manu-

facturers here, but they removed shortly to Soho Mills, downstream, and eventually to Taplow Mills. Clapton Mills were sold in 1855 by the trustees of the late William Venables; "capital well-built brick, boarded and slate Paper Mill, average water power equal to 5 engines, machine room, engine house, working room, store-rooms, spacious upper floors, new chimney 140ft. high, large detached rag-house with sorting room above. Also on same head is a Half-Stuff Mill, water power working 2 rag engines; iron pump, draining chest, half-stuff racks, etc.; Substantial detached family residence near mill, pleasure grounds, gardens, ornamental waters, etc. let to G. H. & F. E. Venables for tenure of 14 years unexpired at June 24, determinable in 7 years. Yearly rental £550. Lessees are covenanted to insure for £4800, keep in repair, and pay rates and taxes. Freehold".

Electroplated ware (spoons, etc) were made here in 1861, about 200 persons, chiefly boys, being employed by Francis Higgins; and three years later Mr. John Unite, of the London tarpaulin firm used the Mill House as a country residence, letting out a portion of the mill, first to Messrs. T. B. Ford's for half-stuff, with beaters, then to Alec Stacy, the woodflour man, who had one or two narrow escapes from firing the mill. They used the south portion of the present mill, over the water-wheel; and about the turn of the century Mr. Unite's sons adapted the main portion for making tarpaulins, tents, sail-cloth, rick-cloth, and seat covers for the open-top London buses, and in place of the millstones they installed a big chaff-cutter the products from which served as a return load for their vans to town where it provided feed for their horses.

Large, glass roofed workshops erected east of the mill were filled with rows of sewing machines; and these and machines in the main body of the mill, (which extended about as far again as it does now, as well as having an east wing), were coupled by straps to shafts running near the floor, and electrically driven with a dynamo turned by the water-wheel. The latter had, of course, driven all the other equipment direct. Messrs. Unite closed down in 1911, and Messrs. Wainwright reproduction furniture and panelling manufacturers, took the premises and they appear to have blossomed into the Tudor Manufacturing Co. Workshops were converted for carving and polishing the woodwork, but it was found that the waterwheel would not normally produce sufficient electricity, and a turbine was installed in its place.

Some remarkable work was done under the super-vision of Mr. Keep, who still lives nearby; panelling for the *Aquitania*, the C.P.R. boats and the English smokeroom of the *Imperator* (later the *Berengaria*); and Mr. Keep himself went to Hamburg and fitted the panelling in the latter ship. They also put a beautiful hammer-beam roof in the *Halmonzora*. Lathes, circular and band saws, planing machines, etc. were driven by the mill, nearly 200 persons being employed; but owing to a dispute with the Union in 1919 the business closed down.

Just afterwards, when a cheap class of panelling was being done, repairing motor bus bodies, etc.,

two men from the Midlands, as a result of a griev-ance, set fire to the workshops, which were burnt out, only the mill being left standing. Mr. Beaufoy took the premises, and adapted the turbine to provide light for the Mill House (now called "Clapton Revel") and Mr. Keep's cottage; but the property now belongs to L. A. Bratt, Esq., who has further improved the House.

The remaining mill building is a remarkable old structure bearing signs of various alterations. With one red brick and two white wooden storeys, and a shallow slate roof, it has large square windows; and the corner posts, etc. are strengthened with big timbers previously used elsewhere. At the south end is a narrow pit-room between the outer wall and wheel room with a similar cubby hole about 2ft. wide the other side of the wheel house and very massive old walls between. Measuring 16ft. diameter by 10ft. with a 7ft. fall, the breast wheel had wooden L-shaped buckets and the sills for the bearings can still be seen. Both pit-wheels, or fly-wheels, about 14ft. by 18ins. were at a higher level, not on the main axle-shaft; and another fly-wheel outside the mill probably provided a belt drive to the workshops. A big vertical "flash" inside the mill, worked by gears, has been replaced by one outside; and the by-pass sluice with tiled canopy like a well cover, makes an ornamental fall down to a pool.

Two pairs of millstones were side-by-side immedi-ately over the water-wheel, and there is a tradition that one of them bore the date 1818; but the floor was cleared and repaired when installing the turbine beneath. The other mill which Bryant shows, was just north of the present one, where a second mill-pond is transformed into a lake; and this was most likely one of the four corn-mills in Wooburn for which millers made returns in 1798; but the Wooburn millers and paper-makers in early directories are difficult to sort out; and the same is true of Langley's nine mills in the parish in 1797.

Glory or *Upper Glory Mill, No. 426* – 1⅛ m. almost N. of Church

Power driven factory
Maps 1768, (1809), 1822, 1824,
(1847), 1875, 1887, 1914

Eight mills, valued at 104/- yearly, stood in Wooburn Manor in 1086; and Oliver Deyncourt held at least four of then in the 13th century. A water corn mill worth 20/- yearly in 1422, and other mills with their tenants and rentals are named in the transfer of the Bertie estate to Mrs. Du Pré in 1784. *Victoria*

County, Vol. III, records that in 1235 John de la Gloria held in Wooburn, of Oliver Deyncourt, a half fee, known from the 15th century as "Glory Manor", "the Glory" or "Glory Mills"; it was a sub- manor of Wooburn Deyncourt.

An agreement was made in 1256 by which Isabel

and Alice de la Gloria* were to hold land, and three mills in "Wuburne" of Isabel of Worcester; and this property changed hands frequently; but the Gloria family were in possession during most of the 14th century.

Richard King and Christopher Fisher rented Glory Paper Mills in 1627, they were therefore amongst the first in the country. They leased them to Edward Waller of Beaconsfield at a peppercorn rent for 22 years, but the premises were re-let to Richard King for £50 yearly, when payments were in arrears in 1645. The mill was transferred to Gilbert and Susan Beck to Sarah Peltzer and others in 1751; and is incidentally named Glory Mill by Jefferys in 1768. Freeman Gage Spicer, paper-manufacturer, and his descendants occupied Glory Mill in conjunction with Hedge Mill from about 1820 to 1850, and then took Lower Glory Mill as well, for a few years. William Wilds was resident occupier about 1860, followed by Messrs. Grosvenor, Chater & Co; the Glory Paper Mill Co. Ltd., until about 1890; and Messrs Dunster & Wakefield who failed in 1893. Thence onwards Messrs. Wiggins, Teape & Co. Ltd. have been the proprietors.

Three steam engines, one a big old beam engine which could be seen working from the roadway, were used by Messrs. Dunster, but the wheel-house remains even today a wonderful old structure of brick and timber hidden away amongst modern buildings. The fall was about 7 feet.

On Sunday morning in 1900 or 1901 the old mill was gutted by fire and had to be reconstructed; but the present extensive mills of yellow brick were erected during the years 1916/7, chiefly by Messrs. Hunt of High Wycombe. The new chimney shaft, some 230ft. high is the largest in the district, the old one, built 1846, having been 140ft. and the best in the valley in its time. Distinctive barrel-shaped roofs of reinforced concrete, a notable feature of the present buildings, induce all moisture to drain away to the eaves instead of dripping over the work; and in 1939 the dun-colour of these roofs gave place to a pleasant green.

Photographic paper, etc. are manufactured here in considerable secrecy; and electric power is provided by the customary steam turbine generator.

Mounted in the yard is a curious old wheel, some 10ft. diameter by 20ft. tread with three sets of iron arms and over 80 narrow buckets; but enquiries are unwelcome, and at the outbreak of hostilities, half a mile of heavy wire and barbed fencing was promptly added to the defences.

Wooburn or *Lower Glory Mill, No. 426* – 6½ f. N.N.E. of Church

Derelict

Maps – 1768, 1793, (1809), 1822, 1875, 1926

Wooburn Mill, in the days of Trade Tokens of which Bucks Museum has a particularly fine collection, had its one special Token, dated 1750. Upon it is the Legend:- "WOBORNE·MIL·HIS·HALF·PENY" and the symbol seems to be a mill-rynd.

Although no other reference to Wooburn Mill occurs in early times, the number of fires that have happened there within living memory have made it a place of note, even in the Wooburn Valley – in fact no one seems to have been able to keep count of them! (One of the earliest recorded mill fires in Bucks was also at Wooburn, in 1698, when "a dreadful fire" completely destroyed William Church's house and mills).

Doubtless Wooburn Mill is upon an early site; and informative adverts. for Lower Glory Mill appeared in 1827/8, when the assignees of James Pegg, bankrupt, offered the premises as a freehold estate.

"Lower Glory Mill, with Dwelling House and Orchard; capital Paper Mill with two waterwheels turned by a fine head of water, patent papermaking machine. Engines, Vats, Screw Presses, Drying Rooms, Store Houses, and Utensils etc. Adjoining the above is a compact and most convenient Corn Mill working 2 pairs of Stones and all incidental gear and machinery complete; and near the mill a genteel Residence called Northcroft Cottage".

A further notice stated there were brick falls to the wheels, and that the mills were upon "the best part of the stream". The land was tythe-free and tax redeemed; and there were 16 acres of fruit trees. James Pegg had occupied the mills for some years, with William Pegg, probably a relative, lower downstream. Venables & Collingwood had Lower Glory Mills in 1830, but in

---

* Or Alina la Glorie, as M.H. Hughes has it in his *Feet of Fines 1940.* Mr. Hughes also gives his dates one year behind *Victoria County* – 1257 instead of 1256, and so on; probably a difference of opinion as to which should count as the first year of any particular reign.

1853 an announcement offered "the late Samuel Collingwood's estate": Paper-mill on River Wye known as Lower Glory Mill or Wooburn Mill having 2 water-wheels; working capability equals 6 engines, plentiful supply of water from artesian wells, Northcroft House, etc.; J.F.G. Spicer acquired the premises, followed by Samuel Healy; John Goodson Turney was there for many years in the latter part of the century; and he is said to have had a fire, and is reputed to have installed the first board-making machine in England. The West Drayton Millboard Co. (Woodbridge & Atkinson) followed and a fire occurred somewhere about 1910. The Buckinghamshire Fibre Board Co. Ltd. had Lower Glory Mill in 1911: but during the Great War, Layman's were there then Via Board; followed by Lavis, who made motor bodies and had a fire in 1929 before going bankrupt. Mr. Major took the premises for flock-making and rags of all colours were hung out to dry in readiness for use; but the seemingly inevitable fire occurred when he was doing a good business. Flock milling is an inflammable trade, and Poyle Mill (Middx.) and one or two others occupied by Mr. Major were burnt.

After rebuilding, Lower Glory Mill was burnt in 1937, before being re-occupied; they were again (1940) refitted, but only some new premises in the rear, engaged on secret munitions work were occupied.

Built of brick on the ground floor, and chiefly timber strengthened with iron girders, above, the buildings stand across the stream, which turned two good wheels side by side, driving separate machinery by shafts and belts; the west one an iron breast-shot some 12ft. diameter by 8ft. with curved buckets; and the other an old all-wooden breast-wheel of the same dimensions with straight unventilated buckets. One axle-shaft passed through the wall and carried a 4ft. cog for a double-chain drive to an 8ft. suspension - type fly-wheel upon a layshaft, probably for driving a row of three large felt or skin washing cylinders (see photo). Beneath the east end is the by-pass in a conduit; and at the side is a smallish red-brick chimney-shaft.

The buildings, of a more pleasing aspect than other Wooburn mills, adjoin a tree-studded garden amidst verdant hills, and alongside Holtspur Hill is the extensive Mill Wood. Wooburn means the winding stream, or as one writer asserts "the winding stream in a valley beneath wooded hills".

Soho Mills, Nos. 288 and 424 – 1 f. S.W. of Church

Power-driven factory
Maps 1768, (1809), 1824, (1847), 1875, 1887, 1914, 1926

Passing beneath the main street near the parish church, and along behind the school wall, the Wooburn or Bourne Stream enters the premises of Soho Mills. Soho is said to have been the cry for calling off hounds for the hare in the 15th and 16th centuries, particularly on the outskirts of a town.

No one familiar with Soho Mills could fail to locate them on the darkest night, for the surrounding neighbourhood is pervaded with a peculiar and rather pungent odour something like that of hot flour; they are not flour mills however, but paper and mill board mills, and have been so far back as records go. In daylight the dark-coloured brick walls of the tall buildings tower up from the narrow footwalk and frown upon the passing traffic with an air of twentieth century industrialism; and a chimney-shaft shoots up aggressively into the sky. A large proportion of the local inhabitants are employed at Soho Mills, and Sheahan noted in 1862 that 70 persons were employed here, although this can be but a fraction of the number now engaged.

George Harrison was the proprietor, with a vat mill in 1823, and possibly Samuel & William Wright, paper-makers at Wooburn in 1830, were here, all other Wooburn mills being accounted for in that year. Later on, Charles Venables (junior) had Soho Mills in conjunction with Cliefden Mills, Taplow, but he eventually failed. For six years the mills were idle, but in 1860 Messrs. Thomas Stephens & Green opened up, and this firm now known as Thomas & Green, Ltd., is still there. Straw was largely worked until 1894, the amount of straw available locally being one of the attractions of the site, whilst another was the excellent water power (for which Mr. Spicer says the site was originally chosen) and also the good supply of spring and artesian well water. Rents also very reasonable, the site being a little apart from the industrial portion of the valley.

Rags, esparto and wood pulp were worked, good and medium quality papers being produced, chiefly coloured; and at one period at the close of the century the firm were also occupying Princes Mill, next on the river, probably for half-stuff. In 1911 two 63ins. machines were employed for white and coloured

Writings and a wide variety of high-quality papers, amounting to 60–70 tons per week. For 45 years, from 1886 to 1931, Mr. Thomas Wheeler who passed away in 1936, was the engineer.

Electric power is now generated by steam and, as might be expected, the premises no longer come within the classification of watermills; indeed Mr. Wetherhead, foreman at Hedsor Mills, stated that when he started as half-time worker at Soho in January 1881 at the age of eleven, a very early type of water turbine provided the power. This was in a small mill situated just behind the present big buildings that flank the roadway, at the spot indicated by Bryant and Lipscomb. These tall buildings contained the straw boilers, which revolved; then the "stuff" passed down to the lower floors to the cleaner and cooler, etc; thence in boxes to the beaters. A man broke the pulp with a rammer – a heavy lump of iron on a stick; and during the Great War bamboo was utilized for wood pulp, owing to scarcity of other materials.

Fuller's Mill, Princes Mill, or *Jackson's Upper Mill, No 287* – Nearly 5m. W.S.W. of Church

Foundations remain

Maps – 1768, (1809), 1824, 1875, 1926

Half a mile below Soho Mills the Bourne Stream passes beneath the Cookham road, and follows the village street of Cores End. The term "End" means and endship, or hamlet – not necessarily the end of a parish or district.

Princes' Mill was the last building on the left, where a cart-way passes through a yard to the meadows beyond. The neat brick-built Mill House abutted on the roadway, on what is now the grass verge with the mill behind it, standing across the water. Quite a picturesque little mill of the old days, wooden boarded with tiled roof, it stood for some seven years empty and a little forlorn, looking for an occupier who never turned up. In September, 1936, the search for a tenant was abandoned and the mill demolished, followed later by the house, this being one of the few watermills pulled down in the county within the last twenty years.

The loop-stream passed beneath the mill, driving an iron breast, or low-breast, wheel of about 8ft. tread within the building, the "flash" being built into the wall. Machinery was driven by line shafting and belts; iron vats and brick-built settling tanks were in the middle of the mill; and the main stream ran at the end of the yard.

The Wooburn paper-makers were frequently mentioned without the names of their mills, but one of the Pegg family was probably here in 1823; from 1830 till his death in 1841 Thomas Lunnon had Prince's Mill (Fuller's Mill as named on Bryant's Map), and in that year it was advertised as follows:-

"a vat mill known as Fuller's situated by the high road, in Wooburn Parish a mile from the Thames, 3 miles from Maidenhead and G.W.R. station, 3 from Marlow and 5 from Wycombe. Water supply equals 3 vats; machine, engine, and working houses, picking and finishing rooms, sizing room, spacious drying loft. Also a Half-stuff or Millboard Mill with one engine, two millboard tables. Full-sized paper-machine and vat, with drying cylinders, glazing rolls and extra pressrolls, by Donkin. Ibbottson's patent knott strainer by Donkin, 2 stuff chests with agitators, and waterwheel with iron shaft to drive same. New steam boiler (high pressure), lead retorts and pipes, bleaching chests and rag boilers, in perfect order for immediate manufacture of PAPER. Residence attached; garden, orchard, meadows, stables, chaise house, etc. Lease, 9 years unexpired. Rent £315. Auctioned by order of executors of late Thomas Lunnon".

Also included in the sale were:-

"gunny bagging, sack tyers, Smalt's blue alum, resin size, felts and felt stretching machine, dandy rolls, iron hand-stuff pressing box, millboard rollers with cast iron framing and brasses, copper stuff-lifters, prepared clay, etc."

If the Half-stuff mill was upon the same premises as the vat mill, they must both have been pretty small, for "Prince's" was not a very big affair altogether. The Venables family next occupied this and Lower Glory Mill, later renting Clapton mill also; but in 1856, the plant and machinery were auctioned – 60 ins machine by Donkin, two stuff chests, high pressure steam engines of 18 h.p. and 10 h.p.; two boilers, one Cornish 20ft. by 5ft. 6ins.: six rag beating and washing engines, etc; Messrs. Thomas & Green Ltd of Soho Mills later utilized the premises for grinding the half-stuff with beaters; and Messrs. Jackson's of Gunpowder Mill finally had Prince's Mill, this and the former sometimes being called Jackson's Upper and Lower Mills. When last used Prince's was a complete hand-made board mill, without machine; it had an electric motor of 100 h.p. and Mr. Jackson expressed the interesting opinion that it was originally built as a flour-mill because of its height and layout. An advert.

in 1911 stated the Bucks Handmade Millboards, Panel Boards etc.; were made; whilst at Lower Mill were two 76ins. machines, Brown and Grey Machine-made Millboards, Fibre-boards, Leather -boards, etc. being produced. Seven vats were used, with water and steam power.

Gunpowder, Eggam's Green, or Jackson's Lower Mill, No 285 – 6½ f. W.S.W. of Church

Power driven factory
Maps – 1768, (1809), 1822 1824, 1875, 1926

It is appropriate that this, the only mill known to have manufactured gunpowder in Bucks, should be styled Gunpowder Mill, but the actual date when this industry was pursued on the premises seems to be lost. The industry is very old; Maxwell in his *Highwayman's Heath* giving voluminous details of Gunpowder mill and attendant explosions on Hounslow Heath, says the first gunpowder in England was made there, by William of Staines in 1346 for use at Crècy, where cannons were first used for discharging stone cannon balls. Ingredients for gunpowder (nitre, sulphur and charcoal) are prepared in pots and vats, etc.; pulverised in drums, sifted in cylinders, and ground in powder-mills, all the revolving machinery being driven by the water-wheel in far off times. The powder-mill was an important item of the machinery, corresponding with the mill-stones of a corn-mill; and it consisted of a circular trough or pan of turned cast iron, surrounding an upright shaft or standard. Upon the latter was a horizontal spindle carrying two cast-iron edge-runners or rollers, one close to the standard and one nearer the periphery of the pan and as their name implied the runners were like millstones travelling on edge instead of lying flat. These iron rollers were generally employed latterly to reduce the risk of sparks (stones having originally been employed); the driving cogs were always iron to wood, for the same reason; and this being a dangerous process, powder-mills are kept apart, with thick walls to prevent an explosion passing from one to another. (Several very large bedstones from edge-runner stone mills for the preliminary breaking down of sulphur, survive to this day on the Middlesex marshes around Stanwell, a typical one mounted on a deep bed of concrete being 8ft. 3ins. in diameter and 16ins. thick, which makes the corn-mill stones at neighbouring mills look quite insignificant!) Further processes, pressing, sifting and glazing etc. follow, with the aid of other machines and agitators, before the powder is finally dried by air currents.

More than a century ago, Gunpowder Mill was converted for paper-making; William Pegg had it in 1826, when a quantity of special rope was stolen from him, and in 1845 an advert. of Eglean's Green Mill Wooburn, appeared:-

"The late William Pegg's Paper and Millboard Mills, farm implements, iron paper wagon, full-sized fire-engine; immediate possession, ½ mile from the Thames known as Gunpowder Mills. Water supply equals 3 vats, Machine, Boiler, Working, Drying and Rag Houses. Also Millboard Mill, 1 engine, 4 millboard tables, 2 press rolls, 3 chests, rope yard and bins, cutting house, 2nd and 3rd rags, baggings, flocks, vitriol, machine wires, rag knives, old mill shaft".

Later, an advert offered force feed pumps, 12ft. cast iron fly-wheel, spur and mitre wheels, etc., "removed from paper-mills in Wooburn Green neighbourhood" – probably from Gunpowder Mill.

Messrs John H. Jackson (now Jackson's Millboard and Paper Co. Ltd.) acquired the mills about 1870 from the Pegg family by marriage; and the premises enjoy the distinction of being the first camouflaged mills in Bucks – practically the whole premises, including chimney shaft some 200ft. high being painted in shades of green, black and red, and presenting an unusual spectacle from the neighbouring hillside.

The 1822 Ordnance marks the premises paper-mills; some copies of Bryant's 1824 map are inscribed "Higham's Green and Mill" and others "Eggams Green and Mill"; and the spot is now called Egham's Green and is in the Bourne End portion of the parish. The mills, situated east of Furlong Road, are now steam turbine operated and very extensive with an average sized low-breast wheel for driving glazing rolls, but disused: formerly they were of brick and wood construction with two wooden wheels driving beaters and paper-machines, etc.; the wheels being of moderate dimensions for the fall was slight.

Hedsor Upper Mill – 1 m. S.W. of Wooburn Church

Working
No map reference

Hidden behind the houses on the left of the Cookham road, is this mill of red brick with yellow painted wooden upper walls; but being upon the same premises as the older mill, which can be better seen, 100 yards down the road, it is easily overlooked or mistaken for an outbuilding.

Lunnon's probably held the mill from the time of erection, and possibly a previous mill also; the dates 1811 and 1878 are cut in the brickwork of the present structure, also 1854 near the sills and on the arch over the waterwheel. William Lunnon had Hedsor Mills in 1830 and Thomas Lunnon had Fuller's Mill.

A strong mill-head turns straight into the enclosed wheel-house from left bank of stream as shown in diagram [diagram missing] in which other machinery can be seen; and the latter is fully described in the introductory chapter to paper and mill-board making [see Appendix 2].

Over the office-door, the name of Lunnon's, who are described as Licenced Paper-makers, is still inscribed in old fashioned Victorian lettering; but Messrs. Jackson's acquired the premises in 1918 and are still in possession. A feature of special interest is the comparatively modern electric tramway which linked the Hedsor Mills with Gunpowder and Prince's by an overhead two-wire system, with little 4 wheeled electric engines now disused; the cables now convey electricity from the parent mill (Gunpowder) to this one.

Although called Hedsor Mills, these have been for some years in the Bourne End district of Wooburn, owing to an alteration of parish boundaries; and it should be noted the terms "Upper" and "Lower" Mill were applied to Prince's & Gunpowder until the closing of the former; and are only of recent adoption as regards Hedsor Mills.

In 1911 Messrs. T. & W. Lunnon (Hedsor Mills, Bourne End) had one 70ins. machine and 8 tables, making Millboards, Hand and Machine including Hand-made pure Rope-boards.

Hedsor Lower Mill, No. 286 – Nearly 1⅛ m. S.W. of Church

Burnt out remains
Maps 1768, (1809), 1824, 1875, 1926

Hedsor Mills were believed to be the only remaining hand-made bookbinders' board mills in the British Isles in 1939, the hand-made process being retained in the Upper Mill just described; but at the end of August 1940 on a Saturday night the Lower Mill was mysteriously gutted by fire. All the timber machinery – the wallower being the only iron piece among the gears and shafting – was charred beyond repair, all the weather-boarding burnt off, leaving only a black skeleton framework standing on the red brickwork base. Despite the wet and dampness pervading every corner of the mill and the abundant water supply, the whole building was blazing in a matter of minutes. Previously, between fifty and a hundred years ago, a less serious fire had occurred, the machinery being saved. Bearing the dates 1853, TL WL 1874, and WL 1806, the Lower Mill, perhaps more than the other, was a last surviving example of the little old-fashioned millboard mills working in the county, and may be regarded as typical of the smaller rag and half-stuff mills of days gone by. Painted in stone colour with russet tiled roof, the building had a square chimney-shaft at the rear.

According to Mr. Spicer, Hedsor Mills were established for paper-making in 1752, but later produced only boards. In 1824 Bryant marked "Hedsor Mill, Upper Bone End". Messrs. Thomas & William Lunnon occupied them as far back as 1823, and although Mr. William Lunnon died in 1836 and Mr. Thomas about 1841, the original name of the firm persisted until the business passed to Messrs. Jackson of Egham's Green, the present owners, in 1918. At the sale of Fuller's Mill in 1841 it was hinted that the purchaser might be granted lease of Hedsor Mills.

"Situated by the high road in the parish of Hedsor, ¼ mile from River Thames, and about the same from Fuller's Mill comprising Millboard mill, working four tables and one engine with work house, finishing room, roll house, drying lofts, cutting houses, etc. A PAPER MILL working two engines and one table with work house, finishing room, drying lofts, etc. Dwelling house with walled gardens. The use of vats, chests and presses, fixtures and utensils would be included in purchase".

In 1888 a board machine was installed, all classes of millboard being made from rope, hemp, brown and other waste paper; and all details of machinery are incorporated in the introductory chapter or depicted in the accompanying diagrammatic plan. Behind the mill, controlled by a large pair of sluices, is the by-pass, which rejoins the river ere passing beneath road to follow the shortest route towards Father Thames.

Farewell old-time mill-board mill, which the Americans offered to purchase and remove just before the war!

Hedsor Old Mill – 1⅛ m. S.W. of Wooburn Church

Foundations and wheel remain
Maps 1768, (1809), 1875, 1926

Two mills were appurtenant to Hedsor Manor (not listed in Domesday) in 1492; and were alienated by Sir Edmund Peckham in 1555 to Thomas Godfrey and his heirs. The mill lands with free fishery passed in 1611 from Walter and Elizabeth Wilcox to Robert Lee, whose descendants conveyed the mills in 1650 to William Hyde and others.

The Old Corn Mill adorned the west bank of the stream (which separated it by a few yards from Lower Mill) with the tiled Miller's cottage (bearing the date 1757) standing betwixt it and the roadway. Over the stream is a low-breast wheel of 15ft. diameter by 5ft, with 8ins. wooden floats and ventilated wooden sole-plates of similar size, the floats being upon iron staves keyed behind the shrouds. Three sets of slender iron arms secure the wheel to a square iron shaft, and a complete iron cog wheel has its arms clamped to those of the water-wheel, the drive being taken into the mill by layshaft; and in front of this cog or spur is a much smaller one secured to the end of the axle, beyond the journal, and driving another layshaft, with a dog-clutch. The axle is almost in line with that of Lower Mill with dividing wall in mid-stream.

Robert Lunnon was the miller in 1798; but in 1853 William Garner was the corn-miller at Bone End (now Bourne End), this being Hedsor Old Mill which was then the only independent corn-milling business below Bowden Mill; and Richard Tubb occupied the premises in 1860. From the seventies to the present century Messrs T. & W. Lunnon worked it, but Messrs Jackson's on acquiring the premises in 1918 demolished the corn-mill and only the water wheel and an iron crown-wheel and wooden stone-nut remained in an outhouse in 1940.

Lower Mills, Bourne End – 1¼ m. S.W. of Church

Gone
Maps 1768, (1809), 1875, 1926 (Mill House)

At the Lower Mills, the property of and worked by Mr. Morley in the 'sixties, situated about 50 yard from the Thames, on the Wooburn Stream or River Bourne, is a 300ft. artesian well supplying water of purer quality than the brook; and of especial interest is the fact that the water was drawn by the water-wheel of the paper mill, thus adding yet another to the varied tasks our mill-wheels have performed.

Lower Mills were an extensive premises, used principally for millboard making, about 60 people being employed; and adjoining the mills, pleasingly situated on the banks of the Thames were Mr. Morley's house and gardens, a mile above Cookham Toll Bridge.

Probably – as Mr. Spicer implies – this is not a very early mill site, for the final 200 yards of the Bourne Stream are at right angles to its general course; in fact the well-known Blessing's Ditch leading down to Hedsor Wharf, near to which pile-dwellings were found is no doubt the old river bed.

Mrs. Caroline Angell had the mills in the first half of last century for hand-made paper. Mr. Morley followed and installed a machine, but was unsuc-cessful; then Chadwick, Bros & Co. took the mills for a time, but failed. Mr. Chadwick was listed in 1877, as a paper-maker, but Messrs. Jackson and Smith took over about that date, as paper and mill-board makers and became the Buckinghamshire Millboard Co. Ltd, occupying the premises until the 'nineties, when the mills were closed down and completely demolished. Mr. Wetherhead of Hedsor Mills, who worked for the latter company after leaving Soho, recalled the Bourne End Lower Mill as a hand-made brown paper and millboard concern, worked by one water-wheel and steam; but they were seriously handicapped by the Thames at flood time. Generally speaking the building was similar to Hedsor Mills, of brick and wood, but with a very tall chimney shaft Now the site is occupied by beautiful rock gardens, which one hopes the Military have not destroyed, belonging to the Mill House.

This brings us down to the Thames, and we now revert to the Back Stream loop at High Wycombe ere leaving the valley of paper mills.

HIGH WYCOMBE

Upper Marsh, or *Marsh Green Mill* – 1 m. almost E.S.E. of Church

Back Stream or *The Dyke*
Working
Maps 1768, (1809), 1822, 1875, 1887, 1926

Sheahan stated in 1862 that 16 paper and corn mills stood on the Wye or Wyke, and its tributary the Dyke Stream, presumably meaning in High Wycombe parish. Since Flint Mill, on the Dyke stream from Hughenden had by that time probably vanished, it is assumed Sheahan referred to "The Dyke," or Back Stream; and this would make a total of sixteen mills if we include Lord's on the West Wycombe boundary or if the two at Bowden are reckoned separately, the others being Ash, Temple, Millbank, Pann, Rye, Bassetbury, Marsh, King's, Loudwater, Snakeley and Hedge on the main stream; and Marsh Green, Beech and Treadaway on the Dyke.

Marsh Green Mill stands at the bend in Back Lane, which follows the Back Stream from Bassetbury to the *Happy Union P.H.* at Loudwater where the two arms of the stream, divided just above the Market hall, re-unite. Situated west of the lane, Marsh Green Mill has a very substantial Mill House (lately occupied by Lady Redesdale and Unity) immediately south of it, backing on to the mill-yard. Of white-painted brick and some weather boarding, with tile roofs, the mill is not displeasing in appearance, when viewed from the slopes of Keep Hill.

Since the fire in the summer of 1935, which gutted part of the mill, it has been overhauled, and has four pairs of stones and modern elevator equipment; the building, believed to be very old, contains substantial old timbers throughout, and the machinery is partly of old-fashioned wooden construction. Enclosed at the east end is a very good 12ft. all-iron overshot wheel, 10ft. wide with three sets of arms, still in

service although steam is also installed; a large 8-armed mortice pit-wheel drives an iron wallower, large stone-nuts turn the two pairs of water-driven stones with bridge-trees parallel to the axle tree; and a layshaft geared to a bevel beneath the great spur drives conveyor screws and mixers etc. by belts. The sluice leads away beneath the lane, as does the mill-tail after tunnelling under the mill-yard.

Thomas Edmonds of Pann Mill also had Upper Mill and Lower Mill in 1798; William Howard was a paper-manufacturer at Marsh Green in 1823; whilst Mr. Allnutt, owner of the paper-mill ransacked at Marsh Green in 1830, probably belonged to the Kentish paper family of that name. *Pigot's* listed Zachariah Allnutt at Bassetbury, the name probably being applied to the district in general, not the mill, although William Fryer was named at Upper Marsh in 1842. Perhaps Allnutt packed up after the riot, to be succeeded by Fryer, who seems to have partnered one of the Edmonds family. Abraham Turner was a paper-maker and rag-merchant at "Upper Marsh" in 1864, Ben Darvill being simultaneously a corn miller at Marsh Green; probably this, the only mill in Marsh Green was divided between corn and paper milling, for the term "Upper Marsh" seems to have applied to this establishment, which is marked Upper Marsh Mill on the 1822 Ordnance.

Ben Darvill, junior, is listed in 1877, followed by his sons; William Whencup was the miller in 1903, but David Basset, of Maidenhead and Bassetbury, was here till about 1930, when Mr. G. J. Mason, miller, baker and farmer took over to grind poultry food – layers' and growers' mash, etc.

Lower Marsh or *Beech Mill* – Nearly 1¾ m. E.S.E. of Church

Gone
Maps 1768, (1809), 1822, 1824, 1875

Beech Mill stood in Wycombe Marsh, below Beech Hill, which overlooks the industrialised valley between Wycombe and Loudwater; it was close to the little ford upon Beech Road, which leads from King's Mead Road (Back Lane) towards Wycombe Marsh

Mill on the main road. Otherwise called Lower Marsh Mill, it is marked as such upon the original Ordnance; but other maps do not name it.

Always used for the manufacture of paper, so far as records show (although Thomas Edmonds was a corn miller at "Lower Mill in 1798 – a rather doubtful identification), Beech Mill is marked "Paper Mill" on Bryant's 1824 map.and was occupied by William Street until mid 1823, when furniture, animals, carts, and mill equipment were offered for sale; and Henry Kingston confirms that Street had a mill on Wycombe Marsh before Saunders.

Five years later the property was advertised as:-

"Valuable Paper-mill, cottages and meadow land. Never failing stream of water, in parish of Chepping Wycombe. Valuable lease of very complete PAPER MILL, with water wheels, fixtures, machines, utensils, in Lower Marsh, late in occupation of Mr. George Crofts, Beech Mill paper manufacturer. Well supplied with spring water, unexpired lease for 16 years at £238 per annum including machinery."

George Crofts was a paper manufacturer at Wycombe Marsh in 1823; and in 1839 Lower Mills, Wycombe Marsh were occupied by Edwin Morby (Morley?) who advertised writing and handmade paper, etc. by direction of the Sheriff. Morley & Saunders were here in 1842; and Thomas Harry Saunders occupied Beech Mill as a paper-maker from the 'fifties to the 'nineties – owner the Rev: M . Geneste – being established at Rye mill throughout this period and for some years later. These two mills were the last vat mills in the district, according to Mr. Spicer, being converted to imitation hand-made paper in 1891.

At about the turn of the century, the Corporation of Wycombe bought Beech Mill and demolished it in connection with their sewage scheme, although the actual mill site in field O.S. 40 to the west of the ford, is unoccupied to this day; and a stream bed, probably the mill-stream, emerges from a culvert on the bank of the main stream, from beneath the spot where the mill seems to have stood.

Fennels, *Overshot* or *Treadaway Mill* – 2⅝ m. almost E.S.E. of Church

Gone
Maps 1768, 1793, (1809),
1822, 1824, 1875 1926

Treadaway Mill stood at the foot of Treadaway Hill on the slopes of which is Fennel's Wood; and on Bryant's map it is called Fennel's Mill. The term "Overshot", on the 1822 Ordnance, has been applied to the mill periodically until recent years; but the local millers prefer to call it Treadaway. Standing close to the roadway at the north corner of the Loudwater station cross-roads, Treadaway Mill has a white-washed brick ground floor, with two whitish weatherboarded floors above, and a hip-gabled roof.

A neat brick and flint house bearing the inscription "Prospect Place, 1877", stood behind the mill, separated therefrom by the mill-stream, with the by-pass running behind the house, the sluice-gate being in the by-pass instead of in the bank of the stream; a water-wheel was within a projecting bay at the east corner of the mill. Stream and the mill-tail rejoined before the reunion of the two streams; and the wheel was a small iron overshot – hence the name, for overshot wheels were unusual in the Wycombe Valley. This wheel is believed to have driven the millstones in corn-milling days whilst paper was made in the other half of the building with the aid of a breast wheel situated above the overshot on the stream.

In a series of sale announcements in 1830 the mill was offered as follows:-

"Valuable copyhold estate. Two-vat paper-mill with 10ft fall, called Overshot Mill in High Wycombe parish; and adjoining corn-mill, property of Miss Ball. Dwelling, fishing, etc.:"

This was presumably Mary Ball of Loudwater, miller, in the 1830 directory, in which year Ann Crutch was a paper maker at Over Shot Mills, – a spinster's alliance perhaps!; and John Ball, miller, was listed at Loudwater in 1842. A later notice announced the sale at Treadaway Mill of a large iron bleaching boiler, rags, layboards, felts, wrappers, flocks, 50 glass carboys, etc. etc.

Augustus Gaviller, paper maker of Overshot Mill, is listed around the half century, and some time later it was agreed between the occupiers to work in 48 hour turns, the same as at Bassetbury; but 50 or 60 years ago T. B. Ford (blotting), Henry Wheeler (paper) and James Saunders (corn) were all using this comparatively small building. Saunders was there from about 1860, and his son eventually had the mill; then Levi Hillsden, son of the Wycombe millwright at Dexter Foundry, shared the building with a paper-miller. At another period, one tenant had the water in the daytime one week, for twelve hours, and at night-time the next week. Hillsden was still there in the

Fennels, Overshot or *Treadaway Mill*

early 'nineties, but the paper business closed down before he left. David Basset, who was at Bassetbury from 1910 or earlier, had Treadaway Mill for corn, for a time, later concentrating on Marsh Green and Bassetbury, whilst Treadaway was tenanted by William Hoath, and then cleared out to be succes-

sively used by a road haulier, a chair and cabinet maker and an electrical business.

About 1886 the mill was burnt out, which probably caused the cessation of paper-making; in the twenties it was partly gutted, and in 1935 it was again burnt, a month or two after the Marsh Green fire, having been rebuilt after the previous fires, and this no doubt accounts for the fact that the gutted mill was seen to be an iron-framed building when the wooden debris was dismantled from it. For some time this gaunt framework stood by the roadside, with some of the lower brickwork intact, and also the little overshot wheel remaining in its pit to the last; but the County Council bought the site and refused to allow reconstruction, on the pretext of wishing to rebuild Back Lane as a sort of Loudwater by-pass, although they should gave known this to be impracticable. The Back Lane is a notoriously unsatisfactory site for a road, for, in the words of Sheahan, "the river at times causes great alarm and inconvenience to the mill owners, as the soil, without any previous cracky appearance, suddenly falls in, carrying very exten-sive chasms, and letting escape, in some vast subter-ranean passages or tunnel, immense quantities of water. In 1857 a farmer had a narrow escape of having his two horses and a plough swallowed up, as the ground gave way to that extent. Some of the mill-owners have introduced iron piping projecting a foot above the level of the water, which at time acts as a vent for fixed air and a load roar is heard" The council has failed at Bledlow, Simpson and Wolverton, amongst other places, to build a new road in the vicinity of water without causing extensive and destructive floods; and although it demolished Treadaway Mill 10 years ago, it has still not embarked on the proposed road.

In 1939, "Prospect Place" which survived the mill was cleared out and demolished.

HUGHENDEN – 1½ m. N. from High Wycombe

Dyke Stream or *Hughenden Brook*

Millfield Wood – Approx ¼ m. N.N.E. of Church

Gone
Millfield Wood on 6" map

Location given above is of the supposed mill site, not of Millfield Wood, which is on the hillside about three furlongs east of the church; and the only available explanation of this name is that in the fields near Church Farm, west of the main road, is a loop stream with some slight foundations which might have belonged to a mill. This alleged site was pointed out to me when enquiring about another mill, and was not suggested to explain the name of the wood, which had not been mentioned during the conversation. It is not a generally known site, for no mill has stood there for a couple of centuries; and one cannot assume positively that the wood is named after it, especially as there is a Mill Field on the far side of the wood (O.S. 148 – a not very probable windmill site because it is below the brow of the hill).

The Dyke Stream marked Hitchendon Brook on Henry Kingston's map, and arising from springs in the fields near the *Harrow P.H.* has not infrequently flooded the road for considerable periods.

Flint Mill – ¼ m. S. of Church

Gone
Map – 1822

"A watermill in Hughenden is named in 1279" says *Victoria County, Vol. III.* It was then held by Adam de la Penne, and previously by Walter Bluet, but no later reference to this early mill has been found.

Another account mentions that "on this stream once stood a mill by Old Ford Lane, and the head-water surrounding a small island fills up when there is sufficient water in the stream"; and of this same little stream, Mr. R.S Downs says in *Records of Bucks, Vol. V.*:- "The little babbling brook which meanders through the park, though too small to be entitled to the name of a river, yet with its little cascades and rustic bridges, lends a pleasant charm to the landscape, as it races on its way to join the Wye at Wycombe. Upon its banks formerly stood the old Flint mill. It is well known that the late Earl Disraeli had a great partiality for high-sounding titles, and accordingly he was wont to designate this brook 'the ancient river Kishon'".

In addition to Millfield wood, which seems too distant from Flint Mill to be associated with it, there are Upper and Lower Millfield, and Millfield Grove at Hughenden. Flint Mill, which is named on the 1822 Ordnance, has been gone a great many years, and no millers' names have come to light.

Glenister's Waterwheel – 3 f. N.N.W. of Church

Wheel remains
No map reference

The long list of Wycombe mills, opening with a more or less private concern at West Wycombe, terminates with a purely ornamental wheel in Messrs. Glenister's premises on the Hughenden road – a wheel which scarcely merits inclusion for it never drove a mill, but it comes in a similar category to Mr. Taylor's wheel at Aylesbury.

Mr. Glenister had his wheel made at the end of last century by a jobbing millwright named Baldwin of Naphill, to ornament his garden which he laid out very nicely at the same time. About 5ft. diameter,

with iron buckets, and fed by a proper sluice for diverting the stream, the wheel pumped water to Mr. Glenister's house for a number of years, but since his death the garden and terrace have been much neglected, and the wheel stands idle and rusty – a curiosity waiting to ensnare the seeker after lost watermills!

The Dyke Stream meets the River Wye close to the Temple Mill site in Bowdrey's Lane, bringing our Wycombe pilgrimage to a close in the heart of the town.

BURNHAM – 3 m. E.N.E. from Maidenhead
West Mill – Site unknown

Cress Brook (?)
Gone

A mill eventually known as West Mill stood on that portion of Burnham Manor which came to the Lascelles. First named in 1260, it was included in the claim for dower made by Cristiana de Gessenna against Richard "King of the Romans". Bestowed by him on Burnham Abbey in his foundation Charter of 1266, the property was described as the mill, fishery and land which were John de Boveney's. In !535

when a rent of 14/8d was paid for Wetsmill to Earl Huntingdon, of Cippenham Manor, together with fishery valued at 40/-, a 21 year lease was obtained by William Tredway; but a lease in 1578 speaks of Westmill as the *former* mill. Probably it was situated on the Cress Brook which, rising in the west of Burnham parish, flows by Dorney Church and Lower Boveney to join the Thames near Eton Wick.

BURNHAM

Two Mile Brook

Burnham Mill, Aymill, or *Haymill* – 1 m. S.E. of Church

Working
Maps 1768, (1809), (1847), 1875, 1902

A mill in Cippenham, called Aymill, was given with the chapel there to Burnham Abbey by Richard, King of the Romans (the Earl of Cornwall, who was claiming the throne of the "Two Sicilies" – Naples and Sicily – the emperor of which styled himself King of the Romans to establish his authority over Italy); and in the grant was included the water-course made by the grantor, leading from the mill to Burnham Abbey through Cippenham Manor. Henry III confirmed the grant in 1268, but later the right of the grantor to divert the water-course came into question, His son (Edward, Earl of Cornwall), however, confirmed to the Abbey the mill and water-course so fully that no diversion could be made to Cippenham Manor or elsewhere. Moreover he granted power at any time to stop the course of the water which used to flow to the Manor, and to close all breaks at will. This

concession, although ratified by Edward III in 1328 did not protect the abbess from citation before Cippenham Court in 1395 for obstructing the water in Aymill Brook at le Parke Burne and allowing it to overflow the land of tenants; and incidentally Edward the Miller was fined at the same time for taking excessive toll.

Rent of the mill in 1535 was 1¾d. but it was doubled in the grant to William Tildesley of the site of the abbey, when the mill was used for brewing. Paul Wentworth granted a lease to John Lidgold in 1565, reserving to himself the millpond and fish, and use of the pool for breeding cygnets and keeping swans.

Part of the miller's duty was to scour the brook leading to the Thames from millpond to Weedrake at Lake End Green, and down to the river, but Lidgold neglected this task and Wentworth's house was not kept sweet and clean from annoyance of foul water. Consequently a presentment for neglect was made at Cippenham Court, and after a final warning in 1583 Wentworth turned the miller and his wife and five children out of doors.

Meanwhile the mill is mentioned in a sheet of Churchwarden's accounts in Burnham parish register, dating from 1549, (as is proved by a report of the purchase of the "mass boke in Englyshe" meaning the first Prayer Book of Edward VI. published on Whitsun Day of that year). Amongst several items for road repairs is the following:- "It: to Jhon Ive for mendynge and gravelyng of ye hy way be tweyne amyll and the Kyng's hy way XX s." Except for the mention of Aymill as a place, in 1638, and Emill in 1707, no later reference seems to occur, although in 1701 James Price of Burnham, miller was jailed for not finding securities and fined £40 for another offence. Aymill continued to appear on the maps; except Bryant's and Lipscomb's which give "Burnham Mill"; and within the last century it has been spelt Ah Mill and Ashmill, but the recognised title has been for a long time Haymill.

Of white-painted woodwork with tiled roof, it adjoins a modernised Mill House; and faces the Great Western main line, from whose embankment it is seen to excellent advantage (especially as there is a fine mill pond of several acres which from the intervening roadway is comparatively obscured by the surroundings.

Midway along the mill building, is an all-iron overshot wheel of about 8ft. diameter by 6ft., driving 2 pairs on the first floor by a wooden upright shaft. The wheel has its own room, with water coming in almost at first floor level; and in a pit-room are the usual pit wheel and large morticed spur, the iron stone-nuts being fore and aft; beneath the spur is a crown wheel for driving the accessories. The by-pass coming round the mill joins the tail-water before passing beneath road and railway; and on the 1822 Ordnance and on Cruchley's map this stream spring and rain fed from near Burnham Beeches Station, is designated Two Mile Brook. There existed formerly a "*Two Mile Public House*" on the main road beyond which at Cippenham Green, the brook divides – one branch to Eton College and one to Dorney Common & Boveney Lock.

For many years this, the only mill in the neighbourhood, has been in the family of Rogers (not connected with the Buckingham and Aylesbury Rogers), although occupied by Henry Round, 1798 and the Hilman family in the middle of the last century. Now the Rogers Bros. do a little grist milling but are largely engaged in the coal business.

STOKE POGES – 2m. North From Slough
Domesday Mill – Site unknown

Farnham Brook

Gone

"Domesday" mentions a mill held of William son of Ansculf by Walter, for 4 shillings; but its low value suggests a horse-mill or cow-mill, although there is a good stream – Farnham Brook – on the west boundary of the parish, and a lake – possibly artificial in the Park. An alternative site is north of Farnham Mill Pond, where Bryant & Lipscomb mark a mill in Stoke Parish, with a pond above it but total absence of written references to a mill for hundreds of years scarcely supports

Bryant's somewhat indistinct symbol.

An anonymous history of the parish printed about 1900, argues that two families of De Molines connected therewith were related because one had a mill-rynd on their coat of arms, and the other some wavy lines denoting surging water as in a mill-pond: and incidentally a place-name Wynsmerehull occurs in Stoke Poges, which might be a corruption from Windmillhill.

FARNHAM ROYAL – 2m. N.W. from Slough

Farnham Royal Mill – 1½ miles S.S.E. of church

Farnham Brook or *Mill Brook*

Gone
Maps 1768, 1793, 1801, (1809), 1824, (1847)

In 1086 a mill was attached to Farnham Manor, having been built since the time of Edward the Confessor by Ralph Tallebosc; and first mention of it as a watermill occurs in 1309. The Earl of Shrewsbury

in 1539 leased the mill and "le Oysle Browne Close" to Nicholas Cowper, *alias* Monsfraye, and in 1560 Anthony Reade obtained a lease of it which short reverted to William Cox. Commissioners were sent to

Farnham in 1572 to enquire into damage done to Crown property by raising the mill pond; and Anne Twiste, the royal laundress and Thomas Twiste, groom received a grant in 1585 of Farnham Watermill and closes for 21 years from Queen Elizabeth. In 1609, when David Salter, was in possession, another commission enquired into lands attached to the mill, which was then granted to Sir Edmund Coke, Chief Justice, by James I. Mr. Salmon "of the mill" held 40 acres in 1635, and the "lands of ffarnham Mill" amounted to 40 acres in 1638. William Herring of Stoke Poges was indicted for putting posts and a gate across the road to Farnham Mill, on Stoke Field: and 12 years later Robert Kingome of the Mill House was mentioned, and the Godolphin family possessed the manor and watermill in 1741.

The large 1801/2 Farnham Royal, Upton & Stoke Poges map at the Bucks Museum names it "Baylies Watermill – tenant, Robert Mason". No other mill is depicted; but Robert Mason is listed as a miller at Salt Hill in 1798 and 1830, at which time he also had a windmill, and at Farnham Royal in 1843. The watermill stood upon the Farnham Brook, just inside the present Recreation Ground on the Bath Road and the old Mill House remained until 10 years ago with a mill-stone in the doorway. Exactly when and how the mill disappeared is not known, but the late Mr. Ben Burton met a man 60 or 70 years ago who said his mother had known the miller's wife.

Farnham Brook, running due south, joins the Common ditch or Colenorton Brook at Eton, with a branch – Willow Brook – towards Black Potts.

UPTON-CUM-CHALVEY – Southern Outskirts of Slough

Mill Ditch

Domesday Mill – ¾ mile S.S.W. of church

Gone
No map reference

At Domesday, one mill at Upton was valued at 4/-; and in 1263 Guy de Chancens held 12 acres of land and a mill at Chalvey and Upton. This was later held by the Prior of Merton and Andrew de Chancens; in 1443 Henry VI leased that part of Upton which included the mill, etc., from the Priory to help endow his College at Eton with tithes. The Reverend R.V.H. Burne, M.A. states in his *History of Upton cum Chalvey, 1913*, that the site of the village mill and fishery is near the railway bridge and Black Potts (from black pot – a basket-work eel trap) – a spot

which is now in Eton parish – and adds that there is no mention of the mill in 1535. Perhaps it had disappeared, for there seems to be no later record, beyond the name Mill Ditch which occurs in an interesting recitation of the parish boundaries in 1739, wherein the Ditch is said to divide the parishes of Upton and Datchet (as it did until the present century). Mill Ditch runs from Mark Bridge to Black Potts, but "Mark" has now deteriorated to Mirk, which becomes more appropriate as Slough's industries develop!

DENHAM – 2m. N.W. from Uxbridge

River Colne

The Durdent Manor Mill – Approx. 1½ miles N. of church

Gone
No map reference

Flowing down from Colney Heath and several points near Hatfield according to state of weather and springs, *via* Rickmansworth, meeting the county boundary about 2 miles above Denham village, the Colne watered the east side of Denham Durdent Manor, first mentioned in 1166; and Stephen Springall (*Country Rambles Round Uxbridge*, 1907) said it is crossed by at least 222 bridges.

Besides apparently owning at one time the Denham Town Mill, the Manor had a small fulling mill on the Colne alongside Harvill (now Harefield)

Moor, and due west of the wharf and lock of that name. John Child was granted this property for 7 years for 5 marks per annum in 1500 A.D. by Thomas Durdent who fled into hiding 12 years later because of a felony. To evade the law he ostensibly sold the Manor to William Newdigate and let all his land except the fulling mill, to various parties. Thomas Durdent, Junr. then came into possession of the mill and retained the profits from it for life.

Nothing further seems to be recorded about the mill, which does not appear upon a map of 1620; but the latter shows that a plot on the river bank, north of a house now called "The Fisheries" was Millcroft; the square field reaching almost to the Mill End Road was Mill field, and the wood alongside the road and touching the river higher up was Milldell Wood.

John or Johannes was the miller in 1334/7 and the Manor, which was old and in need of repair in 1377 is said to contain lath and plaster walls to this day, with some mural frescoes.

Abbot's Mill, *New Mill* or *King's Mill* – 1½ miles N. of Church

Working

Maps: 1768, (1809), 1824, 1842, 1875, 1887, 1914, 1926

At the end of Willowbank is a footpath leading through the New Mill premises to the Rickmansworth branch of the Grand Junction; and here we have, for the second time in Bucks a New Mill alternatively known as King's Mill.

In 1798, the two Denham millers, apart from Nash at the Town Mill were Jnº Hill and Samuel Hill. William & Henry Hull were the owners and millers at New Mill from 1830 to 1855, when they advertised it as a double water corn-mill; five floors; iron columns etc.; built of brick and slate. William King acquired the premises; and his son Harry eventually had the mill. Both were great farmers, and they had the assistance of Mr. Cox (who drives the mill lorry to this day) and his father before him. William King's sheep once beat the Queen's at Slough Cattle Show and the comment passed round "King beats Queen". His son kept pigs on the island behind the mill and fed them on stale flour returned from the bakers, but this being white flour it failed to fatten them, for want of nourishment. King's are believed to have installed the roller gear; and the premises are now sometimes styled Uxbridge Roller Mills, being much nearer to Uxbridge than Denham.

At Ivy House Farm, William King and Mr. Cox's father once cut, thrashed and ground corn, and made bread from it in one day! Success however had its drawbacks, for in the early 'seventies Mr. King was the victim of a succession of incendiary fires at the Farm, one or two being very destructive, and a tramp who admitted causing one of them was only saved from severe handling by police intervention.

Mr. Veech, a Scotsman, took over the farm and mill during the First World War, but was run down and killed by a motorist; and more recently, Mr. Cornwell has been the proprietor.

As a milling concern New Mill is a fine building of yellow brick and slate, with three conspicuous ventilating cowls, but its flat front, unrelieved by the picturesque nooks and corners that make watermills attractive to the eye, frowns somewhat harshly on the landscape. Brick-built extensions at either end house two large waterwheels; and when working the swirling, foaming waters accompanied by the familiar beating and lashing of water around the wheel, brings back something of the milling days of yore to the beholder. Unlike the average, New Mill is adorned with a plaster panel bearing both name of builders and date of erection

BUILT 1836
J. PENN, ENGINEER;
J SHOPPEE, BUILDER

whilst upon the chimney-shaft is a panel inscribed 1903.

Strictly speaking, King's Mill is driven by the Grand Junction Canal, which links up with both the Colne and the Fray river hereabouts. Colne joins canal half a mile upstream, and a little lower a branch without sluices comes straight off the canal, forming a wharf directly behind the mill, for loading barges, with a backwater for parking same; and a sluice then discharges into the by-pass and mill-tail of Denham Old Mill. The wharf pool feeds both New Mill wheels *via* flashes (no sluice); and the nearby lock-gates are dated 1864.

The east wheel, still in situ, is a 16ft. by 8ft. breast-shot with three sets of arms bolted into the centres, upon an 8ins. square fluted iron axle-shaft. About 36 L-shaped iron buckets are bolted to wooden starts and positioned to give narrow ventilating slots right across the wheel, in keeping with Fairbairn's original principles.

A larger heavy-duty wheel the other end was superceded about 1925 by water-turbine and electricity, the existing wheel being for auxiliary work.

The Abbott's Mills – 1½ m. S.S.E of Church

(1) The Cornmill of Denham on the Colne, or Old Mill

(2) Fuller's Mill, or the New Mill

Gone

Gone

No map references

From the voluminous History of Denham by the Reverend R.H.Lathbury. M.A. we learn much about the early Denham mills that would otherwise be obscure.

The Abbott's Mills stood together upon a site between King's Mill and Mr. Mercer's mill, and were burnt down at an uncertain date in the 18th century.

Both mills were granted by the lord of the Manor to Roger Tinctor – that is, Roger the Dyer, of Uxbridge – in 1303 for fulling cloth and grinding corn. Seventy years later, Roger Morcok was granted a piece of ground called the Dyeing Mill Eyot, or Tentour's Eyot, with the dyeing works (fulling mill) upon it, adjoining the Old Mill, for 21 shillings per quarter. In 1837 the corn mill, at that time utterly out of use, was called the Old Mill, and 11 years hence it was "so old that no one would hire it." The New Mill" was then the only one in use in Denham.

Although these mills amongst others were upon Denham Manor, the Abbott was in a position to let these two in particular; and in 1455 the cornmill being now in repair, he let both to William Clyfford for 10 years (*History of Denham* pp.161–2. On p.461 a similar account says the mills were let to William Staynsford in 1455 for 10 years). The agreement was as follows:-

"This indenture made the 17th day of December 33 Henry VI between Edmund Kyrton, Abbot of the Monastery of the Blessed Peter of Westminster on the one part and William Clifford of Woxbrigge (Uxbridge) in the County of Middlesex, miller, on the other part, witnessed that the aforesaid Abbot has granted and let on lease to the aforesaid William Clifford his two mills in Denham in Woxbridge, County of Buckingham, situate in one building under one roof, viz, one mill for fulling cloth and the other a watermill, with all the lands, woods, fisheries, etc.

William Clifford to hold the mills and have the profits etc. from next Xmas for 10 years and to pay the Abbot 13 marks sterling at the four quarters of the year. and the aforesaid Abbots etc. will repair, mend, maintain and keep in order at their own charge the 2 aforesaid mills, perfectly soundly and sufficient in all points and in all matters below water and above ... but the aforesaid William Clifford and his assigns shall repair, mend and keep in good order all the various Cogges, Ronges, and Trundelys, the aforesaid Abbots etc. and their successors will give and find the aforesaid William Clifford a sufficient quantity of timber to such amount as the said Edmund shall consider necessary. And the aforesaid abbots etc. shall give the aforesaid William Clifford one suit of the Abbots' journeyman's livery as often as the aforesaid Abbots shall give suits of livery to other lease-holders.

If the rent shall be one month behind the aforesaid Abbots shall enter the mill and distrain, and if behind for a year the aforesaid Abbots shall enter the mill etc. and take them back".

Kyrton resigned in 1462 to be succeeded by George Norwych. John Slyng tenanted the New Mill in 1388 for £8 per annum, whilst Walter Holting had the Old Mill apparently in 1391, and John Dudle the Abbot's Mills jointly five years later; William Clifford was tenant and Edward Bernard the miller of the Fulling Mill in 1478 in succession to Thomas Roberde; and John Fabyan had both in 1501.

The Manor accounts for 1388/9 show that John Slyng received one load of straw valued at 8d. but did not pay for it because it was for the repair of the mill, which was evidently thatched. Neither the Abbots' cornmill nor the cornmill near the church, to be mentioned later, paid rent, being in disrepair, but one of them produced a little corn, 2 quarters 4 bushels of wheat being sold at 4/- a quarter (10/-) 3 pecks 3 meslin at 4d. a bushel (1/3d) and tithes on the profits of the mill 2/11½. (Maslin is a crop usually consisting of a mixture of wheat and rye). At the Reformation, the Crown of course seized the Manor.

Medemill Mill – Approx. 1½ miles S.S.E. of church

Gone
No map reference

The Medemill stood near the site of Mr. Mercer's mill, later Procter's Garage: it was not the Abbot's mill and does not stand out prominently in the history of the Manor although belonging to it and repaired by the Abbot; nor did the Manor use it.

So far back as 1388 it was "much out of repair" and in 1370 the Lord of Colham was "stopping a certain watercourse at the Medemill to the injury of his neighbours, so he is on the mercy of the Court". Also, it was presented that the millers were then shutting the watergates of the said mill, whereby the flow of water was so hindered that the King's high-road was flooded to the detriment of the neighbours, etc. In 1377 Medemill was let for one rose chaplet; later, after repairs had been effected, it was let out on lease; and in 1396 a red rose rent valued at ¼ d. was paid. Up to 1492 the Lord of Colham paid this rent, probably an ancient right of his, to the Manor, but the Abbot had the right of letting out the mill, and his bailiff collected £6–13–4 rent from Richard Clyfford at that time. Probably this was not a Domesday mill, or the manor would have used it to grind the tenants' corn; and the name may be derived from Medler or Med-leys.

Roger Morcok tenanted the mill in 1401, Walterus Dyer 1430, William Dyer 11 years later, Richard Clifford being the miller, and William Staniford in 1450, whilst John Fabyan was miller in 1501. (It will be observed that the millers' names and other details coincide with the Abbot's Mill particulars; but the Reverend R.H.Lathbury, whose book is very exhaustive, is apparently satisfied that Medemill is a different one).

Two early mills unidentified may be mentioned here, since they are probably one or other of the foregoing; in 1340 the Lord Abbot was bound to make a bridge at the Broken Mill, and it must not be made to the detriment of his neighbours; in 1478 Drugo Brudenell was tenant of a mill quite in ruins, called Chaweyes-myll.

Now we come to the most interesting, if not unique record of the cost of repairs to the Medemill and the Mill of Denham in the late 14th century – probably 1388:-

"Wages of John Bourne 1½ days for setting
   up the wall of the Medmill @ 4d per day   6d
"Ditto to John Trewe, 3 days thatching the
   same @ 4d a day   1/0
"Wages of a man helping the same   6d

"Purchase of ½ hundred laths for the same   3d
"¼ cwt. of stantis nails for the same   2d
"200 lathnails bought for the same   2d
"Wages to John Sawyer engaged for 5 days doing
   the work on the . . . ? at the Medmill etc.   2/6
"To Richard Drawe, hired for 4 days @ 5d
   a day   1/8
"By purchase of iron for making 2 . . . ? for the
   said mill   3/6
"Purchase of iron for making a pin, etc.   2/0
"Purchase of iron for making a new spindle for
   the corn mill, the old one being allowed for   1/8
"By purchase of rongs for the cornmill   10
"By wages to Richard Pynston for 2 days,
   John Trewe 2½ days, Adam Middlemore for
   ½ day, felling and lopping timber in the parks,
for making new cogwheel at the cornmill
   @ 4d each per day, etc. etc.   1/8
"Costs of carting the said timber from the
   parks to the mill   1/0
"Paid for making cog wheel and the repair
   of the said water wheel, by agreement, all
   things considered   1/16/8
"Bracing up and binding the said cogwheel
   with iron bolts and bands, iron and nails for
   the same purchased   3/4
                            2/17/5

"Costs connected with Denham Cornmill.

"Paid to Robert Thurston removing old
   woodwork of the mill, trimming and sawing
   new timber for the same, putting new
   millstone into position making the mill
   ready for grinding the whole of the
   carpenter's work to be   10/0
"½ hundred gross of nails bought for the work   6
"Bracing up the cogwheel with iron bands   9
"Purchase of iron for making new . . . and
   spindle for the mill, the old iron being
   allowed for   2/3
"Purchase of steel for making 2 mill-bills   10
"Workmens' wages for making same   6/6
"By hire of a cooper for 1 day to hoop the
   hopper of the mill   4
"Expences of 36 men hired as for 1 day
   cleaning out and digging the sand out of
   the watercourse between the said mill and

the park gate for better flow of water everything included   5/4

"For the hire of Thomas Wyke for 12 days, John Franklin 4½ days, Richard Clark 3 days, John Norhampton 4½ days, on the same job – stopping up also a hole or well opposite the water-net of the mill – also ramming some fresh work at the mill, where the soil had been removed, in addition to the assistance of Walter

Holtyng for 4 days, who took nothing for his trouble, 4d a day each   8/0

"For bread, beer and cheese for 26 men who assisted at the said work for 1 day by request   1/4

"Paid to Robert Thurston for a brass socket on which the spindle or axle of the mill-wheel runs   1/6

—————
1/17/7

Old Mill or *Mercer's Mill* – 1½ miles S.S.E. of Church

Used as garage
Maps: 1768, (1809), 1842, (1847), 1875, 1887, 1914

Denham Old Mill, which became Procter's Garage, stands shorn of much of its former glory, just west of the river and canal on the Oxford road. Located at the corner of Willowbank it is large, and square built with dormer windows in the tiled roof; but the walls are now stuccoed and a yawning entrance-way admits such motor-cars as are not in too much of a hurry to stop.

"In crossing this bridge" (the old seven-arch bridge by Mercer's Mill) "we notice much prettiness at its upper part – foaming water from mill, weeping willows all around, grassy island all afore, trees of cypress both erect, water spreading wide and clear, picturesqueness every weir" -Springall in 1907.

In the west wall of the garage can be seen the bricked up arch where the big wheel, probably overshot, was formerly turned by a third share of the canal water, which also feeds New Mill, and Fountain's Mill, Uxbridge; but the building is cleared out and largely reconstructed within. The by-pass runs behind

the mill, under Willow Walk, to meet its opposite number from New Mill. The pleasing Old Mill Cottage and Old Mill House survive in Willowbank, behind the mill-building, with doorways set back in little nooks; and west of the mill is *Old Mill Café* in which is preserved an old wooden belt drum together with a note that the Old Mill dates from 1699 and was dismantled in 1929.

D.C. Webb was owner and Henry Stevens miller in 1842. Stevens and Mercer were afterwards proprietors until the First World War. Henry Mercer (whose family were mill-owners interested also in Thorney Mill, Iver: West Drayton Mill; and Fray's Mill, Uxbridge), was the last miller, eventually driving the millstones by steam power. Captain Adams of the R.A.F. then became owner and remodelled all the buildings. The Colne divides a mile below the Old Mill, which it approaches from the west, the main stream forming the county boundary for a while, and the Colne Brook deviating into Bucks.

IVER – 2½ m. S.S.W. from Uxbridge

Colne Brook

Iver Mill – ¼ m N.N.E. of Church

Sluices remain
Maps 1768, 1824, (1847), 1862

Iver Mill, (named in Bryant's map) and all succeeding mills in the extreme southern corner of Bucks are upon the Colne Brook, which pursues its course a mile or so within the County boundary, whilst the River Colne, first forms the boundary from Uxbridge, then deviates into Middlesex to join the Thames at Staines.

The site of Iver Mill is just behind "Bridgefoot House" in Delaford Park, where the weir and sluices exist; the Manor of Delaford, to which it belonged, seems to date from around 1250 A.D. In 1362 the Bailiff was ordered to put right the way at Iver Mill, he having diverted it. The rents of Iver Manor, to which Delaford was subsidiary, being really only a tenant holding, included in 1547 the farm of Iver Mill and water appertaining (except fishery), leased to John Williams for 50 years from December 1528 at £3. 6. 8.

Iver and Thorney Mills were mentioned in a pamphlet of 1641 supporting a project to bring the waters of the Colne to London, the rent of Iver Mill then being £16. Edward Trigg was the miller of Iver in 1695, Stephen Batten had a mill in Iver in 1784; and William Allum was the miller in 1798.

About 1800 Iver Mill was a large cotton spinning manufactory occupied by Mr. Thomas Dickinson and worked by water, alongside the big Georgian house called "Bridgefoot, with detached picking rooms and store room. The Lysons said that in 1801 the mill contained all apparatus including upwards of 2,200 spindles, 57 persons being employed there, and they added "this was the old Iver corn mill, of which remains can still be seen". Dickinson's venture was short-lived, and in 1844 "the late Mill site was included in Mr. Charles Clowe's property, and in 1847 only the Thorney paper mill and an oil mill were working". Apparently this is overlooked by Messrs. Ward & Block who later state that it was burnt in 1850; the oil mill was in the same building as the papermill. Joseph Hyde and Robert Jennings were millers at Iver in 1830.

The Colne Brook, says Stephen Springall, was far stronger years ago, except in droughty weather, giving the miller less anxiety than it eventually gave the Thorney miller downstream, so that Iver Mill "went round merrily enough, and successfully coped with all the corn which the jovial farmers on the surrounding land were able to bring to it. But about the year 1850 the old mill had a blaze up, until it had all blazed down, and Iver Flour Mills now scarcely remembered, for its lane of approach is closed up and the site well-nigh obliterated, the yet sonorous and musical water-fall alone telling as to where the mill once stood".

Although only two mills seems to marked upon the maps at Iver, three are claimed to have existed in Messrs. W.H. Ward and K.S. Block's voluminous *History of Iver* (1933) where they suggest that all three were located upon Domesday sites, and were valued at 42/- (about £11 in our money) Describing the third as Huntsmoor Mill, situated in Huntsmoor Park, and probably belonging to the minor manor of Cornwall, they omit to state what kind of mill this was, nor do I find any record of the millers in the directories; but in 1865, say the above authors, it was burnt out, leaving only the sluice gates etc. to mark the site. Several cartographers – Culliford 1842 in Gyll's *History of Wraysbury*; also Bryant, and Lipscomb mark all the mills known and admitted to have stood in the vicinity, but none within Huntsmoor Park; and in the writer's view, Messrs Ward & Block are barking up the wrong tree and are confused over Kelsey's Old Flour Mill (burnt Jan. 29, 1873) or Yiewsley New Mill, which adjoined a house called "Huntsmoor Weir"; but both these mills were in Middlesex – not Bucks. Finally, Stephen Springall, whose *Country Rambles Round Uxbridge* 1907 covers every known West Middlesex mill and others with meticulous accuracy, omits all reference to "Huntsmoor Mill" although he gives the particulars of Iver Mill. There is or was a Fuller's Field in the parish near Potter's Close and the Homestead.

Thorney Mills; Paper and Oil – 1⅛ m N.N.E. of Church

Derelict

Maps 1768, 1793, (1809) 1822, 1824, 1842 (1847), 1862, 1875, 1887, 1926

A fine old wooden-walled building, jutting forth into a narrow part of the Thorney-Drayton road, west of the Staines railway line is Thorney Mill, reminiscent of Weirhouse Mill near Chesham, to be described later.

North of the fairway with substantial yellow-brick, three-floored Mill House facing it from the south, Thorney Mill has the familiar louvred upper walls of paper-milling days and a great rickety tiled hip-gable roof, dark and broken with age, stretching the whole of its length from north to south, with projecting loading loft built into roof. Former white walls are grey from neglect; an idle chimney shaft, and broken windows boarded up, speak silently of the passing out of business of this giant among watermills. The empty ground floor, about 120ft. × 30ft. is of brick, with iron columns supporting the joists; but massive old timbers can be seen in the drying room above, which is open to the roof, like some great country barn, and it can only be the rugged strength of this old building that induced one firm after another to enlist its services in a district where modern factory premises have sprung up within walking distance. Even today the mill is serviceable, but for the tiles slipping from the roof.

Obviously erected as a paper-mill, the present building was occupied by John Owen, 1842 (paper), at which time it was either new or reconstructed according to an advertisement, Mary Ann Lane, paper manufacturer in 1853–4, Thomas Philps being foreman; and although Charles Venables, paper-manufacturer, had an address at Iver Lodge, this was probably Venables, Senior, of Wooburn and Taplow, who may have acquired the Lodge as a residence in retirement. William Edwards and Frederick Weidenbach Whichelo were resident-occupiers in 1864; and Price & Co. were paper-makers here from 1877 or earlier; during the Great War millboard was made here. For a short while the premises served as a paint works; and finally for the manufacture of iron water pipes of 2 or 3ins. diameter for use in factories, etc. An improvised hoist is constructed of these tubes in the yard, but the top tube has bent under the strain! It is believed that the wheel was used by the mill-board makers, and the river water for cooling the pipes; the wheel – a breast type of iron with 3 sets of 8 iron arms and L-shaped wooden buckets – is still in the wheel-house, with a crank-and-chain controlled sluice alongside it. At its outer side, over mid stream, the wheel drove an overhead counter shaft passing through the wheelhouse wall to carry an external drum, which probably received an engine drive; no pit-wheel or other direct drive is provided within the mill.

Now the entrance gates bear the faded inscription: "Iver Tube Works", and this concern closed down in 1923. The by-pass is east of the mill; and the mill stream immediately west. Thorney was probably one of the three Domesday mills in Iver; and one existed at the side in 1388 when, through the bailiff's default, the highway there was damaged by flood. Farm of Thornton Mill was leased in 1519 for 30 years to William Duffield for ¾d., but the mill rent was £25 in 1641; and by a remarkable coincidence Frank Duffield & Co. occupied the mill around 1910 for manufacture of Brown and Royal Hands. In 1701 a paper-maker

was established in Iver – probably at Thorney – in 1779 Richard Abrook made coarse paper at this mill; and Nicholas Mercer used it for paper-making until the half century. Mr. Mercer, a descendant of Nicholas, and owner of the invaluable large-scale 1842 map of the Colne and its tributaries – an original drawing some 9 feet long, which he kindly loaned to me – was born at the Mill House and believes his ancestor established the present mill-building.

Now we turn separately to Thorney Oil Mills, which were contemporary with the Paper Mills from about 1842 until the middle fifties. These were on the same premises if not actually in part of the main building; and Mr. Mercer agrees that both concerns were at this site; and that the mill was used for linseed crushing about a century ago. The list of mill owners and occupiers on the 1842 map gives Thorney Mill, oil and paper -owners Trustees of Edward Wright (listed as a paper maker 1830); occupier, James Wright who lived at the Mill House. Thorney Oil Mills were advertising the same year in the name of J.E. Wright, seed crusher; in 1848 they were described as spacious premises for sale "in the parish of Iver and county of Bucks", thus disposing of a less precise advert which mentioned West Drayton; and in 1853 Walter Graham was seed-crushing at Thorney Oil Mills. Thence onwards we hear only of the paper-mill, which once again settled down to its own routine – and shall we say, to its own *smells*, for linseed mills are indeed a landmark to anyone whose nose is in working order! So are the "noisome" stampers which rise and fall on the bags of linseed in a pit, like the early stampers in the paper mills.

COLNBROOK* – 3½ m. E from Eton)

[Colne Brook]

Langley Marish or *Colnbrook Mill* – 150 yards S.E. of Colnbrook Church

Gone
Maps: 1842, 1847, 1875

A mill in Colnbrook is named in 1274 – "Lucas de Baton, of the City of London, holds a mill in this town, or near it". – and in the 16th and 17th centuries two water-mills – probably under one roof – belonged to the Bulstrodes. In 1697 John Lee of Wraysbury, who had purchased them from Thomas Berenger, passed them to John Midgley and Thomas Gilbert; and John Fyce was the miller of Langley Marish in

1710. The only mill standing within living memory was at the end of Mill Lane at the east end of the town, and was worked by Thomas Cane in 1791; Issac Cane, baker, with Thomas Ayliff, miller, in 1798; Mark Alpheus Westaway in 1842, when it belonged to John Harcourt Powell; followed by Westaway's descendants till the sixties; and finally William Oakey Gurney was proprietor; the marriage

* A parish formed in 1853 out of parts of Langley Marsh (in which Colnbrook Mill stood) Iver, Horton, and Stanwell (Middx); but at the 1934 reshuffle, Colnbrook was once more absorbed. Gill (*History of Wraysbury*) says the bounds of Colnbrook, which belonged to the Middlesex Hundred of Spelthorne, were run over every 20 years – they needed it, but one wonders *which* bounds were run over!.

of his son James, corn dealer of Langley is recorded in the Medmenham Parish Registers in 1883.

In the early hours of Sunday morning, March 15, 1896, a disastrous fire occurred and "the old timbers flared and blazed away until reduced to ashes, and it has not been rebuilt" (Springall).

Colnbrook Mill stood beyond the present Georgian "Mill House" divided from it by a drive in to the yard of Old Tan House Farm, which entrance seems to have been roofed by an upper storey. The mill probably spanned the stream which divides house from roadway; the waterway is bricked; one guide of the "flash" existed in 1940, and the wheel seems to have been a 10ft. quarter shot, 9ft. wide. A by-pass around the farm isolated the buildings upon an island. Gill says Isaac Cane, milling here in 1830, inhabited an old house adjoining, which was demolished prior to

1862; and near to this was "a starch house" but he offers no suggestion as to a tan mill.

Mussen & Craven made the curious statement in 1853 that "although a market town [Colnbrook] markets have only been held 3 times during the last 50 years; these were for the purpose of *preventing a powder mill being built in the vicinity*. Should a market not be held at intervals, this might take place". From which one gathers that it was illegal to erect these dangerous mills within range of a market town, which is not surprising when one reads that almost every pane of glass was broken in Twickenham and Isleworth etc, on the numerous occasions when the Hounslow Heath Mills exploded and "most parts of London & Westminster felt the shock and imagined it to be an earthquake" Maxwell's *Highwayman's Heath*.

HORTON – 3¼ m. E.S.E. from Eton

[*Colne Brook*]

Medieval Corn Mill and *Fulling Mill*

Gone

Colne Bridge or *Horton Mills* – 3f. E. of Church

Used as factory
Maps: 1763, 1793, (1809), 1822, 1824, 1842, (1847), 1875, 1887

Medieval Corn Mill and Fulling Mill

A mill in Horton worth 20 shillings in 1086, was granted in 1213 for 4 years by William de Wyndleshore (Windsor) to Hamon, son of Henry, and his heirs, although another account says Adam de Caversham had it for 4 years at that date.

In the course of a lawsuit 9 years later Hamon procured a deed giving him the mill and appurtenances and right of grinding for the lord's household, and for the village of Horton; and this is probably the estate held by Adam Horton later in the 13th century.

Reference to John of the Mill of Horton occurs in 1279 and 1286. A century later, when the mill was associated with the Belet portion of the Horton

Manor, the corn-miller, William Blackmore diverted the watercourse near his mill and built a fulling mill which seems to have been the forerunner of the present Horton Paper Mills.

In 1408 it was found by inquisition that the new mill, worth 13/4d. yearly, had been built on the waste lands of Horton Common, and the owners were dispossessed, but they obtained a writ of restoration on the ground that Blackmore built the mill on his own land; and in 1428 Thomas Melreth held it.

Soon afterwards the mill was held by John Pury, presumably of Horton Pury Manor and leased to Henry Bulstrode, then to various members of the Phipps family during the 17th and early 18th centuries.

Colne Bridge or Horton Mills

Known as the Colne Bridge Mills, these mills of Phipp's were used for various purposes, and the rags collected for paper-making there in the 17th century introduced the London Plague into the neighbourhood, almost simultaneously with a price-cutting campaign on the part of Phipps, whose indifference to other people's interests, served to make him one of

the most unpopular individuals in Bucks at that time.

In 1636 there were twelve paper-mills in Bucks, one of the most important being this same Edward Phipps' mill at Horton. He was Chief Constable of Bucks, and the previous year had been presented at the Ecclesiastical Court for working on Sundays all the year round.

The plague broke out in 1636, and no sooner had

the mills shut down than Phipps added insult to injury by petitioning for aid on account of loss of business; but the J.P's at once cross-petitioned to have these and other papermills destroyed altogether as a public nuisance, although unsuccessful in their demands. It appears that some of the papermakers, Phipps included were paying their workpeople rather handsomely, which of course did more good to the men than it did to agriculture – a workman and four apprentices between them had 45/- per week.

Next year Phippps once more was in disfavour. Complaints were made that his paper could not be written upon with ink, and that he was taking advantage of a monopoly in his part of Bucks and making inferior stuff to sell at lower prices than the Wycombe firms, who were making the best quality papers.

Nothing further seems to have been recorded of these disputes, possibly because the mill was in other hands later in the century, and the next news is that in 1649 Richard West was a paper maker at Horton, and

George Glanville in 1699; William Gibbon, 1738, and in 1791 the Brerewoods of Horton Manor adjoining purchased from the mill proprietors leave for an opening to feed canals in their laid-out gardens from the main river, at an expense of £300.

Names of paper makers at Horton are in the parish registers in the 18th century (as are the Colnbrook millers, owing to Colnbrook not being a parish at the time) and William Pearson was the chief proprietor at that period; but in 1799 John Shepherd, William Ford (corn miller) and William Butler had Horton Mills. A bridge, newly constructed to supercede the ferry at the mill, was to be maintained by the mill owner. About 1800, the mills served in common with Wraysbury Mill, as an iron works, but this did not last long; Wraysbury Mill was converted to paper in 1820; and part at least of Horton Mills – shown separately north and south of each other by Bryant, Lipscomb and Culliford were employed in paper making in 1825, when the following sale notice appeared:

Colne Bridge or *Horton Mills*

"Powerful and never failing supply of water – Horton Paper Mills. The stream is now only applied to five vats and two milled board tables, but the highest authority has declared it capable of working at least 10 or 12 vats. It has four excellent drying lofts."

In 1832, Samuel Tipper of Horton Mills died, then there occurred the 1835 riots, arising from change of mill-masters, unemployment, low wages, and the monstrous poor laws which drove small-holders and aged persons to the pauper houses or "Free Prisons" as the great Cobbett aptly termed them – all of which evils were traceable to the "enclosure", of course, since this was the cause of unemployment and destitution. The storm over the "continuous roll" machines had subsided, but in this new uprising several paper-mills including some on the Colne Brook were burnt down; and many men, convicted of riot and arson were imprisoned or transported, but accounts seem not to indicate individual mills. Henry Tipper was owner-occupier in 1842 but probably Horton Mills were worked by two or more concerns later for in 1853 Messrs. Keen & Co. were printers of shawls, silks and de laines at the "New Print Works" whilst Messrs. Tipper & Co., who employed 60 persons printing shawls remained at Horton Mills until business declined and finally ceased in 1859; Timothy Healy was also given as a millboard manufacturer in 1854. With the shawl printing works dismantled, the whole property was purchased by Edward Tyrrell (excepting one factory for making boards, and a right of water-course which was reserved by Colonel Williams, lord of the Manor; and Tyrell's new tenants Ladell & Ibotson, of Wraysbury and Hythe End Mills, downstream occupied the premises as paper manufacturers. The mills were then described as having "factory houses" behind them for employees; the factory itself was apparently much as it is now, with a tall central chimney. Drying lofts and cutting departments were provided, steam coppers, vats, 4000 printing blocks, slate-topped tables, etc. Some of this equipment belonged to the print works, part of which became a place of worship holding 250 persons, and containing a harmonium.

No tenants were then mentioned for many years but in 1828 the Mills again appear as a going concern, occupied by Cellulose Products (1926) Ltd. and the mills have for some time been engaged in the making of glazed tiles by Granitese (Gt. Britain) Ltd.

Somewhere about 1928, Mr. Wooster, whose father had Coleshill Windmill and various watermills, inspected the premises; he tells me the watermill building existed and had two big breast-wheels in good condition, but the machinery had been cleared out (not burnt). A little later a paper firm took the mills, installing a steam engine out the front, visible from the roadway, but the water was unsuitable for paper; the mills were therefore vacated once more, and were empty on and off for some years until the tile factory was established.

Viewed from the Colne Bridge, on the Stanwell road, Horton Mills, standing back north of the road, partly white-walled with drying-room louvres and shallow slate roofs, presented a pleasant spectacle in summer-time (until a new spate of commercial jerry-building broke out alongside the roadway in 1944), and still more attractive 50 years ago when a lovely ancient moat 80 yards square, surrounded by an orchard, existed between entrance-way and river. Even now the reflection of dark woodland shadows, white walls and blue sky contrast happily in the still waters of the broad silent stream.

WYRARDISBURY – 3½ m. S.E. from Eton
[Colne Brook]

Culvett, Coltnett or *Wraysbury Mills, No 290* – 5f. almost E.N.E. of Church
Working under power
Maps 1768, (1809), 1822, 1824,
1842 (1847), 1862, 1875, 1887, 1926

Of the two mills that stood in Wyrardisbury in 1086, it is recorded that the lord of the Manor held them and tenants could grind corn there; and the present mill (or its predecessor) is fully dealt with in Mr. G.W.J. Gill's voluminous *History of the Parishes of Wraysbury and Horton and Town of Colnbrook, 1862*, and in *V.C.H. Vol: III*. In 1289 John de Remenham and his wife possessed a mill in Wraysbury; William atte Stoke had it in 1325 and in 1547 George Bulstrode of Horton held Coltnett or Culvett watermill as free tenant of Wraysbury Manor; it remained in the family for about a century.

As far back as 1605, Wraysbury Mill was a paper manufactory, thus figuring amongst the first ten or twelve paper mills in the county; but the premises also served as corn, iron, copper, silk and snuff mills at one time or another. The Bulstrodes claimed to own Wraysbury Common near the mill in 1627 and one imagines that common and mill presented a vastly different scene in those far-off days. Twenty years later William Sandford and Robert Brome had two mills here; in 1725 John Leader and James Meeres were paper-makers of Wraysbury; then we read of William Pearson, paper-maker, doubtless the same who occupied Horton Mills. Ralph and John Crowder joined him presumably as owner-occupiers, and Pearson seems to have had only part of the mill in 1758, for in the meantime Judge Carter held a mill at Wraysbury.

In 1755 complaint was made that the damming up of the water in the mill-stream had flooded Wraysbury Common and made the ford over the Colne dangerous; and another account says Richard Streatley, tenant of the mill dammed the stream in 1756, in which year his son Richard and R. Carter took the corn-mills (presumably Wraysbury) for £32 per annum. Henry Bullock was paper-making here in 1760, followed by his son John and grandson Henry, who died in 1840.

Meanwhile part of the premises served as an iron mill, tenanted by Jukes Colson paying £1.16.0 in 1772; five year later a conversion to copper milling was carried out by The Gnoll Company who took their name from Gnoll Castle in Glamorganshire, which belonged to a property owner at Wraysbury. Again in 1790 the premises were fitted out as an iron mill being purchased by Thomas Williams and tenanted by George and Thomas Glascott, London brass and iron founders with Thos. Ashby in charge of a corn mill; but the place was entirely closed in 1820 (the intention being to transfer to Taplow Mills), and was refitted later for paper-making. During Glascott's tenancy, Mr. Ashby was served with a writ, in 1801, to surrender his holding in the mills, and William Gyll bought them. The Ordnance of 1822 marks "Copper Mills" whilst Bryant depicts three mills upon three arms or loops in the stream. All three were west of Copper Mill Road and north of the present Southern Railway line; and they all appear on Culliford's map.

In 1830, when Glascott & Co. had reappeared as copper-millers, one or more buildings was used as a silk mill, about which no details have come to light. Mr. Williams at this period sold out to P. Grenfell, M.P. with whom he was associated at Temple House Coppermills, Berks, whilst Mr. Glascott worked the mills until his retirement in 1841; and Buckland's map shows that Ashby & Williams owned the mills, Ibotson's being the occupier, in 1845. The brothers Ibotson had leased them the previous year at £600, but this partnership was dissolved shortly, Richard and Percy having taken the Poyle Mills in Middlesex

for paper-making before 1830. In the sixties when Col. Williams was owner and Ladell & Ibotson proprietors, paper was produced from linen rags and cotton with a steam engine patented by the lessees, who owned their own plant and machinery. They pressed paper; rendered rags by steam drying, and used patent strainers, bleaching machinery and slate cisterns; and all equipment was of the best and most modern kind. About 40 men were employed at £2 a week (whilst farm labourers' wages were 5 shillings) and 60 women – they made printing paper for books. newspapers, charts, plates, etc; besides drawing paper and expensive paper-hangings. No fatal accident occurred for the 50 years prior to 1861, when the superintendent was unfortunately caught in the machinery and killed.

Behind the mills at that date was a very fine Black Italian Poplar tree, nearly 80ft. high; and the old ferry-road to Horton could still be traced by the mill, as it headed for the bank of the Colne, which it followed. The river bed was 10ft. deep at the mill-tail, and 3 to 6ft. deep downstream with plenty of trout which were not affected by chemicals, the stream then being quite clear.

In 1888, Messrs. Isaac Warwick & Co, established themselves as paper makers – Mr. Warwick de Buriatte being latterly at the Mill House – and they remained until about 1935. The trading name was that of Mr. de Buriatte's sons – Isaac and Warwick; and a former employee said steam-power was employed – turbine he believed. In 1907 they turned out strong paper boards for lining railway carriages, by which Springhall probably meant roof linings; and they were using one 64ins. machine in 1911 for manufacture of Printings, Middles, Printer's boards, cover paper and cardboards. The Bell Punch and Ticket Co, then occupied the premises which on March 19, 1938, were partly gutted by a big fire; but the business continues as before, under the old title of Isaac Warwick.

Extensive and far from picturesque, the buildings are of tarred galvanised iron and pink brick, with iron and brick chimneys; and the reconstruction since the fire has heightened the contrast between mills and surrounding countryside. From the river bridge by the Station however, the dignified Mill House appears between an array of overhanging copper-beeches and laburnums, with a flower-bedecked lawn sloping down to the water, which Mr. Gill says was known in 1807 as the Colnet or Colne Stream or Mill River. He adds that floods were an annual occurrence, especially in 1809; and he records that on June 17, 1857 the paper-mills served the novel purpose of accommodating a big concert to raise funds for a church organ.

Hythe End Mill or *Ramie Fibre Mill* – 1⅜ S.E. of Church

Converted to factory
Maps 1768, 1793, (1809), 1824, (1842)
1847, 1862, 1875, 1887, 1926

A second mill stands in Wraysbury, near the junction of Colne Brook with the Thames, at Hythe End, this being the last mill on the former stream, and the lowest-lying and most southerly in Bucks, standing only 50ft. above sea level, and very nearly due west of the old Crystal Palace. Probably one of the two Domesday mills in Wraysbury, little seems to be recorded about it, perhaps because it is covered in a general way by references to the mills of Wraysbury.

Hythe End Mill was more or less subsiduary to Wraysbury Millls, in the same ownership for long periods – indeed Gyll repeats much of his information about Wraysbury Mills in relation to Hythe End – water-course blocked by Carter and Streatley, sale of mills by Ashby to Gyll, which he says occurred in this case in 1762, Ashby continued to use the premises in connection with a brewery. Ralph Carter had acquired the mills from Philip and John Harcourt by deed of 1740; and in 1812 Ralph Dun had a corn-mill "at Iver or Wraysbury", probably meaning Hythe End, which is the only mill not accounted for at that date; and 20 years later another complaint was made against Robert Ashby re height of water, when a stone marking maximum height was erected near Hythe End Green bridge, in a field on the Staines side, bearing the title "F.T. 1832", followed by a long inscription (quoted by Gyll, p.87 of his *History*). In 1842 Messrs. Skidby & Ashby were the owners; Ralph & Percy Ibotson the occupiers.

Messrs Ladell & Ibotson held the mills in their own fee in the sixties, for manufacture of mill-boards by steam and water, employing 25 men and a few women, rising by 1865 to 35 men and 45 women. The firm purchased Hythe End Mills from Mr. Ashby; and they were described by Gyll as having paper warehouses and machinery corresponding to Wraysbury Mills but smaller, and approached by a little lane very muddy in winter. Both establishments worked day and night except Sundays in those days, and Hythe End Mill, well and successfully managed, produced coarse boards from rope and was adjoined by a waste ground which provided a convenient site for spreading rags to bleach in the sun and wind. Culliford marks one mill-building on his map in Gyll's *History*; and Gyll says the Wraysbury-Hythe End road had been raised for a length two miles at a cost of £242 (not £242,000 as it would be if done by a modern County Council contractor!)

The Mills, occupied by Fred Cullingford in 1877, and the Hythe End Co. in the nineties, are approached by a bridle road leaving the Staines road, by the Feathers P.H. heading towards the ferry for Egham.

Colne Brook discharges into the Thames alongside the ferry stage; and Stephen Springall, in his excellent and entertaining notes on the Colne mills (*Country Rambles Round Uxbridge*, 1907) provides the following most interesting details of the period.

"We see growing on our right", he says, speaking of the approach from the main road "a big bed of tall plants, a species of nettle which yield a marketable fibre, as the old mill opposite may declare. This . . . is a rather peculiar mill and its operations differ from all other Colne mills. It receives a raw herbaceous substance very similar to bass or raffia, so well known to gardening folk. Various operations with the machinery and the water of the Colne bring the substance to a soft silky fibrous nature, and instead of nettles or bass or raffia, there is wound on bobbins a strong and valuable fibre thread, which is dispatched to a manufactory to be made into such different things as mantles for incandescent light, blankets for warmth and wear, scarves for soft silky comfort, fabrics for fashionable ladies and many other things.

"For several years the old mill was wholly and utterly abandoned and presented a most doleful appearance with not a sign of human life anywhere about it. But again there is life and animation, for the old big wheel has had its accumulated silt removed and merrily it goes round at the swish of the Colne waters. Just beyond this Ramie Mill, we get to the ending of the Black Park Channel which, crossing the lane almost at its end, runs into the Colne and so to the Thames. Water from Bell Weir on the Thames passes *under* the Colne here, below the mill, where it is siphoned in pipes, and the same at Staines Mustard Mill. Just opposite Ramie Mill is also a place where Colne Water flows straight into an aqueduct in connection with Staines Reservoir."

The nettle-like plant, I should imagine was the Rhea nettle, utilised on the lines of flax; or the Russian Rami – a strong plant of the cotton family with fibre suitable for weaving. Today, adjoining the stuccoed Mill House, a factory, believed to incorporate some remains of the mill, is occupied by M.S.S.Recording Co. Ltd; and jerry-building and commercial exploitation proceed apace regardless of the decencies of

beauty spot preservation. The Colne meanwhile tumbles over the sluices in the rear, and finds ten or a dozen outlets into the Thames, including the "Crick" (River Crane) which runs out at Samuel Kidd's former flour-mill at Isleworth.

CHESHAM

River Chess

Early Mills on Bury,
Higham and Chesham Manors
Latimer Corn and Fulling Mills
Payne's Mill

Sites unknown
Gone

Bury Manor

A mill on Chesham Bury Manor was bestowed on Missenden Abbey in the 12th century by Richard de Sifrewest, although in 1202 he was in litigation with Adam, one of the Abbots, and secured that he, Richard, should have the grinding of a moiety of his demesne corn free at that mill, and the Abbot, the grinding of the other moiety. This mill, omitted from Domesday, and not specifically called a watermill, is not mentioned again; but the Manor was combined with Higham Manor in 1490, so that its mill, if remaining, would lose its identity. Possibly this was the mill given by Queen Eddid (Edith?) to Alsi, valued 6/8d., for this is not in Domesday, the only one of that value in Bucks being at Milton Keynes.

Higham Manor

Brictric, a man of Queen Edith (Edward the Confessor's wife) held Chesham Higham Manor until the Norman, Hugh de Bolbec of Whitchurch seized it; in 1086 there was a mill worth 10/- later described (1312) as a watermill leased at fee farm; and it passed to the De Veres, direct descendants of William's henchmen and consequently the recipients of many favours. Descending with the Manor the property was described as "two mills" in 1481, both under one roof in 1580. *Victoria County Vol. III*, add that "two watermills continued to be mentioned amongst the appurtenances of the Manor in the 17th and 18th centuries, and may be identified with two of the present three flour mills Lord's, Cannon's and Weirhouse . . . the three mills were in possession of the Cheynes family at the death of Francis Cheynes in 1645, with land called Cannon Mead".

Chesham Manor

Two mills valued at only 3/- and received by the Bishop of Bayeux from two "sokemen" or vassels, seem to have been on Chesham Manor, but absence of future references suggests they were not water-driven. Two springs in Chesham arose in Highamead Meadow, (doubtless on Higham Manor), and on Frogmore Farm, to meet at the town; and there were three open wells or springs in the town, one in Church Street called Bridewell, another at the entrance to Duck Alley near Townfield Bridge, and a third, now lost, in Waterside near the Gasworks.

Latimer Corn and *Fulling Mills*.

Latimer, together with Ashley Green, Chartridge, Waterside, etc., were included in Chesham civil parish in the olden days of milling, although now seperated. Two watermills stood on Latimer Manor in 1323, one corn and one fulling, leased at 60/- and 28/6d. but no mention of them occurs after 1335, The miller of Latimer however, is mentioned more than once in the Chesham Parish Registers – 1562, Edward sonne of the myller of Latymarsh died; 1563. December, Thomas, miller of Latimer, died: 1563 January Thomas Meredew miller of Latimer myll, died. (N.B. January followed December since the year, until 1752, began on March 25 and ended March 24th.

Payne's Mill

In 1275 Laurence de Broc died seized of Payne's Mill in Chesham, leased to Missenden Abbey for 15/-; and in 1286 the Broc's estate included a fulling a corn mill; and the latter may been in Latimer since the compilers of the *County History* appear to obtained their references from the Latimer deeds.

Probably no mill has existed in the hamlet for centuries, but the stream is looped as it passes between the Chenies road and Latimer village; although there seems from the original Ordnance to have been a realignment of the main road at this point, which may have been accompanied by changes in the course of the stream.

Old Bark Mill, or The Tan Mill – ½ f. S.E. of Church

Gone
No map reference

A fire at Water Lane Steam Mills in 1942 brought to light in the local press some details of its early predecessor – Old Bark Mill or The Tan Mill, which gave place first to a water saw mill over a century ago (eventually aided by steam) and later to the above mentioned steam factory. Mr. John Garrett (or Garrett-Pegge) – "old Johnnie Pegge" they called him, for he lived to a very advanced age, was the owner and was listed as a tanner in 1830 and 1842.

The mill stood on the Chess in Water Lane, which forms a short cut from the Missenden road to the Town Bridge in Germain Street; and the stream runs under the above road by the *Queen's Head P.H.*, thence dividing into millstream and by-pass at the corner of Water Lane (which probably years ago was an inundated cartway or ford), rejoining just above Town Bridge.

Old Bark Mill stood north of Water Lane, overlooking the back gardens of Church Street; and evidence of the tanning work is stated to have been found on the site of Germain Street School, and in Red Lion Street nearer the Town Hall; the nature of the work may be surmised by referring back to Olney Tan Mill. A brief note in *Country Life* (Oct.13. 1944) stated that a "tanning millstone", illustrated, was corrugated on the edge (presumably an edge-runner) for grinding bark; and was similar to the cider mills of Herefordshire, where it was found, except for the grooves on the crushing edge. *Rural Industries of England and Wales vol IV*, explains that bark was usually stripped by the local saw-mill and sold to the tannery – hence the link between timber and boot trade at Chesham. Oak bark was ground into small pieces by a crushing machine at the tannery, then immersed in a clear water vat for several days.

Cow hides having been soaked in lime pits to loosen the hair, so that it can be scraped off with a knife, are thoroughly washed to free the lime; then immersed in tannin-pits containing ground oak bark in a stronger solution in each pit. After this come finishing processes not directly connected with the bark mill; and some tanneries specialise in the somewhat different processing of sheep skins.

Some interesting speculations could be indulged in from the records of millers and tanners in the Chesham Parish Registers, but it will suffice to mention the family of Grover who may have been either tan-mill proprietors or employees.

1581 John Grover, tanner, marries Joan, daughter of Richard Tookfer; 1585 Nehemiah, a son born (folowed by other children); 1599, John Grover tanner dies. 1606, Nehemiah, son of John Grover deceased, marries Deborah, daughter of Dabney, deceased. 1618 Nehemiah Grover dies; 1619 son born to Deborah Grover, widowe, late wife of Nehemiah Grover deceased; and so on. Other tanning families were named Ware, Potter and Hepburn.

Water Lane Mill – ½ f. S.E. of Church

Now a factory
No map reference

Prior to a fire about 50 years ago, Water Lane Mill – successor to Old Bark Mill – was water and steam driven; and the late James Nash, who had celebrated his ninetieth birthday when he obliged me with a few details in 1942, worked the watermill portion between 1865 and 1870.

The building was of brick, he told me, and the wheel was about in the centre, in an open pit surrounded by a rail, so that one could look down on it as it worked. Mr. Nash who passed away in November 1944, believed it was the same wheel that had worked the Bark Mill. Only the small circular saw was water-driven, by the usual belt, owing to the limited power, the larger saws being steam driven.

The fire occurred, as is not unusual, on a Saturday night; and it is recorded that the Reverend E.C. Boultbee worked at the fire all night, returning home found that a son had been born to him. Nevertheless he conducted the morning service as usual. The old building stood amongst trees where scores of rooks nested; and before the fire they all left like rats deserting a ship, so tht Mr. Wright, senior, who noticed this, anticipated disaster. It was always William Wright's mill as long as Mr. Nash can remember; but before the fire Mr. Nash had joined the marines as might be suspected from his tall spare upright figure at so advanced an age. He stood almost at "attention" whilst in conversation. Prior to his Water Lane experiences Mr. Nash was employed half-time at Shute's Silk Mill, schooling half day and working in the afternoon. This was a spinning mill, driven by a big beam engine, on the site of the Royal Bucks Laundry, near the gas works, and it apparently existed in 1831 when J.A. Cox

was a silk throwster with a mill at Waterside. Returning from service, Mr. Nash worked in Bates' Steam Saw-mills for 28 years. These had never been water-driven, being situated on the opposite side of the Moor road from Canada Works; neither had Thomas Wright's sawmill, near *the White Horse P.H.* between the London and Amersham roads; nor Charles Wright's saw mill at Townfield Yard, between the Town Hall and the gas-works. Finally Mr. Nash worked at Canada Works until recent years.

Messrs William Wright & Sons Ltd., are now proprietors of Water Lane Mill, which suffered another serious fire in the main building on the evening of Whit-Monday 1942, while closed for the holiday, but this structure, also of red brick was steam driven.

CHESHAM BOIS – 1¼ m. S.S.E. from Chesham

[*Chess*]

Amy Mill – 7½ f. N.N.W. of Church

Mill House remains
Maps 1768, 1793, (1809), 1822, 1824, 1842, (1847), 1875, 1887

Amy Mill

In the church Registers we find the following:

"1592 – John Carter of the fullynge myll was buryed the XV day of July Aº Dni 1592.

"The wife of one that had taken the fullyng myll of William Carter was buryed the viij day of September Aº Dni 1592.

"1596 – Danyell Tappinge fuller, was buried the Tenthe daye of Januarii Aº Dni 1596.

"1616 – John Dell of Amee Mill buryed the vj of Aprill Aº Dni 1616.

"As far back as the middle of the 16th century", it is stated in C.E. White's *Church and Parish of Chesham Bois 1889*, "the fulling and dyeing of cloth was actively carried on at the mill, to which reference is frequently made in the Registers; but the fuller's business having become extinct the mill is now used for the production of flour, etc.".

This seems to imply that Amy Mill, named by Jefferys, is the old fulling mill under a new guise, and in support, we may note that the mill stands at the foot of Fuller's Hill.

In 1826, Amy Mill is mentioned in connection with a diversion of the Amersham road, when the Amy Mill Close and Orchard, and Mill Field were occupied by Thomas Wright, the miller, who was there in 1798 or earlier. In 1838 Amy Mill was advertised by the exors. of Th.Wright as a Freehold Water Corn Mill with residence and fishery; strong head of water power, and good roads adjoining.

Mr. James Nash believed that Mrs. Charlotte Fox of Lord's Mill preceded the Rose family at Amy Mill; and that he was correct is proved by W. Holland's large map of 1842, on which she is named as tenant and John Iggulden the owner. George Rose senior, who was killed by his steam engine at this mill in January 1845, apparently took over in 1842, for he was named at Amy Mill in the directory that year; and *his* son George was described as a corn-miller here in 1853. He owned Bois Steam Mill in 1864, and had Canada, Lord's and Amy Mills, all on the same stream in 1877; and *his* son George had Canada and Lord's Mills eventually.

Amy Mill, Mr. Nash said, was a white wooden structure with an internal wheel, for both flour and saw milling, the flour business being conducted by George Rose to the last; whilst Robert Biggs worked the saw-mill portion for making cricket bats, etc. but it was demolished during Mr. Nash's younger days' and the flour business transferred to the new Bois Mill, now Canada Works, opposite. Some say that Amy Mill was largely brick, and was steam-driven when pulled down; apparently it was considered obsolete. The mill site is now occupied by a large pink brick house of dignified design called the Big House, or Amy Mill House, with the original little mill house adjoining it, and stream and by-pass behind.

Bois Mill, Rose's Mill or *Canada Works* – 7½ f. N.N.W. of Church

Working by power
Maps 1824, (1847), 1875, 1900

In the extreme north corner of Chesham Bois parish is Bois Mill standing, as Amy Mill did, on the present outskirts of Chesham, the sites being opposite one another, across the road. Bryant has the title "Amy Mill" against Bois Mill, possibly it was regarded merely as an adjunct of Amy Mill at that period.

Built of chequered red and black brick, with slate roof, chimney shaft, and iron-framed windows it is used for woodturning in such articles as children's spades, garden fencing, etc. and is said to have acquired the name Canada Mill from the fact that George Rose who occupied it for many years (grandson of the original George Rose of Amy Mill) visited Canada just before or after taking charge of the premises. He is incidentally reputed to have been the first man to drive a motor car through Chesham – a tiller-steered machine.

Probably father and son, both of whom had the mill, were progressive men, turning from one trade to another at their mills according to what seemed most profitable at the moment, for the present building was erected as a flour-mill, according to Mr. Nash. In 1853 George Rose the father was already established here as a corn-miller, but the following year he describes himself as a miller, meal man, corn dealer and saw miller of Bois Mills, the sawing probably being done only at Amy Mill. He is believed to have worked Bois Mill first by water, then by steam up to 50 years ago, for corn-milling; but his son converted to saw-milling, whilst the corn business was pursued at Lord's Mill, which his grandfather rented 50 years previously.

George Rose is listed as a paper miller at Bois Mill in 1864, and the same directory stated that the Waterside mill included a paper mill. Mr. Nash

Bois Mill, Rose's Mill or *Canada Works Mill*

assured me that Rose had no interest in Elliott's paper-mill (also known as Bois Mill, although not in Waterside) and none of the other Waterside mills was manufacturing paper in 1864; we must therefore assume that Rose did produce paper at the mill under notice although it cannot have been for very long, nor on a big scale.

The application of the name "Bois" to more than one mill causes some confusion, not lessened by the fact that Bates' Steam Mills were also called Bois Steam Saw Mills, but it appears that neither water-mill generally went by the name of Bois amongst millers, one usually being called Rose's and the other Elliott's. Roses Mill is however marked Bois Mill on the 6 inch Ordnance (1900).

In 1877 Rose describes his various premises as Amy Mill, Bois *Steam* Mill, and Lord's Mill, confirming Mr. Nash's statement that Bois was not a watermill in his time. Bryant & Lipscomb depict it as a watermill (1824) but Holland, 1842, omits it altogether, bearing out Mr. Nash's contention that no building existed there in his childhood.

Thomas Hearn acquired Canada Mill many years since, and still conducts it under the title of the Canada Works Ltd. The by-pass to Bois mill is the open stream alongside the Moor road, with the mill-tail discharging into it just below the mill, beneath which it passes down a cemented slope; and at the end of a pleasant green on which horses graze while children play around them is the ancient Lord's Mill.

Lord's Mill or *The Three Gable Mill* – 5½ f. S.E. of Church

Working by electricity
Maps 1793, 1824, 1842, (1847), 1875, 1926

The 17th century Lord's Mill on the corner of Chesham Moor Road – one of the three Bucks water-mills noticed by the Historical Monuments Commission is by repute the oldest non-ecclesiastical building in the parish; and is distinguished by its three half-timbered gables, and the Elizabethan stack of chimneys on the adjoining Mill House; although the brickwork is now plastered over on the front walls. The roofs are tiled, and the windows lattice framed.

At its reconstruction ca 1660, the mill was owned in common with Cannon's and Weirhouse Mills, by the Cheynes family, and further particulars are briefly mentioned in my references to Higham Manor.

Within living memory a huge eight armed low-breast or undershot wheel, about 25 feet in diameter, reaching up to the eaves, similar to the Bassetbury wheel but narrower, was outside the rear of the mill (facing the town). the stream being turned at right angles to lay on to the wheel; and a very small illus-tration of this is in the Artists' reference work *I See All, Vol: IV, p.1965.*

The footing for the bearing of this wheel exists, and also the sluice which was close behind the wheel, in line with the river bank, with a fixed weir immedi-ately above it leading away round the wheel and beneath the Mill House.

Now the water runs straight in on to a broad all-iron "overshot" within the mill, about 9ft. wide and 6ft. diameter, somewhat like that at Weirhouse. The layout is conventional with a morticed pit wheel, the

Lord's Mill or *The Three Gable Mill*

gearing being all iron except for morticed stone nuts (front and back of the mill, in a wooden enclosure) and crown wheel upstairs. From the latter a layshaft drives the usual pattern sack bollard, and the machines, including a big old two-sack dresser now disused; at the back of the mill another layshaft conveying power *to* the crown wheel from a belt coupled to an electric motor.

Nowadays the latter works full time, water power being discarded ever since the present wallower was installed about 1932, because of water shortage and trouble repeatedly experienced with meshing of gears and trueing up of brasses. Indeed they preferred hard old oak rather than brass for axle-tree bearings, etc.; and used to cut blocks from the oak beams of the mill, and fashion them to suit – new oak from the builder's yard was useless.

A curious feature about the mill, according to tradition, is that like some of the ancient tithe barns of the West Country, she stands on the ground without foundations.

The three Waterside millers in 1798 were John Bailey, James Tuffnall and Aaron Moody, Bailey having the largest business and Tuffnall the smallest. John Fox, was the miller in 1830; and about 12 years later Mrs. Charlotte Fox, after a spell at Amy Mill, returned to Lord's – "Old Lady Fox" they called her, for she lived to be very old and remained till 1858,

when the following advert appeared:

"Water Cornmill and Farm for sale at Chesham Bois, on river Chess. Two waterwheels, 3 pairs stones and whole of going gear, dwelling house, adjoining large barn, cowhouse and stable; 56 acres of land. Close to Chesham Meadows (6 acres) adjoining Chesham Common. Above property is let to Mrs. Fox, who has occupied it for many years at £110 per Annum"

Two curious statements here call for comment (1) that the mill was in Chesham Bois and (2) that it had two wheels; but it is beyond dispute that Mrs. Fox rented no other mill in the 'fifties and had occupied Lord's Mill for some years past; one assumes that one water wheel was in the position of the present one and the other was the big wheel, the stream being divided.

George Rose of Amy and Bois Mills took over Lord's as well, his grandfather having been there until 1842, according to Holland's map, when John Garrett was the owner. Rose, senior, and Mrs. Fox seem to have exchanged mills, a not unknown occurrence; and the Rose family, and Frank Jewers ran the business until about 1910 since when Messrs. W.E.Wright & Sons, the corn merchants of Germain St. have occupied the mill for grist work.

Canon's or Cannon's Mill – 1m. S.E. of Church

Disused
Maps 1768, 1793, (1809), 1822, 1824,
1842 (1847), 1875, 1887, 1926

Next down the Chess stream after Lord's Mill is Cannon's Mill towards the end of Waterside, a combined farmstead and mill for many years occupied by Mr. Alfred Gee, who was the last miller.

Formerly belonging to the Cheynes family, together with adjoining land to the west, known as Cannon Mead, the mill stands on a very old site; the present building is whitewashed brick, with wooden upper walls and shallow slate roof. Bestriding the stream, it is built on to a millhouse with adjoining cottage below the right bank of the stream almost face to face with the weir and sluice gate, so that it looks as though a flood would wash the cottage away; actually the by-pass is turned and led away behind the cottage and mill.

Cannon's Mill shares the distinction with Weirhouse (next downstream) and Wolverton and Haversham in the north, of having its stones set in a

row and geared to a horizontal driving shaft running the length of the mill. An all-iron over-shot wheel, of larger diameter but not so broad as those at Lord's and Weirhouse, carries a large iron spur pit-wheel which engages an iron pinion above it, on the end of the driving shaft; and four pairs of underdriven stones are controlled by iron bevel stone-nuts sliding up and down, and geared to mortice bevel crown-wheels, the bridge trees and frames being at right angles to mainshaft. Along the front of the wooden enclosure or housing containing this machinery, is a long conveyor receiving meal from the stones. Between first and second pairs of stones is the upright shaft geared to a small crown wheel, and carrying, on the first floor, a belt drum and two crown-wheels, the upper of which is smaller. The drum drives a subsiduary upright shaft mounted above the water-wheel close to the lever-controlled flash; the lower crown-

Canon's or *Cannon's Mill*

wheel drives a layshaft at the back of mill (over-looking the mill cottage and facing Chesham), this shaft being coupled by belts to chaff-cutter and grind-stone. The upper crown-wheel is geared to a layshaft forward, from which a very long belt drove a big old flour dresser at the end of the room, beyond the mill-stones, but this was disused when roller-milling made it uneconomical to produce flour; and the belt is now coupled to the spindle of an elevator close by; another drum on this layshaft controls the sack-hoist. Practically all the machinery is of iron, except the crown-wheel, cogs, and bevel on the sack-hoist layshaft.

Although the mill is idle, a pair of stones nearest

the road are workable, but all windows in the building have been broken by destructive passers-by for a public footpath runs though the mill yard.

Robert Ball had the mill from 1830 or earlier until the 'seventies, (William Lowndes, owner) after which Alfred Gee occupied it until his death in 1937. His miller then went to Weirhouse Mill; and Mr. West, who lives near by and was born about 1870 at the Mill Cottage has been in charge of the fishing and ditches on the property all his life, and his father before him.

Mr. Delaney who took the premises as a farmer and dealer does not think it would be profitable to put the mill to work.

Warehouse or *Weirhouse Mill* – 1¼ m. almost S.E. of Church

Working
Maps 1768, (1809), 1822,
1824, 1842 (1847), 1875, 1887, 1926

The third of the three mills in Chesham on the Cheynes estate was the Weirhouse mill, which has gone by this name right back to Jefferys' time, although usually spelt "Warehouse" in paper-milling days – a fine big white-boarded and tiled structure jutting out against the roadway so that it catches the eye of everyone travelling along the Latimer road.

John Allnutt, perhaps related to Allnutt of Marsh Green, was a paper-maker her in 1830; Daniel Elliott succeeded him, and John Elliott, who afterwards had Bois Mill, downstream, was owner-occupier in 1842; but 7 years later the effects of Weirhouse paper-mill were for sale:- resin, soda, half-stuff, rags, machine felts, dandy glazing rolls, bleaching chest, 80 gallon copper, rag boilers, stone retort, liquid blue, etc. By direction of F.Bell. Later that year the mill was to let, for use as a corn mill or any other purpose agreed upon. Apply Mr. Dodd of Chenies. But the premises continued as a paper-mill under Anthony Banks, until finally sold in 1858:

"Weirhouse Paper and Corn-mill, Chesham. Plant and working items of a 2 Vat Paper Mill. By Auction. Small water-mill. Excellent mechanical Vat press of great power in complete order; 40ft. of 2 inch iron shafting with riggers. Wooden vats, pulp strainers and lifters; powerful wet and dry pressers. Crab and ropes and pulley; slated bleach cisterns. Copper bleach pump, copper-hand stuff strainer, paper-moulds; double steam copper, treble-lines, sides and standards; scales, layboards, 21 large canvas curtains in drying loft; paper tables. Arnott's stove, rag-duster and case. Usual implements and utensils of a hand-made paper mill. One pair 4ft. peak; I pair 18ins. cullen stones (a corruption of Cologne from whence this class of stone was obtained) with laying shafts, iron arm riggers and driving straps. Stage and corn hopper, sack tackle, carts, horses.

John Clare (1864) was probably the first corn-miller as such; but the late Mr. Percy W. Puddephatt's father William, acquired the mill before Clare had been there very long; and he is believed to have put in the present wheel; his son laid out the ornamental streams and falls around the garden of the Mill House, the real by-pass being round the back, with the mill-tail inside hedge against roadway.

Mr. Percy Puddephatt passed away in 1936, aged 84; and owing to the death of the miller about the same time difficulty was experienced in carrying on. The late Mr. A.W. Pope, a well-known local coal merchant eventually rented the mill, employing Mr. Gee's miller as stated, whilst a dairyman rented the farming portion of the premises and Mrs. Puddephatt remained in the Mill House. In 1877, Fred Payne, baker and miller, of High Street, had the use of the mill, apparently by arrangement with Mr. Puddephatt. End-on to the road with the well-built Mill House, separate across the yard, the mill is of brick, with white painted woodwork above, and a long deep tiled roof setting off the white walls and the pointed yew tree dotted about the grounds; but the Chesham side is very much disfigured by a long galvanised iron fence alongside the roadway. This is a pity, for it is a big imposing old mill when seen to advantage, the main building being about 90ft. by 27ft.; and in the drying room beyond, the louvres are retained in the long white walls, verifying that hand-made papers were produced; and a feature of the louvre panels is that they have no diagonals to ensure rigidity.

The existing wheel – a broad all-iron overshot with three sets of arms, smaller in diameter than breadth, is beneath the main ground floor, which is at "cart level" to facilitate loading, and is fed by a big cast-iron pentrough, 8 or 9ft. wide, mounted on strong oak piers. Placed near the roadway, it carries an iron spur gear, the same as Cannon's Mill, with a big iron driving shaft at higher level running the length of the main building and receiving its power through a large spur with a double set of iron rod spokes rivetted into the tyre and having the appearance of an early pattern bicycle wheel – a type of spoking more favoured for belt-wheels in factories.

Three very substantial morticed crown wheels on the shaft are geared to iron stone-nuts which are each swung in and out of mesh by lever and yoke as in windmill practice; and the stones are on the "cart level" floor. Between second and third driving wheels is a large iron and wooden drum from which a belt ascends to the ceiling of the stone-floor, where it drives two shafts, belt coupled, and a third on the floor above. Two sets of sack-gear are provided – one from the stone floor where the portable machines are also driven; and one from the upper floor, where dresser and cleaners are situated.

Warehouse or *Weirhouse Mill*

Numerous and capacious bins are provided by partitioning the upper floors, the mill being big enough to handle a very good corn-business; and some surprisingly massive old timbers are contained within the mill, which had probably been standing 200 years.

When water was high in the river Mr. Puddephatt used to disconnect all machinery over night and let the wheel run free till morning, but like all Bucks' streams it is not so powerful nowadays, owing to neglect and to having been choked with tar from the road. The wheelhouse has plenty of head-room, as though it might have contained a big breastshot

wheel at one time.

About thirty years ago, when water failed in a drought, a Crossley Gas Engine was put in, with its own generating plant; and when the town gas was brought along they switched on to this supply, but the wheel has always been the main string, and was used exclusively by Mr. Pope, trade not being extensive.

The late Mr. Todd miller and manager of Chenies Mill, a very capable all-round man, fitted new cogs at weir house some years ago, when the machinery was badly cut up; and he is believed to have repaired other mills in the valley from time to time.

Blackwell Hall Mill – Nearly 1⅞ f. E.S.E. of Church

Gone
Maps 1768, (1809), 1824, 1842, (1847)

First mention of a mill at Blackwell occurs in the 13th century, with another reference in the 15th; at which time the Earls of Surrey may have owned it, for *Victoria County* records the mill under the heading of Latimer Manor, and the site is now just within the new parish of Latimer, established 1898, having formerly been in Chesham parish.

Neither Jefferys nor the 1822 Ordnance named the mill, but Bryant gave "Blackwell Hall and Mill" and Holland included it in 1842.

Although not standing within living memory, its former existence is known to a number of old people locally, one or two even claiming to have seen the foundations, which were above the Blackwell Hall

Lane Bridge; and Mr. West, of Cannon's Mill, told me he knew an old man who had worked at Blackwell Hall Mill.

Pigot in 1830 said "the Chess works three corn-mils and the machines of four others for making paper, one of which belonging to Mr. George Stevens, works on a very large scale". What a pity then that an advert of Sept: 1841 offered :-

"the house furniture, Paper-mill implements and effects – plough and ploughing boards, dry press boards, scales, felts, 100 gallon copper, rags, wrap-pers, soda, resin, manganese, oil, coal, woollen rags. By direction of George Stevens who is quit-ting this country".

Holland described this as a paper mill, owner the Reverend G. Street, no tenant; but George Howard was listed as a paper maker here in 1842, by Pigot's.

In 1844, at Blackwell Hall Mill, the effects of a paper maker were auctioned; 50 reams of shop paper, hand-stuff and sago, farina, (apparently a yellow starchy dye) and resin, vitriol; etc.; and we may assume the mill was demolished about a century ago.

Elliott's Mill or Bois Mill – 1m. E.S.E. of Church

Mill House remains
Maps – 1768, (1809), 1822, 1824, 1842

Held by De Bosco or Du Bois in the 13th century the Bois Manor was granted to the ubiquitous Sir John de Moleyns about 1340, other claimants having been ignored. Later the Cheynes family held the property, but the paper-makers where eventually proprietors of their own mill.

A Domesday Mill worth 3/- was attached to the manor of Chesham Bois; in 1310 a watermill was mentioned and in 1585 Francis Cheynes accused Henry Gorsom, "a disorderous and contentious person", of keeping away from the mill a laden horse and its master whom Gorsom had "stroken and verie evellie abused". In 1592, says *V.C.H. Vol. III*, "the mill was used for fulling and although the name of Bois Mill still lingers, water power has long since ceased to be applied for commercial purposes and the Mill House is a private residence".

Situated a half a mile downstream from Blackwell Mill, Elliott's is marked "Paper Mill" on Jefferys' map, Elliott's Mill" on the 1822 Ordnance, and "Chesham Bois Mill" by Bryant. Richard Elliott was owner-occupier making paper in 1842 having been here from 1830 or earlier; John Elliott was listed as a paper manufacturer of Bois Mill in 1853 (and at Waterside ten years previously) and *Records of Bucks* noted in 1854 that "Mr. Elliott has a fine specimen of the bittern, taken near Chesham, in his collection" adding that a bittern's nest and eggs were found about that time on Marsworth reservoir. (The bittern is now even more rare, due to the draining of the marshes and the activities of so-called "sportsmen"). Probably the next five years or so witnessed the closing down of the mill, which Mr. Nash said was occupied by Elliott to the last. The Mill House, stuccoed and thickly covered with creeper, stands at the roadside, approached by a long loop in the stream, across which the mill stood.

CHENIES – 4m. S.E. from Chesham)

[*Chess*]

Cheynes or *Chenies Corn Mill* – ¼ m. N. of Church

Disused
Maps 1768, (1809), 1822, 1824, (1847), 1875, 1887, 1914

It will afford all true lovers of "the olden time" some pleasure to know that the last miller of Chenies – Mr. Boughton – delivered his flour in a big old wagon drawn by three horse abreast, a sight which few of the present generation are likely to have encountered along the road; A man named Dancer drove the wagon, and the employed miller until about 1927 was the late Mr. James Todd, who passed away in 1938, aged 84, after being at Chenies Mill for 30 years, and previously at Clewer Mill (Berks). Mr. Todd, much in demand as a soloist in his young days, later found himself popular as a mill repairer, owing to his skill, as already mentioned.

George Dodd was the proprietor in 1798 and 1843;

and in 1848 Chenies corn-mill was described as adjoining the papermill and working two pairs of French Stones, dressing and bolting machines, profitable grist connection, residences and grounds. Leased from Duke of Bedford, apply John Dodd; but neither ownership nor tenancy changed for many years. Eventually Mr. John Boughton of the Manor House had the mill, followed by a son who ran it until about 1935. Another son, also born at the mill, has the agricultural engine-yard near Chalfont station.

Now the mill buildings are used by W.W. & H. Fitch for dairy farming, but the mill itself is locked up, with machinery *in situ*.

The Ordnance of 1822 gives Cheneys Mill, but Bryant calls it Chenies Corn and Paper Mills, an important point for this seems to be the earliest evidence of a paper mill at the site.

A good head of water is provided by a long embanked mill-pond west of the Flaunden road, with a sluice in the left bank leading to a long by-pass. At the road bridge the stream divides into two, the left arm passing beneath the mill to drive an inside wheel, whilst the other runs down a fall where another disused wheel is situated in the open, on the paper-mill site.

Both wheels, broad iron overshots, are fixed with a baulk of timber passed through them, although the stream flows over the outer wheel all the time. The inner wheel drove the customary upright shaft and three pair of stones – large ones either side and a smaller pair in the middle. On the first floor is a morticed crown-wheel driving an iron belt shaft for dresser and other machines. The other wheel has a three-throw crank attached to its axle, as at Shardeloes Mills, near Amersham, for pumping water up the village street to the main road, (where there is a reservoir with an overflow into the meadows), a considerable task, since the reservoir is 150ft. above the mill. This is the Duke of Bedford's main but the Water Company obtained permission to couple it to their own pipe on the London road and thus supply the village from their water works.

Rather square-built, of light-coloured brick, with a slate roof and skylights, the mill adjoins an old half-timbered mill cottage; and a quarter of a mile downstream is a copse called Millfield Spring, the word "Spring" being the local name for a spinney all the way along the Bucks-Herts. border.

Chenies Paper Mill – ¼ m. N. of Church

Wheel remains
Maps – 1824

Bryant who provides the earliest record of a paper-mill at Chenies, seems to be the only cartographer who notices this establishment, which stood alongside the corn-mill, the outdoor wheel remains.

George Dodd, probably father or grandfather of John Dodd, leased the mills from the Duke, from 1830 or earlier, until 1848 when the premises were auctioned.

"Chenies Mills, late property of George Dodd deceased. New erected and very superior range of buildings extending a length of 178 feet adapted expressly as a FIRST RATE PAPER MANUFACTORY. Water equals 4 engines*; good quality of water for washing fine papers, drying lofts, coal cellars, shaving house, boiler house, bleaching house, steeping house, rag-house etc. etc. Four-drinier patent paper machine, waterwheel, 3 engines; Chests, pressed, etc.".

Further equipment was advertised the following year; complete machinery; fixtures etc. of paper mills;

48ins. paper-machine and vat, with Drying Cylinders, Glazing rolls, press rolls, copper cylinder for heating vat, brass knot-strainer, 3 vacuum pumps by Donkin. Nine-foot steam boiler with iron furnace etc.; Brickwork includes boiler chimney. Piping, shafts and brasses, cisterns, finishing tables, half-stuff press, cutting bench, fire engine and buckets, 5 muskets with bayonets, quantity cast iron. Apply John Dodd

All first class equipment down to the 5 muskets with bayonets for coping with rioters, but probably the shortest lived paper-mill in Bucks nevertheless.

In 1813, the Reverend St. John Priest described Mr. Dodds's irrigation scheme – the only one of its kind in Bucks, in the field between the mill-pond and main road. A gulley called a floater was cut parallel and close to the river bank with lateral branches every 40 feet. These baulks are 30ft. long; and 40 feet from the main floater is a parallel drain – on a lower level – intervening grade 1 in 12 – with 30ft. baulks intervening grade 1 in 12 – with 30ft. baulks interspersed between the others and gradient from floater branch

* i.e. rag engines.

194

to drain branch is the same. The drain rejoins stream below bridge; and every so often the land was thus flooded over, and cropping was as follows; March-May 10 ewes grazed = £20. Then water land. Mow it. Water again, and second hay crop = 6 loads of 18 cwt each = £33. Nov- Dec Graze 4 cows = £44. Also graze 2 horses. The cows progressed better on the hay from this ground than on barley meal. Cost per acre for irrigating at that time was £25; St. John Priest said

results were remarkably good.

If this has little bearing on watermilling, it at least typifies the enterprise of our millers, the only apparent snag being the gullies would make mechanical mowing difficult.

The River Chess, which forms the County boundary near the mill, later enters Hertfordshire to join the Gade just below Croxley Green windmill, when the Gade immediately joins the Colne.

LITTLE MISSENDEN– 2½ m. W.N.W. from Amersham

River Misbourne

Little Missenden Mill or *Deep Mill* – ¾ m W.N.W. of Church

Used as house
Maps; 1675, 1768, (1809), 1822, 1824,
1842, (1847), 1870, 1875, 1887, 1914

"There cometh a brook almost from Missenden, passeth hard by Hagmondisham, leaving it almost by full south, on the right ripe, and after running downe by the valleis of Chilterne towards Colne Streame".

Thus wrote Henry VIII's Antiquary Leland, although the Misbourne actually had its source in recent generations beneath the kitchen of Rignall's Farm along the Hampden Valley some distance above

Little Missenden Mill or *Deep Mill*

Missenden. Occasionally the stream rises higher up the valley near the ancient blacksmith's shop and in 1765, when one Timothy Theobolds aged 90 was buried, the Rector wrote in the Parish Register that he was informed by this man's father that 11 or 12 years before Timothy was born (i.e. about 1663) "ye springs were yn so high as to rise and run in Hampden Bottome. The like did not happen since, till March 1764 wn after 6 months almost contind wet ya rose and ran in Blackett Field with a Current sufficient to have drove any overshot mill.

Flowing behind the village and through the beautiful Abbey grounds (now to be carved up and destroyed by the Bucks County Council for the benefit of road hogs) to form a fine artificial lake, and beneath the London road near the so-called "Little Abbey" – a Victorian mansion – the Misbourne feeds the big mill pond of Deep Mill, now intersected by the railway embankment, the building of which put the mill out of action. Beyond the railway bridge the old red brick building with iron clamps in walls and sky-lights in tiled roof, is a prominent landmark on the right.

The moiety of a mill at Missenden was mentioned in 1220; and in 1506, a miller of Missenden – possibly of Deep Mill – was burned at Buckingham in the course of the Lollardist religious persecutions. He was Robert Cosin, otherwise known as "Father Robert" or Robert the Miller.

At the Dissolution, Deep Mill seems to have belonged to Missenden Abbey; in 1545 it was granted to Richard and Robert Tuberner; later to Anthony Nyxe, a miller who sold it in 1584 to William Fleetwood. The mill descended in his family with the Manor of Great Missenden and therefore presumably belonged at one time to Prime Minister Fleetwood.

Probably Edward Nash, a contemporary miller to John Darvell, (both at Little Missenden in 1694) was at Deep Mill; and John Stone was the miller in 1798. Job Pearce was the miller in 1830, when two men were charged with stealing some sacks and 20 bushels of wheat valued at £10, which they tried to persuade him to grind for them. Then the Clarke family rented from George Carrington, and later owned, Deep Mill, whilst also interested in Wycombe Heath and Great Missenden windmills; but in 1891, when the Metropolitan Railway threw their embankment across the middle of the mill pond, James Nash was renting the premises; and he removed to Wycombe Heath Windmill.

Meanwhile the Met. being short of material for embankments, excavated a large meadow downstream beyond the *Royal Oak P.H.*, and this might easily be mistaken today for another mill-pond; they also cut the present stream-bed from the Suffolk Bridge to the Church, the original course being near the main road under some bushes.

Marks of the water wheel at Deep Mill are still visible on the present outer wall, but the wheel was probably enclosed originally; and the stream ran closer to the building than at present, discharging beneath Deep Mill Lane where part of the parapet of the old bridge can be seen alongside the existing bridge. The west end of the building is weatherboarded; the other end, facing the embankment, and having the general appearance of a toll-house, is an additional sitting-room with French doors, designed to overlook the pleasant mill-pond but the embankment rudely cut off the view.

No mill machinery remains, except for a bin or two in the roof, but curious carvings of wheatsheaves survive on some old beams.

Ogilby's London-Banbury Road Map of 1675, in the earliest series of accurate road maps ever made, marks Deep Mill, which is thus named by Jefferys and on the 1822 Ordnance; but Bryant calls it "Little Missenden Mill", for it was mainly on the Little Missenden side of the parish boundary, the Mill House being in Great Missenden – a very odd arrangement in the case of a self-contained building which did not bestride the stream.

In 1821, when Mr. Hour was the miller, a chalyabeat spring impregnated with iron was found in the mill garden, alongside Steep Hill.

Mill End Mill – 3½ f. E.S.E. of Church

Used as dairy
Maps; 1768, (1809), 1824, 1842, 1870, 1875, 1887, 1926

Mill End Mill appears to contain some of the oldest machinery in Bucks, although the age of mill equipment is a difficult thing about which to speak positively. Certainly all the machinery except the mill-wheel is of early design and ancient appearance.

Passing beneath the building, which is mainly of half-timbered red brick with tiled roof, the stream was laid on to a six-armed iron "overshot", 10ft. wide and 8ft. diameter, upon a wooden axle, by means of a wide wooden pentrough, with by-pass outside the

Mill End Mill

mill, but trough and wheel bearings appear to have given way, and the mill became disused at the end of the Great War. A small iron pitwheel, with wooden felloes and cogs – an unusual type – drove a massive old timber upright shaft, the top gudgeon pin of which is carried in a large plummer-block upon a cross-beam.

The great spur, on the ground floor, is exceptionally large, and entirely of wood, driving two pairs, with mortice stone nuts, wood to wood; and immediately over the spur, between it and the ceiling is a large morticed crown-wheel which received a drive for the horizontal steam engine installed 50 years ago when the river failed. (Some say the stream dries up every seven years, and others that its failure to flow is a portent of disaster, maintaining that it dried before the Boer War, the 1914, and the 1939 Wars; but in 1939 it was only dry above Great Missenden, where the Bucks Water Board had choked it with chalk sludge. (On the other hand it was totally dry when Peace came in 1945!)

Some most interesting gear is upon the upper floor of the mill, with its broken and decaying ceilings, where the upright shaft is splayed out into a big square head and all the machinery is of wood. From the upper face of a big four-armed crown-wheel a bevel-pinion upon a lay shaft was driven, the latter being coupled to the dresser and machine by belts; and a fine old solid wood crown wheel, smaller and just above the first, drove another layshaft extending over the wheel-room below. The teeth of the latter crown-wheel face upwards and engaged with a rare half-lantern pinion – that is to say a wooden disc with cylindrical teeth, lying parallel to its spindle- probably the only pinion of its kind in the County, and reminiscent of the full lantern pinions used in medieval wind-mills. Whether this is a genuine old relic or an improvised fitting of later years it is difficult to say, but it certainly is in keeping with all the wheel-work to be found on this floor, and seems to take us back to the glorious days of cloth sailed "peg" mills, wooden-walled ships and long-haired cavaliers!

Mill End Mill

Actually the present building is thought to date from 1600 A.D. or thereabouts; but the house, standing end-on to the road is much later, and is believed to replace a little miller's cottage the foundations of which are behind the mill.

The Amersham Rent Roll shows that John Darvell had the mill in 1692, at which time it is called Darvel's Mill, and an adjoining mead, probably on the other side of the road was called Mil Moore; the following year Darvell was indicted for altering a justice's warrant and fined £5! Joseph Sibley had become miller by 1798; and his family occupied the mill until after the Great War, when the late Arthur A. Sibley moved down to Amersham Upper Mill. He was the last miller, and Mr. T. Varney fitted up the premises as a dairy, but gave up in 1943.

Mr. A.A. Sibley who called it Town Mill, whilst others call it Little Missenden Mill, passed away in 1938, and his brother, Charles (who had partnered him) at the end of the same year at the age of 79.

AMERSHAM

Town Mill or *Upper Mill* – 3 f. W.N.W. of Church

Disused

Maps; 1768, (1809), 1822, 1824, 1842, 1847, 1875, 1887, 1926

Town Mill marks the northern extremity of that delightful village street of Amersham, which Leland described in 1540 as "a right praty market town on Friday, of a streete well builded with tymbar".

The ancient mill and the back part of the Mill House are of half-timber and brick, dating from about 1550 A.D., the front block being a later Georgian addition; and it is one of the three pre-1700 water mills recorded in Bucks by the *Hist. Mon. Comm.* In the upper storey at the rear is an eight-light mullion window, and an original dormer window remains in the attic.

A long mill-pool provided a good head of water for an all-iron "overshot" 9ft. by 7ft., with three sets of four arms and fairly narrow-mouthed buckets. Layout of machinery has been considerably altered from time to time; so that when closed down, at the death of Mr. A.A.Sibley, the ground floor arrangement was most unusual, if not unique. An extension of the axle shaft passes straight through the wall of the wheel-room, which is towards the east end, and carries an iron bevel pinion; and from this a layshaft runs towards the north wall and engages with a bevelled stone-nut. From the end of the shaft a belt communicates with another layshaft upstairs.

The other pair of stones are not coupled to the

Town Mill or *Upper Mill*

wheel, but receive a long belt drive from a small engine room beyond the wheel-room; and in this case also a layshaft drove the stone-nut. The engine, supposed to have been an oil-driven type, of foreign make, is missing. All ground-floor machinery, as at Mill End, is enclosed, with hand wheels for controlling the stones and feed, projecting through the partition; and the "flash" is adjusted by an iron lever, slotted at intervals for a pin to set it in various positions, and protruding up through the floor.

Upstairs, belts drive grindstone, chaff-cutter, bolter and shaker – the latter having a reciprocating motion applied by crank and strap. On the middle of the layshaft is a skew gear driving another shaft crossing it at right angles – the only example I have encountered in Bucks – the latter shaft being belt-coupled to the sack-bollard.

Last mill to do a corn trade on the Misbourne, this is reputed to have been a paper-mill in the past, but no louvres are fitted to the wooden portion of the upper walls. Altogether a typical old country mill, with mellowed tiles on the roof, in olden days it looked on to a ford, the bridge in front of the building, with millstones embedded in the road surface, being of no great age comparatively.

For about a century, probably from 1772 when Messrs. W. & G. Weller acquired the local brewery, the mill was owned by them; and the Gregory family were the millers for a hundred years to about 1860, William Gregory being in charge for 46 years until the business changed hands, William Sibley till the 'nineties; and the late A.A. Sibley last, in conjunction with Little Missenden Mill. He advertised home-made bread guaranteed made from pure stone-ground flour; and a special poultry meal, but the premises are now privately occupied.

Malt Mill – 1f. W.N.W. of Church

No map references

In 1504 there was a malt mill at Amersham, which *Victoria County* suggests may be the present Town Mill, since it was in the same ownership as the brewery and malt house (Messrs. W & G Weller) for about a century; on the other hand Town Mill was not used as a malt mill in Messrs. Weller's time, if at all. Edward & William Weller were maltsters at Church End in 1842, and were in all probability, then using a waterwheel at this site. Brewery and malthouse – now dismantled, are opposite the Church at the foot of Rectory Hill; and behind the brewery, looking on to the fields behind the High Street is a century-old brick building of warehouse type placed across the stream, which local inhabitants and millers believe to have been a water-driven mill for cracking down malt some 50 years ago, but inquisitive eyes were unwelcome in those days and they did not actually see the interior.

A tantalising document of April 25, 1766, from which the "plan hereunto annexed" is missing, thus leaving the mill site in doubt, describes a mill to be built near to Lower Mill and leased at £12 a year – thus it could not have been Robert Eeles' mill. Nor do the dimensions coincide with Quarrendon Mill; consequently the above Malt Mill seems indicated. *Records of Bucks, Vol. XIII, 1940* states that William Holding the lessee undertook to build:

"one Good and Substantial Water Corn mill, eighteen feet wide in the Clear and twenty feet . long in the clear, and the Brick work eighteen feet high to the plate, with two pairs of French stones and two bolting mills, with Sack tackle and all other wheels belonging, sufficient to drive the same". Landlord to allow "rough timber, bricks, tyles etc." to value of £100; lessee to keep everything in repair *except* "the French stones, spindles, Jacks and footbrasses to the same belonging, Feeders, hoops, bins and bin-ladders, bolting mills, pulleys and ropes, meal troughs and sack-ropes all which are agreed to be appraised and valued at the end of the said term by two indifferent persons".

In *Records of Bucks* surprise was expressed that the Misbourne should be expected to drive three mills in half a mile; and I would add that the mill was extraordinarily small – in fact smaller than the Shardeloes pumping mill; and if she was indeed relegated to malt-cracking for a brewery one cannot be surprised! Further reference in the 1945 volume of the same journal quotes particulars of an earlier mill, adding "this is not the mill at the west end of the town, but one near to the point where the road to Chesham turns off; it will be seen that in 1624 this mill was in very bad repair:-

"Saunders his watermill, and mille meade contayneth

2ac. 2ro. 35 pe. worth per annum	£ 20.0.0
The present rent whereof is per annum	£ 6.0.0
Which valued at 20 yeares purchase is	£120.0.0".

Silk Mill Lower Bury or *Bury End Mill* – 3 f. E.S.E. of Church

Used as road-house
Maps; 1675, 1768, (1809), 1822, 1824, 1842, (1847), 1875, 1887, 1926

Standing against the *Chequers P.H.* at the foot of the London hill, on the east side, is Bury Mill which went by this name as early as 1504, although some rebuilding has since taken place.

For generations the Drake family, of Shardeloes, who owned practically the whole of Amersham town until after the Great War, were owners of the mill, which is now known the "Mill Stream Café" and is run as a road-house; and Capt. T. Tyrwhitt-Drake very kindly supplied some particulars, printed in *Records of Bucks, Vol: XIII, 1938* concerning Lower Mill. These comprised accounts of the "Several Working Utensils, Goods and Chattels" of Robert Eeles the younger, which were "lying or being in or about the Mill", in 1755, 1771 and 1778; and it appears there were two pairs French stones and one pair Cullins; and "Three Flower mills with ropes to drive them; three handcarts to drive the wheat and flower about the Mill, etc.". In 1771 Eeles had bought a French stone and placed it under the Cullin; and in 1778 he enumerated a Dressing machine with shaking Screens, two Wheat screens, Flour Cloths and all the usual paraphernalia.

Capt. T. Tyrwhitt-Drake discovered in 1940 further items, including an agreement by which Henry Goodspeed leased the mill for 21 years; and a little later it was described as The Culling Mill with culling bills and boxing Chissell. William Mourton and William Charsely under an agreement "for New Building a paire of Brest Mills before Midsomer 1696", and they were "to do all Milwright's work of any nature whatsoever, and to fell all the Beech and Crab tree to be used at the Mill"; to find all sawing work; load all timber and find all labourers to dig up the Old Mill and put in the New Mill. Mr. Drake to pay £60 in three sums of £10 and a final sum of £30 "when the Mill is finished."

Robert Eeles, Junr. made some proposals on an undated paper, as to the terms on which he would take the Lower Mill:-

"the Mill and Banks to be put in good repair; a Parlor and room to be built over the Mill; Mill tail to be warft (embanked) with Slabs or Bricks; River below Mill to be sunk so that Wheels shall be laid a foot lower; an arch for Carriages to go over; Backwater to be turned down Berry Mead; yard pailed in; pipe laid from Mill pond to wash house; rent advanced from £30 to £35 a year if all these things are done to my mind."

Mr. Eeles did not think that the Mill would keep a man without lowering the Mill tail whilst also retaining wheels at existing height, for it would not otherwise do a Stroke of Business; and Mr. Drake presumably agreed, for Eeles became tenant.

In 1692 the Amersham Rent roll shows that Peter Parker occupied Lower Mill to which an additional barn was shortly added. Later occupants were John Eeles 1798, Samuel Allen and Son, Thomas Rayment, Geo. Dyer, William Challacombe (considered to have been the last real miller,) 1877 and 1891, and J.J. Wheelhouse 1895. Robert Eeles may have been miller in 1791, when he was listed as a "mealman".

At about the turn of the century when the new Station Road was laid out, the by-pass was obstructed and blocked, and the mill consequently put out of business; but whether the occupier was compensated no one seems to know. At any rate neither he nor the proprietors of the *Chequers P.H.* had their legitimate compensation for the subsequent flooding of premises, which was due to the flood water having to pass through the wheel-house for want of a proper channel. In fact it was a case of the river occupying the wheel-house instead of the Wheel-house occupying the mill!

Always used for corn-milling except for a spell of silk weaving a century ago, Bury mill-wheel was an "overshot", enclosed in centre of building, with millstones above, but eventually the premises stood completely empty, with water rushing through the wheelroom. About 1934 they were reconditioned and fitted with dance floor and galleries, etc., and if the mill is disfigured by advertisement signs it at least enjoys a respite from the breaker's axe.

Of warm red brick and tile, with some half-timbering, and now adorned with lead lattice windows, the mill is indicated upon Ogilby's Road Map of 1675. In the 1820s it is marked Silk Mill, thus joining the chain of silk factories – mainly steam – up and down the County a century ago; and Robert Gibbs gave an excellent outline of local silk weaving in his *History of Aylesbury*, with particular reference to that town's steam and hand-loom mill, which doubtless functioned similarly to the watermills; whilst Sir R. Phillips said there were 60 water driven silk-mills and 130 steam in the United Kingdom in 1841.

The Chinese made silk over 3000 years ago; they conveyed it to Persia, the Byzantines to Greece, the Moors to Spain, the Normans to Sicily, the Flemings to Spitalfields, London. Looms were used in Egypt 2000 B.C. and introduced in England about 1131–33, although probably not called "looms" until Sir Thomas Lombe invented a new silk mill for which he received £14000, in 1732. The warp or length of material, might consist of 8000 strong threads, largely made on Arkwrights' pattern spinning frame; and the weaver, who had two treadles, depressed one,

thus raising the alternate threads of the warp above the others. A jerk of a handle drove the shuttle through the opening in the warp, carting with it the weaker thread of the weft (usually made on Crompton's "mule"); a batten pulled by the left hand tightened the thread; and the action was reversed; the shuttle returned, and so on. Preliminary processes such as manufacture of the thread were not performed at the mill. Power looms made hard silk; hand-looms the finest and more delicate; patterned silk as well as plain were produced. Machinery for the former, invented by M. Jacquard and fitted to the figure-pattern looms was so intricate, said Gibbs, as to be "incomprehensible". He explained that it depended on a series of perforated cards, which presumably permitted different control rods to raise and depress different threads of the warp, as the pattern developed; the general principle appears to have been similar to that of the big train indicator machines on Southern Railway termini in London which anyone may grasp by watching closely when operated. Power-looms in a watermill were doubtless belt-driven from lay shafts, as in steam silk-mills.

At the erection of the London Transport garage, a stream was found, probably part of the old by-pass; and Millshot Drive, and an adjoining house, are named after the mill.

Impey's Mill or *Quarrendon Mill* – 1¼ m. almost E.S.E. of Church

Disused
Maps; 1768, 1793, (1809),
1822, 1824, 1842, 1875, 1887

Quarrendon Mill, near the eastern boundary of Amersham, stands at the end of a cart-track down some fields, probably acquiring its name from the Querendon's or Quarrendon's, who had rights in Amersham in the 13th century; and it is interesting that the name Querendon is said to be derived from the old English *cweorn-dün*, mill hill. Not that this necessarily signified a windmill, for it might refer to a horse-mill, or the hill might be named after the water-mill which probably existed before Domesday.

Of pale red brick with two floors and shallow slate roof picked out with dormers, this longish building placed end-on to the left bank, contains some old machinery, but not the mill-wheel. this appears to have been a rather large breast-wheel, perhaps 15ft.diam. upon a square wooden axle outside the end of the building; the other end incorporates the mill cottage. Arrangement of machinery is conven-

tional, with two pairs Peak and one pair burr. Except for the morticed eight-armed pit and great spur wheels, all gears, bridges and bridge-trees are iron, with the usual screw adjustments, the bridges being tangential to the great spur; and the three pairs of stones have spouts leading down to a horizontal screw mixer mounted along the front of the machinery room.

The peak stones were of feathered-edge type, with short deep furrows around the periphery; and upstairs is a layshaft driven from a morticed crown-wheel on the upright shaft, which has a large universal joint midway up. This layshaft carries several drums and projects through the wall as though to receive an auxiliary power drive, whilst disengagement is achieved by lifting a beam on which the inner end of the shaft rests. Part of a wire and brush cleaner exists; and the sack-bollard and its drum in the dummy floor in the roof, are of wood. Mill-race and by-pass are now lined with brick and concrete, doubtless reducing risk of flooding from congestion of water-ways.

John Impey, corn-miller, had the building in 1842, in succession to Joseph Impey (1798) and old people locally still call it Impey's Mill, although the name Quarrendon dates from time immemorial. Philip Goddard was afterwards the miller followed by George and Arthur Williams and eventually by Mr. Venner, the last miller.

Philip Goddard, probably father or grandfather of the above, and Thomas Rayment of Bury Mill were active supporters of their trade, their names appearing in several agreements devised at public meetings in High Wycombe and Amersham. They

supported sale of corn by Imperial Measure; protested against infringements of water rights by the Grand Junction Canal Co.; and aroused opposition to the Anti-Corn Law League, which condemned the Corn Law as a Bread-Tax racket of the landlords (who certainly supported it), whilst some of the millers claimed that it "exalted the manufacturers at the expense of the farmers" It was of course a tariff measure, so appealed as it still would, to a section of conservative or reactionary traders and farmers.

Bryant (1824) gives "Quarrington Mill" as does the 1850 directory, but this is obviously a temporary misnomer, now fortunately corrected. The mill, disused since about 1910, is now occupied by Mr. Thompson, an egg dealer.

CHALFONT ST. GILES – 3 m. S.E. from Amersham

[Misbourne]

Chalfont Mill or *The Old Mill* – 3½ f. N.N.W. of Church

Disused
Maps; 1768, (1809), 1822, 1824, 1842, (1847), 1875, 1887

Three mills, one paying 5 ores, and two others nothing, stood on the Manor of Chalfont St. Giles and were held by Manno the Breton in 1086. In 1247 a watermill is mentioned but by 1349 it was in a ruinous state. By 1814 there existed two watermills, one being of course the present, and they were owned by George Palliser, Lord of the Manor; possibly the two were under one roof, for the existing site seems to be the only one in the parish.

The existing building claims to be the oldest mill in the county, whilst the cottage adjoining dates from the early 17th century, and had its walls painted (now papered over) with a series of rural studies, one of which was entitled "The Windmill". The paintings had become quite unintelligible from smoke and damp, and a picture on the ceiling is black with age, so that only one or two details can be distinguished. Tradition has it that years ago an itinerant labourer and artist tarried at Chalfont Mill to perform some small tasks for the miller; he was accommodated at the mill cottage, and in return for his keep, illuminated the walls with these fresco paintings which, in the circumstances, probably did not depict any particular windmill. Some editions of *Black's Guide* state that the paintings dated from 1665. The claim of the mill itself to antiquity is difficult to understand, for externally it is of no great age and much newer than the cottage and barn adjoining, nor does the interior look exceptionally ancient.

Chalfont Mill so named on the 1822 Ordnance, is very picturesquely situated, on the right side of Mill Lane, which runs down to a ford from the Aylesbury turnpike, from whence the big rickety old black barn with sagging tiled roof can be seen adjoining the timbered and yellow washed mill cottage and pink brick mill. An old chimney-shaft – relic of steam milling days – stands beside the mill, and behind it the pine woods rise upon the steep hillside. The ford is part of the by-pass stream which comes round the mill from the sluice; whilst the mill-stream formerly passed beneath the west end to drive an inside wheel long since discarded. A concrete retaining wall now stops the water short of the mill, and a new cut in the bank leads to a turbine, believed to be of horizontal type, situated in an annex at the corner of the mill, the present mill-tail then discharging by a culvert under the road. This turbine did not drive the mill; it merely operated two belt-driven pumps which supplied water to a neigh-bouring mansion.

Some of the mill machinery remains between wheel room and cottage; the usual pit-wheel and upright shaft etc. driving two pairs of stones, machinery – including bridge-trees – being of wood, with the exception of the mortice-bevel pit-wheel and the wallower. The steam engine is believed to have been over the wheel-room, in which case the wheel will have been "overshot".

Chalfont Mill or *The Old Mill*

Peter Parker was miller in 1798; in 1842 J. & H. Gurney were the millers, and William Morten the owner; the Gurneys remained, and used the steam engine in the 'nineties, after which Mr. Pocock employed someone to work it, and finally a man named Cox used it for his own purposes only. Now Mr. Gurney is the owner, and the premises are let to Mr. H. S. Williams, poultry and dairy farmer.

CHALFONT ST. PETER – 4½ m. S.E. from Amersham [Misbourne]

Silk Mill, Fulling Mill or *Chalfont St Peter Mill* – 1f. N. of Church

Foundations remain
Maps; 1822, 1824, 1842, (1847)

A mill worth 6/- stood on Chalfont St. Peter Manor in 1086, later passing to Missenden Abbey, and being again mentioned in 1291. On the estate claimed by Geoffrey Bulstrode in the early 14th century against the Prior of St John of Jerusalem, was also a water-mill which is long since lost sight of, but there seems no reason to suppose these mills to have been else-where than upon the present site. This is just north of the village, 200 yards above the ford which existed across the High Street – the main London and Aylesbury road – well into the present century.

Thomas Price was the miller in 1689; Thomas Belch 1699; and in 1710 a letter to the sheriff's officer complained that several persons had failed "to keep their river banks between Aylesbury and Chalfont St. Peter to the damage of Mr. Wyrley's Mill". John Harding was the miller in 1798.

Standing west of the road, a building evidently

representing the mill is marked "Silk Factory" on the 1822 Ordnance, and Bryant calls it "Silk Mill"; but its history seems to be wrapped in a mystery which is not lessened by Holland describing it as a Fulling Mill on his excellent 1842 map, owner John H Hibbert, and proprietor Henry Brewer. William Hatch was a corn miller at Chalfont St. Peter in 1853, and David Russell the following year. Possibly the building stood empty for a long time after this, for it is not now remembered as a working mill, nor does any further mention seem to occur in the directories until the present century, when the Mill House is listed. Said to have been a brick structure standing north of an alley leading to the fields, it is known to have been a corn-mill at the last; but nothing beyond a double archway foundation over the river survives. As a fulling mill probably this was the last in Bucks, besides being the only one to follow on after a silk mill.

IVER – 2½ m. from Uxbridge

[*Misbourne*]

Chalfont Mill, Noke Mill or *Oak End Mill* – 4⅞ m. N.N.W of Church

Gone
Maps; 1695, 1768, (1809),
1824, (1847) 1870, 1875.

Upon Oakend estate stood a small mill which disappeared many years since. Morden 1695, called it Chalfont Mill, placing it in Burnham Hundred, whilst Iver is in Stoke Hundred. Jefferys has Oak Mill. Bryant marked it Oak End Mill in 1824 and had it in Iver Parish; the 1875 Ordnance gave it as a saw watermill.

From Messrs W.H.Ward and K.S.Block's excellent *History of Iver* it appears that the district of Noke or Noake Mill, later Oak End, was a detached electoral division of Iver parish until 1861, when merged with the new ecclesiastical parish of Gerrards Cross; in 1895 the latter became a civil parish. Thus Bryant, obviously more reliable than the vague Morden, is verified.

William Gould sold part of the estate in 1727, but Henry Gould died at Noake Mill in 1739; and the estate passed to the Hibbert family, who had Chalfont St. Peter Mill. Meanwhile, a miller, Richard Playtor, is recorded in the 17th century; and in 1852 a "Capital Corn and Flour Mill in first-rate order" was advertised. "Steam and water power. Excellent house, garden, three cottages. Enquire Mr. Chas. Hilton, Oak End, Chalfont St. Peter. To Let". Note this is not actually stated to be Oak End Mill, which Holland did not have on his map; and Mr. Hilton might have had Chalfont St. Peter Mill whilst residing at Oak End.

Mill Lane and Mill Wood; both south of the mill-site, are named after the mill; and I am informed the House was formerly called Mill House and the mill adjoined it.

DENHAM

[*Colne*]

Moorhouse Farm Mill – Approx 1m. W.N.W. of church

Working
No map reference

Below Oak end Mill comes another almost equally obscure, yet still working mill for no map or directory indicates its presence. Situated midway between the Tatling End Road and Denham Golf Club Halt, a good mile from the Church, on a cart-track now closed at the turnpike end, the mill is in the outbuildings of the farm, end-on to the west bank of stream; the mill-race approaches the rear of the barn, turns east beneath a brick-built wheelhouse, rejoining the mainstream just below a little sluice-gate. The 12ft. breast-wheel, all of iron, is divided into two pieces through the spokes, with three sets of six arms and 30 straight buckets, one of which was of wood when inspected. A 2-piece morticed pit-wheel of domed construction, 7ft. 6ins. diam. engages a pinion at axle level, whose shaft enters the barn to turn a morticed bevel; and alongside this is a capstan wheel engaging the usual "flash".

Engaging with the bevel, again at axle level, is a pinion driving an abnormally long counter-shaft reaching from end to end of the lengthy barn, this shaft and the spur being encased after a man was unfortunately killed by the gear. A long belt against the west wall couples the shaft to a pair of millstones on a high hurst-frame, with a large hopper in the loft above; another belt drives an oat-crusher, to which a grindstone is also attached; a third engages the chaff-cutter. The remaining two-thirds of the counter-shaft, with a half-way bearing, is belt coupled to a swede-cutter and also in an annex, to a vertical single-cylinder pump to fill an overhead water-tank for the farmhouse. Another belt formerly turned a dynamo for lighting; but main electricity is now available.

In the middle of the big yellow brick and tiled barn, which is mainly an open cart-shed, a thresher was formerly stationed, to work by water, but this is gone. All belt wheels, pinions and shafting are of iron. On the face of the barn is the inscription

B. H. W. W.
1886

commemorating Benjamin Way, owner of the property; but there probably was a previous mill in view of the obstacle that milling rights would present to the erection of an entirely new wheel. The walled mill-tail, in which young trout abound, looks pretty old; and the picturesque farmhouse is mentioned in 1496, when Peter Peckam bought it.

The present owner, Mr. James Lipscomb, succeeded his father, and I am indebted to his sister, Miss Lipscomb and their neighbour Mrs. Crouch, from whom I heard of the mill, for a most interesting and enjoyable afternoon at Denham.

Denham Cornmill or *The Town Mill* – ¼ m. S. of Church

Used as residence
Maps; 1768, 1793, (1809), 1822, 1824, 1842, (1847) 1875, 1887, 1914, 1926

One of two watermills appurtenant to Denham Manor in 1086 and valued at 10/- was doubtless the Town Mill, held by Martin de Capella in the 12th century and John de Bohun in 1275.

In common with other Denham mills it brought no rent in 1377, being out of repair. Richard atte Terne was the miller in 1401 and Hugo Bereacre in 1440; Roger Tyler, farmer, had the mill in 1478; and Willelmus Atkyns, Richard Okeborne and Johannes Bourton were millers in Denham 11 years later; Alice Berakere was miller and brewer in 1501, when Johannes Berakere, Johannes Blakeman, Henricus Wolff and Thomas Ellys were also millers in the parish; and these people being almost the only ones whose calling was stated in the Compotus Rolls evidently ranked as of some importance.

Eubold le Strange appears to have held this and the Abbey Mills in 1330; and 30 years later the Lord Abbot "stopped the flow of water at Denham Mill whereby the high-road is flooded", but there is some confusion between the Town Mill and the cornmill on the Colne, which are often not clearly distinguished. In 1454, when the Abbot of Westminster held the mill, the overlord was declared unknown; and William Bowyer, coming into the property from the Peckhams after the Dissolution, valued the mill at £4. Lord Strange of Knockin passed the Denham Manor mills to the Earls of Derby, from whom they

came to the Chandos family in the early 17th century.

Denham Cornmill, or as Bryant calls it, Denham Farm and Mills, stands west of the Uxbridge road, outside the village; and house and mill are across the stream make a pleasing group with their curious Dutch gables, especially since the red brick had been plastered and painted white and the old fashioned shutters green. The roof is of slate and the date 1857 is on a panel on the wall

Joseph Nash was the miller in 1798; Edward Nash, 1843; and the Hamaton family for the latter half of the century, eventually erecting the existing chimney. Wm. Edwin Hamaton, the last miller, afterward became overseer at Colham Mills (Uxbridge, Middx.) downstream. Meanwhile, the next tenant cleared out the mill gear – millstones not rollers, and commenced manufacturing size paste, a considerable number of girls being employed; but some 10 years ago the late Rector, Mr. Battisford, took over the buildings for a residence, renovated and modified them, adopting the name "Weller's Mead". Mr. Harold W Swithingbank acquired the Court and mill in 1885; from the Lambert family, the previous owners being the assignees of Thomas Hamlet. About a mile east of Denham Mill the Misbourne Stream joins the Colne, which in turn enters Middlesex to meet the Thames near Staines.

LANGLEY MARSH – 2 m. E. from Slough

Black Park Pond Stream

Black Park Saw Mill – 2 m. N. of Church

Working
Map –1875

Situated only 20 miles from London, Black Park Lake and its surroundings can rightly be called one of the beauty spots of Bucks; the lovely beech woods reach right down to the water's edge, casting dark, sombre reflections in the silent lake and giving it almost a tropical aspect on a hot summer's day. In the midst of this setting of natural beauty, and especially as this is our very last water mill site, it seems a pity to introduce the unharmonious name of Langley Marsh – a relic I imagined of the pseudo-Cockney jargon of Slough until I discovered that it is a recent revival of a medieval landlord name, Meres or Marreys – and I therefore take the liberty of reverting to what appears to have been the accepted name of the parish a century ago, Langley Marsh.

Really there are two mill sites here, one either side of the Fulmer road at the west end of the lake, but as they are estate saw-mill sites and the one mill replaced the other a single heading will suffice. The original mill stood close by Saw Mill Cottages, east of the road, and probably was water-wheel driven, since the fall was small. Eventually, however, the mill was transferred to the yard of Rowley Farm, west of the road, where it is incorporated in the curious red-brick building finished with ornate and somewhat grotesque barge-boards, terminating in a sort of figure-head either end.

Water is conveyed to a 22 h.p. turbine in this building by an underground pipe 19ins. diam.

obtained from America; and leading up from the turbine a shaft carries a mortice-spur wheel to drive the stone-nut for a large pair of stones (disused) on the first floor. They took 20 minutes to grind a sack of flour that in a kibbling machine can be scratched through in 5 minutes, which only shows that if you want a job done properly you must have patience. The iron bridge-tree was screw-adjusted; and a shaft on the first floor drove a saw sharpening machine. A main shaft from the turbine to a smaller building adjoining, drives an interesting early pattern Worssam (Chelsea) vertical saw with reciprocating motion – quite a novelty in these days. This has a 24ins. saw bench with gear drive; and a circular saw is also employed.

In the big old tiled barn across the yard, almost like a tithe barn, is another rare curiosity – a stationary threshing machine of similar design to present-day road threshers, mounted upon a frame, but disused; it is by Ransome, Sims and Jefferies, 1859.

Water supply is from the 13½ acre lake which has two other outlets – a pipe line to Langley Park and a general safety valve which was enlarged after the bank burst during the wet season of 1903; and the mill-tail discharges by way of George Green, beneath the canal near Langley, through Riching's Park, past an obscure mill site near Colnbrook, by Horton and Wraysbury and so into the Colne Brook just below Hythe End Mill, within hale of Father Thames.

HORTON – 3¼ m. E.S.E. from Eton

[*Colne Brook*]

Pile Mill or *Poyle Mill* – ¾ m. N.N.E. of Church, on original ordnance

Gone
1822

½ m. N.N.W. of Church, on Bryant and Culliford's maps

1824, (1847), 1862

A mysterious building called Pile Mill appears only on the original 1ins. Ordnance, standing west of the Colnbrook road, in open bleak country, just short of that town at the spot occupied by Mildridge Farm, formerly Milldridge Farm which dates back to Jeffery's time (1768). No signs exist of a former mill, although a longish by-pass surrounds the farmstead; this is stated by Mr. Wicks to be of assistance in preventing flooding, and he thinks quite possibly

there was a mill. It would have been in Horton parish, since it disappeared ere the realignment of boundaries in 1853, and there the matter would rest but for the difference of opinion of the cartographers, for Bryant places Poyle Mill (not to be confused with the modern mill of that ilk in Middlesex) just above New Butts Farm on the same brook and same side of the road where there is a loop-stream; but Bryant himself does not name the mill; leaving this venture to

Culliford, who is probably wrong. We can only add that the streamlet follows the road into Horton, through Wraysbury to Hythe End. It can never have had a powerful flow in such flat country; nor can this be the early Horton corn-mill site for it is not near the present mills.

Thus appropriately enough we launched our water-mill quest in the north-west of the county, and terminated in the south-east. Practically every known type of watermill has come to our notice, and the reader will, I hope, have found sufficient of interest in the foregoing to encourage him to seek out the forgotten watermills, secluded and hidden away, as well as those more popular landmarks about which so much more has been written – the glorious windmills.

Appendix 1
Introduction to Corn Watermills

Having treated somewhat exhaustively of windmill history and economy, it is hoped that a single chapter will suffice to embrace a corresponding introductory survey of corn watermills.

Difference of opinion seems to exist as to who invented watermills or the waterwheel. Fairbairn believed that the immense quantities of water in Egypt and Assyria, coupled with need for irrigation in drier parts of those countries, led to contrivances for turning water to good account as a source of power; and added that Vitruvius, (Roman architect and author of De Archetum c. 16 BC) mentioned both irrigating and corn-grinding mills. Another contention is that the Greeks devised a horizontal (vertical axle) waterwheel in 450 B.C., without gears, and the Romans were the first to gear watermills; although the Romans being only copyists, of a somewhat unintelligent "Nazi" mentality, the present writer doubts very much whether they originated anything.

To continue from Fairbairn, he mentions that Whittaker in his *History of Manchester* records an alleged Roman watermill foundation unearthed in Manchester; and he expresses the opinion that the Dutch early adopted water tide-mills* but considered windmills more serviceable in their well winded country, when invented.

From the ensuing chapters it will be seen that numerous English watermills were in service in Saxon times – indeed in no case does the origin of many "Domesday" watermills in Bucks appear to be recorded, although it is clear that most if not all were pre-Norman, some perhaps predating the county itself, which it is thought to have been founded under King Offa in 802 A.D. The Normans another Nazi-minded race destroyed some Buckinghamshire mills, but probably built none; and the reduced value in *Domesday Book* of certain watermills indicates the probable course of William's roundabout march of pillage and plunder from Hastings to London, which is thought to have been via Wallingford, Princes Risborough, Aston Clinton, Waddesdon and the Claydons to Buckingham, thence to Wolverton, Olney and Lavendon. A section seems to have branched from Aston Clinton to Cublington, Linslade and Brickhill and another via Iver, Taplow and Wooburn. All the "Domesday" mills of Bucks, totalling some 130, are indicated in the text, with values; and in this connection it should be mentioned that one shilling in 1086 (date of Domesday Book)

would be equal to 3 shillingsworth of goods by weight in 1939, and more than this in general value.

Mr. W Pennington Storer observed *(Records of Bucks. Vol. 2)*, that

"In feudal times existed not the class of millers who now exist between growers and bakers. The lord of the manor where there was a stream usually (perhaps invariably) had his mill – a grist mill, receiving the corn of the tenants, and returning it ground; a certain customary portion being retained under the name of toll, as a recompence for grinding, though sometimes money payments were received instead. In some Manors tenants were obliged to grind at the Manorial mill; and there is an instance upon record of a tenant who was presented at the Court Leet for refusing to do so. 'To bring grist to one's mill' is a phrase which one supposes originated in the feudal custom"

Another note (in Vol. 11, p.30 adds that the lord of the Manor generally farmed out his mill or mills to a tenant whom he permitted [to] make a fair profit; but some millers, taking advantage of monopoly, took too much profit and were presented at Court Leet, by the "tithingmen" for so doing. When the miller took toll in kind he measured or struck off his portion of meal with a stick somewhat resembling a truncheon, and called a "strike" and there is an amusing story about taking an excess or unauthorised toll, which in some districts is called "hanging up the cat". A miller out with his mill-boy, met a customer on his way to pick up some meal, and sent the boy back with him to hand over the produce. "Be sure and hang the cat up" said miller to boy, thinking the customer wouldn't understand. Arrived at the mill, the boy went upstairs for something; and customer promptly took a strike of meal from one of the miller's sacks and popped it into his own. On his way home he met the miller, who enquired politely whether the meal was all right. "Yes, thanks", said customer pleasantly, "*and I hung the old cat up*"!

A curious note on corn prices at Wycombe occurs in the Domestic State Papers relating to March 1622 (1623 New Standard – the year having counted from March 25 to March 24 in those days, until 1752).

"The midle sorte of wheat wch. was at viis. or thereabouts ys nowe at vs.vid. or lesse. Barley beinge at 4s. the bushell ys the dearer because it is

---

* Worked by tidal waters, and so not found in Bucks.

the comon foode of the poore, and that the seede tyme is not yet paste. Beans and peas and oats are fallen. in diverse p'ishes the p'ishon's have of their own purses bought Rye at London, to serve the poore wth. all, and solde it them better cheape than they bought yt."

Right for feudal times until about 1750, practically all watermills had a separate wheel for every pair of stones, hence two or three Domesday mills (i.e. wheels) are listed in Bucks villages where in some cases only one site is known, *vide* this illuminating picture by Fairbairn of medieval rural life:-

"In the early stages of civilisation, when industrial progress was at a low ebb, and in those days when the whole population was trained to war, and a miserable system of tillage existed, mills were little in demand, with the exception of corn and fulling mills; the former to grind oats and barley, and the latter to mill a rough description of serge or blanket. At that period, mill architecture was out of the question, as the dwellings of the retainers, and those employed in the field or manufactory, were mere hovels ... Mills were simply sheds, with water wheels having straight floats, and a long conduit or spout to carry the force of the water descending from the high fall against the float boards below. In process of time . . . a new description of mills was introduced to meet the requirements of a superior class to those under the feudal system, who were chiefly engaged in war and plunder. At this period mills were improved and enlarged, but there were no attempts at architecture; and what is still more surprising, the engineers and millwrights of those days appear to have had no idea of the advantages derivable from large waterwheels, but contented themselves with additional wheels to meet the demand of additional work. On these occasions every pair of millstones and every pair of fulling stocks had their own separate water wheels, and these were multiplied according to the demands or necessities of the trade"

Smeaton (1724–1792) of lighthouse fame, Fairbairn suggests founded the practice of concentrating his water power on one wheel; John Rennie (1761–1820) builder of Waterloo Bridge, followed suit with steam power at Albion Mills; and Fairbairn himself (1789–1874) adopted the practice at the notable Catrine Cotton Mills in Ayrshire where two fifty-foot wheels have been driving a single 18 foot spur-wheel for nearly 120 years, the mill-head and tail race being single. The wheels naturally increased in size; and at Catrine they occupy a separate commodious wheel-house, thus removing dampness from the mill-building besides facilitating repairs – a plan which would strongly have recommended itself to Mr. William Cripps, who considered that the wheels should at least occupy an external lean-to and not obstruct the mill interior.

All this time, waterwheel design was developing, especially from 1750 onwards, before which date most wheel were "undershot" with straight radial floats, partly because a fast-running wheel was thought to be essential, and it was known that "over-shot" wheels were more limited in speed; but the weight of the water in the buckets of the latter wheels is a great asset, as will be explained, if a sufficiently high fall of water can be provided. Then came the steam engine, introduced in Bucks around 1840; but water power is not totally supplanted here even yet. Beam engines with a great overhead rocking beam linking the piston of a vertical cylinder with the connecting-rod, worked very slowly and steadily, with a sweet almost silent motion, at very low boiler pressure (only 10 lbs. per sq. in. up to the 'forties) were employed for several generations. High pressure direct-coupled engines appeared in watermills before the turn of the century, mostly of a crude form, followed by efficient variable-expansion engines, and finally by both water turbines and steam turbines, and some crude oil engines, which will be recorded under appropriate mill-headings. Water turbines in general differ from water wheels in being submerged in ...

[remainder of the text missing]

Appendix 2
Introduction to Paper and Millboard Mills

Paper was made from cotton rags in 1100 A.D. according to Dr. Johnson, and from linen rags in 1170. Its manufacture was introduced to Europe by the Moors, who had paper-mills in Spain in the 12th. century, the Egyptains having made it "centuries before the Christian era", in the words of Haydn, who says they made it of cotton in 600 A.D. Sir Richard Phillips said it was made from the Papyrus shrub until 700 A.D. and Dr. Ure suggested that the Chinese, who manufactured paper from bamboo, had first made it from vegetable matter, at a time when the Egyptians still used papyrus.

Earliest known paper-mill in England was near Stevenage, Herts. in the late 15th. century; and Caxton printed on paper made at Paper Mill Mead, near Hertford. At the end of Wynkin de Worde's edition of Bartholomaeus *De Proprietatibus Rerum, 1494*, its thin paper, made by John Tate in England is commended.

Sir John Speilman's mill for making coarse white paper at Dartford in 1580 is recorded by Stow; and Speilman attempted to prove that Her Majesty's patents granted him sole right to make paper in England. The Privy Council retorted that he was a German, and did not build the first paper mill, moreover he had *leased* a mill to a man whom he now petitioned against; he had caused a great nuisance by employing numbers of vagrant women to beg for rags in London, some of whom stole property as they went along.

In general, we made only brown paper until the French began to manufacture writing paper here in 1690, although the notorious Phipps of Horton, Bucks, had already made a very poor quality writing paper, whilst others near High Wycombe had made a good quality. Thence onwards paper-making proceeded apace in Bucks, which has always shared with Herts, Kent and the North the honours of the paper industry; and many historical facts concerning the 18th. century paper-makers will be found under individual mill headings.

Until about 1800 all paper was made in sheets by hand; but at that date M. Piere Didot purchased a model paper machine from Monsieur Robert, and sold the invention to Henry and Charles Fourdrinier, who brought it more or less to perfection and had it manufactured by Brian Donkin, the noted engine and machinery maker of Bermondsey; but the Fourdriniers, to whom the greatest credit was due, were never recompensed. They are said to have been at that time at Hemel Hempstead, where an important law-suit occurred between one of the other paper-mills and the Grand Junction Canal Co. over interfer-

ence with water rights, alleging that the Company drew off an excessive amount of water from the river and failed to return it; and probably as a result of this, a Gauge House was erected near the *Cowroast Inn* at Northchurch, where a continous record is kept of the rise and fall of the canal. It is illegal, except by agreement, for the flow of water either to be stopped or drawn off, above a mill, or obstructed below the mill-tail, and the necessary provisions of the Act frequently led to actions and disputes.

Conversely, "divers persons" were apt to proceed against the millers and paper makers over their handling of the mills; and in 1636 an interesting petition was presented against Phipps of Horton and others alleging that

"the grounds and highwayes adjoining to these Milles have been much anoyed and overflowed by the hygh penning upp of the waters far above the size, (sides?) wheras the sayd grounds are killed, and the sayd wayes rather become passages for boates than highwayes for men and horses to travile. The fishes in the Rivers have bine and are dayly destroyed and hindered from striving upp by reason of the double Wheeles of the sayd Milles running near to the bottom to the depth of about an inch and a half with great violence, and allowance are made soe narrowe and layde soe hygh as the ffishes can by no means passe.

The bordering inhabitants are much anoyed by the hideous noyse of the hammers of the paper milles, which goe dayes and night, even on Sunnedays, which are heard two or three miles off. The noysome smells of the sayd infectious ragges are soe offensive as they are cented afar off. The Corne markets neere adjoining to those milles are much decayed, for that their former corne milles are converted to Paper Mills, for yt allbeit for a shewe they have Corn Mills at the sayd Paper Mills yett their carelessnesse in grinding the same for their greater profitt otherwaies, and the feare of the inhabitants to bring their Corne hither for danger of infection by their noisome ragges, doth cause them to go farther".

For the first 60 years of the last century an excessive Excise Duty (part of the "Tax on Knowledge") was imposed on all manufactures of paper; and it may have been a sign of the times that the period more or less coincided with that of the Corn Laws (otherwise known as the Bread Tax) the "enclosure" or Land Thievery Act; and the Window Tax, or Tax on Health. In 1830 the Excise Duty or Paper Tax of £15 per ton was accompanied by the Newspaper Stamp duty of 4d. a copy, and the Advertisement Tax of 3/6d. For the purposes of the tax every mill had an official number, which I have given, where known, in the individual mill headings; and to simplify collection and checking no paper-mill was permitted to make mill-board, and vice versa. Sometimes the duty worked out at three times the total wages of the workmen; and instead of purchasing English books, foreign countries obtained a copy and reprinted, which enabled them to sell at about one-third of our price, especially in America where Trollope states they always stole the copyright without paying the author a penny-piece.

Unfortunately at the repeal of the Paper Tax in 1861 the makers did not at once reduce prices, and foreign makers jumped into our market and did considerable damage. We were at about that time, importing 32 million lbs. of rags, and exporting 20 million lbs. of paper. Sir R. Phillips said in 1841, a ream of paper was 18 quires of 24 sheets, and 2 quires of "outsides" of about 20 sheets each, which approximates to the present-day ream of 480 sheets. But a printers ream is 21½ perfect quires or 516 sheets; and a perfect ream of printing demy paper weighed from 18 to 24 lbs.

It will be necessary to describe briefly the two general processes of paper making – hand and machine – but it may first be mentioned that according to Mr. A. Dyke Spicer's *The Paper Trade* 1907 the very first continuous roll machine was installed at Frogmore, Herts, in 1803, the second at Two Waters, Herts, 1804, and the third at Marlow, 1804 or 5. Six were installed in 1805; and by 1840, 190 were at work. In 1804 ten tons of machine-made paper were produced in the United Kingdom; and 15,000 tons were hand-made; but production of machine-made overtook hand-made in 1824; and at the half-century twenty-nine papermills worked in Bucks – more than any other county except Kent, Lancashire and Yorkshire – out of a total of nearly 400. Owing to amalgamations and so-forth the total diminishes as time goes on; thus there were about 300 in 1880 and 200 in 1910, but production increases.

Paper riots had of course caused many outlying mills to convert to corn before 1850; and the railways to some extent brought about further closures, owing to the advantage accruing to mills adjoining the line over those of the beaten track.

A century ago most paper mills sorted and prepared their own rags; now they buy them, if used, ready sorted. Women sorted the rags in the sorting-room, into fines or firsts, old white sheets, etc; seconds, clean slightly coloured; thirds darker and dirtier; outshots bad coloured whites; prints, coloured stuff; new cuttings; mixed linen and cotton; and blues, blouse rags and blue stuff. Other materials utilized were gunny (bagging and bales), and rope – manila from railways and ships.

Seams were cut off in some cases, otherwise soft parts would wash away before the seams rotted and rags were then put on a wire gauze table or hurdle, with a sharp knife over it, and bunches of rag pulled across the knife to shorten them before going to the machines, so that they did not wind round the spindles, etc.; the dirt fell through the gauze to a drawer. In early days the rags passed to the rag-machine or "rag-devil" a tearing machine not much used now; then to the more modern "breaker" (for machine-made boards) in which knives or prongs running against each other at speed tear the material into smaller particles but without further tearing the fibres; and thence to the "duster" for further cleaning. This is a wire drum some 5ft. in diameter with prongs inside it and a revolving worm or pronged spindle in the middle; and the whole is enclosed in a dirt collecting box. From the duster to a slow revolving spherical boiler, driven by an external cog-ring, pressed to 20 or 30 lbs. of steam, where the material is in a soda solution for some twelve hours, to extract resinous matter, etc. Rags are bleached in chloride tanks, but in the earliest days they were merely wetted and laid out on the grass in the sun.

Now the rags are ready to be beaten to pulp, and at this stage the material is known as "half-stuff"; very often the process at this point was performed in small auxiliary mills, known as "half-stuff" mills.

Next comes the pulping process, which has involved three successive methods; first the "stamper" – the very earliest machine used in paper making – a system of hammers actuated by water – driven cams. This was the "noisome" machine complained of in 1636; and it is stated that 16 stampers fed one pulp vat and took two or three days to deal with a charge; the vat produced 130 lbs. paper a day or 45,000 lbs. per annum. Secondly, the Hollander, a device imported from Holland for paper making – not millboards – and consisting of a large vessel containing knives opposed by other knives upon an internal roller; and thirdly the "beater" or rag engine which still serves even for machine-made paper. Beaters and pulp engines, which developed from the Hollander are often mounted in pairs, one higher than the other, so that the pulp can be passed on for a second beating in the pulper, which "rubs up" the material after beating, without tearing the fibre and they are generally upon a stage or platform.

In the appended rough plan of Hedsor Mills [*missing from manuscript*] showing the principal machines, A is an old wooden clasp-arm water wheel 12ft. in diameter by 10ft. 4ins. tread, of the usual low-breast type, driving a big wooden pit-wheel in the Lower Mill. On the upright shaft are the iron wallower B and a big old wooden spur C; and the cog-ring of roughly hewn teeth on the under face of the latter drives the beaters DD which are at one side of their respective ribbed cast iron tanks EE, these tanks being on a stage, so that the pulp may be drawn of at a stop valve. The actual beater is a drum, usually 2 or 3ft. in diameter, and a similar width, in which closely spaced radiating knives are set laterally, revolving at about 150 to 200 revs, per minute. Beneath the drum is an adjustable iron slide with about a dozen lateral knives, which can be raised or lowered by the hand-wheel F to vary the aperture. Slide and floor of the tank are a little inclined, and a hinged board G, secured to the drum case by a string, regulates the flow of pulp down the slope, whilst an attendant pushes the pulp up the other bay of the tank with a big wad on the end of a long beater stick when filling, after which it runs round of itself. Pulp is drained off, and in some cases passes through a "knotter" or strainer to remove conglomerates of fibres, or "knots" which are held back when the pulp is jolted through a series of slits in the strainer. Round chests HH receive the pulp, and in each is a revolving agitator I and from the chest a vatman continually feeds the square vat J which has a "hog" – and a horizontal four-vane spindle across it. From this vat the paper-maker "crouches" or scoops pulp out of a wire mesh frame or bottom-mould, having first placed a frame or "deckle" around it. The mould is placed on the press and on the top is laid a grid or a top mould. The saddle of the press (the press board), swings from an arm L, with a counter balance weight, and when brought into position is screwed down so that the water is squeezed into a trough below. From the mould or press the board is tilled onto a press plank or "couch plank" (pronounced "cooch") and a felt laid over it; alternate boards and felts are tipped or couched until a "post" of 32 boards is formed, and a press block placed on top. This was in the old days passed to a big Samson hand-press M, standing about 8ft. high where the boards, were left to "weep", but nowadays there isn't time for this refinement! When this press was screwed down as far as possible by hand with a tommy-bar, the winch or capstan N reaching from floor to ceiling, was brought into use;

this was driven by a wooden shaft some 30ft. long running across the ceiling from a cog at the top of the wooden upright shaft and engaged by a counter-balance lever O; and the rope P was looped onto the tommy-bar a number of times and tightened by the capstan.

Nowadays the big hand presses are discarded when pressing is necessary, in favour of hydraulic presses QQ. The sheets are next laid off onto a board to keep the pack rigid, and felts returned to the vatman for future use. Truck rails R are laid between brick sets in the floor, for the "planks" to be slid along when conveying a "post" of boards to the press; they were not used for wheeled trucks as far as is known.

Large scale paper making by hand involved a variation of this process, three men being employed at the vat instead of one. The vatman took up the wire frame, which had very closely spaced parallel wires, with cross wires about half an inch apart, if making "laid" paper; "wove" paper is made upon a woven fabric base. Placing the deckle upon the frame he plunged the whole into the vat and in lifting it out, imparted a curious "shake" which was the secret of his trade; and placed the mould in the press. This "shake" served to discharge superfluous pulp over the deckle; but the vatman might suddenly lose his "shake" for ever, and thus be incapacitated for the work. After preliminary pressing, a "coucher" took the frame from the vatman; the "layer" seized a warm damp felt from a trestle and laid it down, and the coucher turned over the mould to deposit the sheet, and returned the mould to the vatman; the layer then laid another felt on the pack, and so on until the "post" was complete. Hydraulic pressing followed, and the felts were returned to the trestle by the layer. Sandwiched between two boards the "post" was then left in another press for several hours to "weep" or drain, then taken out and left to dry, and finally separated and in some cases gelatine sized, one sheet at a time in a tub. More often resin size is added to the pulp engine; and it may be mentioned the pulp is sometimes heated by a "pot-hole" heater under the vat, or by steam pipes.

In the Upper Mill an extremely interesting hand-made board process is performed by Mr. Bowers, approximating as nearly to this old paper-making process as anything now to be seen in England. Pulp is dipped directly out of the tank; the mould is rested on a bench S, and a saddle is then pressed down upon it by means of a long lever T, which meets a stop, to prevent excessive pressure. This is Mr. Bower's own adaptation; and the only drawback is *monotony* for he has performed these movements daily for 16 years!

After pressing and laying, boards are taken to the steam heated drying room upstairs and spread out on the "trebles" which consist of ropes or lines U, stretched between poles V which are secured with pegs in posts W, being pushed up first one side then the other after laying the boards on the lines. Sheets of hand-made paper were not laid flat across the limes but slung in batches of four or five sheets together over individual lines with a big wooden T-piece called a "cross" to hank like washing; and it is now usual for boards to be vertically suspended from self-gripping metal clips fixed to cross bars between the poles as at X. No iron or metal must come in contact with paper, however, because of staining, and the only rope that will not stain is cow-hair covered – hence references to "hair-lines" in the advertisements.

After drying of hand-made paper still further processes followed; it went next to the picking room where girls picked out all the bits of metal and buttons, and other blemishes with a sharp knife. Thence to the glazer, who laid down alternate sheets of paper and polished zinc; several quires were then put into the press together, and finally the sheets were again separated and re-examined in the finishing room, or "saile", retaining its old French name from early paper – making days. They were then stacked in the stock room.

Old time drying rooms had vertically louvred walls in which large slotted panels slid along in grooves inside a slotted wall, on the principle of sliding ventilators, so that draught could be regulated; the Lower Mill has this pattern, but Upper Mill has horizontal pivoted louvres controlled by a vertical wooden shutter-rod like windmill sails.

Finally menu and showcard boards etc. are glazed between steel glazing rolls Y, one above the other and driven by steam-generated electricity and (one pair for preliminary dressing of paper only by a 12–13ft. all-iron breast wheel Z, with buckets 10ft. 4ins. wide fed directly of the main stream); but in some cases paper passes round a very large cylinder, as much as 18ft. diameter, if glazed one side only, as for bag paper. This cylinder was not employed at Hedsor.

Beaters in the Upper Mill are electrically driven; and between the two mills are a group of settling tanks in which rope, years ago, was left to soak until disintegrated for hand making, a slate being let into each wall so that the date for refilling could be posted up.

At extreme left of diagram is a stamping bench for cutting out shaped boards such as discs; and at the extreme right an edge runner mill or clay mortar, driven by iron gears from a cog ring just above the great spur, for preparing China clay which helps to produce an art surface. Also an old-fashioned pump in the corner of the building, driven by the water-wheel for raising water, and the latter after use is discharged over the wheel.

Turning to machine-made, pulp is pumped into the stuff chests, and flows through the machine to emerge in the finished roll as shown in the more or less self-explanatory diagram of Fourdrinier and modern machines. In the former, which cost about £1000, a copper slide regulates the flow through a 5ft. wide slot onto the endless wire mesh belt, with an endless deckle-strap at either side; through the adjustable couch-rolls where a press felt or woven wire draws off some of the moisture, so that the sheet will come off the wire intact, and onto another endless felt and through the iron or brass covered press-rolls to the reel. The backwater lifter consists of a number of L-shaped pipes for picking up superfluous water at one side of a trough beneath the wire and passing it through the hollow axle-shaft to a tank on the far side, where it can be utilized again. The Fourdrinier did the work of 12 large vats – 6 tons of paper a week, at the rate of 36ft. a minute.

More modern machines are an elaboration of the same principle. Pulp contained in a vat fitted in some cases with two "hogs" is fed onto the wire over a breast-roll and passes over a vacuum suction box in front of the couch rolls; thence to the first and second press-rolls, the latter having an endless felt damp collector. The paper follows the course marked by arrows, through a long series of steam drying cylinders, (introduced by Crompton in 1821) with long felts above and below, each of the latter having two drying cylinders of their own. Smoothing cylinders come next, then cooling rolls, followed by a series of calendar rolls immediately short of the reel. During the later days of water power the speed of these machines was increased from 150ft. to 550ft. of 126ins. paper per minute; and incidentally the Ibotsons, of Wraysbury etc. made various improvements to paper machines.

By 1850 so much paper was used that the supply of rags became permanently inadequate; esparto grass was found serviceable, and was prepared in a "potcher" – a vessel like a large rag-breaker, after drying, dusting and boiling. In 1870 wood pulp was adopted, newspaper being made from "machine-pulp", i.e. pulp ground from wood blocks by sand-stones or from bark shaved from timber logs in a water driven bark mill; and magazines from "chemical-pulp" – chippings dissolved in chemicals. Books were made from esparto; writing paper and bank notes from linen and cotton; drawing and photographic from rags; good quality manila from flax. Esparto sometimes could not be used owing to its fatal effects upon trout, especially before purifying systems came into vogue.

Paper is often bulked with China clay; and colouring is generally added in the beating engine. Bleaching powder was invented by Tennant in 1799; but chlorine gas was also used in a slate-lined chamber for a similar purpose, the pulp then passing to an earthenware still, containing oxide of manganese, salt and vitriol. Watermarks are put in by a "Dandy roll" which has the desired device upon it; or these rolls could also be used minus watermark for imparting a hand-made appearance to "machine-made".

Great strides have been made in paper manufacture with the advent of steam reciprocating and turbine engines, but the foregoing remarks are mainly applicable to water-mills, with which we are primarily concerned.

I am particularly indebted to Mr. Wetherhead, foreman of Hedsor Mills for kindly correcting this rather difficult chapter, but it should be mentioned that he is a life-long mill-board man, and does not claim an authoritative knowledge of paper making. Technical terms such as "layboard", for example, found in paper-mill adverts but not mentioned in the chapter are, he explained inapplicable to mill-board making and are outside his scope.

Appendix 3
Bibliography

Anon	*History of Stoke Poges*	ca 1900
Aylesbury News and Advertiser		1839 etc
Barley R.E.	*Romance around Stony Stratford*	1928
Baxter J.H. D.Litt	*Medieval Latin Work List*	1934
Beckman Prof. J.	*History of Inventions, Discoveries*	
	and Origins 2 Vols.	1846
Bennett R. and Elton J.	*History of Corn Milling* 3 vols	1898
Bennett Rev. F.W.	*Bletchley 100 Years ago*	1926
Bennett Rev. F.W.	*Bletchley*	1933
Blyth W.	*England's Improvement or Reducement*	
	of Land to Pristine Fertility	1652
Bradbrooke W.	*Watling Street in Bucks*	1902
Bradbrooke W.	*History of Fenny Stratford*	1911
British Archaeological Assn	*Journal of the B.A.A. Vol III*	1941
Brontë C	*Shirley*	c 1845
Brown J.H. and Guest W.	*History of Thame*	1935
Browne Willis	*History and Antiquities of Buckingham*	1755
Bucks Archaeological Society	*Records of Buckinghamshire* 14 vols	1854–1944
Bucks Archaeological Society		
(Records Branch)	*Feet of Fines*	1941
Buckinghamshire Herald		1792
Bucks Advertiser and Aylesbury News: Bucks, Beds & Herts Chronicle; Bucks		1820–58, 1874, 1879,
Chronicle & Advertiser; Bucks Chronicle & Bucks Gazette, Bucks Gazette &		1881, 1895
Beds Chronicle: Bucks Gazette, Windsor & Eton Express; Bucks Herald & Uxbridge		
Advertiser & Windsor & Eton Journal etc.;		1820–1858, 1874,
		1878, 1879, 1881,
		1895
Buckinghamshire Parish Registers	Vol 35 (Wing)	1897
Bull F.W.	*History of Newport Pagnell*	1900
Burne Rev. R.V.H; M.A.	*A History of the Parish of Upton*	
	cum Chalvey	1913
Camden W.	*Britannia*	1695
Carr-Gomm F.C.	*Records of Farnham Royal*	1901
Clarke A.	*Windmill Land* 2 Vols	1916
Clear A.J.	*History of the Town and Manor of Winslow*	1890
Cole N.T.	*I Remember. 1855–1937*	1937
Cole Rev. W; M.A.	*The Blechley Diary*	1765–7
Ebblewhite E.A.	*Parish Registers of Great*	
	Hampden 1557–1812	1888
Eland G.	*The Chilterns and the Vale*	1911
Eland G.	*Old Works and Past Days*	1921
Eland G	*In Bucks*	1923
Enclosure Award	*Marsh Gibbon*	1841–52
Fairbairn Sir W.	*Mills and Millwork*	1878
Farrar Rev C.F.	*Ouse's Silent Tide*	1921
Finch W. Coles	*Watermills and Windmills*	1933
Finnemore J.	*Social Life of England* 2 Vols.	1902
Foster B.	*Pictures of English Landscape*	1863
Fowler J. K.	*Echoes of County Life*	1892
Fowler J. K.	*Recollections of Old Country Life*	1894
Fowler J. K.	*Records of Old Times*	1898
From Various Sources	*Note on Slough and Upton*	1893

Gaskell C.M.	*Records of an Eton Boy*	1883
Gentleman's Magazine		1752, 1805
Gibbs R.	*Bucks Miscellany*	1891
Gibbs R	*History of Aylesbury with its Borough* and *Hundreds, with the Hamlet of Walton*	1885
Gibbs R	*Record of Local Occurrences 1400–1840 A.D.* 4 Vols	1879
Graves H.	*Way about Buckinghamshire*	1903
Guest Rev. A.N.	*Stantonbury Tales*	1924
Gyll G.W. J.	*History of the Parish of Wraysbury and Horton and the Town of Colnbrook*	1862
Harman H.	*Buckinghamshire Dialect*	1929
Harrison J.T.	*Historical Buckingham*	1909
High Wycombe Directory and Guide		1875
Hilton Rev. S.	*The Story of Haversham*	1937
Holloway J.	*History of Whitchurch*	1889
Hughes M.W.	*A Calendar of the Feet of Fines for the County of Buckingham 1196–1260*	1940
Hissey J.J.	*Across England in a Dog Cart*	1891
Imperial Magazine	1760	
Inclosure Acts relating to Buckinghamshire 4 Vols.		
James W. and Malcolm J.	*General view of Agriculture in the County of Buckingham*	1794
Johnson S.	*Dictionary of the English Language*	Ed. 1764
Keefe H.J.	*A Century in Print*	1939
Kellys Directories (Bucks)	1854, 1864, 1877, 1891, 1895, 1899, 1903, 1907, 1911, 1915, 1916, 1920, 1928, 1931, 1933, 1935, 1939	
Kingston H.	*History of Wycombe, my Native Town*	1848
Kropotkin Prince.	*Field. Farm and Workshop*	1909
Larking Rev. L.B.	*The Knights Hospitallers in England*	1851
Lathbury Rev. R.H.	*History of Denham*	1904
Lipscomb G.	*History of Buckingham*, 4 vols,	1847
Marshall E.	*On the Banks of the Ouse*	1887
Martin C.T.	*Catalogue of the Archives in the Muniment Room of All Souls College, Oxford*	1877
Mee A.	*I See All*, 5 vols.	ca 1935
Ministry of Agriculture	*Agriculture*	January 1944
Mitchell C.S.	*Building Construction*	1894
Mitton G.E.	*Buckinghamshire and Bedfordshire*	1929
Moreton Rev. C.O.	*History of Waddesdon and Over Winchendon*	1929
Morley J.	*The Life of Richard Cobden 2 Vols.*	1881
Manuscript Copy of Poll taken at Election of 1784		1784
Musson and Craven's Directory		1853
Native Resident	*Haddenham 50 Years Ago*	c 1931
Northampton Mercury		1720, 1833
Oldham E.F.	*Fenny Stratford Year Book and Directory*	1908
Page E.W.	*Some Datchet Charities*	1924
Page W.	*Victoria County History*, 4 vols.	1905–27
Parker J.	*Early History of Wycombe*	1879
Parker T.J.	*Quainton 50 Years Ago*	1915
Parsons Dr. F.G. F.S.A.	*Old Records of Monks Risborough* 3 vols	1937
Phillips Sir R.	*Million of facts*	1841
Phipps Rev. P.W.	*Chalfont St Giles*	1896

Pigot's London and Provincial Directories — 1823, 1830, 1842

Plaisted Rev. A.H. — *English Architecture in a Country Village* — 1927

Plaisted Rev. A.H. — *The Manor and Parish Records of Medmenham* — 1925

Plaisted Rev. A.H. — *The Parsons and Parish Registers of Medmenham* — 1932

Railway Magazine — October 1939

Ratcliff O. — *History and Antiquities of the Newport Hundreds* — 1900

Ratcliff O. — *Illustrated Guide Book of Olney and Weston Underwood* (Revised) — 1887

Ratcliff O. — *Olney Almanack* (Revised) — 1907

Ratcliff O. and Brown H. — *Olney, Past and Present* — 1893

Registers of Electors of Aylesbury Borough and Hundreds 1802, 1804, 1818, 1832, 1835, 1840, 1852, 1857

Register of Electors for Buckinghamshire 1831, 1843, 1845, 1864

Richmond R. — *Leighton Buzzard and its Hamlets* — 1928

Rose W. — *Village Carpenter* — 1937

Rose W. — *Good Neighbours* — 1942

Roundell Rev. H. — *Lecture on Buckingham* — 1864

Royal Commission — *Historical Monuments of Bucks* — 1913

Salter Rev. H.E. M.A. — *The Boarstall Cartulary* — 1930

Salzmann L.F. — *English Industry in the Middle Ages* — 1913

Saunders J.E. — *Reflections and Rhymes of an Old Miller* — ca 1935

Scott J.W.R. — *The Countryman* — Autumn 1943

Sheahan J.J. — *History and Topography of Buckinghamshire* — 1863

Shephard Rev J. M.A. — *Old Days of Eton Parish* — 1908

Silvester Rev. T. — *Manuscript History of Buckingham Vol 2* — 1826–30

Society for the Protection of Ancient Buildings — *English Windmills* Vol 2. — 1932

Spicer A.D. — *The Paper Trade* — 1907

Springhall S. — *Country Rambles Round Uxbridge* — 1907

Staines J. — *History of Newport Pagnell* — 1842

Stow J. — *Survey of London* — 1603

Stowe Park Sale Catalogue — c 1922

Sutcliffe J — *Treatise on Canals and Reservoirs etc.; instructions for designing and building a corn mill* — 1816

Thayer W.M. — *From the Tan-yard to the White House* — 1885

Topographer — — — — — — — 1789

Turner S — *History and Manners of the Anglo Saxons*

Tyringham Estate Sale Book — 1906

Universal British Directory of Trade and Commerce — 1791–3

Ussher Rev. R — *History of the Parish of Westbury* — 1913

Walker, Brown, Lightbody, Davis and Burn — *Working Drawings and Designs in Mechanical Engineering etc.* — ca 1870

Ward W.H. and Block S.K. — *History of Iver* — 1933

Waters. E.C. — *Genealogical Memoirs of the Chesters of Chicheley*, 2 vols. — 1878

West Sir L — *History of Wendover* — 1909